The Origins and Development of the English Language

The Origins and Development of the English Language

Thomas Pyles

UNIVERSITY OF FLORIDA

HARCOURT, BRACE & WORLD, INC.

New York • Burlingame

Contents

Preface

This book aims to be a fresh and up-to-date account of English historical linguistics. Though much of the material would be of interest to the general educated reader, the book is designed especially for the advanced undergraduate course in the history of the English language. The treatment is, however, sufficiently detailed to be useful to graduate students of English preparing for qualifying examinations.

Our primary concern is the internal history of our language, presented in a chronological treatment of its phonological and grammatical development from prehistoric times to the present. Purely external history, so admirably treated in other books, is thus purposely kept to a minimum—a few paragraphs here and there in the chapters dealing with Old and Middle English. Though hundreds of words are cited throughout, vocabulary accretions as such, along with the cultural and political forces leading to their adoption, have been dealt with in a single final chapter.

The treatment of writing is somewhat fuller than is usual in works of comparable scope. Its relationship to speech is explored in detail, with the hope of dissipating a good many popular misconceptions which plague the professional student of language.

A good deal of attention has been given to British and American differences, certainly more than is customary in books of American provenience. Interesting and sometimes significant as such differences are, they are nevertheless viewed in what the writer hopes is a proper perspective and without any trace of nationalistic bias. For it is the English language, wherever spoken by those whose mother tongue it is, which is our concern. Neither British nor American linguistic provincialism has much place in a world as cozy as Telstar and jets have made ours, whether we like it or not.

Early Modern English—the language of Shakespeare and the Authorized Version of the Bible (commonly called the King James

Bible), so like our own that we are sometimes unaware of subtle and important differences—has been treated in more detail than is customary in books attempting to cover developments in our language in the millenium and a half stretching from the first English settlement of Britain in the mid-fifth century to our own day. Perhaps because of its very familiarity, the study of the speech of this early yet modern period has often been considered somehow less important, or at least more expendable, than that of earlier periods. The similarities between it and current speech can be quite deceptive, however, as anyone who has had to listen to the exegetical flights and fancies of badly informed commentators knows perfectly well.

Obviously this book owes much to contemporary linguistic scholarship. Without the painstaking labors of fellow students of the language, the writer could have laid little claim to up-to-dateness, for one man can only do so much. But it is also indebted to the works of distinguished predecessors who have dealt with much of the material here surveyed. It is often difficult to tell precisely where one's indebtedness to others ends and one's own contribution begins. In any event, I am eternally grateful to the goodly company of scholars living and dead whose works I have read and learned from.

I am also, and more immediately, indebted to Dr. Kenneth G. Wilson, of the University of Connecticut, who read the entire manuscript and made some very wise and helpful suggestions; to an unidentified reader for his sage and heartening comments; to Dr. John T. Algeo, of the University of Florida, for reading one of the more troublesome chapters and giving me the benefit of his opinions concerning a number of points; to my son, Thomas Pyles, Jr., for asking discerning questions about certain early chapters which he read and for listening with apparent interest to my disquisitions in answer, some of which subsequently got into the text; to my chairman, Dr. C. A. Robertson, of the University of Florida, who encouraged me through every stage in the writing of the book; and to my wife, who made life run as smoothly and agreeably for me as it could possibly have done under the circumstances.

T. P.

The Origins and Development of the English Language

CHAPTER I

Facts, Assumptions, and Misconceptions About Language

LANGUAGE, man's greatest intellectual accomplishment, is immeasurably ancient. We may be fairly sure that man was already making use of the complicated and highly systematized set of vocal sounds which go to make up language when the woolly-haired rhinoceros and the mammoth roamed the earth. Archaeologists have shown that man was using tools in those far-off prehistoric days, a fact which presupposes his ability to hand down knowledge of their construction and use to his descendants. How long it took him to acquire this ability we have no way of knowing.

THEORIES OF THE ORIGIN
OF LANGUAGE

It is just as well not to speculate overmuch on the ultimate origins of language, since we have absolutely no information on the subject. The earliest languages of which we have any records are already in a high stage of development. The same is true of languages spoken by primitive peoples. The problem of how language began has naturally tantalized philosophical minds, and many theories have been advanced, to which waggish scholars have given such fancifully descriptive names as the pooh-pooh theory, the bow-wow theory, the ding-dong theory, and the yo-he-ho theory. The nicknames indicate how seriously the theories need be taken: they are based respectively on the notions that language was in the beginning ejaculatory, echoic (onomatopoeic), characterized by a mystic appropriateness of sound to sense in contrast to being merely imitative, or made up of grunts and groans emitted in the course of group actions and coming in time to be associated with those actions.[1]

We cannot know, then, how language began; we can be sure only of its immense antiquity. However man started to talk, he did so a breathtakingly long time ago, and it was not until much later that he devised a system of making marks in or on wood, stone, and the like to represent what he said when he talked. Compared with language, writing is a newfangled invention, although certainly none the less brilliant for being so. But it is merely symbolization of the sounds man makes in speaking, and thus not really language at all, though for convenience' sake and by long tradition we speak of written language in contrast to spoken language. The earliest writings (in Sumerian) go back only about five thousand years, but man had been talking, as we have seen, for hundreds of thousands of years before these first documents.

WRITING AND SPEECH

No system of writing which would be comprehensible to more than a few people can hope to accomplish all that we accomplish when we speak. As we shall see later, such phenomena as pitch and what is conventionally but confusingly called juncture are symbolized in writing with varying degrees of satisfactoriness. We can, in fact, indicate certain types of junctures (the pauses or halts that we make in speech) more satisfactorily in writing than we ordinarily do in speaking. For example, "grade A" may well be heard as "gray day," but they are distinguished from each other when we come to write them. But we cannot show in ordinary writing the difference between *sound quality* 'tone' and *sound quality* 'good grade' (as in "The sound quality of the recording was excellent" and "The materials were of sound quality")—a difference which we make very easily in speech by strongly stressing *sound* in the first instance and the first syllable of *quality* in the second.

The conventions of writing differ somewhat, but not really very much, from those of ordinary speech. For instance, we ordinarily write *was not, do not, would not*, although we usually say *wasn't, don't, wouldn't*. Furthermore, our choice of words is likely to differ occasionally and to be made with somewhat more care in writing than in ordinary, everyday speech. But these are purely stylistic

[1] For a good, readable discussion of these theories, with some additional speculations, see Otto Jespersen, *Language: Its Nature, Development and Origin* (New York, 1922), Chapter 21, "The Origin of Speech."

rather than linguistic matters, as is also the fact that writing tends to be somewhat more conservative than speech.

A DEFINITION OF LANGUAGE

For our purposes language may be defined as systematized combinations of sounds which have meaning for all persons in a given cultural community. For those languages which have been recorded (and there are some which have never been written down), writing is the graphic representation of these combinations of sounds. This definition of language does not include gestures, facial expressions, and other body movements which, though they play a part in communication, will normally not be considered in this book.

Perhaps the most important word in our definition is *systematized*. We speak in certain patterns, or according to a certain system. Thus, according to the sound-system of Modern English, the consonant combination *mb* never occurs at the beginning or at the end of any word. As a matter of fact, it did occur finally in earlier stages of our language, which is why it was necessary in the preceding statement to specify "Modern English." Despite its complete absence in this position in the sound-system of English for at least six hundred years, we still insist—such is the conservatism of writing habits—that the *b* be written in *lamb, climb, tomb, dumb,* and a number of other words. But this same combination, which now occurs only medially in English (as in *tremble*), may well occur in final or even in initial position in the sound-systems of other languages. Initial *mb* is indeed a part of the systems of certain African languages, as in Efik and Ibibio *mbakara* 'white man,' which in the speech of the Gullahs —Negroes living along the coastal region of Georgia and South Carolina who have preserved a number of words and structural features which their ancestors brought from Africa—has become *buckra.* It is notable that the Gullahs have simplified the initial consonant combination of this African word to conform to the pattern of their native English speech.

The sounds of a language recur again and again according to a well-defined system, not haphazardly, for without system communication would be impossible. The same is true of all linguistic features, not sound alone. Thus, according to the grammatical system of English, a very large number of words take a suffix written -*s* to indicate plurality or possession (in which case it is a comparatively recent convention of writing to add an apostrophe). This suffix is variously pronounced. *Duck,* for instance, adds the sound which is usually indicated by *s*; *dog* adds the sound which is usually indicated by *z*; and *horse* adds a syllable consisting of a vowel sound plus the *z* sound.

Words which can be thus modified in form for the purposes specified are traditionally called nouns. They fit into certain definite patterns in English utterances. *Alcoholic,* for instance, fits into the system of English in the same way as *duck, dog,* and *horse*: "Alcoholics need understanding" (compare "Ducks need water"), "An alcoholic's perceptions are faulty" (compare "A dog's perceptions are keen"), and the like. But it may also modify a noun and be modified by an adverb: *an alcoholic drink, a somewhat alcoholic taste,* and the like; and words that operate in this way are called adjectives. *Alcoholic* is thus both adjective and noun, depending upon the way it functions in the system of English. Such an utterance as "Alcoholic worries" is ambiguous because our system, like all linguistic systems, is not completely foolproof. But the headline "President-Threatening Alcoholic Worries U.S. Agents," while certainly no model of English style, is not really ambiguous, but only momentarily irritating. We know at second glance that *Alcoholic* is here a noun, the subject of a verb *Worries* (rather than the modifier of a plural noun *Worries*) because of what follows in the pattern: *U.S. Agents,* the object of *Worries.* What we have here is the most frequently occurring of all English sentence patterns: subject-verb-complement.

FOR DIFFERENT LANGUAGES,
DIFFERENT SYSTEMS

It is obvious that every language must have its own system, though it may share certain features with other languages. What has been said of the capacity of the typical English noun to add a sibilant suffix for pluralizing or indicating possession is, for instance, not at all true of the typical Modern French noun, which has no possessive form and which in isolation remains unchanged in the plural. The fact that singular *ami* and plural *amis* are written differently is merely a historical feature of the French writing system. The two forms are actually identical in speech except when *amis* is "in liaison," that is, followed by a word beginning with a vowel sound, in which case the normally "silent" *-s* is pronounced. The French noun, then, would require a definition different in some of its details from that of the English noun.

Pidgin English and other languages spoken by primitive peoples are just as systematic as English, or as Classical Latin for that matter. Since system in languages *is* grammar in its widest sense, it is obviously impossible for there to be a grammarless language. When Dr. Johnson remarked that English had no grammar, he was thinking of the complicated system of word-endings of Latin as constituting grammar. It would have been remarkable if anyone had thought otherwise in his day. But the fact is that English "The fire cooks the meat," Melanesian Pidgin "Fire i-cookim abus,"[2] and Latin "Ignis carnem coquet" all have grammar. The systems are of course different, but no one system can be said to be superior to another. In the sentence from Pidgin, for instance, the ending *-im* of the verb indicates that a direct object follows; in "The meat cooks," no such ending would be used: "Abus i-cook." This ending is a systematic grammatical device indicating the same grammatical relationship as the accusative ending *-em* (with which it of course has no connection) of the Latin noun. In the system of English, the position of *meat* in the sentence indicates the same grammatical relationship. Position is, however, relatively unimportant in Latin: "Carnem ignis coquet" means the same thing as "Ignis carnem coquet," inasmuch as the direct object is clearly labeled by the ending. To reverse the meaning (with nonsensical effect) one would have to change only the *form* of the words, as follows: "Caro ignem coquet." The order of the words makes no difference. In English (as also in Pidgin), the same reversal in meaning is accomplished without change of form, but of word order only: "The meat cooks the fire."

The acquisition of language—that is, the mastery of one of the complicated linguistic systems by which man, and man alone, communicates—is an arduous task. But it is a task which normal children all over the world seem not to mind in the least. It is not of course claimed that a child of four or five has acquired all of the words he will need to know as he grows up. What is true is that he has rather fully mastered the system by means of which he will speak of many things for the rest of his life. The immensity of his intellectual accomplishment can be appreciated by anyone who has learned a second language as an adult.

[2] This sentence, with spelling slightly modified, is taken from *Hands Off Pidgin English!* (Sydney, Australia, 1955), by Robert A. Hall, Jr., to whom I am also indebted for the other grammatical statements about Melanesian Pidgin English in this text.

DO BIRDS AND BEASTS
REALLY TALK?

Language, it has been implied, is an exclusively human phenomenon. Many of the lower animals are physically just about as well equipped as man to produce speech sounds, and some—certain birds, for instance—have in fact been taught to do so. What we call our speech organs are actually organs with primary functions quite different from the production of speech sounds, functions such as the ingestion and mastication of food. But no other species has ever developed a system of sounds which even remotely resembles human language. It is man alone who has adapted certain organs in such a way that he can talk about the manifold things which concern him, ranging all the way from food, shelter, and sex to transubstantiation, relativity, and existentialism.

LANGUAGE SYSTEMS
ARE CONVENTIONS

The systems which operate in the world's many languages are, it is important to remember, arbitrary and conventional; that is to say, there is usually no connection between the sounds we make and the phenomena of life. This is to some extent true even of the comparatively small number of echoic words, like *bow-wow*, which seems to those of us who speak English as our native language to be a fairly accurate imitation of the sounds made by a dog, though it is highly doubtful that a dog would agree, particularly a French dog, which says *gnaf-gnaf*, or a German one, which says *wau-wau*, or a Japanese one, which says *wung-wung*.[3]

The common man thinks unquestioningly that his language is the best—and so it is for him, inasmuch as he mastered it well enough for his own purposes so long ago that he cannot remember when. It seems to him more logical, more sensible, more right—in short, more

---

[3] The reader interested in the sounds made by foreign animals will do well to look into Noel Perrin's instructive and highly amusing "Old Macberlitz Had a Farm" (*New Yorker*, January 27, 1962, pp. 28–29), and the erudite comments by the ambassador from Norway, Paul Koht (in a letter to the editor of the *New Yorker*, February 24, 1962, p. 125), from which he may acquire from a native speaker valuable information about the sounds uttered by Norwegian cows (*mmmøøø*), sheep (*mæ*), pigs (*nøff-nøff*), and other creatures. Norwegian hens very sensibly say *klukk-klukk*, though doubtless with a heavy Norwegian accent.

natural—than the way foreigners talk. But, as we have seen, there is nothing really natural about any language, since all these highly systematized and conventionalized methods of human communication must be acquired. There is, for instance, nothing natural in our use of *is* in such a sentence as "The woman is busy." The utterance can be made just as effectively without the meaningless verb form which is conventional in English, and some languages do get along perfectly well without it. This use of *is* (and other forms of the verb *to be*) was, as a matter of fact, late in developing and has never developed in Russian and the other languages of the Balto-Slavic group.

To the speaker of Russian it is thus more "natural" to say "Zhenshchina zanyata"—literally "Woman busy"—which sounds to our ears so much like baby talk that the unsophisticated speaker of English might well conclude (and how wrong he would be!) that Russian is strictly a childish tongue. It will be noted also that the system of Russian manages to struggle along without the definite article, which in most other Indo-European languages has developed out of the demonstrative pronoun. As a matter of fact, the speaker of Russian never misses the definite article—nor should we if its use had not become conventional with us.

To our hypothetical common man, calling the organ of sight *eye* will seem to be perfectly natural and right, and those who call it anything else—like the Germans, who call it *Auge*, the Russians, who call it *glaz*, or the Japanese, who call it *me*—he is likely to regard as either perverse or simply unfortunate because they do not speak languages in which things are properly designated. The fact is, however, that *eye*, which we pronounce exactly like the nominative form of the first person singular pronoun (a fact which might be cited against it by a foreign hypothetical common man), is the name of the organ in question only in our present English linguistic system. It has not always been so. Londoners at the time of the accession of King Edward III in 1327 pronounced the word with two syllables, the vowel of the first syllable being that which we pronounce nowadays in *see*. In the course of the fourteenth century the final unstressed vowel sound (pronounced like the *-a* in *Ida*) was lost, though we continue to this day to write it, calling it "silent *e*." And, if we chose to go back to King Alfred's day, we should find yet another pronunciation and, in addition, a different way of writing the word from which Modern English *eye* has developed. When a

Scottish plowboy says "ee" for *eye*,[4] he is not being quaint, or whimsical, or perverse, or stupid. He is merely using that development of a variant form of the word (one which had approximately the vowel sound of *date*) current in his own linguistic system—a perfectly "legitimate" pronunciation which happens not to occur in that type of English spoken in the southern part of England and, for reasons which have nothing to do with "good" or "bad," by educated speakers of English all over the English-speaking world. Knowledge of such changes within a single language should be sufficient to dissipate the notion that any one word or any one form of a word is more appropriate except in a purely chronological and social sense than any other word or form.

WRITING IS NOT LANGUAGE

Misconceptions about language are very widespread and by no means confined to hypothetical common men. Very often these false notions grow out of a confusion of writing with language. It is, for example, quite generally supposed by English-speaking people that their language is a "difficult" language, or at least more difficult than, say, Spanish. The fact is that all languages are about equally difficult to acquire. It is true, however, that some languages have writing systems which are in one way or another less efficient than those of other languages. This fact has nothing to do with language itself, for, as we have observed, writing is but a symbolization of language.

Nevertheless, such words as *through, though, bough, rough,* and *cough* are time and again cited as evidence of the devilishness of the English language, inasmuch as, though all are spelled with *-ough,* all have different vowel sounds, with a final consonant occurring in the last two which is nonexistent in the first three. "How can the poor foreigner ever learn such a language?" it is asked.

All that is really proved by such examples is that English has a highly conservative spelling system: our spellings frequently indicate pronunciations which have not been current since Middle English times. But as *language,* English would be no easier if we wrote *thru, tho, bow, ruf,* and *cawf.* Immigrants forced to learn the language "by

---

[4] As in Robert Burns's "To a Mouse":

Still thou art blest, compared wi' me!
The present only toucheth thee:
But och! I backward cast my e'e . . .

ear," as we all learned it as children, would not confuse these words in their speech any more than we do—though of course they would have some difficulty in reading and writing.

Out of this confusion of writing with language emerge such notions as that of the late Senator Robert L. Owen of Oklahoma, who believed that a new international alphabet would remove all language barriers and hence bring about universal brotherhood and understanding—the underlying assumption being that understanding inevitably brings about agreement. With the best will in the world, Owen invented such an alphabet—a "global alphabet," he called it—and conducted a long crusade to have it taught in the Oklahoma school system. He claimed that "through it I can teach any reasonably intelligent man Chinese in two months. . . . It is a means by which we can teach the English language to all the world at high speed and negligible cost."[5] The first of these claims is true only in the sense that, if both parties knew Chinese to begin with, the senator could have taught his pupil to *write* that language in his "global alphabet"—quite a different thing from teaching him the Chinese language. As a matter of fact, Chinese could be written in any alphabet and frequently is written in the Roman alphabet.

How far this sort of misconception can go is illustrated by the editorial pronouncement of a metropolitan daily newspaper,[6] commenting upon the various spellings of the name of a now happily forgotten Iranian premier as *Mossadegh, Mossadeq, Moussadek,* and *Musaddiq.* The editorial writer concludes that "if no agreement can be reached on the spelling of one man's name, consider how much greater is the problem of translating accurately the fine shades of meaning in an address by a statesman of Pakistan, Turkey, or Ethiopia."

Now, no one would deny the difficulties of accurate translation, but these have nothing whatever to do with the way a word (in this instance a proper name) is transliterated from one alphabet into another. The name of a great Russian writer whom English-speaking people know as *Chekhov* is written in other spelling systems according to the various ways of transliterating Russian, which uses the Cyrillic rather than the Roman alphabet: the French write *Tchékhov*; the Italians, *Čechov*; the Germans, *Tschechow*; the

[5] Cited by Leonard Bloomfield in "Secondary and Tertiary Responses to Language," *Language,* XX (1944), 49.

[6] The Jacksonville *Florida Times-Union,* October 28, 1951, p. 8.

Swedes, *Tjechov*; and the Spanish, *Tchejoff, Tchekov,* or *Chejov.*
The fact that these variant writings give a fairly close approximation
of the Russian pronunciation to one familiar with the phonetic and
orthographic systems of the languages cited is all that is really
important. The writer himself wrote his name Чехов, which, despite
its strangeness to our eyes, does not indicate that Russian is an
uncommonly difficult language or that, in the interests of international "understanding," the Russians ought to adopt our way of
writing—or, for that matter, that we ought to adopt theirs. Names,
like all other words, were in existence long before anybody ever
wrote them, and the way one writes them is purely and simply a
matter of tradition. Had the Russians long ago settled upon Chinese
ideograms as the basis of their writing system, their language would
have had precisely the same development which it has had, and the
great writer would have had the same name as that under which he
is known to us. When, in 1928, Mustafa Kemal Pasha (later Kemal
Atatürk) as president of Turkey substituted the Roman alphabet for
the Arabic in writing Turkish, the Turkish language changed no
more than time changed when he introduced the Gregorian calendar
in his country.

THE NOTION OF LINGUISTIC CORRUPTION

Another widely held notion is that there are ideal forms of languages, these being thought of as "pure," and that existing languages
represent corruptions of these. Thus, the Greek spoken today is supposed to be a degraded form of Classical Greek rather than what it
really is, a development therefrom. Since the Romance languages
are developments of Latin, it would follow from this point of view
that these also are corrupt, although this assumption is not usually
made. Those who admire or profess to admire Latin literature sometimes suppose that a stage of perfection had been reached in Classical
Latin and that every divergent development in Latin was indicative
of steady and irreparable deterioration. From this point of view the
late development of Latin spoken in the early Middle Ages (sometimes called Vulgar, or popular, Latin) is "bad" Latin, which,
strange as it may seem, was ultimately to become "good" Italian,
French, Spanish, and so on.

It is obvious that such notions, despite their tenacity, are completely invalid. They are based to some extent upon yet another

notion—that languages which make use of complicated systems of endings for case, tense, mood, gender, and the like are superior ("more expressive of fine shades of meaning" is a frequent description) to those which, like English and French, do not. This notion is particularly dear to the hearts of those who have a smattering of classical learning and who in support of the supposed superiority of the classical languages point to the fact that Greece and Rome produced great literature. But literary excellence has little or nothing to do with language *as* language. Speakers of English have also produced some rather great literature at various stages in its development, as all the world agrees: *Beowulf* in Old English, *Troilus and Criseyde* and *Sir Gawain and the Green Knight* in Middle English, and *Hamlet* and *Paradise Lost* in Modern English. Literature of high quality may be written in any language provided some of its speakers are interested in, and capable of, writing such literature.

Instead of retaining a complicated system of inflections (variations in the form of words, usually by means of endings) such as we find in Latin, Greek, and Sanskrit, many modern languages make use of other devices to indicate grammatical relationships—word order, for instance, and what Charles Carpenter Fries in *The Structure of English* (New York, 1952) and elsewhere has called "function words," which include words traditionally called prepositions, auxiliaries, conjunctions, articles and words which may be substituted for them (such as possessive and demonstrative pronouns), and adverbs of negation and degree. Latin *pater Caroli* 'Charles's father,' for instance, came to be expressed in French, Spanish, and Italian respectively by *le père de Charles, el padre de Carlos,* and *il padre di Carlo* 'the father of Charles.'[7] The Latin genitive has been completely lost in the languages derived from Latin, its function being performed by a preposition meaning 'of.'

This loss of the genitive in the Romance languages ought to be—and doubtless is—considered degenerative by those who believe in linguistic corruption. Inflectional complexity is dearly beloved by those who fancy that they know their way about, even if somewhat gropingly, in the classical languages. Such persons are likely to regard English, which, though it has retained its genitive, has lost most of its other inflectional devices in the course of its development, as crude and barbarous. If this were the sole criterion for their judg-

[7] Note that English, which has never lost the genitive inflection, can use either construction.

ment, they would of course be logically committed to a similar low opinion of the Romance languages.

Indo-European, the origin of practically all the languages of Europe as well as some Asiatic ones, was even more complex than the classical languages. In addition to the case forms found in most Latin nouns, for instance, the Indo-European noun had also an instrumental, a locative, and a vocative form, the last two of which survive only very rarely in Latin. Now, carrying to its logical conclusion the point of view of such linguistic commentators as have been cited, we really ought to speak reconstructed Indo-European. Think of the "fine shades of meaning" which might be expressed by the locative, the vocative, and the instrumental cases!

As a matter of fact, however, most of us get along very well without these shades. We do not in the least miss the various uses of the almost lost subjunctive mood in English, and are impatient when we must use the subjunctive in speaking languages which have preserved it, such as German, French, and Spanish. Many American speakers of English nevertheless feel that there is something inherently virtuous about using the subjunctive in the "If I (he, she, it) were" construction, and that the altogether adequate "If I (he, she, it) was" is "bad" English. Teachers, whose influence upon the recent development of English has been considerable, are doubtless to some extent responsible for our retention of the subjunctive, which once had a number of other functions as well, now happily forgotten. These other uses were lost long before Americans came to regard as "good" English that prescribed for them by those whom they consider to be authorities, rather than that which they actually hear (but frequently fail to notice) from persons of good standing.

Because we hear so much of "pure" English, it is perhaps well that we examine this particular notion in some detail before passing on to more important matters. When Captain Frederick Marryat, an English novelist, visited the United States in 1837–38, he thought it "remarkable how very debased the language has become in a short period in America," adding that "if their lower classes are more intelligible than ours, it is equally true that the higher classes do not speak the language so purely or so classically as it is spoken among the well-educated English." Both statements are nonsense. The first is based upon the captain's apparent notion that the English language had reached a stage of perfection at the time America was first settled by English-speaking people, after which, presumably because of the innate depravity of those Englishmen who brought their language to the New World, it had taken a steadily downward course, whatever that may mean. One wonders, also, precisely how Marryat knew what constituted "classical" or "pure" English. It is probable that he was merely attributing certain superior qualities to that type of English which he was accustomed to hear from persons of good social standing in the land of his birth and which he himself spoke. Any divergence therefrom was "debased": "My speech is pure; thine, wherein it differs from mine, is corrupt."

In our own day these concepts of linguistic purity and corruption survive, so that even so highly sophisticated a fictional character as Dr. Peter Alden in George Santayana's *The Last Puritan* (New York, 1936) is made to say of his son's speech, "I should like his English to be fundamentally pure; then all the abominable speech he will have to hear will seem to him absurd and amusing. . . ." (p. 80). If instead of "fundamentally pure" Dr. Alden had said "aesthetically pleasing to persons in our station of life" or "highly cultivated" (in contrast to ordinary "abominable" speech), no one could quarrel with such a statement of his personal preferences. To claim that these preferences are for what is "fundamentally pure" is quite another matter.

That the equally sophisticated author himself had the same notion of educated speech as pure and of common speech—actually more conservative in many details than educated speech—as debased is indicated by a good many pseudolinguistic pronouncements of his own throughout the novel, as in his description of the speech of Fräulein Irma, a German governess, as "British—musical, colloquial, and pure" (p. 91).[8] Santayana, who spent much of his life in the

---

[8] Santayana, as might be expected of one with his cultivated use of English, uses *colloquial* in the sense 'familiar, easy-going, informal,' the meaning which it still has among the highly educated. It is notable that in common usage the word has come to mean 'regional' or 'local' (doubtless because of the phonetic similarity of *colloquialism* and *localism*). Hence a word which for many denotes a quality altogether attractive and desirable (and in fact usually unavoidable) has come frequently to denote what is supposed to be bad, as in the statement of one described in an Associated Press news item of September 6, 1953, as a voice coach for various eminent actors and actresses: "If you speak with a nasal twang or a colloquial accent . . . you are handicapping yourself, no matter what your business."

United States, seems here to be implying that the development of the English language in America has been somehow inferior to that which has occurred in England. Somewhat different these developments have certainly been, but it would be impossible to determine by any objective standards that one has been good and the other bad, though one type of English may be more pleasing than another to a given person or group. It is indeed likely that most of us, for reasons which have nothing to do with language as such, would prefer Sir John Gielgud's reading of Shakespeare to that of, say, Marlon Brando. It is ironical that in a number of details Brando's native speech resembles that heard in the Globe Theatre of Shakespeare's day more closely than does Gielgud's—for instance, in its retention of *r* before consonants and in final position and of the so-called "flat *a*" in words like *path, staff, master,* and perhaps in its intonation as well.

THE QUESTION OF USAGE

The concept of an absolute and unwavering, presumably God-given standard of linguistic correctness (sometimes confused with "purity") is so widespread, even among the educated, as to merit some attention here. Those who subscribe to this notion become greatly exercised over such matters as the split infinitive, the "incorrect" position of *only*, and the preposition ending a sentence. All these supposed "errors" have been committed time and again by eminent writers and speakers, so that one wonders how those who condemn them know that they are bad. Robert Lowth, who wrote one of the most influential English grammars of the eighteenth century (*A Short Introduction to English Grammar,* 1762), was praised by one of his admirers for showing "the grammatic inaccuracies that have escaped the pens of our most distinguished writers."

One would suppose that the usage of "our most distinguished writers" would be good usage. But Lowth and his followers knew, or thought they knew, better; and their attitude survives to this day. This is not, of course, to deny that there are standards of usage, but only to suggest that even in the reputedly democratic society in which we live any set of standards which are to have validity must be based on the usage of speakers and writers of generally acknowledged excellence. These would nowadays almost inevitably be persons of education, though it has not always been so; other ages have not placed so high a premium on mere literacy as our own. Distressing as it may be to all idealists, what we think of as "good" English has grown out of the usage of generations of well-born and well-bred persons many of whom could neither read nor write. In the late fifteenth century, William Caxton, obviously a highly literate man, used to submit his work to the Duchess of Burgundy (an English lady despite her French title), who "oversawe and corrected" it. We have no information as to the speed and ease with which the Duchess read, but it is highly likely that she was considerably less literate than was Caxton himself. Yet to Caxton the "correctness" of the usage of a lady of the court was unassailable, whereas he would seem to have had little faith in what came naturally to him, a brilliant son of the bourgeoisie. His standard of excellence was the usage of persons of good position—quite a different thing from our own servile obedience to the mandates of badly informed "authorities" who, when not guided by their own prejudices, attempt to settle questions of usage by the same methods as those which were employed by Lowth and his followers in the eighteenth century.

LANGUAGE AND NATION

Another fondly held belief is that a language somehow expresses the collective "soul" of its speakers. Certainly no one would deny that the external history of a nation may be reflected in its word stock; this the history of the English language demonstrates eloquently. But this is not the same thing as supposing that the attitudes toward life and the habits of mind of a people are reflected in the grammatical structure of their language. Such a thesis as Otto Jespersen's "As the language is, so also is the nation"[9] is quite indefensible, though still believed so tenaciously that to gainsay it is likely to bring down coals of fire on one's head. If it were merely a notion held by a lunatic fringe of society, there would be little point in mentioning it here. But the fact is that it is as widely believed by otherwise educated people as the equally untenable notion that climate affects language, which, if true, would mean

[9] *Growth and Structure of the English Language,* 9th ed. (Oxford, 1954), p. 16.

among other things that we ought to talk faster and louder in winter than in summer.[10]

Because it has vitiated much of our thinking about language, one more popular misconception must be mentioned—the notion that certain languages are more "expressive" than others. Now the fact is that all languages are about equally expressive, if by the term we mean 'efficient for purposes of communication.' It is obvious that members of one linguistic community will not need or want to express all that the members of another community might consider important. In short, the Eskimo feels no need to discuss Zen Buddhism, the quantum theory, or the single tax. But he can talk about what is important to his own culture, and doubtless with greater efficiency in some instances than can the anthropologist who must describe that culture in, say, English—a language which might well impress the Eskimo as being quite "primitive" because it has only one widely used word for the frozen vapor which falls in white flakes (*snow*), whereas his language has many words for many different kinds of snow. Furthermore, he can make a good many grammatical distinctions in his language that we are not in the least concerned with making in ours. These also doubtless seem so essential to him that, if he ever gave the matter a thought, he might well regard English as sadly deficient in its grammar as well as in its word stock.

BEWARE THE LAY LINGUIST

One of the most important tenets of the layman's linguistic creed is that any thoughtful, well-educated person, no matter what his special training may have been, is competent to make authoritative pronouncements about the language which he speaks or, for that matter, about any language with which he has a passing acquaintance. The late Leonard Bloomfield, an authority on American Indian languages, tells of being informed by a physician that

[10] Witness the following statement from Miriam Chapin's *How People Talk* (New York, 1947): "It is true that the south seems to soften sounds; witness Louisiana's slurred r's and drawled vowels . . ." (p. 18). Presumably the heat is held responsible for these phenomena, though it should be pointed out that the loss of *r* under certain circumstances is paralleled in eastern New England and in England. As for the drawl, whatever the term means, Noah Webster reprobated his fellow New Englanders for their "drawling, whining cant" in his *Dissertations on the English Language* (1789), though the drawl is now supposed to be characteristic of Southern American speech.

Chippewa has only a few hundred words—a patently fantastic statement to make concerning any language. Says Bloomfield, "When I tried to state the diagnostic setting, the physician, our host, briefly and with signs of displeasure repeated his statement, and then turned his back to me."[11] This was a more or less typical (to adopt Bloomfield's term) "tertiary response to language"—that encountered when one tries to enlighten a speaker who has made a statement about language (a "secondary response") which is open to question. As we proceed, we hope it will become increasingly obvious that the study of language, like language itself, has order, discipline, and system, and that consequently the layman's opinions about language are no more reliable than his opinions about medicine, physics, or engineering.

The linguistic commentator with a heavily authoritative air about matters of usage is usually to be distrusted when his pronouncements deny social acceptability to locutions that we have read in reputable books and heard from the lips of reputable speakers. Thus, when the writer of a syndicated newspaper column solemnly informs his linguistically insecure readers that it is incorrect to say "There were 400 people present" because one should never use *people* after a number, but only *persons,* we are quite justified in asking how he knows this. And, inasmuch as there could not possibly be any way of knowing other than by divine inspiration, we are equally justified in assuming that the current preference of a large majority of educated speakers for *people* in such a construction is sufficient to establish it as "correct," that is, in good usage. Likewise, when we come upon lists of words which practically everyone is supposed to mispronounce, we are surely justified in asking ourselves how the compilers of such lists know how the words ought to be pronounced, unless they too are divinely inspired by a linguistic Jehovah who watches over the destiny of the English language.

The plain fact is that there has been an appalling lag between attitudes toward language and the brilliant research which the present century has seen. In no way has this fact been more strikingly illustrated than by the furor of indignation which met the publication of *Webster's Third New International Dictionary* in 1961. Newspaper and magazine editors, as well as critics who should have known better, exposed the fact that they did not know what a dictionary is supposed to be, namely, a record of the words of a lan-

[11] "Secondary and Tertiary Responses to Language," p. 49.

guage, though no really complete record could ever be made. It was apparent that otherwise educated people believed that it should be only a record of what they thought of as "good" words, though it would be very difficult to arrive at any complete agreement among the critics themselves as to which words are "good," and therefore worthy of recording, and which ones "bad," and by the same token unworthy. Magazines which pride themselves on their modernity in the arts and sciences took a stand on language that was little in advance of the prescriptivism which has flourished among linguistically naïve and insecure people since the eighteenth century. The whole sorry business has been chronicled in *Dictionaries and* That *Dictionary* (subtitled *A Casebook on the Aims of Lexicographers and the Targets of Reviewers*) edited by James Sledd and Wilma R. Ebbitt (Chicago, 1962)—a work which should, but will not, make a good many popular pundits hang their heads in shame.

The nineteenth century concerned itself largely with establishing the relationships of the various Indo-European languages, of which a résumé will be given in Chapter IV. But before the end of that century the first three volumes and a large part of the fourth volume (it was published originally in sections) of that great monument of English scholarship, *A New English Dictionary on Historical Principles,*[12] had been published, Henry Sweet had laid the groundwork for the study of English phonology, and the American Dialect Society had been formed. The first quarter of the present century witnessed the appearance of most of the great descriptive, analytical, and historical work of Otto Jespersen, the German Karl Luick, the Dutchmen E. Kruisinga and H. Poutsma, and the Englishman H. C. Wyld, among others. In 1921 appeared Edward Sapir's *Language: An Introduction to the Study of Speech,* a valuable and learned work with not a single diacritical mark or phonetic symbol, and in 1933 Leonard Bloomfield's great *Language,* a revised and enlarged version of his *Introduction to the Study of Language* (1914). Bloomfield's book has been of tremendous influence; it has in fact been called the Bible of American structural linguistics.[13]

[12] Now usually called the *Oxford English Dictionary* (see p. 47, n. 35). It lists a great many words which must have been considered "bad" at the time.

[13] Bloomfield and Sapir were both, it should be noted, students of exotic, specifically American Indian, languages. They perceived the tremendous importance of linguistic structure far more clearly than could those whose studies had been confined to the similarly structured Indo-European languages.

In 1951 appeared *An Outline of English Structure* (Norman, Okla.), by George L. Trager and Henry Lee Smith, Jr., and, in 1952, Charles Carpenter Fries's *The Structure of English*. Trager and Smith concern themselves primarily with a description of the phonology of English, though they also treat morphology (the inflectional system) and syntax (the combining of forms to make phrases and sentences). Fries concerns himself almost wholly with English sentence structure. These have proved to be highly germinative works. Books exemplifying the structural principles laid down in them include Archibald A. Hill's *Introduction to Linguistic Structures* (New York, 1958), Charles F. Hockett's *A Course in Modern Linguistics* (New York, 1958), H. A. Gleason, Jr.'s *An Introduction to Descriptive Linguistics*, rev. ed. (New York, 1961), Harold Whitehall's *Structural Essentials of English* (New York, 1956), and W. Nelson Francis' *The Structure of American English* (New York, 1958). Paul Roberts in his *Understanding English* (New York, 1958) has with considerable success attempted, in his own words, "to relate the complicated data of linguistic science to the equally complicated purposes of the course in English for college freshmen"; the little volume by Whitehall is also designed for college students. James Sledd's *A Short Introduction to English Grammar* (Chicago, 1959) is a successful compromise between the traditional and the new, utilizing as it does the most useful features of both.

The transformational, or generative, analysis of Noam Chomsky, developed out of the important work of Zellig S. Harris exemplified in his *Methods in Structural Linguistics* (Chicago, 1951), is a more recent approach to the study of syntax, quite different from that of the structural linguists, who conceive of the sentence as a combination of classifiable elements in sequence. Chomsky's *Syntactic Structures* (The Hague, 1962), a formidable work full of abstract symbols and mathematical phraseology, has for its purpose the formulation of principles which will, in his own words, "generate all of the grammatical sequences of L [a given language] and none of the ungrammatical ones." Chomsky attempts a "rigorous account of the process by which a grammar generates sentences,"[14] by means of "transforms," or syntactic structures which closely parallel other syntactic structures: thus "John's avoidance of publicity" is a transform of "John avoids publicity," as the passive construction "Publicity is

[14] "A Transformational Approach to Syntax," *Studies in American English* (Third Texas Conference on Problems of Linguistic Analysis in English [Austin, Tex., 1962]), p. 126.

avoided by John" is a transform of "John avoids publicity." (Perhaps the clearest exposition of transforms is that given by Gleason in Chapter 12 of his *Introduction to Descriptive Linguistics.*) Chomsky is concerned only with the grammar of current English. Any thorough-going historical application of the system will require many years to make.

It is obvious that the study of English grammar, or English structure, has been lively and productive—that there are, in fact, a number of grammars of English, not *a* grammar that as yet explains anything so complicated as any language. But public attitudes have remained comparatively unaffected by all this scholarly activity, to some extent perhaps because the materials and methods are difficult and popularizers have been lacking. The fact seems to be, indeed, that in the opinion of the public the linguist is, or at least ought to be, concerned wholly with matters of usage and, since he is at least held to be an expert on language, if a pretty poor booby in other respects, he ought to make up his mind about such matters as the incorrectness of *it's me*, split infinitives, *ain't, finalize, to contact,* and other similar trivialities.

Thus, in a period which has witnessed the most exciting linguistic research since the days of Rask, Grimm, and Bopp, whom we shall encounter in a later chapter, otherwise educated people—people who would scorn to believe in a Ptolemaic cosmology and who pride themselves on knowing a lot about atomic fallout and outer space—have remained practically unaffected by it all. It must of course be admitted that such research is not spectacular except when it utilizes machines of one sort or another, as in machine translation.

We shall later examine in somewhat more detail the beginnings of some of the more preposterous notions about English usage, notions which are responsible for still-current linguistic attitudes. For the time being it is sufficient that we be warned that we shall learn little about language unless we reject such erroneous attitudes as have been the subject of much of this chapter.

One requirement for even an elementary understanding of language is that we understand its relationship to writing, with which it is often confused. Writing is nevertheless of the utmost importance, and it is obviously necessary to have some understanding of its history and its conventions before we go very deeply into an examination of the development of the English language. These will be treated in some detail in the following chapter.

CHAPTER II

Letters and Sounds
A Brief History of Writing

WRITING, as we have seen, is a product of comparatively recent times. With it, history begins; without it, we must depend upon the archaeologist. The entire period during which men have been making conventionalized markings on stone, wood, clay, metal, parchment, paper, or any other surface to symbolize their speech is really no more than a moment in the vast period during which they have been combining vocal noises systematically for the purpose of communicating with each other.

IDEOGRAPHIC AND SYLLABIC WRITING

There can be no doubt that writing grew out of drawing, the wordless comic-strip type of drawing done by savage peoples. The American Indians made many such drawings. It is not surprising that certain conventions should have developed in them, such as horizontal and vertical lines on a chief's gravestone to indicate respectively the number of his campaigns and the number of wounds he received in the course of those campaigns,[1] or the lines rising from an eagle's head to indicate that the figure represents the chief of the eagle totem, in a "letter" from this chief to the president of the United States (represented as a white-faced man in a white house).[2] But such drawings, communicative as they may be in a narrow sense once one

[1] Cited in Holger Pedersen, *Linguistic Science in the Nineteenth Century,* trans. John Webster Spargo (Cambridge, Mass., 1931), p. 143.

[2] Reproduced in E. H. Sturtevant, *An Introduction to Linguistic Science* (New Haven, Conn., 1947), p. 20, from Henry R. Schoolcraft, *Historical and Statistical Information Respecting the Indian Tribes of the United States.* There are many excellent reproductions of such drawings in Chapter 2 ("Forerunners of Writing") of I. J. Gelb's *A Study of Writing* (Chicago, 1952).

understands their conventions, give no idea of actual words. Any identity of wording in their interpretation would be purely coincidental. No line, no element, even remotely suggests speech sounds, and hence such drawings tell us nothing of the language of those who made them. When such use of symbols standing for ideas which can be pictured—rather than for the sounds which go to make up words— reaches a more or less wholly conventional stage, it becomes ideographic, like Chinese writing, in which every word has a symbol based not upon the phonetic structure of the word but upon its meaning.

Another method, fundamentally different, probably grew out of ideographic "writing": the use of the phonogram, which is concerned with sound rather than with meaning. Ultimately, by a sort of punning process, pictures came to be used as in a rebus—that is, as if we were to draw a picture of a tie to represent the first syllable of the word *tycoon* and of a coon to represent the second. In such a method we may see the beginnings of a syllabary, in which symbols, in time becoming so conventionalized as to be unrecognizable as actual pictures, are used to represent syllables.

FROM SEMITIC SYLLABARY
TO GREEK ALPHABET

Semitic writing, the basis of our own and indeed of all alphabetic writing, was not itself alphabetic; rather, it was a syllabary, using symbols for syllables consisting of a specific consonant plus any vowel. Since Semitic had certain consonantal sounds not found in other languages, the symbols for syllables beginning with these sounds were readily available for use as specific vowel symbols by the Greeks when they adopted for their own use the Semitic writing system, which they called Phoenician, using even the Semitic names of the symbols, which they adapted to Greek phonetic patterns: thus *aleph* 'ox' and *beth* 'house' became *alpha* and *beta* because words ending in consonants (other than *n*, *r*, and *s*) are not in accord with Greek patterns. The fact that the Greeks used the Semitic names, which had no other meaning for them, is powerful evidence—if such were needed for what nobody doubts anyway—that the Greeks did indeed acquire their writing from the Semites, as they freely acknowledged having done. The order of the letters and their highly similar forms are additional evidence of this fact.

The symbol A, which from our modern point of view the Semites and the early Greeks drew lying on its side, indicated in Semitic a syllable beginning with a consonantal sound which did not exist in Greek, or for that matter in any other Indo-European language. Its Semitic name was 'aleph, the initial apostrophe here indicating the consonant in question; and, because the name means 'ox,' it has been thought to represent an ox's head, though interpreting many of the Semitic signs as pictorial characters presents as yet insuperable difficulties.[3] By ignoring the initial Semitic consonant, the Greeks adapted this symbol as a vowel, which, as we have seen, they called *alpha*. *Beth* was ultimately somewhat modified in form to B by the Greeks, who wrote it and other reversible letters facing in either direction; in the early days of writing they wrote from right to left, as the Semitic peoples usually did, and as Hebrew is still written.[4] From the Greek modifications of the Semitic names of the first two letters, the word *alphabet*, as everyone knows, is ultimately derived.

THE GREEK VOWEL SYMBOLS

The brilliant Greek notion of using as vowel symbols those Semitic syllabic symbols which began with non-Greek sounds gave them an alphabet in the modern sense of the word. Thus, Semitic *yod* became *iota* (I) and was used for the Greek vowel *i*; at the time the symbol was taken over, Greek had no need for the corresponding semivowel with which the Semitic word *yod* began. Just as they had changed *aleph* into a vowel symbol by dropping the initial Semitic consonant, so also the Greeks dropped the consonant of Semitic *he* and called it *epsilon* (E), that is, *e psilon* 'e simple, or *e* without the aspirate.' Semitic *ayin*, symbolizing a syllable beginning with a guttural consonant nonexistent in Greek, became for the Greeks *omicron* (O), that is, *o mikron* 'o little.' Semitic *heth* was at first used as a consonant and called *heta*, but the "rough breathing" sound which it symbolized

[3] See Gelb, pp. 140–41.

[4] Sometimes the early Greeks would change direction in alternate lines, starting, for instance, at the right, then changing direction at the end of the line and going from left to right, and continuing this change of direction throughout. Solon's laws were so written. The Greeks had a word for the fashion—*boustrophedon* 'as the ox turns in plowing,' a wondrous word indeed, which may even be used in English if one is skillful enough to steer conversation in such a way as to make occasion for its use. Those who are fortunate enough to find such occasion stress the first and third syllables (respectively *boo* or *bough* and *fee*).

was lost in several Greek dialects, notably the Ionic of Asia Minor, where the symbol was called *eta* (H) and used for long *e*. The vowel symbol *omega* (Ω), that is, *o mega* 'o big,' was a Greek innovation, as was also *upsilon* (Υ), that is, *u psilon* 'u simple.' *Upsilon* was born of the need for a symbol for a simple vowel corresponding to *vau* (F), which was used for the semivowel sound written *w* in English. This sound was lost in Ionic, as also in other dialects, and *vau*, which came to be called *digamma* because it looked like one gamma on top of another, ceased to be used except as a numeral—but not before the Romans had taken it over and assigned a different value to it.

THE GREEK CONSONANT SYMBOLS

Practically all of the remaining Semitic symbols were used for the Greek consonants, the Semitic values of their first elements remaining for the most part unchanged; the same was true of their graphic forms.[5] *Gimel* became *gamma* (Γ), *daleth* became *delta* (Δ), and so on. The early Greek alphabet ended with *tau* (T). The consonant symbols *phi* (Φ), *chi* (X), and *psi* (Ψ) were later Greek additions.

THE ROMANS ADOPT THE GREEK ALPHABET

The Ionic alphabet, adopted at Athens, became the standard for the writing of Greek, but it was the somewhat different Western form of the alphabet which the Romans, perhaps by way of the Etruscans, were to adopt for their own use. The Romans used a curved form of *gamma* (C), the third letter, which at first had for them the same value [g] as for the Greeks, but in time came to be used for [k].[6] Another symbol was thus needed for the [g] sound. This need was

[5] A good idea of the shapes of the letters and the very slight modifications made by the early Greeks may be obtained from the charts in Gelb, p. 177, and Pedersen, p. 179. Gelb also gives the Latin forms, and Pedersen the highly similar Indian ones, Indian writings from the third century B.C. onward being written in an alphabet adapted from the Semitic.

[6] Letters enclosed in square brackets are used as phonetic symbols. In this chapter no letters will be so used without further explanation unless, as in the present instance, they are ordinarily used with the same values in current English spelling or their values can easily be inferred from the context in which they appear. The brackets are unnecessary in discussing prehistoric sound-changes, as in the following chapter, since it is obvious that the letters are under these circumstances used exclusively as phonetic symbols.

remedied in time by a simple modification in the shape of C, resulting in G: thus C and G are both derived from Greek Γ. The C was, however, sometimes used for both [g] and [k], a custom which survived in later times in such abbreviations as *C.* for *Gaius* and *Cn.* for *Gnaeus*.

Rounded forms of *delta* (D), *pi* (P), and *sigma* (S), as well as of *gamma*, were used by the Romans. These were not Roman innovations; all of them occur in Greek also, though the more familiar Greek literary forms are angular (Δ, Π, and Σ). The occurrence of such rounded forms was doubtless due in early times to the use of pen and ink; the angular forms reflect the use of cutting tool on stone.

Epsilon (E) was adopted without change. The sixth position was filled by F, the Greek *digamma* (earlier *vau*). The Romans gave this symbol the value [f]. Following it came the modified *gamma*, G. H was used as a consonant, as in Semitic and also in Western Greek at the time the Romans adopted it. Thus the Romans could not indicate the distinction in vowel length made by the Asiatic Greeks when, after the loss of [h] in their dialect, they chose to use its symbol for long *e*.

The Roman gain in having a symbol for [h] was slight, for the aspirate was almost as unstable a sound in Latin as it is in Cockney English; ultimately, as in Greek, it was lost completely. Among the Romance languages—those derived from Latin, such as Italian, French, Spanish, and Portuguese—there is no need for the symbol, since there is no trace of the sound, though it may be retained in spelling because of conservatism, as in some French and Spanish words, for example French *heure* and Spanish *hora* 'hour' (but compare Fr. *avoir* with Sp. *haber* 'to have').

Iota (I) was for the Romans both semivowel and vowel, as illustrated respectively by the two *i*'s in *iudices* 'judges,' the first syllable of which is like English *you*; the prolonged form of this letter, that is, *j*, did not appear until medieval times, when the minuscule form of writing developed.[7] The majuscule form of this newly shaped *i*, that is, J (for whose uses see p. 33), is a product of modern times. *Kappa* (K) was used in only a few words by the Romans, who, as we have seen, had already ascribed to C the Greek value of this symbol. Next came the Western Greek form of *lambda*, L, corresponding to Ionic Λ. M and N, from *mu* and *nu*, require no comment. *Xi* (Ξ), with the value [ks], following Greek *nu*, was not taken over into Latin; thus in the Roman alphabet O immediately followed N. *Pi* (Π) was adopted in a

---

[7] In ancient writing only majuscules (capital letters) were used.

rounded form, P; it was therefore necessary for the Romans to use a tailed form of *rho* (P), as the early Greeks also had sometimes done, thus R. Q (*koppa*) stood for a sound which had dropped out of Greek, though the symbol continued to be used as a numeral in that language. The Romans used it as a variant of C in one position only, preceding V; thus, the sequence [kw] was written QV—the *qu* of printed texts. *Sigma* in its rounded form S was adopted unchanged. *Tau* (T) was likewise unchanged. *Upsilon* was adopted in the form V and used for both consonant and vowel.

The symbol Z (Greek *zeta*), which had occupied seventh place in the early Roman alphabet but had become quite useless in Latin because of rhotacism (see p. 95, n. 40), was reintroduced and placed at the end of the alphabet in the time of Cicero, when a number of Greek words were coming to be used in Latin. Another form of *upsilon*, Y, was used in such words to indicate the Greek vowel sound, which was like French *u* and German *ü*. *Chi* (X) was used with the Western Greek value [ks], the sound of Ionic X being represented in Classical Latin by CH, just as TH and PH were used to represent Greek *theta* (Θ) and *phi* (Φ) respectively. Actually these were accurate enough representations of the Classical Greek sounds, which most scholars agree were similar to the aspirated initial sounds of English *kin, tin,* and *pin.* The Romans in their transcriptions very sensibly symbolized the aspiration, or breath-puff, by H. The sounds symbolized in Latin by C, T, and P apparently lacked such aspiration, as *k, t,* and *p* do in English when preceded by *s,* for example *skin, sting,* and *spin.*

LATER DEVELOPMENTS OF THE ROMAN AND GREEK ALPHABETS

Even though it lacked a good many symbols for sounds in the modern languages of Europe, the Roman alphabet was taken over by the various European peoples, though not by those Slavic peoples who in the ninth century got their alphabet, called Cyrillic from the Greek missionary leader Cyril, direct from the Greek. The Greek missionaries, sent out from Byzantium, added a number of symbols for sounds which were not in Greek, for example Ш for the sound spelled *sh* in English. B was used for [v], which sound the symbol also symbolized in some positions in Greek; a modification, Б, was used for [b]. *Sigma* was written C in later Greek, and C has thus the value [s] in the writing of those Slavic peoples—the Russians, the Bulgarians, and the Serbs—who use this alphabet. Those Slavs whose Christianity stems from Rome—the Poles, the Czechs, the Slovaks, the Croats, and the Slovenians—use the Roman alphabet, adapted by diacritical markings (for example Polish *ć* and Czech *č*) and by combinations of letters (for example Polish *cz, sz*) to symbolize sounds for which the Roman alphabet naturally made no provision.

THE USE OF DIACRITICAL MARKINGS

In various ways the Roman alphabet has been eked out by those who have adopted it. Such un-Latin sounds as the *o*-umlaut and the *u*-umlaut of German are written *ö* and *ü*; as we have seen, Y had been borrowed by the Romans from the Greeks for the sound indicated by the latter. The *ä* as now pronounced does not differ from the sound indicated in German by *e*; for instance, *Bäder* 'baths' and *geben* 'to give,' which have the same long vowel; and *Hände* 'hands' and *senden* 'to send,' which have the corresponding short one. Other languages also use the dieresis—the superposed dots—to indicate vowel quality: Danish, Icelandic, Norwegian, Swedish, Slovak, Albanian (*ë* only), and, among the non-Indo-European languages, Estonian, Finnish, Hungarian, and Turkish. Its occasional use in English and French writing, as in *preëminent* and *Noël* respectively, is for quite a different purpose—to indicate that two adjacent vowel symbols are to be pronounced as separate sounds.

Other expedients are the acute accent marks of French *é*, of Czech and Icelandic *á, é, í, ó, ú,* and *ý*, of Hungarian *á, é, í, ó,* and *ú* (with double acute accent marks for *ő* and *ű* also), and of Polish *ó, ć, ń, ś,* and *ź*;[8] the grave accent marks of French *à* and *è*; the circumflex accent marks in French *â, ê, î, ô,* and *û* and Roumanian *â* and *î*; the wedge of *ě, č, ň, ř, š,* and *ž* in Czech; the tilde of Portuguese *ã* and *õ*[9] and of Spanish *ñ*; the cedilla of French, Portuguese, and Turkish *ç* (in Turkish it symbolizes the sound usually spelled *ch* in English); the bar of Polish *ł*; and the circle of Swedish and Norwegian *å* and Czech *ů*. There are still other, less familiar diacritical markings. Lithuanian makes very free use of such devices.

[8] Acute accent marks are also used in Spanish, but only to indicate stress where it might otherwise be in question; they do not indicate either the quality or the quantity (relative length) of the vowels which they are placed above.

[9] To indicate nasal vowels. For the same purpose Polish uses a hook under the vowel symbol (*ą, ę*); so does Lithuanian, for purely historical reasons, inasmuch as the nasalization has been lost in that language. French uses no special marking for this purpose.

THE USE OF DIGRAPHS

Digraphs (pairs of letters), or even longer sequences like German *sch*, have also been made use of to indicate un-Latin single sounds, such as those which we spell *sh, ch, th*, and *dg*. In *gu*, as in *guest* and *guilt*, the *u* has the sole function of indicating that the *g* stands for the initial sound of *go* rather than what we might expect it to represent before *e* or *i*, as in *gesture* and *gibe*. The *h* of *gh* performs a similar useful function in *Ghent*, but not in *ghost* and *ghastly*. English makes no use of diacritical marks save for the rare dieresis, preferring other devices such as the aforementioned use of digraphs and of entirely different symbols for mutated (umlauted) vowels: for example English writes *man, men*; compare the German method of indicating the same vowel change in *Mann, Männer*.

ADDITIONAL SYMBOLS

Furthermore, as has been noted in the case of the Cyrillic alphabet, other symbols have been used, such as the runic þ (called *thorn*) and ƿ (called *wynn*) used by the English, along with their modification of *d* as ð (called *eth*), all now abandoned as far as English writing is concerned. The þ and the ð were adopted by the Scandinavians, who got the alphabet from the English. They used the former symbol at the beginning of a word, where it indicated the initial sound of *thin*, and the latter in all other positions, where it indicated the initial sound of *thine*. Subsequently the first of these sounds became [t] (or [d] in words regularly lacking stress, such as pronouns and definite articles) except in Icelandic, which alone uses þ. In modern times ð came to be written *d* by the Scandinavians, but Icelandic reintroduced ð in the nineteenth century.

The ligature œ, which indicated a single vowel sound in post-Classical Latin, was used in early Old English for the *o*-umlaut sound (as in German *schön*). When this sound was later unrounded, there was no further need for œ in English. It was, however, taken over by the Scandinavians, who have long since given up the symbol, the Danes having devised ø and the Swedes using ö. It is sometimes used in English in a few classical loan-words (words taken by one language from another), for instance *amœba* and *cœnobite*.

For the vowel sound of *cat*, the English used the digraph *ae*, later written prevailingly as a ligature—that is, as æ. This digraph they also got from Latin, in which the classical value (as in Ger. *Kaiser*, from *Caesar*) had long before shifted to a vowel sound roughly similar in value to that which the English ascribed to it. The *æ* was called *æsc* 'ash,' the name of the runic symbol which represented the same sound, though it in no way resembled the Latin-English digraph. When in Middle English times, beginning around 1100, the sound indicated by *æ* was lost, the symbol went out of use. Later, in the sixteenth century, the sound developed again, but the old way of indicating it was not revived; instead, *a* was used. Today *æ* is used in Danish, Norwegian, and Icelandic. It occurs occasionally, with a quite different value, in loan-words of classical origin, like *encyclopædia* and *anæmia*.

THE GERMANIC RUNES

In the early Middle Ages various script styles—the "national hands" —developed in those lands which had been provinces of the Roman Empire. But Latin writing, as well as the Latin tongue, all but disappeared in the Roman colony of Britannia, which the Romans had perforce practically abandoned even before the arrival of the English. These Germanic invaders of a land whose population was predominantly Celtic had available to them when they wished to write, which was certainly not very often, the twenty-four runes, to which they added six. These runes, in the beginning associated with pagan mysteries—the word *rune* means 'secret'—were angular letters intended originally to be cut or scratched in wood[10] and, though perhaps ill adapted to any sustained composition, served well enough for inscriptions, charms, and the like. Their close similarities to both Greek and Latin symbols make it obvious that, though the order of the symbols is quite different,[11] they are derived from the Roman alphabet, with which the Germanic peoples could easily have acquired familiarity, or from some early Italic alphabet akin to the Roman alphabet.

THE EARLIEST ENGLISH WRITING

Although St. Augustine and his Roman missionaries must have written the sixth-century Italian script, this hand never established itself in England. The script used in the Old English manuscripts is based

[10] The word *write* is akin to the German word *reissen* 'to tear.' *Book* is generally thought to be related to *beech*. It has been plausibly suggested that the runes were originally scratched, cut, or torn in strips of beechwood or in the bark of beech trees.

[11] As modified by the English, the first group of letters consists of characters corresponding to *f, u, þ, o, r, c, g,* and *w*. The English runic "alphabet" is sometimes called *futhorc* from the first six of these.

upon the Irish modification of the Roman alphabet. This so-called Insular hand was used for English writings until the Norman Conquest. It is generally accepted that the Irish, whose conversion to Christianity antedated that of the English, taught the English how to write. The Insular hand is still used in the writing of Irish Gaelic.

To read Old English in the Insular hand of the manuscripts requires little adjustment for the modern student, once he becomes accustomed to the aforementioned *æsc*, the peculiar forms of *f, g,* and *r,* the *eth,* the runes called *thorn* and *wynn,* and the three forms of *s,* one of which, called "long *s,*" looks very much like an *f* in modern typography except that the horizontal stroke does not go through the top of the letter. This particular variant of *s* (ſ) was used until the end of the eighteenth century save in final position, printers following what was the general practice of the manuscripts.

THE LATER FATE OF THORN, ETH, AND WYNN

The earliest English texts—those written before 900—used the digraph *th* instead of þ. Toward the end of the Middle English period, around 1400, the same digraph—the Roman transliteration of *theta*—was gradually reintroduced, and English printers regularized its use instead of the single symbol which for centuries had supplanted it. Similarly, *u* and *uu,* used for [w] in early manuscripts, were supplanted by ƿ, which continued in use for a long time, though not quite so long as þ. The earlier English symbol, *uu,* had in the meantime been adopted on the Continent, whence it was brought back to England by Norman scribes in a ligatured form as *w.* The origin of this symbol is accurately indicated by its name, *double-u.*

The þ was used in Old English for both the initial sound of *thin* and that of *thine.* Even before the introduction of þ, the English had crossed the Irish *d,* presumably to represent the second of these sounds, though actually they used the symbol to represent precisely the same two sounds for which they used first *th,* then þ. From a phonetic point of view, it would have made excellent sense to use þ exclusively for the first of these sounds and to write the ð within words to indicate the second, which never occurred initially or finally in Old English;[12]

---

[12] It occurs initially in current English only in *the, this, that, these, those, they, their(s), them, then, there, though, than, thus,* the more or less archaic *thou, thee, thy, thine,* and the more or less literary *thence* and *thither. Thither* is also very frequently pronounced—usually in reading aloud, for the word can hardly be regarded as current in spoken English—with the initial sound of *thin.*

but to do so would hardly have occurred to our ancestors, who would have regarded the two sounds merely as positional variants of a single sound. Even so, the situation was not really so bad—again from a phonetic point of view—as the modern use of the single digraph *th* for no fewer than three different sounds, as in *thin, thine,* and *thyme* (traditionally pronounced *time,* though a new pronunciation based on the spelling is occasionally heard, mainly from younger-generation speakers). The *ð* gradually disappeared during the Middle English period, but *þ,* as we have seen, continued in use until the very end of the Middle Ages.

In a few words *y* (which *þ* in its later form had come to resemble) was used as a representation of *þ*; for example *y*^t was used as an abbreviation for *that*[13] and *y*^e for *the*. The latter abbreviation survives to our own day in such pseudoantique absurdities as "Ye Olde Choppe Suey Shoppe," in which it is usually pronounced as if it were the same word as the old nominative second person plural pronoun *ye*. Needless to say at this point, there is no justification whatever for such a pronunciation. The two words were carefully distinguished, and would have been even had they been printed identically. The fact is, however, that they were also carefully distinguished in printing, as in writing, by the superior *e*, either following the *y* or directly over it, for the definite article. Though *y*^t could hardly be read as any other word, it too was always written with the superior *t*.

YOGH

The Old English symbol *ȝ* was an Irish form; *g* entered the English alphabet later from the Continent. In late Old English *ȝ* had three values, as we shall see (p. 110). In Middle English times it acquired a somewhat different form, *ȝ* (called *yogh*),[14] and was used for two sounds which came to be spelled *y* and *gh* later in the period. Old

[13] Old English used a crossed *thorn* as an abbreviation of the same word.

[14] This symbol, which continued to be written in Scotland long after the English had given it up, has been mistaken for *z*—the symbol which printers, having no *ȝ* in their fonts, used for it—as in the pronunciation of the names *Kenzie* (compare *Kenny,* with revised spelling to indicate a pronunciation somewhat closer to the historical one) and *Menzies*. Pronunciation of the second name as *men-yeez* survives, particularly in Scotland, though the usual English pronunciation follows the makeshift spelling with *z*. For other examples of this erroneous interpretation of *ȝ* as *z*, see Otto Jespersen, *A Modern English Grammar on Historical Principles* (Copenhagen, 1909–49), I, 22–23.

English, for instance, wrote ȝeldan 'to yield,' cniht 'knight,' and þurh 'through'; early Middle English wrote the same words ȝelde(n), cniȝt, and þurȝ; later Middle English (as in Chaucer) wrote them yelde(n), knyght, and thurgh.[15] The characteristic conservatism of Modern English spelling is reflected in our retention of the gh in writing, though the earlier phonetic symbolism of this digraph (the same as that of ch in German) has been lost in all types of English save Scots for so long that the modern speaker of English must laboriously learn how to articulate the sound in question when he studies German. Nevertheless, we go on writing words which once contained the sound just as if it had survived, and such sensible spellings as tho, thru, and nite meet with widespread disapproval.

After the Norman Conquest, the French form g supplanted Old English ȝ to indicate the "hard" sound in English words; and, with the introduction of French words into English, the newer symbol was used also with the value which it had in Old French before e and i, for instance gem and age—the same value that it has in Modern English. Modern English thus preserves in loan-words what was formerly the French value of g before the vowels e and i; in Modern French the older sound has become that of the final consonant of rouge, or the medial sound of English measure. No native English words, incidentally, begin with this older sound. It occurs initially only in loan-words, for example gentle and juggle (Old French), generate[16] and judicial (Latin). In Latin, as we have seen (p. 25), the letter i was used both as vowel and as semivowel. It was only as the Romance languages developed from Latin, however, that there came to be a really sharp differentiation in the pronunciation of these two sounds, the semivowel coming to acquire the sound preserved initially in such loan-words as judge (from OF iuge, ultimately Lat. iudex)—that is, a sound identical with that of the final consonant of the same word and popularly referred to as "soft g." Hence the identity of sound indicated by j

[15] Note that one of the two sounds written in early Middle English with yogh was in Old English written not with the earlier form of that letter, but with h. Later these different sounds were differentiated in writing, as they had been in Old English.

[16] Note that we pronounce the g before e and i in Latin loan-words (and before y in those which are ultimately Greek, like gymnasium) in the Old French way, as we also pronounce the name of the letter itself. The Romans pronounced the name of the letter gay, the initial sound of which indicates its only value in Classical Latin.

(which, as we have seen, was merely another way of writing *i*) and *g* before *e* and *i*.

THE USE OF J

When the prolonged and curved *i*—that is, the *j*—came into being, it was used merely as a variant of *i* in final position, especially when preceded by another *i*, as in Latin *filii*. The dot, incidentally, was not originally part of minuscule *i*, but is a development of the faint sloping line which came to be put above this insignificant letter to distinguish it from the strokes of contiguous letters such as *m, n,* and *u,* as well as to distinguish double *i* from *u*. It was later extended by analogy to the *j*, where, because of the different shape of the letter, it performed no useful purpose. Since English scribes used *y* for *i* in final position,[17] the use of *j* in English was long more or less confined to the representation of numerals, for instance *iij* for *three* and *vij* for *seven*.

The present use of *i* for vowel and *j* for consonant was not established until the seventeenth century. In the King James Bible (1611) and the First Folio (1623) of Shakespeare, for instance, *i* is used for both values. For a long time after the distinction in writing was made, however, the feeling persisted that *i* and *j* were one and the same letter: Dr. Johnson's *Dictionary* (1755) puts them together, and this practice continued well into the nineteenth century.

THE USES OF U AND V

It was similar with the curved and angular forms of *u*—that is, *u* and *v*. Although consonantal and vocalic *u* came in Latin to be sharply differentiated in sound early in the Christian Era, when consonantal *u*, hitherto pronounced [w], became [v], the two symbols *u* and *v* continued to be used more or less indiscriminately for either vowel or consonant. When *v* came to be used in English in Middle English times, the scribes followed the Continental practice of using either symbol for either value; as a general thing, though, *v* was used initially and *u* elsewhere, regardless of the sound indicated, as in *very, vsury* (*usury*), and *euer* (*ever*), except in the neighborhood of *m* and *n*, where for the sake of legibility *v* was frequently used in other than initial position. Continental printers in time came to use *v* and *u* for consonant and vowel respectively, and before the middle of the

[17] Compare *marry* with *marries* and *married; holy day* with *holiday.*

seventeenth century English printers were generally making the same distinction. As with *i* and *j*, catalogues, indexes, and the like put *u* and *v* together well into the nineteenth century; in dictionaries *vizier* was followed by *ulcer*, *unzoned* by *vocable*, and *iambic* was set between *jamb* and *jangle*. Many editions of old texts, particularly those used in schools, substitute *j* and *v* for *i* and *u* when these indicate consonants, and *u* for initial *v* when this indicates a vowel, representing, for example, *iaspre*, *liue*, and *vnder* as *jaspre* 'jasper,' *live*, and *under*. Except for the passage reproduced from Banckes's *Herball* in Chapter VII, this practice will here be followed when older writers are cited, as also for citations of individual words from older periods. The matter is purely graphic; no question of linguistic evidence is involved.

The consonant sound [v] did not occur initially in Old English, or, for that matter, in any other Germanic language in its oldest form.[18] Old English used *f* for the [v] which developed internally, as in *drifen*, 'driven,' *hæfde* 'had,' and *scofl* 'shovel.' Except for a very few words which have entered Standard English from Southern English dialects, in which initial [f] became [v]—for instance *vixen*, the feminine of *vox* 'fox'—no Standard English words of native origin begin with [v]. Practically all our words with initial *v* have been taken from Latin or French. No matter how familiar such words as *virtue* (Latin), *visit* (Latin), *very* (French), and *voice* (French) may be to us now, they were once regarded as foreign words—as indeed they are, despite their long naturalization. The introduction of the letter *v* (that is, *u*) to indicate the prehistoric Old English development of [f] to [v] was an innovation of Anglo-Norman scribes in Middle English times: thus the Middle English form of Old English *drifen* was written *driven* (that is, *driuen*).

OTHER ROMAN CONSONANT SYMBOLS IN ENGLISH

B, *d*, *h*, *k*, *l*, *m*, *n*, *p*, *r*, *s*, *t*, and *x* ([ks]) have been used throughout the history of the Roman alphabet to represent the same (or in some instances approximately the same) sounds which they symbolize in English today, though it should be remembered that the breathing originally indicated by Latin *h* was lost in Latin (see p. 25) and that hence

[18] In Modern German the letter *v* regularly occurs in initial position as a writing for [f], for instance *Vater* 'father.' German [v] in initial position is a late medieval development from [w], as the retention of *w* in the spelling indicates, for instance *Weg* 'way.'

the symbol has no phonetic significance in those Latin-derived languages which retain it here and there in their spelling.[19] Its use to indicate the aspirate in English (and the other Germanic languages as well) is due to scholarly tradition, for the aspirate had been lost in Latin long before the Germanic peoples learned to write.

The later influence of Classical Latin caused French scribes to restore the *h* in many words, for instance *habit, herbage,* and *homme,* though it was of course never pronounced. It was also sometimes inserted in English words of French origin where it was not etymological, for instance *habundance* (mistakenly regarded as coming from *habere* 'to have') and *abhominable* (supposed to be from Lat. *ab* plus *homine,* explained as 'away from man, hence bestial.') When Shakespeare's pedant Holofernes by implication recommended this latter misspelling and consequent mispronunciation with [h] in *Love's Labour's Lost* V.i.26 ("This is abhominable, which he would call abbominable."),[20] he was in very good company, at least as far as the writing of the word is concerned, for the error had been current since Middle English times. Writers of Medieval Latin and Old French were similarly misled by a false notion of the etymology of the word. Because of the influence of writing, *h* has gradually come to be pronounced in all English loan-words from French except *honor, honest, hour,* and *heir.* Pronunciation of *herb* without [h] is, however, still usual in American English; less usual, though by no means uncommon in American usage, is omission of [h] in *humble*—a pronunciation regarded by Dickens as old-fashioned, not to say vulgar, in the British speech of his day, otherwise there would have been no point in his indicating Uriah Heep's pronunciation of the word as *'umble.* In *humor,* present usage wavers; pronunciation of this word without [h] is certainly commoner in educated American speech than in Standard British English.

Names in *H-* from the classical languages were somewhat more

---

[19] Portuguese uses *h* purely as a diacritic in the combinations *lh* and *nh,* symbolizing the sounds which Spanish has chosen to indicate by *ll* and *ñ* and Italian by *gl* and *gn* respectively, for example Latin *filius* 'son,' Portuguese *filho,* Italian *figlio.* Spanish, French, Italian, and Portuguese all use *ch,* with differing values.

[20] This (with correction of an obvious printer's error) and subsequent quotations from Shakespeare's plays are from the First Folio (facsimile ed., London, 1910) with the line numbering of the *Globe* edition (1891) as given in Bartlett's *Concordance.* Roman type will be substituted for the annoying italic used for proper names occurring in speeches in the Folio.

familiar in Middle English times in their French than in their classical forms; Chaucer, for instance, has *Omer, Ector, Ercules,* and *Eleyne,* along with such inverted spellings as *Habradate* (for *Abradates*) and *Helie* (*Eli*)—the last of Hebrew origin—indicating equally well that [h] was not pronounced in such words. The classical forms, with *H* written and pronounced wherever called for by the classical etymology, became much more usual after the Renaissance, though *Ector* and *Omer,* which looks deceptively Mohammedan when spelled *Omar* (as in the name of General Omar Bradley, born in Missouri), survive in the southern American hill country and the areas settled therefrom. It is not surprising that those lowland Scotsmen who colonized the "King's plantation" in Ulster and whose descendants crossed the Atlantic and settled the Blue Ridge, the Appalachians, and the Ozarks should have been little affected by the classical culture of the Renaissance. *Ellen* survives in all parts of the English-speaking world; it is thought of not as a variant of *Helen,* but as a separate name.

UNETYMOLOGICAL H AFTER T

During the Renaissance *h* was inserted after *t* in a number of foreign words, for instance *throne,* from Old French *trone.* The French word is from Latin *thronus,* borrowed from Greek, the *th* being, as we have seen (p. 26), the normal Roman transliteration of Greek θ. The English respelling ultimately gave rise to a change in the initial sound, as also in *theater* and *thesis,* which earlier had initial [t]; similarly with the internal consonant sound spelled *th* in *anthem, apothecary, Catherine* (the pet forms *Kate* and *Kit* preserve the older sound), and *Anthony* (compare *Tony*), which has retained its historically correct pronunciation in British, but not in American, English. The American pronunciation of *Anthony* is precisely parallel with the universal English pronunciation of *anthem* and the other words cited. It is sometimes heard even in reference to Mark Antony, where the spelling does not encourage it. The *h* of *author,* from Old French *autor* (modern *auteur*), going back to Latin *auctor,* was first inserted by French scribes, to whom an *h* after *t* indicated no difference in pronunciation. When in the sixteenth century this fancy spelling began to be used in the English loan-word, the way was paved for the modern pronunciation, historically a mispronunciation. It was almost inevitable, in the light of the slavish subservience which even partially literate people show toward writing, that the *th* should be given a value which it has in native words which were written with þ in Old and Middle English.

Elizabeth, Arthur, and *Dorothy* were formerly pronounced with [t], as the pet names *Betty, Art,* and *Dot* indicate. *Thomas* and *Theresa* have remained unaffected by their spellings; a spelling pronunciation of *Esther* is occasionally heard from the half-educated, but not from either cultured or illiterate speakers. *Thames* as the name of an estuary in Connecticut is frequently pronounced as the spelling seems to indicate it should be. Such is the effect of literacy divorced from tradition. But, as we have seen, the same thing has happened many times in the history of English, and is in no wise indicative of a particularly American form of linguistic depravity. In *Waltham,* for instance, the *t* and the *h* are in different syllables from a historical point of view, the *-ham* being from Old English *ham* 'home, village' with shortened vowel. The two symbols have, however, been mistakenly regarded by people familiar with spelling—not by illiterates, we may be sure—as constituting the digraph *th;* hence, on both sides of the Atlantic, frequent pronunciation of this word with the medial consonant of *lethal*—just as if one were to pronounce *courthouse* as *cour-thouse. Gotham,* when used as a nickname for New York City, is invariably pronounced with the same medial consonant, though in British English, as the name of a town in Nottinghamshire, it continues to be pronounced *got 'em. Chatham,* which is parallel in structure, always has medial [t], though there is an overcareful American pronunciation as *chat-ham* doubtless regarded as an educated improvement upon *chat 'em.*[21]

THE DIGRAPH PH

H after *p,* according to Latin custom (see p. 26), was used in a good many English words of Greek origin to indicate the post-Classical value of Φ in Greek, as well as replacing *f* in a few words not from Greek, for instance the proper name *Ralph,* previously and still to a large extent in England pronounced to rime with *waif.*[22] (The *l* is also

[21] A precisely similar misinterpretation of *s* and *h* as constituting a digraph occurs in *Lewisham* and *Evesham,* in which pronunciation with the medial consonant of *banish 'em* rather than with medial [s] has become practically universal, though in the beginning such pronunciation was parallel with the childish misreading of *mishap* to rime with *bishop.*

[22] As in Act II of W. S. Gilbert's *H.M.S. Pinafore:*

> In time each little waif
> Forsook his foster-mother,
> The well-born babe was Ralph—
> Your captain was the other!!!

mere window dressing from a historical point of view.) Ordinarily, however, *ph* indicates genuine Greek origin.

THE DIGRAPH CH

H after *c* was used by French scribes, or by English ones under French influence, to indicate the initial sound of *child* (OE *cild*) in all words regardless of their origin; following a short vowel the trigraph *cch* (supplanting earlier *chch*) was commonly used in Middle English times—*catch* appears as *cache, cacche,* and *cachche*—but *tch* had come to be usual under the same circumstances by the sixteenth century. *Ch* was also, as we have seen, a transliteration of Greek *chi* (X), pronounced [k] in *chorus, machination,* and the like, and was sometimes inserted under classical influence in words where it did not belong, for example *schedule* (from OF *cedule*), for which Noah Webster recommended the American spelling pronunciation with initial [sk],[23] as if this were a Greek loan. *Schism,* though ultimately Greek, was taken from Old French *cisme,* the spelling of which was in the sixteenth century made to conform to the Greek original. The word is, however, still pronounced with initial [s] by cultured speakers, but pronunciation with [sk] is frequently heard nowadays.

THE DIGRAPH GH

H after *g* has been discussed in another connection (pp. 31–32); *gh* also came to be used—or rather misused from a purely rational point of view—after 1400 to indicate "hard *g*" in some English words, the practice surviving in *ghost* (OE *gast*–ME *go(o)st*), *aghast,* and *ghastly.* It also occurs in words of exotic origin as a transliteration of non-Roman symbols indicating non-Roman sounds, for instance *ghazi* and *ghoul,* and in *gherkin* and *Ghent,* where it performs the genuinely useful purpose of indicating that these words are not to be pronounced like *jerkin* and *gent.*

THE DIGRAPHS SC AND SH

In early Old English times *sc* symbolized [sk], but during the course of the Old English period the graphic sequence continued to indicate the later development of [sk] into the sound symbolized from Middle English times to the present by *sh.* The *sh* was an innovation of Anglo-Norman scribes (OE *sceal*–ME and ModE *shall*), who earlier had used

[23] The British English pronunciation with the first syllable as *shed-* is also erroneously based upon the misspelling. The historically correct pronunciation would begin with [s].

s, ss, and *sch* for the same purpose. The digraph *sc* thus occurs after the Old English period only in borrowed words. In those ultimately Latin or Greek, regardless of their immediate source as far as English is concerned, *sc* may indicate either [s] or [sk], depending upon the following sound, for example (with [s]) *scion, science, scene,* (with [sk]) *scandal, scorpion, sculpture, scripture.* English words of Scandinavian origin use *sc* for [sk] before *a, o, u,* and *r,* for example *scald, scowl, scurf,* and *scrape;* under other circumstances English uses *sk* in Scandinavian loans, for example *skill* and *bask.* In *scent* and *scythe* the *c* is a late and an etymologically altogether unjustifiable insertion; in the latter word, as well as in *scissors* (OF *cisoires*), there has been confusion with Latin *scindere* 'to cut' (past participle *scissum*).

THE SEQUENCE WH

Middle English scribes preferred the writing *wh* for the phonetically more accurate *hw* used in Old English times, for example Old English *hwæt*–Middle and Modern English *what.* For a large part of the English-speaking world the *h* in the graphic sequence *wh,* save for the exceptions noted in the last sentence of this paragraph, has no phonetic significance; it is, however, significant as far as the speech of northern England, Scotland, Ireland, and most of the United States is concerned. Spoken differentiation of such pairs as *whale–wail, when– wen,* and *which–witch* in American English is doubtless attributable largely to the influence of those Ulster Scots, or Scotch-Irish as they are sometimes misleadingly called, who began arriving in America in large numbers around the end of the first quarter of the eighteenth century and who settled first the Pennsylvania back country and subsequently a large part of the country away from the Atlantic Coast.[24] Notions of "correctness" based upon spelling have to some extent restored the [hw] in areas where [w] is historically to be expected. In *whole* (OE *hal*) and *whore* (OE *hore*), the *w* indicates what was a dialectal pronunciation which seems to have become fairly common in the sixteenth century; the unwritten [w] of *one* and *once* is of the same dialectal origin; in *who, whom, whose* there has been loss of earlier [w].

[24] For the geographical distribution of [hw] and [w] in the eastern United States, see Raven I. McDavid, Jr., and Virginia Glenn McDavid, "*h* Before Semivowels in the Eastern United States," *Language,* XXVIII (1952), 41–62, and Raven I. McDavid, Jr., "Our Initial Consonant 'H'," *College English,* XI (1950), 458–59.

C *AND* K

Under French influence, scribes in Middle English times used *c* before *e* and *i (y)* in French loan-words, for example *citee* 'city' and *grace*, with an earlier French value of this symbol [ts], later becoming [s]. Now, as we have seen, *c* in Old English writing never indicated [s], but only [k] and the sound in Middle English times written *ch*. Thus, with the introduction of the newer French value, *c* remained an ambiguous symbol, though in a different way: it came to represent [k] before *a, o,* and *u* and before consonants, and [s] before *e* and *i* (*y*). *K*, used occasionally in Old English writing, thus came to be increasingly used before *e* and *i* (*y*) in Middle English times (OE *cyn(n)* 'race'—ME *kin, kyn*) to indicate the stop sound, so that *c* might be reserved for the sibilant, as in *certain* (compare *curtain*, with *c* indicating [k] before *u*). *Ck* is usual for [k] after short vowels, but the ending -*ick* has been simplified to -*ic* in *music, critic, physic,* and the like. In recent loans, with final stress, the French spelling is used, as in *critique* and *physique*, which are regarded as different words from *critic* and *physic*.

Z *AND* S

Z was sometimes used in Old English times in loan-words, in which it had the value [ts]—as such alternate spellings as *dracontse–draconze* 'dragon-wort' indicate—the same value which the symbol has to some extent in Italian (for example in *grazie* "thanks") and always in German (for example *Zeit* 'time'). The French also wrote *z* for the consonant sequence [ts], and the Modern English value of the letter reflects the Old French loss of [t] in this sequence. When this occurred, words which had been spelled with *z* could be spelled with *s*. The French change in sound and spelling thus made *z* available for the sound which it represents in both French and English today. Although occurring in English mainly in loan-words, *z* came to replace *s* in a number of native words, for example *freeze* (ME *fresen*), but with little consistency (compare *cheese*, from ME *chese*). Neither the symbol nor the sound which it came to symbolize occurs initially in native English words, save dialectally in the southwestern counties of England. Confusion of *ʒ* with *z*, leading to miswritings and ultimately to mispronunciations, has been discussed in another connection (see n. 14).

THE SEQUENCE QU
AND THE DIGRAPHS GU AND DG

French scribal practices are responsible for the Middle English spelling *qu*, which French inherited from Latin, replacing Old English *cw* (that is, *cp*), as in *quellen* 'to kill,' *queen,* and *quethen* 'to say,' which despite their French look are all native English words, in Old English respectively *cwellan, cwen,* and *cweðan.* Also French is the writing *gu* (see p. 28), in which the *u,* earlier pronounced in Central French, was used in some words as a mere diacritic to indicate "hard *g*" before *e* and *i* (*y*). This usage did not become really common, however, until well into the Modern English period, around 1650. The *u* has also been inserted before *a* in *guard,* where there is no real excuse for it. Also French in origin is the digraph *gg,* supplanting in other than initial position Old English *cg,* later written *dg(e)* (OE *ecg* 'edge'–ME *egge*).

THE VALUES OF VOWEL SYMBOLS

Our knowledge of the scholarly pronunciation of Latin in the early Middle Ages is obviously an important basis for our reconstruction of the pronunciation of English in its earlier periods. The vowel symbols were used in our earliest writing with the values which these symbols had in the Latin alphabet as acquired by the English from the Irish missionaries—for instance, *a, e,* and *i* were approximately as in the later English loan-words *mirage* (never as in *rage*), *fete* (never as in *mete*),[25] and *machine* (never as in *mine*). *O* and *u* when they symbolize long[26] vowels have had approximately[27] the same values in earlier periods which they now have in *rode* and *rude,* though both letters have symbolized other sounds as well. The other three vowel symbols, however, approximate their Latin values much more closely

[25] In natural English speech pronounced the same as *fate,* though a desire to be "correct" on the part of those who have had a smattering of French in school has given rise to an affected pronunciation riming with *bet.*

[26] Here, as always in learned usage, *long* refers solely to the length, or duration, of the sound, without implying any difference in quality. We have no concern here with the practice of dictionaries intended for the general public which use the macron—traditionally a symbol of length—over the vowel of, say, *cate* to differentiate this word from *cat.* In such unscientific usage, the macron indicates primarily a qualitative difference. The vowel of *cate* is obviously not a lengthened variety of the vowel of *cat,* but instead a quite different vowel. From our point of view, the vowel of *cad* must be regarded as a somewhat lengthened variety of the vowel of *cat;* what qualitative difference exists is so slight as to be insignificant.

[27] In comparatively recent times the long vowel symbolized by *o* acquired a so-called off-glide which the native English-speaking student of foreign languages must learn to leave off if his pronunciation is to be acceptable. He must not, for instance, pronounce French *rose,* Italian and Spanish *rosa,* and German *Rose* with the *u*-glide which many of us have in English *rose.*

in other writing systems than they do in Modern English. Because of a radical change in English long vowels which occurred in the course of the fifteenth century (to be discussed in Chapter VII), the long sounds indicated by these symbols acquired qualities quite different from their former ones. *Name,* for instance, which used to have the vowel sound of Modern English *father,* now has the vowel sound of Middle English *feet,* whereas Modern English *feet* has the vowel sound of Middle English *riden* 'to ride.' As a consequence of the retention of earlier spellings for shifted sounds, the vowel symbols *a, e,* and *i* have acquired for us values quite different from those which they have in all other languages using the Greek or Roman alphabets. This fact is undoubtedly one of the reasons why foreigners, to whom these symbols are pronounced approximately as we would pronounce *ah, ay,* and *ee,* are so often confused by English spelling.

DOUBLE LETTERS

To indicate vowel length, Middle English writing frequently employed double letters, particularly *ee* and *oo,* the practice becoming general in the East Midland dialect late in the period. These particular doublings have survived into our own day, though of course they do not indicate the same sounds as in Middle English. As a matter of fact, both *ee* and *oo* were ambiguous in the Middle English period, as every student of Chaucer must learn. One of the vowel sounds indicated by Middle English *ee* came generally to be written *ea* in the course of the sixteenth century; for the other sound *ee* was retained, alongside *ie* and, less frequently, *ei,* spellings which were also used to some extent in Middle English. An earlier value of the writing *ea* is preserved in *yea, break, great,* and *steak,* and an even earlier value survives in the shortened vowels of *death, head, deaf,* and a number of other words in which *ea* stands for the short vowel sound usually symbolized by *e.*

Double *o* came to be commonly used in later Middle English times for the long rounded vowel of the word *awe,* a vowel which developed out of Old English long *a.* Unfortunately for the beginning student, the same double *o* was used for the continuation of Old English long *o.* As a result of this duplication, *rood* 'rode' (OE *rad*) and *roode* 'rood' (OE *rod*) were written with identical vowel symbols, though they were no more nearly alike in pronunciation than are their modern forms. Final unstressed *e* following a single consonant also indicated vowel length in Middle English, as in *fode* 'food' and *fede* 'to feed'; this corresponds to the "silent *e*" of Modern English, as in *case, mete, bite, rote,* and *rule.* Doubled consonants, which indicated consonant length in earlier periods, began in Middle English times to indicate also that a preceding vowel was short. Surviving examples are *dinner* and *bitter,* as contrasted with *diner* and *biter.* In the North of England *i* was frequently used after a vowel to indicate that it was long, a practice responsible for such spellings as *raid* (literally a 'riding,' from OE *rad,* noun), *Reid* (a long-voweled variant of *red,* surviving only as a proper name), and Scots *guid,*[28] as in Robert Burns's "Address to the Unco Guid, or the Rigidly Righteous." In the Modern English period, though there are instances as early as the thirteenth century, *a* has also been widely used after *o* for the same purpose of indicating length of the preceding vowel, as in *road, boat,* and the like. After *e,* as we have seen in the preceding paragraph, *a* had a qualitative as well as a quantitative function.

O *AND* OU *FOR* U

Short *u* (as in *put*) was commonly written *o* during the latter part of the Middle English period if *m, n, u (v, w)* were contiguous. The Middle English writings *sone* 'son' and *sonne* 'sun' thus indicate the same vowel sound that these words had in Old English, when they were written respectively *sunu* and *sunne. O* for *u* survives in a number of Modern English words besides *son,* for example *come* (OE *cuman*), *wonder* (OE *wundor*), *monk* (OE *munuc*),[29] *honey* (OE *hunig*), *tongue* (OE *tunge*), and *love* (OE *lufu*), which last, if it had not used the *o* spelling, would have been written *luue* (as indeed it was for a time) until the seventeenth-century distinction of *u* and *v.* Beginning earlier, but becoming usual in the fourteenth century, the French spelling *ou* was used to represent English long *u,* for example *hous* (OE *hus*), and sometimes short *u* as well. Before a vowel the *u* of the digraph *ou* might well be mistaken as representing [v], for which the same symbol was used. To avoid confusion (as in *douer,* which was a possible writing for both *dower* and *Dover*),[30] *u* was doubled in this position—that is, written *uu,* later *w.* This use of *w* would of course have been unnecessary if

[28] The original long vowel, as in *food,* has undergone shortening in Standard English *good.*

[29] But Middle English *nonne* 'nun' (OE *nunne*) has returned to the earlier way of indicating its vowel sound.

[30] To use an apt example supplied by Jespersen, *Modern English Grammar,* I, 89.

u and *v* had been differentiated as they are now. *W* also came to be used instead of *u* in final position. *U* occurs in this position in *you* and *thou*, but both words were frequently written with *-ow* in former times.

Y *IN OLD AND MIDDLE ENGLISH*

The letter *y* was exclusively a vowel symbol in Old English, having the value of Modern French *u* or German *ü*; the consonantal value of the letter as used since Middle English times was indicated in Old English, as we have seen (n. 15), by *g* (that is, ʒ). Later pronunciation of the Old English vowel without lip-rounding caused it to fall together with *i*, so that *y* might be used for both vowel and consonant. In other words, Middle English scribes used *y* for one of the values of ʒ (see p. 31) and also, for the sake of legibility, as a variant of *i* in the vicinity of stroke letters, for example *myn homcomynge* 'my homecoming.' Late in the Middle English period there was a tendency to write *y* for long *i* generally. *Y,* as we have seen (p. 33), was regularly used in final position.

RENAISSANCE RESPELLINGS

Certain Renaissance respellings, for instance *throne* (p. 36) and *schedule* (p. 38), which have ultimately effected changes in traditional pronunciations, have already been mentioned. *Debt* and *doubt* are likewise fancy respellings of *det* (Middle English, from Old French) and *dout* (ME *doute*, also from Old French), the *b* having been inserted because it was perceived that these words were ultimately derivatives of Latin *debitum* and *dubitare* respectively; similarly with the *c* in *indict* and the *b* in *subtle*. If those learned men responsible for such respellings thought to effect a change in pronunciation like that which Shakespeare's schoolmaster Holofernes recommended,[31] they have not been successful so far as these words are concerned.

Comptroller is a pseudolearned respelling of *controller*, taken by English from Old French. The fancy spelling is doubtless due to an erroneous association with French *compt* 'count.' The word has fairly

[31] In the passage referred to on p. 35, he speaks of those "rackers of ortagriphie [orthography]" (for to him, as to many after him, spelling set the standard for pronunciation) who say *dout* and *det* when they should say *doubt* and *debt*. "D, e, b, t, not d, e, t," he says, unaware that the word was indeed written *d, e, t* before schoolmasters like himself began tinkering with spelling.

recently acquired a new pronunciation based on the misspelling. *Receipt* and *indict*, both taken from Anglo-French, and *victual*, from Old French, have been similarly remodeled to give them a Latin look; their traditional pronunciations have not as yet been affected. *Parliament*, a respelling of the English loan-word *parlement* (a derivative of Fr. *parler* 'to speak'), has also quite recently acquired a pronunciation such as the later spelling seems to indicate to literate, if unsophisticated, speakers—a pronunciation occasionally heard from such high-powered speakers as television and radio news commentators, who have tremendous prestige in modern life.[32] It is not unlikely that many who have previously used the traditional trisyllabic pronunciation will in time mend their ways and adopt the four-syllabled one based on the contemporary spelling. This may well seem to them more "correct" for the very reason that it is so based. It is thus obvious that in a period of widespread (if perhaps only thinly spread) literacy, misunderstanding of the true relationship of writing to speech can bring about changes in language.

Another such change of long standing has resulted from the insertion of *l* in *fault* (ME *faute*, from Old French), a spelling suggested by Latin *fallita* and strengthened by the analogy of *false*, which has come to us direct from Latin *falsus*. For a while the word continued to be pronounced without the *l*, riming with *ought* and *thought* in seventeenth-century poetry. In Dr. Johnson's day there was wavering, as Johnson himself testifies in the *Dictionary*, between the older *l*-less and the newer pronunciation with *l*. The eighteenth-century orthoëpists indicate the same wavering. These were men who conceived of themselves as exercising a directive function; they recommended and condemned, usually on quite irrelevant grounds. Seldom were they content merely to record variant pronunciations. Thomas Sheridan, the distinguished father of a more distinguished son named Richard Brinsley, in his *General Dictionary of the English Language* (1780) decides in favor of the *l*-less pronunciation of *fault*, as does James Elphinston

---

[32] The spelling pronunciation is not exclusively American, as one might expect it to be. In the English Angel recording of *H.M.S. Pinafore*, George Baker, who sings the role of Admiral Sir Joseph Porter and is described in the accompanying booklet as "perhaps the greatest patter singer who has ever lived," manages to pronounce the *i* (in the lines "I grew so rich that I was sent/ By a pocket borough into Parliament"). It is highly improbable that the pronunciation is intended to characterize Sir Joseph as a self-made man.

in his *Propriety Ascertained* (1787). Robert Nares in his *Elements of Orthoëpy* (1784) records both pronunciations and makes no attempt to make a choice between them. John Walker in his *Critical Pronouncing Dictionary* (1791) declared that to omit the *l* made a "disgraceful exception," for the word would thus "desert its relation to the Latin *falsitas*." The history of the *l* of *vault* is quite similar.

SPELLING PRONUNCIATIONS

Regardless of the method by which they have been taught, or have taught themselves, to read, it is likely that most literate people attribute sounds to the letters of the alphabet. This is to put the cart before the horse, for, as should be perfectly clear by now, letters do not "have" sounds, but merely symbolize them. Nevertheless, the literate person is likely to feel that he does not really know a word—say, a name that he has not heard clearly—until the question "How do you spell it?"— much more frequently asked under such circumstances than "How do you speak it?"—has been answered.[33]

A knowledge of spelling has been responsible for changing the pronunciation of certain words whose written forms for one reason or another do not indicate pronunciations which had become traditional. For instance, simply because it occurs in writing, the *t* of *often* has come to be pronounced once again, as it was in earlier days and up until well into the seventeenth century,[34] though the pronunciation

[33] This is amusingly illustrated in the 1960 motion picture version of H. G. Wells's *The Time Machine*, when the Time Traveler, projected hundreds of thousands of years into the future, asks a beautiful blonde Eloi girl what her name is. Inasmuch as the English language has by an unexplained miracle not changed in the least during this vast space of time, the girl understands him perfectly and replies "Weena." "How do you spell it?" immediately asks the Time Traveler. This is too much for Weena, who has no notion of spelling. Wrinkling his brow and taking careful thought, the Traveler proceeds to trace the letters *W, E, E, N, A* in the earth, thus making the name somehow more "real" than it had previously been for him, and presumably for the illiterate girl as well. In justice to H. G. Wells, it should be stated that the incident does not occur in the story as he wrote it.

[34] Jespersen, *Modern English Grammar*, I, 275, is probably overstating somewhat when he says that the *t* seems to have been "always" mute in the eighteenth and nineteenth centuries, for Walker, though he records only the "offen" pronunciation, states in the introduction to his *Dictionary* that in this word "the *t* begins to be pronounced." Though within the memory of the present writer such pronunciation has been considered affected—

with *t* is not yet recorded by all current dictionaries. So widespread is it, however, that it is probably safe to predict that in another generation or so only philologists will get the point of the *orphan–often* dialogue in Gilbert and Sullivan's *The Pirates of Penzance*, culminating in Major-General Stanley's question to the Pirate King, "When you said 'orphan,' did you mean 'orphan'—a person who has lost his parents, or 'often'—frequently?" This will of course make no sense with the restoration of the *t* in *often*; the words will no longer be homophones, or even near-homophones as they are in American English with the *r* of *orphan* pronounced. *The Oxford English Dictionary*,[35] whose *O* installments were published in the early years of the present century, records only the pronunciation without *t*, but adds the comment that pronouncing the *t* is "now frequent in the south of England, and is often used in singing."

Reanalysis of the compound *forehead*, with restressing of the second element and the *h* pronounced, was also in the beginning due to a mistaken notion of the relationship between writing and speech. This pronunciation is, as far as I can tell, universal among younger-generation speakers, and is, it must be admitted, perfectly natural with them, since they learned so to pronounce the word long before they knew how to spell it, the analytical pronunciation having originated, though at first frowned upon, at least a generation ago. Reanalysis of *breakfast* as *break* plus *fast* would be quite parallel to what has happened in the case of *forehead*.

Such is the misunderstanding of writing as it is related to speech

---

nouveau riche, as it were, and hence lacking "status"—it must now be considered both "Queen's English" and "President's English." I have not heard Elizabeth II pronounce the word, it is true, but both her father and her uncle, the duke of Windsor as Prince of Wales, used the form with *t* in public addresses. The usage of two kings should be sufficient to establish a pronunciation as Standard English.

[35] The title of this work, one of the monuments of English scholarship, will be hereafter abbreviated *OED*. It is still frequently called the *NED* from its older title *A New English Dictionary on Historical Principles*. Its first installment (*A* to *Ant*) was published in 1884; its last—*Wise* to *Wyzen* (*X* to *Zyxt* had already appeared in 1921), in 1928. It was reissued in 1933 with a new title page and a supplement of additions and corrections made necessary by the fact that publication of the work had extended over a period of nearly half a century. It is, as the newer title indicates, published by the Oxford University Press.

that many people suppose that the "best" speech is that which conforms most closely to the notions which they have acquired about the writing system, though this supposition has not as yet been extended to such words as *through* and *night*. Because of mass education, what is essentially a secondary factor—writing—has begun to affect pronunciation more than it ever did before. This tendency is, as we have seen, quite the reverse of what happened in earlier times, before English spelling became fixed, when writing was made to conform to speech. To put it in different terms: whereas in previous periods the purpose of writing was conceived to be the visual representation of speech, nowadays many conceive speech—ideally, at any rate—as the oral representation of writing.

Words which we have never heard spoken we must necessarily pronounce as their spellings seem to indicate, assuming that there is no dictionary handy. There are no grounds for reproach if a child reads *misled* as if it were the preterit of a hypothetical verb *to misle*. The great scholar W. W. Skeat of Oxford once declared that "I hold firmly to the belief . . . that no one can tell how to pronounce an English word unless he has at some time or other *heard* it," and refused to hazard an opinion on the pronunciation of a number of very rare words—among them *aam, abrus, abactinal,* and *acaulose*—going on to say, "It would be extremely dishonest in me to pretend to have any opinion at all as to such words as these."[36] A number of common, everyday words which for one reason or another have become less used than they formerly were have acquired pronunciations based upon their written forms, for instance *clapboard*, pronounced like *clabbered* until fairly recently, but now usually analyzed as *clap* plus *board*; the same sort of analysis might occur also in *cupboard* if houses of the future should be built without cupboards or if builders should think up some fancy name for them, like "food preparation equipment storage area."[37] A number of generations ago, when a grindstone was much more a part of daily life than it is now, the word rimed with *Winston.*

It is similar with proper names which we have not heard spoken. Our only guide is spelling, and no one, particularly no American, is to be much blamed for pronouncing *Daventry, Shrewsbury,* and *Ciren-*

---

[36] Quoted in *Funk and Wagnalls New Standard Dictionary of the English Language* (New York, 1925), p. 2762.

[37] This is not outside the realm of possibility. In luxury advertisements *kitchen* is sometimes "food preparation area."

cester as their spellings seem to indicate they "should" be pronounced; as a matter of fact, many English people treat in exactly the same way these words, whose traditional pronunciations as *daintry, shrowsbury,* and *sissiter* (or *sizziter*) have become somewhat old-fashioned. Although, as all educated Americans are perfectly well aware, the colleges at Oxford and Cambridge whose names are written respectively *Magdalen* and *Magdalene* are still called *maudlin,*[38] a London bus conductor would be baffled at the request to be put down at "Tibald's" Road; it would be necessary to pronounce *Theobald* as spelled, for the pronunciation indicated by Pope's spelling "Tibald" (in reference to the Shakespearean commentator Lewis Theobald) is now quite old-fashioned, if not altogether archaic.

[38] The pronunciation is based on Old French *Madelaine,* whereas the written forms are Latin. Compare Caius College, Cambridge, named for an English doctor named Keys who adopted a Latin written form for his name.

CHAPTER III

The Sounds and Spelling
of Current English

IN ASMUCH as the Roman alphabet was inadequate for the writing of Old English and had to be eked out by additional symbols like *æ* and *þ*, it is not surprising that, with these symbols lost to us and a number of new sounds having developed, it should be even more inadequate for the phonetic representation of Modern English. We have, for example, only five vowel symbols, *a, e, i, o,* and *u*; that this number is wholly inadequate is indicated by the fact that the first of these alone may have as many as eight different values, as in *cat, cate, calm, any, about, care, call,* and *was* (riming with *fuzz*). In our treatment of English sounds we shall have recourse to a way of writing in which the same symbols are used consistently for the same sounds, rather than continue as heretofore to use the awkward expedient of using riming words or of referring to the initial consonant of, say, *thy* in order to distinguish this sound from the phonetically different though identically written initial consonant of *thigh*.

We have just mentioned "same sounds," and it thus becomes necessary to point out that what are commonly regarded as the same sounds may vary from language to language. In English, for instance, the vowel sound of *sit* and the vowel sound of *seat* are distinctive. There are many pairs of words, contrastive pairs as they are called, the difference in which resides solely in a distinctive quality which these sounds have for us: *bit–beat, mill–meal, fist–feast, lick–leak,* to cite only a few such pairs. But in Spanish this difference, so important in English, is of no significance at all; there are no such contrastive pairs, and hence the two vowels in question are felt, not as distinctive sounds, but as one and the same. The native speaker of Spanish, when he learns English, is as likely as not to say "I seat in the sit" for "I sit in the seat"—a mistake which would be impossible, except as a slip of the tongue, for the native speaker of English.

THE PHONEME

What in any language is regarded as the "same sound" is actually a group of similar sounds which make up what is known as a phoneme. A phoneme is thus the smallest *distinctive* unit of speech; it consists of a number of allophones, that is, of similar sounds which are not distinctive. Thus, speakers of English regard as the "same sound" the sound spelled *t* in *tone* and *stone*, though actually a different sound is symbolized by the letter *t* in each of these words: in *tone* the initial consonant is aspirated, that is, followed by a breath-puff, which may be clearly felt if one holds one's hand before one's lips when pronouncing the word; in *stone*, this aspiration is lacking. Nevertheless, both sounds belong to, or are allophones of, the English phoneme [t],[1] which differs according to the phonetic environment in which it occurs, or, to put it in another way, the allophones occur in what is called complementary distribution.[2] There are in English no pairs of words the members of which are distinguished solely by the presence or absence of the aspiration; hence, from a phonemic point of view, the two *t*-like sounds in English are the same because they are nondistinctive. They merely occur in different environments, one initially, the other after *s*. But the two sounds might well be phonemic in other languages, and in fact are: in Chinese, for instance, the difference between aspirated and unaspirated *t* is quite significant, the aspiration or the lack of it distinguishing between words otherwise identical, just as *t* and *p* in English *tone* and *pone* do. Greek, as we have seen (p. 26), had different symbols for these sounds, Θ and T, and carefully differentiated them, whereas the Romans had only the unaspirated sound represented by Greek T—that which is preceded in

---

[1] It is customary to write phonemic symbols within slanting lines, or virgules. In this book we shall ordinarily use rather "broad" phonetic transcriptions, enclosed in square brackets. These will show only the gross characteristics of speech, and hence will be practically always the same as phonemic transcriptions; in other words, nonsignificant, or allophonic, features will as a rule not concern us any more than they would if the transcriptions were labeled as phonemic by putting them within slanting lines.

[2] There are other allophones of the phoneme written *t,* for instance as it occurs in American English medially in *item, little,* and *matter,* in which it is very like [d], and in a certain type of New York City speech in the same position as a glottal stop, that is, a "catch" in the throat, notably in *battle* and *bottle.*

English by *s*. It was not until the classical period that they transliterated Θ by TH and presumably tried to pronounce *theta* in loan-
words as an aspirate, that is, as [t] plus [h].

In Old English the sounds represented in Modern English by *z, v,*
and *th* as in *thy* were not phonemic, but merely allophones of *s, f,*
and *th* as in *thin* which occurred only medially (as in *nosu* 'nose,'
delfan 'to delve,' and *baðian* 'to bathe'). There were no contrastive
pairs like Modern English (initially) *seal–zeal, fan–van, thigh–thy,*
(medially) *loosing–losing, luffing–loving, ether–either,* and (finally)
loose–lose, luff–love, mouth (noun)–*mouth* (verb) for the simple reason that the sounds in question which are now contrastive occurred
in Old English in complementary distribution.

A METHOD OF TRANSCRIBING
ENGLISH CONSONANTS

Each of the following conventional spelling symbols enclosed in
square brackets—some have been thus used before—is the usual letter
in ordinary writing for the distinctive sound which it symbolizes and
will therefore be readily understood when thus used as a phonetic or
a phonemic symbol, though variant spellings will be supplied:

[b]   as in *bub, bheesty*
[d]   as in *dud, bdellium, dhow*
[f]   as in *fife, phantom, rough, off, Chekhov*
[h]   as in *ha, who,* school-Spanish *Don Quixote* (as "Donkey
      Hoty"), *junta* (in the pronunciation of many newscasters
      who have "had" Spanish)
[k]   as in *kick, car, khaki, chasm, masque, sacque*
[l]   as in *lull, llama*
[m]   as in *mum, comb, solemn*
[n]   as in *nun, mnemonic, pneumonia, comptroller*
[p]   as in *pup, hiccough*
[r]   as in *rear, rhomb, catarrh*
[s]   as in *sis, science, cereal, schism, psyche, Worcester*
[t]   as in *toot, Thomas, ptomaine, phthisic, victuals* (that is,
      "vittles"), *slapped* [-pt]
[v]   as in *valve, of,* British *nephew*
[w]   as in *won, one, ouija, boudoir, suite*
[z]   as in *zoos, lose, xylophone, Missouri, Quincy* (Mass.), *czar*

Note that, although a conventional spelling symbol like those which have been listed, *g* has no single value in ordinary writing, where it may indicate the initial sound of *get* or of *gem* or the quality of the *n* in *ring*. The International Phonetic Association approves [g] for the first of these values, but [g], if limited to this single value—which happens to be that which we first think of as the "sound of *g*"—will do perfectly well for our purposes:

[g]   as in *gag, guard, ghost*

Because *y* was used exclusively as a vowel symbol in Old English, it is best to use here another symbol—that conventional in the alphabet of the International Phonetic Association—for what is usually thought of as the "*y*-sound" in Modern English, thus:

[j]   as in *yet, hallelujah, onion, bouillon*

In addition, other consonantal symbols are needed, and the following will be used:

[ŋ]   as in *sing, sink*

[š][3]   as in *shush, schist, sure, issue, nation, chamois, Lucian, passion, anxious, ocean, precious, luscious, fuchsia, nausea, luxury* [-kš-]

[ž][4]   as medially in *leisure, azure, delusion, luxurious* [gž], *equation,* and initially and finally in a few French loans, such as *gendarme* and *rouge;* the sound seems to be gaining ground, perhaps to some extent because of a smattering of school French, though the words in which it seems new to me are, with the exception of *centrifuge* and *menagerie,* not of French origin, for instance *rajah, adagio,* and *cashmere*

[č][5]   as in *church, itch, nature, cello, Czech*

[ĵ][6]   as in *judge, George, gem, gin, gyrate, Giovanni, soldier, grandeur, educate;* common in television and radio usage, though regarded by many as nonstandard, in *congratulate*

[3] The International Phonetic Association's symbol is [ʃ].

[4] IPA [ʒ].

[5] IPA [tʃ].

[6] IPA [dʒ].

[θ]⁷ as in *thin, chthonian*
[ð] as in *then, bathe*

A CLASSIFICATION
OF ENGLISH CONSONANTS

Consonants may be classified according to their place of articulation (labial, dental, velar) and their manner of articulation (stop, fricative, liquid, nasal, affricate), and according to whether or not vibration of the vocal cords, or "voice," is or is not a component of articulation. Thus [p], [t], and [k] are voiceless stops, or explosives, so called because in their production an actual stoppage is made at a given point in the mouth and is then broken down by an explosion of breath with no accompanying vibrancy. But, if vibrancy is added to the articulations necessary to make these sounds, the resulting sounds are what are usually called voiced stops, [b], [d], and [g]. With stoppage at the lips, the result is [p] or [b]; hence these are called respectively the voiceless and voiced labial stops. With stoppage made by tongue against teeth (more accurately, at the point where the gums meet the teeth), the result is [t] or [d]; hence these sounds are called respectively the voiceless and voiced dental (or, more accurately describing English articulation, alveolar) stops; the more general term, *dental,* will here be used. With stoppage made against the velum, or soft palate, which may be discerned by running the tongue back along the roof of the mouth until it reaches that part which is soft and spongy, the result is [k] or [g]; hence these sounds are called respectively the voiceless and voiced velar stops. Both [k] and [g] have palatal (more forward) varieties, depending upon contiguous vowels, as in *kin* contrasted with *calm* and *give* contrasted with *gone,* but these differences will here be ignored since the sounds in question are in complementary distribution: one symbol for each is sufficient.

⁷ It would really be more appropriate to use þ to indicate this sound in a historical survey of the English language, in which the runic symbol is a traditional writing. It is in fact the symbol employed in the *OED,* in H. C. Wyld's *The Universal Dictionary of the English Language* (London, 1932), in Jespersen's *A Modern English Grammar on Historical Principles* (7 vols., Copenhagen, 1909–49), and in a good many other important works as well. But, because of the general familiarity nowadays with the IPA-endorsed θ for this value—a value which it never had in Classical Greek—I have chosen to use it here rather than be accused of a rage for singularity.

It is similar with those sounds called fricatives, or spirants, in which incomplete stoppage is made at corresponding positions, so that the air must "rub" (Lat. *fricāre*) its way through instead of breaking down a complete obstruction as with the stops; these are [f], [v] (respectively voiceless and voiced labiodental), [s], [š], [θ] (voiceless dental), and [z], [ž], [ð] (voiced dental). Velar fricatives were current in Old and Middle English, as they are still in German, for example *Nacht* 'night' and *nicht* 'not.' One symbol, [x], is sufficient, as in the case of velar [k], [g], and their palatal variants. [č] and [ǰ] are respectively voiceless and voiced affricates, in effect combinations of dental stop and fricative.

Those consonants which are articulated by obstructing the oral passage and allowing the breath and voice to flow through the nose are called nasals, namely the labial [m], with lips completely closed; the dental [n], with stoppage made at tooth-and-gum line; and the velar [ŋ], with stoppage made at velum. The nasals may by themselves form syllables, as in *clapham* [-pm], *rotten* [-tn], *happen* [-pn] or [-pm], and *bacon* [-kn] or [-kŋ].

In [l], classified as a liquid, breath and voice flow out at the sides of the tongue; hence the sound is sometimes referred to as a lateral. Like the nasals, [l] may be syllabic, as in *ripple* and *model*. Also classified traditionally as a liquid is [r], whose similarity of articulation to [l] under certain circumstances is indicated by its historical alternation with that consonant, as in *Sarah–Sally, Katherine–Kathleen*, and the related words *stella* (Latin), *astēr* (Greek), and *steorra* (Old English) 'star.' But there are yet other varieties (allophones) of r: the symbol indicates a fricative after [t], [d], and [θ] (as in *true, drew,* and *three*), in addition to having a suggestion of a trill after [θ]; and in Standard British English between vowels—as in *America, worry,* and *very*[8]—it is usually a tongue-flap. In the general sense in which we have here used *dental* to include [t] and [d] and other alveolars, [r] may be classified as a dental, with voiced and voiceless allophones.

Standard British English has no [r] before a consonant sound (as in *farm, far distances*) and in final position in an utterance (as in "The distance is far"), or, to put it in another way, in this type of speech [r] is pronounced only when a vowel follows in the same word (as in *daring*) or in one immediately following (the "linking r" as in *there*

---

[8] Sometimes spelled "veddy" in caricatures of British speech.

is and *far away*). This loss of [r], stemming from the folk speech of the eastern counties north of the Thames, occurs also in the speech of eastern New England, New York City, and much of the American coastal South. The speech of the last-named region frequently lacks linking *r* as well. Most American speech, however, preserves the sound under all conditions, as does the folk speech of the South and the West of England (see pp. 250–51). An intrusive [r] occurs in the usage of a goodly percentage of the speakers of Standard British English,[9] as in *law*[r] *enforcement.* Essentially analogical with the etymological [r] which is retained before a word beginning with a vowel (linking *r*), this intrusive [r] is also common in eastern New England and New York City, but not in the South, where linking *r* is rare. An intrusive preconsonantal [r] occurs in western Pennsylvania and adjacent regions in *wash* and *Washington.*

Failure to understand that [r] is lacking before a consonant or in final position in Standard British English has led to American misunderstanding of such British spellings as *aren't I,* '*arf* (for Cockney *half*), and *Eeyore,* Christopher Robin's donkey companion,[10] and consequently of the instruction given by the London *Observer* that the Italian surname of Sir Harold Caccia, former British ambassador to the United States, should be "pronounced Catcher" (June 22, 1956, p. 7). Equally puzzling for one whose speech was not *r*-less would be the complaint of the *Evening Standard* that some people pronounce the latter part of Sophia Loren's first name in the English fashion, "to sound like fire" (September 15, 1956, p. 5).

Because of their vocalic quality, the labial [w] and the palatal [j] are called semivowels. Hence many phonemicists write the symbols *w* and *y* (for the *j* usual with historical and comparative linguists)

---

[9] According to Daniel Jones, *English Pronouncing Dictionary,* 11th ed. (London, 1950), pp. xvii–xviii. G. B. Shaw, whose speech lacked this characteristic, deplores the intrusion, incorrectly associating it solely with the usage of the man in the street (in a singularly ill-informed preface which he wrote for R. A. Wilson's *The Miraculous Birth of Language* [London, 1941], p. 19). Shaw's example, equating *Maria Ann* with *Maria ran,* would be about as likely to occur in aristocratic as in common speech.

[10] In Standard British English, *an't,* a variant of *ain't,* is a homophone of *aren't* (and also of *aunt*). The *r* in *aren't I* is thus merely a spelling serving to indicate the quality of the vowel; the same quality is indicated by the *r* in '*arf. Eeyore,* which A. A. Milne could just as well have spelled *Eeyaw,* is what Cockney donkeys presumably say instead of *hee-haw.*

to indicate the transitional sounds, called off-glides, in *mouse* /maws/ and *mice* /mays/. We shall here use [ʊ] and [ɪ] to indicate these off-glides—the same symbols used to indicate respectively the *oo* of *foot* and the *i* of *fit*.

A METHOD OF TRANSCRIBING ENGLISH VOWELS

In what is probably the most familiar type of phonemic transcription for current English, as set forth by George L. Trager and Henry Lee Smith, Jr., in their *Outline of English Structure* (Norman, Okla., 1951), all long vowels of current English are analyzed as diphthongs, or sequences of short vowels and semivowels functioning as off-glides. In this system, for instance, /iy/, /ey/, /ow/, and /uw/ correspond to our [i], [e], [o], and [u] respectively. The nineteenth-century phoneticians, notably Henry Sweet, recorded the off-glides which they heard in such words as *beet, bait,* and *boat,* and Leonard Bloomfield in his groundbreaking *Language* (New York, 1933) also analyzed the long vowels as diphthongal. Kemp Malone in "The Phonemes of Current English," published in his *Studies in Heroic Legend and in Current Speech* (Copenhagen, 1959), points out, however, that "the distinctive feature is not the off-glide but the quality of the vowel and in fact we distinguish the vowels of *beat* and *bit* with ease by their difference in quality whether an off-glided allophone of the former vowel is used or not" (p. 239). It is no part of our present purpose to resolve the matter, even if it were possible to do so. Inasmuch as the off-glides of current English were absent in the older periods with which we shall be greatly concerned, single symbols will serve that purpose best.

For the representation of vowels we shall require, as noted heretofore, more than the five symbols furnished by the Roman alphabet. Furthermore, as the examples given below indicate, a single vowel sound may be represented in various ways in conventional English spelling. This is of course true of some consonant sounds as well, as we have already seen. Our need here, as with the consonants, is for an unvarying symbol to represent a given sound, no matter how it may be written in conventional spelling.

It will be noted that the conventional vowel symbols used within brackets have approximately the same values that they have in the spelling systems of those languages other than English which use the Roman alphabet (see pp. 41–42). For instance, in transcribing Modern

English words we must use [i] for that sound which is written *i* in other languages, but which, except for words recently borrowed by English from these other languages (for example *police*), is most frequently written *e, ee, ea, ie,* and *ei* in Modern English; and we shall use [e] for that sound which is usually written *a* (followed by a consonant plus "silent *e*") or *ai* in Modern English (as in *bate, bait*). English *o* and *u* frequently correspond to the *o* and *u* of other languages, in which case they are transcribed [o] and [u], as in *roll* [rol] and *rule* [rul]. *A* with its "Italian" value in the spelling of English words occurs before *r* and *lm*, in *father* and sometimes in *rather* (always in Standard British English), in certain types of American English after *w* (as in *watch*), and in post-eighteenth-century Standard British English in about 150 other common words[11] in which an older vowel sound, preserved in American English, acquired this value when followed by a voiceless fricative (by [s] in *grass, ask, last*; by [f] in *staff, half, laugh*; by [θ] in *bath*) or by [m] or [n] plus another consonant (*example, command, aunt, dance*). All these examples, like the others listed by Kenyon, were pronounced in Standard British English during the seventeenth and eighteenth centuries precisely as in the speech of most Americans today.

Following are the symbols to be used for vowel sounds:

[ɑ]   as in **ah, alms, art, father, heart, sergeant, Gloucester, ennui, kraal, aunt,**[12] *stop*[13]

[a]   as in eastern New England *ask, half, laugh, path,* and the like; also common in the usage of American actors and (especially) actresses and others who have had training in what used to be called elocution; midway between [ɑ] and [æ], as in both syllables of French *madame*

---

[11] The commonest ones are listed in John S. Kenyon's *American Pronunciation*, 10th ed. (Ann Arbor, Mich., 1961), pp. 179–80.

[12] Pronunciation of this word with [ɑ], though sometimes regarded as a British affectation, is by no means uncommon in American English.

[13] The vowel indicated, which prevails in American English, is also gaining ground in British English. My own observations agree with those of C. K. Thomas, who notes this British use of the unrounded vowel in words like *God, clock, mop, got,* and *collar* in his *An Introduction to the Phonetics of American English*, 2nd ed. (New York, 1958), p. 205.

[æ]   as in *at, plaid, ma'am, Spokane, The Mall* (London),
     salmon, Caedmon, lingerie (more frequently one
     hears [lɑn-]), *draught*

[e]   as in *ape, great, faint, feint, angel, fay, fey, halfpenny*
     ([he]*penny*), *Baal, gauge, gaol, Baedeker, quoit* (as
     pronounced by many players); alone in final sylla-
     bles, *Iowa* (locally), *café, sachet*

[ɛ]   as in *elf, head, said, says, leopard, friend, heifer, bury,*
     Thames, Pall Mall, Reynolds, haemorrhage, phlegm;
     alternating with [æ] before [r] in American English,
     as in *air, ere, their, bear, prayer*

[ɜ]   (occurring only before *r*) as in *urn, earn, erg, bird,*
     word, journal, masseur, myrrh; in words which had
     earlier [ʊr] followed by a vowel, like *worry, hurry,*
     borough, thorough, and *courage,* Standard British
     English has [ʌr], a pronunciation also current, ac-
     cording to Kurath and McDavid, in Metropolitan
     New York and to a lesser extent in other parts of the
     Atlantic seaboard.[14] The [ɜ] of noncoastal American
     speech in such words is also current in British folk
     speech.

[i]   as in *eel, eat, be, mete, camellia, ceiling, lief, people,*
     police, maenad, amoeba, quay, key, British *retch*

[ɪ]   as in *it, sieve, renege, English, gyp, women, build, busy,*
     old-fashioned *teat*; before [r] in *ear, peer, pier, weird,*
     mere, mirror, lyric; unstressed as in (initially) *elude,*
     illume, (medially) *area, material, Israel, Simeon,*
     Ephraim, Nausicaa,[15] (in final syllables followed by
     a consonant) *bucket, topic, biscuit, fragile, dactyl,*
     minute (n.), *college, knowledge, marriage, opposite,*
     legate, portrait, palace, office, lettuce, horses, tortoise,
     old-fashioned *Calais* [-ɪs], some of which also occur
     with [ə]; standing alone finally, [-ɪ] alternates with

[14] Hans Kurath and Raven I. McDavid, Jr., *The Pronunciation of English in the Atlantic States* (Ann Arbor, Mich., 1961), p. 127.

[15] Followed by another vowel, unstressed medial [ɪ] may alternate with [i].
When no other vowel follows, [-ɪ-] and [-ə-] alternate, as in *terrify, maximum,
ceremony, telephone.* In American English [-ə-] is practically invariable in
such words.

[-i], in American English at least, as in *body, money, taxi, Leslie, strophe, Macaulay, Raleigh*[16]

[o] as in *oh, owe, soul, oats, row, roe, yeoman, brooch, sew, though, beau, chauffeur, picot,* American *cantaloupe*

[ɔ] as in *awe, all, aught, ought, broad, for, four,*[17] *or, oar, ore, door, Omaha, Utah, Arkansas*

[u] as in *ooze, to, two, shoe, croup, brougham, move, tomb, Cowper, buhl, cruise, Devereux* [-ru], *Sioux, rheumatic, Lewis, Leveson* [lusn], *lieutenant, bouillon,* old-fashioned *lasso*; alternating with [ʊ] in *room, broom, roof, hoof, coop,* and a few other *oo*-words, and with [ju] after [t] (*Tuesday*), [č] (*chew*), [d] (*due*), [ǰ] (*adjure*), [s] (*sue*), [z] (*resume*), [r] (*ruth*), and [θ] (*thew*)

[ʊ] as in *bull, book, wolf, bosom, would, bourgeois, Boer, worsted* 'cloth'

[ʌ] as in *sun, son, young, blood, does* (v.), frequently in stressed *was*

[aɪ] as in *I, eye, ay, hie, style, stile, buy, by, bye, height, isle, aisle, choir, Van Dyck, Van Eyck*

[aʊ] as in *how, house, McLeod, sauerkraut*

[ɔɪ] as in *oil, boy, Reuter, Boulogne*

[ju]¹⁸ as in *music, butte, beauty, view, few, feud, cue, queue,* Scottish *Home*

---

16 An additional symbol, small capital *i* with a bar running through it, might have been used for the unstressed vowel. We shall, however, for the sake of simplicity ignore the slight difference between the vowels of the first and second syllables of words like *city, rivet,* and *billet* in the pronunciation of many speakers. In final position the unstressed vowel may range from [ɪ] through various gradations to a shortened variety of [i]; if followed by a consonant, as we have seen, it might also be pronounced [ə].

17 Many persons in the United States, Canada, the English Midland, northern England, and Scotland have [o] in *four, oar, ore,* and *door.* Such speakers distinguish *oar* and *ore* [or] from *or* [ɔr], *four* and *fore* from *for, hoarse* from *horse, mourn* from *morn, boarder* from *border,* and use [or] in words written *-oor* (though it is of course not implied that the writing has anything to do with the matter), for instance *door* and *floor.* The distinction of [or] and [ɔr] is a historical one, but is not maintained in Standard British English and in many types of American English, which have [ɔr] in all these words.

18 In American English there is a variant [ɪu] in other than initial position.

[ə] the symbol called *schwa*, used to indicate the "murmur
vowel" of unstressed syllables, as in the initial syllables of *elope* (in which it alternates with [ɪ]), *obey* (in
which it alternates with [o]), *about, sustain*; internally
in *summary, summery, memory, syrupy, dominate* (in
the last of which it alternates with British [ɪ]); in the
final syllables of *Cuba, Goethe, piano*,[19] *window,
borough, bureau, Edinburgh, gallop, stirrup, bias,
famous, judgment, Monmouth, Durham*. It alternates with [ɪ] in the final syllables of *office, lettuce,
palace, careless, Isaac*, and with [ɪ] or [i] in *Miami,
Missouri*, and *Cincinnati*. It occurs in words written
with *r*, with or without *r*-coloring depending upon
whether the speaker is "*r*-ish" or "*r*-less," in initial
unstressed syllables as in *pervade, partake*; in medial unstressed syllables as in *haberdasher, gabar-
dine*; and in final unstressed syllables as in *coward,
shepherd, cupboard*. In *r*-less speech [ə] alone is the
final sound of such words as *bursar, butter, lucre,
nadir, actor, glamour, femur, Tourneur*. Likewise in
r-less speech it replaces final and preconsonantal [r]
in stressed syllables after [ɪ] (*ear, beard*), [ɛ] or [æ]
(*there, cairn*), [ɔ] (*or, form*), [o] for those who have
this vowel before *r* (*four, force*), [ju] (*pure, cured*),
[ʊ] (*tour, bourse*), [aɪ] (*ire, tired*), and [aʊ] (*our,
scoured*)[20]

CLASSIFICATION OF ENGLISH VOWELS

Of the vowels listed above, [i], [ɪ], [e], [ɛ], and [æ], because of the
positions assumed by the tongue in their articulation, are classified as

---

[19] In *piano, window, borough*, and *bureau*, [ə] alternates with a *u*-like
sound, sometimes with a long *o*.

[20] An intrusive [ə] sometimes occurs between consonants in certain
words, for instance between [l] and [m] in *elm, film*, [n] and [r] in *Henry*,
[r] and [m] in *alarum* (an archaic variant of *alarm*), [s] and [m] in *Smyrna*
(in the usual local pronunciation of New Smyrna Beach, Florida), [θ] and
[r] in *arthritis*, and [θ] and [l] in *athlete*. The name of this phenomenon
is *svarabhakti* (from Sanskrit), and such a vowel is called a svarabhakti
vowel. If, however, one does not care to use so flamboyant a word, one
can always fall back on *epenthesis* (*epenthetic*) or *anaptyxis* (*anaptyctic*).
Perhaps it is just as well to say "intrusive schwa."

front vowels, and [u], [ʊ], [o], [ɔ], and [ɑ] as back vowels. Both series have been given in descending order; that is, in relation to the height of the tongue as indicated by the downward movement of the lower jaw in their articulation: thus [i] is the highest front vowel and [æ] the lowest, as [u] is the highest back vowel and [ɑ] the lowest. All the back vowels save [ɑ] and one front vowel, [y], which no longer occurs in English (see p. 108), are pronounced with some degree of rounding of the lips and hence are called rounded vowels.[21] [ɜ], [ʌ], [ə], and [a] are, as regards the position of the body of the tongue, central; they are sometimes called mixed vowels.

FURTHER COMMENTS ON TRANSCRIPTION

In the chapters on Old, Middle, and early Modern English, where we shall have to deal specifically with vowel quantity, colons will be placed after phonetic symbols to indicate vowel length. Where, in dealing with current English, we have no particular concern with vowel quantity, length will not be indicated: the difference in quality between [u] and [ʊ] is usually all that need be noted; similarly with the qualitative difference between [e] and [ɛ], [i] and [ɪ], where the first member of each pair is pronounced with tongue tense, the second with tongue relatively lax, or slack.

In the occasional transcriptions of words in the following chapters, primary stress will be indicated by a vertical mark above the line and preceding the syllable having such stress: thus *sofa* ['sofə] and *about* [ə'baut]. If a syllable has secondary stress, a corresponding mark below the line will be used to indicate it: thus *emanate* ['ɛmə‚net]. With conventional orthography, the familiar slanting accent marks over the vowel symbol (or over the first symbol of a digraph) will be used: thus *émanàte*.

SOME CONCLUDING COMMENTS
ON ENGLISH SPELLING

As far as the unambiguous use of vowel symbols is concerned, Old English writing is by and large phonetic in relation to the Roman alphabet, Middle English writing somewhat less so. It is not until we come to Modern English times that we find such diversity of spellings

[21] Thus we may speak of *putt* (a variant of *put* used in the game of golf) as showing "unrounding" of the earlier vowel sound which survives in its variant. Compare, however, *put, full, bush,* all having rounded vowels, with *cut, gull, blush,* with later unrounding.

for single sounds as have been illustrated by the many examples cited above. Some of the reasons for the present state of English spelling practices have already been discussed. Others will come to light as we explore the development of the English language through the centuries.

CHAPTER IV

The Backgrounds
of English

LANGUAGE tends to change for a variety of reasons. Moreover, this manifold tendency is operating all the time in all languages, though its operations are not perceptible save to a few persons who for one reason or another concern themselves with such matters and who may note changes in word usage and in the pronunciation of individual words (like *ration*, which used to rime with *passion*, but has comparatively recently acquired a pronunciation riming with *nation*) in the course of a lifetime. But such changes as these are really quite minor in relation to the changes in sounds and grammar which take place in the course of centuries—changes which would make the English of Geoffrey Chaucer, if we were happily able to resurrect him, seem very different from our own speech. That of Alfred the Great, who lived about as long before Chaucer as we live after him, would seem quite like a foreign language to all who had not made a special study of Old English.

THE PUZZLE OF LINGUISTIC CHANGE

Passage of time and geographical separation are but contributory factors and not direct causes of linguistic change. Thus, the English language as Americans speak it today has become differentiated from present Standard British English in certain respects in the relatively short time that has elapsed since its speakers became separated, though never really isolated, from the mother country. The English language of the seventeenth century suffered no sea-changes when it was brought across the Atlantic: the first Englishmen to settle in America spoke exactly as they had spoken at home. Nevertheless, changes have certainly come to pass. Those which have occurred in British English are, as a matter of fact, considerably more far-reaching and more fundamental than anything which has happened independently in American English—the treatment of *a* in words of the *staff, glass,* and *path* type, the treatment of *r* preceding a consonant or in final position, and the treatment of the penultimate syllables of polysyllabic words in *-ary, -ery,* and *-ory,* for instance. American English preserves the older British treatment; Standard British English has changed in all these respects since the seventeenth century.

We can say precisely what has happened in any sort of linguistic change, and we can also as a rule say where a particular change occurred and assign to it an approximate chronology. But we can supply a reason only for those changes due to analogy, which is a mental process, even though it need not be conscious. We can describe what happened as "rounding" when Old English *ā* (in *stān, hām, bān,* and so forth) came invariably to be pronounced [ɔ:] south of the Humber, and we can say, on the basis of spellings with *o,* approximately when this began to happen (late eleventh century). But *why* it happened, or, for that matter, why this later sound was "raised" and "fronted" to [o:], as in Modern English *stone, home, bone,* and so forth, we cannot really explain. We can only declare that certain tendencies toward changes of various sorts have prevailed at certain times and in certain places, and that these changes have accomplished themselves, not haphazardly, but with the greatest regularity. We can usually map the exact course of such changes, and we can describe them scientifically in phonological terms.

LANGUAGE FAMILIES

In the discussion of so-called linguistic families which follows, we must bear in mind that a language is not born, nor does it put out branches like a tree—nor, for that matter, does it die except when every single one of its speakers dies, as has happened to Etruscan, Gothic, Cornish, and a good many other languages. When we speak of Latin as a dead language, we are referring to a highly artificial literary language; but spoken Latin still lives in various developments in Italian, French, Spanish, and the other Romance languages.

Hence the terms *family, ancestor, parent,* and other genealogical expressions when applied to languages must be regarded as no more than metaphors. Languages are developments of older languages rather than descendants in the sense in which people are descendants of their forefathers. Thus, Italian and Spanish are different developments of an earlier, more unified language, Latin. Latin in turn is one of a number of developments, which include Oscan and Umbrian, of a still earlier language called Italic. Italic in its turn is a development of Indo-European. Whether or not Indo-European has affinities with other languages spoken in prehistoric times and is hence a development of an even earlier language, no one is prepared to say with certainty; for, as we have seen, we are quite in the dark about how it all began.

Older scholars—and they were to some extent theorists—classified languages as monosyllabic, agglutinative, incorporative, and inflective, these being exemplified respectively by Chinese, Turkish, Eskimo, and Latin. The monosyllabic languages were supposed to represent the most primitive type—a notion which doubtless grew out of investigations into languages of our own Indo-European group, with their large number of monosyllabic roots. But even the earliest (middle of second millennium B.C.) records of Chinese, a monosyllabic language in its modern form, represent not a primitive but actually a late stage in linguistic development. It obviously cannot be inferred from such evidence as this that our prehistoric ancestors prattled in words of one syllable each.

The older scholars also observed, quite correctly, that in certain languages, such as Turkish and Hungarian, words were made up of parts "stuck together," as it were; hence the term *agglutinative*. In such languages the suffixal elements are usually whole syllables having very definite meanings. The inflectional suffixes of the Indo-European languages were supposed likewise once to have been independent words; hence, some believed that the inflective languages had grown out of the agglutinative. Little was known of what were called incorporative languages, in which all sentence elements are combined into a single word; the elements have no independent existence, but can appear only as infixes.

The trouble with such a classification is that, though apparently objective, it is not really so, but is instead based on the out-of-date theory that early man spoke in monosyllables. Furthermore, the difference between agglutinative and inflective was not well defined, and there was considerable overlapping. Nevertheless, the terms are useful and widely used in the description of specific languages or even groups of languages.

A much more satisfactory and more objective classification of languages can be made on the basis of such correspondences of sound and structure as indicate relationship through common origin. Perhaps the greatest contribution of nineteenth-century linguistic scholars was the painstaking investigation of these correspondences, many of which had been noted long before.

Such investigation indicated unmistakably that practically all of the languages of Europe (and hence of the Americas and other parts of the world colonized by Europeans) and some of Asia have in common certain characteristics of sound and structure and to some extent a stock of words which make it perfectly obvious that they have all developed out of a single language spoken in prehistoric times. This earlier language is usually called Indo-European.[1] What it was called by those who spoke it we have no way of knowing, nor do we know what they called themselves. We shall here follow the usual practice of referring to them as the Indo-Europeans, but it must always be borne in mind that the term has no racial connotations; it refers only to a group of people who lived in a relatively small area in early times and who spoke a more or less unified language out of which many languages have developed in the course of thousands of years. These languages are spoken today by approximately half of the world's population.

THE NON-INDO-EUROPEAN LANGUAGES

Before proceeding to a more detailed discussion of the Indo-European group, we may perhaps best delimit it by briefly noting those languages and groups of languages which are *not* Indo-European. Two important groups have names which reflect the Biblical attempt to derive all the races of men from the three sons of Noah: the Semitic (from the Latin form of the name of the eldest son, more correctly called Shem in English) and the Hamitic. The term *Japhetic*, once used for Indo-European, has happily long been obsolete. On the basis of many phonological and morphological features which they share, Semitic and Hamitic are thought by many scholars to be related through a hypothetical common ancestor, Hamito-Semitic; there are

---

[1] *Indo-Germanic* is not now much used except by German scholars. Its coinage was not due to German patriotism; it was intended to do no more than indicate what were thought to be the easternmost and westernmost limits of the geographical distribution of the languages recognized as belonging to the group. Another term, *Aryan,* has been used synonymously. Originally this term referred only to the Asiatic languages of the group. This is still the reference which it has in learned use, where its occurrence is now somewhat rare, *Indo-Iranian* and *Indo-Persian* being the preferred terms.

also those who believe in an ultimate relationship, impossible to prove, between Semitic and Indo-European.

The Semitic group includes the following languages: (Eastern) Akkadian, called Assyrian in the periods of the oldest texts, and later Babylonian; (Western) Hebrew, Aramaic[2] (the native speech of Jesus Christ), Phoenician, and Moabitic; (Southern) Arabic and Ethiopic. Of these, only Arabic is spoken by large numbers of people over a widespread area. Hebrew has comparatively recently been revived in Israel, to some extent for nationalistic reasons.[3] Ethiopic survives mainly in Geez, a Christian liturgical and learned language of Ethiopia, and in Amharic, which is used in state documents in that country. It is interesting to note that two of the world's most important religious documents are written in Semitic languages—the Old Testament in Hebrew (with large portions of the books of Ezra and Daniel in Aramaic) and the Koran in Arabic.

To the Hamitic group belong Egyptian (called Coptic after the close of the third century of the Christian Era), the Berber dialects of North Africa, and various Cushitic[4] dialects spoken along the upper Nile. Coptic is used in the liturgy of the Coptic Christian Church in Egypt, much as Geez is used in the Ethiopian Church and Latin in the Roman Catholic Church, but is not spoken elsewhere. Arabic became the national language of Egypt in the course of the sixteenth century.

Semitic is thus essentially Asiatic, and Hamitic North African. Hamitic is in no way related to any of the languages spoken by Negroes in central and southern Africa, the vast region south of the Sahara. These languages are usually classified into three main groups:

[2] Formerly—and incorrectly—called Chaldean, Chaldaic, or Chaldee. Though he should have known better, the foundations of modern linguistic science having already been laid in his day, Noah Webster thought that "Chaldee," which he believed to be the language of pre-polyglot Babel, was the ancestor of all languages. In his *American Dictionary of the English Language* (1828) he proposed a good many "Chaldee" etymologies which later and better-informed editors have quietly consigned to the wastepaper basket.

[3] Hebrew is not of course to be confused with Yiddish (that is, Jüdisch), a German dialect with many words of Hebrew origin which has come into being since the fourteenth century and has become a sort of international language of the Jews. Newspapers printed in Yiddish use Hebrew characters.

[4] Cush was a son of Ham.

Sudanese, extending to the equator, a large and highly diversified group of languages whose relationships to one another are difficult and in some cases impossible to establish; Bantu, extending from the equator to the extreme south, a large and well-defined group of related languages; and Hottentot and Bushman, remotely related languages spoken by small groups of quite primitive people—though the languages are in no sense primitive—in the extreme southwestern part of Africa. Hottentot and Bushman have no relationship to the other Negro groups, nor is it demonstrable that the Sudanese and the Bantu groups are in any way connected with each other.

Languages belonging to the Dravidian group were once spoken throughout India, where the earlier linguistic situation was radically affected by the Aryan invasion. These are the aboriginal languages of India. They are now spoken mainly in southern India.

The Indo-Chinese group includes Chinese proper and the languages of Tibet and Indochina. Japanese is totally unrelated, though it has borrowed the Chinese written characters and many Chinese words. Attempts to relate Korean to either Chinese or Japanese have not been successful. Ainu, the language of the aborigines of Japan, is totally unrelated to any other language of which we have any knowledge; it is now spoken by no more than a handful of people.

A striking characteristic of the Malay-Polynesian languages is their wide geographical distribution in the islands of the Indian and the Pacific oceans, stretching from Madagascar to Easter Island. The more or less moribund Australian native languages, spoken by only a few Australian blacks nowadays, have absolutely no connection with Malay-Polynesian, nor have the more than a hundred Papuan languages spoken in New Guinea and neighboring islands.

The American Indian languages constitute a geographic rather than a linguistic grouping, comprising many languages showing very little relationship, if any, to one another. It has been estimated[5] that at the time of Columbus' discovery only about a million and a half Indians occupied the huge area north of Mexico, with about forty million more in Mexico and Central America, the Antilles, and South America. A very important and widespread group of American Indian languages is known as the Uto-Aztecan, which includes Nahuatl, the language spoken by the Aztecs, and various closely related dialects.

[5] By P. Rivet, cited by Willem L. Graff, *Language and Languages* (New York, 1932), p. 427.

Aleut and Eskimo, which are very similar to each other, are spoken in the Aleutians and all along the extreme northern coast of America and north to Greenland. The isolation of the various groups, small in number to begin with and spread over so large a territory, may to some extent account for the great diversity of American Indian tongues.

Basque, a very intricate language spoken in many dialects by no more than half a million people living in the region of the Pyrenees, has always been something of a popular linguistic mystery. It now seems fairly certain, on the basis of coins and scanty inscriptions of the ancient Iberians, that Basque is related to the almost completely lost language of those people who once inhabited the Iberian peninsula and in Neolithic times were spread over an even larger part of Europe. Efforts to relate it to Etruscan, a language of which we know very little, to the non-Indo-European languages spoken in the Caucasus Mountains (not mentioned elsewhere here), and to the Hamitic languages have not been successful.

An important group of non-Indo-European languages spoken in Europe, as well as in parts of Asia, is the Ural-Altaic, which falls into two subgroups: the Ural, or Finno-Ugric, which includes Finnish, Estonian, Livonian, Lappish, and Hungarian, among others of less importance; and the very remotely related Altaic—though there are those who deny any such connection. Altaic includes various varieties of Turkish, such as Ottoman Turkish (Osmanli) and that spoken in Turkestan and in the Azerbaijan Soviet Socialist Republic, as well as Mongolian and Manchu.

The foregoing is by no means a complete survey of non-Indo-European languages. We have merely mentioned some of the most important groups and individual languages, along with some which are of little significance as far as the numbers or the present importance of their speakers are concerned, but which are nevertheless interesting for one reason or another. Louis H. Gray lists twenty-six linguistic groups and two isolated languages (spoken respectively in China and India by small groups of people), and comes up with a total of 2796 languages, of which 132 are Indo-European.[6] His figure coincides with that arrived at by the French Academy. But Gray rightly had no faith in such a count, for, as he points out, it is often impossible to reach agreement as to what constitutes a language: the line demarcating dialect and language is difficult to draw, and linguists do not always agree on where it should be drawn. Furthermore, depending largely upon one's

[6] *Foundations of Language* (New York, 1939), p. 418.

point of view, Old English, Middle English, and Modern English might be regarded as one, two (on the basis that the transition from Middle English to Modern English is somewhat less well defined than that from Old English to Middle English), or three. And there are yet further difficulties pointed out by Gray, who concludes that between 2500 and 3500 might be given as an estimate, but admits that such an estimate is "so rough as to be practically worthless."

EARLY STUDIES
OF THE INDO-EUROPEAN GROUP

The concept of an Indo-European group of languages—and subsequently of other groups as well, for the work of the early Indo-Europeanists gave impetus to the study of non-Indo-European languages also—may be said to have grown out of British rule in India. It was this which was responsible for a wider knowledge of Sanskrit in Europe—to all intents and purposes a third ancient language with which to compare Latin and Greek. Latin had previously been supposed to be a degenerate form of Greek. Such an explanation of the correspondences between Sanskrit and the two hitherto-known ancient languages would obviously not do, for India was completely outside the sphere of Greco-Latin civilization.

For this new concept a remarkably versatile man, a veritable eighteenth-century "admirable Crichton," was largely responsible. A former member of Dr. Johnson's brilliant circle, Sir William Jones was at the age of thirty-seven judge of the supreme court of judicature at Fort William (Calcutta) in Bengal after a brilliant career as Orientalist, student of many languages, poet, classicist, jurisconsult, and public official in England, where he had withdrawn as a parliamentary candidate for Oxford University just before election day because of his sympathetic view of the American cause in the War of Independence and his opposition to the slave trade.

Shortly after his arrival in India, Jones founded the Bengal Asiatic Society. In a paper read before that group in 1786, he declared that Sanskrit bore to Greek and Latin "a stronger affinity . . . than could possibly have been produced by accident; so strong, indeed, that no philologer could examine them all three without believing them to have sprung from some common source, which, perhaps, no longer exists," going on to say that "there is a similar reason for supposing that both the Gothick [that is, the Germanic] and the Celtick . . . had the same origin with the Sanscrit."

Before Jones's time a good deal was known of many languages other than the classical ones, and some attempts at classification had been made. A few Europeans, mostly missionaries, had even learned something of Sanskrit, and some of them had noted "affinities," or correspondences, with European languages. As early as the sixteenth century an Italian merchant in India pointed out in a letter the striking similarity of Sanskrit *deva-* 'God' to Italian *dio*; of *sarpa* 'snake' to his *serpe*; and of the numerals *sapta* 'seven,' *astau* 'eight,' and *nava* 'nine' to his native *sette, otto,* and *nove*.[7] Had he been able to hear more of the ancient language known to and used by Hindu scholars of his day, he would have noted other such striking correspondences: in the numerical system alone, for example, *dvau/due* 'two,' *trayas/tre* 'three,' *čatvār-/quattro* 'four,' and *dasa/dieci* 'ten.'[8]

But Jones's clear statement, showing full realization of the relationship of Sanskrit to the principal European languages through a common ancestor, came just when the time was ripe for it, and may thus be said to have been the starting point for modern comparative linguistics. It only remained for more able, if less versatile, men to work out the details necessary to establish beyond any doubt the essential unity of that great group of related languages which we call the Indo-European family.

The first man to present a systematic comparison of a number of these languages was a German scholar with the unforgettable name of Franz Bopp. In 1816 Bopp published a brilliant study of the verbal endings of Sanskrit, Persian, Greek, Latin, and Germanic, and, in installments at intervals from 1833 to 1852, a huge comparative grammar in which he added Old Slavic and Lithuanian to the languages just named. He was later to add Armenian, Albanian, and Celtic. It was Bopp's work which got comparative Indo-European grammar on its feet.

But even before the publication of Bopp's first work the young Danish scholar Rasmus Rask had written a prize-winning essay on the origin of Old Norse in which he recognized the relationship of the Germanic, Hellenic, Italic, and Baltic groups and expressed the belief that Indo-Iranian might also be related. By the time his essay was published, in 1818, he had perceived that Armenian was Indo-European.

[7] Cited by Paul Thieme in "The Indo-European Language," *Scientific American,* CXLIX, 4 (October 1958), 63–74—a fascinating article intended for the general educated reader.

[8] The medial consonant of *dasa* was a palatal fricative approximating the final sound of German *ich*.

It was not until somewhat later that he admitted Albanian to the family.

Rask clearly perceived that sound shifts were regular, not sporadic, and recognized the Germanic sound shift later to be more expertly codified by Jacob Grimm in the second edition of his *Deutsche Grammatik* (1822).[9] This sound shift, to be discussed in some detail later, was in time to be associated with Grimm's name as Grimm's Law.[10] There is, however, some justice in the statement of Otto Jespersen that "if any man is to give his name to this law, a better name would be 'Rask's Law,' for all these transitions . . . are enumerated in Rask's *Undersøgelse* [the essay of 1818] . . . which Grimm knew before he wrote a single word about the sound shift."[11] In any case, the relationship of the Germanic languages, including English, to the other members of the group was now made perfectly clear.

Comparative and historical linguistics thus began with the study of the Indo-European family. Similar study of other languages and groups of languages was to come later, and as a result of the principles educed by the nineteenth-century Indo-Europeanists. Bopp, Rask, and Grimm had laid solid foundations for such studies, among them identifying the Germanic, Balto-Slavic, Celtic, Italic, Hellenic, and Indo-Iranian groups of languages as subgroups of Indo-European, along with the individual languages Armenian and Albanian. There followed in the course of the nineteenth century a series of brilliant and exciting studies, mostly by German scholars, which are still the basis of modern linguistic study. The story is best told by Holger Pedersen in his *Linguistic Science in the Nineteenth Century*.[12] The discovery and deciphering of writings in Tocharian and Hittite, found respectively in East Turkestan and Asia Minor, and the identification of the

[9] By *deutsch* Grimm meant 'Germanic,' not merely 'German.'

[10] It is an amusing irony that this great scholar, who never married, should be best known as the "author," with his brother Wilhelm, of a beloved nursery classic—the famous *Grimm's Fairy Tales*. The brothers Grimm, both of them fascinated by folklore, in the scientific study of which they were pioneers, were the collectors of the stories which have delighted generations of children despite the disapproval of modern child psychologists.

[11] *Language: Its Nature, Development and Origin* (New York, 1922), p. 43.

[12] Translated from the Danish by John Webster Spargo (Cambridge, Mass., 1931).

first of these languages as Indo-European in origin and the second as either Indo-European in origin or a language of common origin with Indo-European[13] are achievements of the twentieth century. They are also discussed by Pedersen in the work cited.

INFLECTION
IN THE INDO-EUROPEAN LANGUAGES

All the Indo-European languages are inflective—that is, all are characterized by a grammatical system based on modifications in the form of words, by means of endings and vowel changes,[14] to indicate such grammatical functions as case, number, tense, person, mood, and the like. The older inflectional system is very imperfectly represented in most modern languages: English, French, and Spanish, for instance, have lost much of the inflectional complexity which was once characteristic of these languages; German retains considerably more, with its various forms of the noun and the article and its so-called strong adjective declension. Sanskrit is notable for the remarkably clear picture it gives us of the older Indo-European inflectional system; it retains much that has been lost or changed in the other Indo-European languages, so that its forms show us, even better than Greek or Latin can do, what the system of Indo-European must have been.

Traces of this inflectional system which survive in varying degrees in other related languages led the early Indo-Europeanists to the discovery of the relationship of languages as widely separated geographically as Icelandic and Sanskrit. Once one understands and makes allowances for the regularly occurring sound changes, the relationship of the personal endings of the verb in the various Indo-European languages becomes perfectly clear. For example, the present indicative of the Sanskrit verb corresponding to English *to bear* runs as follows:

SINGULAR

1 bharā-mi 'I bear'
2 bhara-si 'thou bearest'
3 bhara-ti 'he beareth'

[13] Those who hold to the second of these alternatives, notably the late American Hittitologist, E. H. Sturtevant, hypothesize a parent language called Indo-Hittite, from which both Indo-European and Hittite stem.

[14] As in Modern English *boy–boys; who–whom–whose; walk–walks–walked–walking; man–man's–men–men's; sing–sings–sang–singing.*

PLURAL

1 bharā-mas 'we bear'
2 bhara-tha 'you bear'
3 bhara-nti 'they bear'

The only irregularity here is the occurrence of -mi in the first person singular, as against -ō in the Greek and Latin forms to be cited immediately below. It was a peculiarity of Sanskrit to extend -mi, the regular first-person ending of verbs which had no vowel affixed to their roots, to those which did have such a vowel.[15]

Leaving out of consideration for the moment differences in vowels and in initial consonants, compare now the present indicative forms as they have developed from Indo-European into Greek and Latin, with special regard to the personal endings:

GREEK	LATIN
pherō[16]	ferō[16]
pherei-s	fer-s[18]
pherei[17]	fer-t
phero-mes (Doric)	feri-mus
phere-te	fer-tis
phero-nti (Doric)	feru-nt

[15] This vowel (for example the -a suffixed to the root bhar- of the Sanskrit word cited) is called the thematic vowel. The root of a word plus such a suffix is called the stem. To these stems are added endings. The comparatively few verbs lacking such a vowel in Indo-European are called athematic. The m in English am is a remnant of the Indo-European ending of such athematic verbs.

[16] In Indo-European thematic verbs the first person present indicative had no ending at all, but only a lengthening of the thematic vowel.

[17] The expected form would be phere-ti. The ending -ti, however, does occur elsewhere in the third person singular, for instance in Doric didōti 'he gives.'

[18] In this verb the loss of the thematic vowel is exceptional. The expected forms would be feri-s, feri-t, feri-tis in the second and third persons singular and the second person plural respectively. Compare legō, mittō, scrībō, and other verbs of the third conjugation, all of which have the thematic vowel throughout, for example legis, legit, legitis, and so forth.

Comparison of the personal endings of the verbs in these and other languages leads inevitably to the conclusion that the Indo-European endings had to be as follows (the Indo-European reconstruction of the entire word is given in parentheses):

-ō, -mi	(*bherō)[19]
-si	(*bheresi)
-ti	(*bhereti)
-mes, -mos	(*bheromes)
-te	(*bherete)
-nti	(*bheronti)

Note now in Gothic and Old English the Germanic development of these personal endings:

GOTHIC	EARLY OLD ENGLISH
bair-a	ber-u, -o
bairi-s	biri-s
bairi-þ	biri-þ
bairi-m	bera-þ[20]
bairi-þ	bera-þ
baira-nd	bera-þ

Germanic þ corresponds as a rule to Indo-European t (see p. 93). Leaving out of consideration such details as the -nd (instead of expected -nþ) in the Gothic third person plural form, for which there is a soundly based explanation, it is perfectly clear that the Germanic

[19] An asterisk before a form indicates that it is a reconstruction of what can be assumed to have existed on the basis of comparative study. Since Indo-European was spoken only in prehistoric times, all forms cited as existing in that language are necessarily reconstructions; the same is true of cited forms of any language in a prehistoric stage, for instance Germanic and very early Old English. The asterisk is also placed before a form assumed to have been current during the historical period though not actually recorded. Some of the forms from Greek and Latin in the two preceding footnotes might also have been preceded by asterisks, though labeling them "expected forms" in contrast to the forms which are actually attested gives sufficient notice that they are hypothetical and thus satisfies the claims of scholarly integrity.

[20] From the oldest period of Old English the form of the third person plural was used throughout the plural. This form, beraþ, from earlier *beranþ, shows Anglo-Frisian loss of n before þ.

personal endings correspond to those of the non-Germanic Indo-European languages. A complete comparison of the Germanic languages makes possible a reconstruction of the proto-Germanic endings in the same way that the Indo-European forms have been reconstructed. As has been seen, no guesswork is involved in such reconstruction.

COGNATE WORDS
IN THE INDO-EUROPEAN LANGUAGES

Words of similar structure and similar, related, and in many instances identical meanings in the various languages of the Indo-European group may be recognized, once one knows what to expect in the way of sound-shifting, as cognate—that is, of common origin (Lat. *co* plus *gnātus* 'born together'). Thus all the roots just cited (*bhar-, pher-, fer-, bair-, ber-*) are of common origin, all being developments of Indo-European **bher-*; so, for that matter, are the thematic vowels and the personal endings, though the untrained observer may sometimes find it difficult to recognize the relationship. For cognates, as we have seen, do not necessarily look much alike: sound shifts have occurred in the various languages of the Indo-European group (these languages may also be referred to as cognate) which may make related words as unlike in sound as *father*, Sanskrit *pitā*, and Irish Gaelic *athir*[21]—all developments of Indo-European **pətēr*. Sometimes, however, there is sufficient similarity—for example between *maharaja*, ultimately Sanskrit, and Latin *mājus rex* 'great king'—to be apparent even to the untrained observer.

The most frequently cited cognate words are those which have been preserved in a large number of Indo-European languages; some have in fact been preserved in all. These common related words include the numerals from one to ten; the word meaning the sum of ten tens (*cent-, sat-, hund-*) in various quite dissimilar-looking but nonetheless quite regular developments; words for certain bodily parts (related, for example, to *heart, lung, head, foot*); words for certain natural phenomena (related, for example, to *air, night, star, snow, sun, moon, wind*); certain plant and animal names (related, for example, to *beech, corn, wolf, bear*); and certain cultural terms (related, for example, to *yoke, mead, weave, sew*). It is interesting to note in passing that cognates of practically all of our taboo words—those monosyllables which

---

[21] Indo-European *p*, which corresponds to Germanic *f*, was lost completely in Celtic.

pertain to sex and excretion and which seem to cause great pain to many people—are to be found in other Indo-European languages. Historically, if not socially, these ancient words are just as legitimate as any other words.

One needs no special training to perceive that our *one, two, three* are akin to Latin *ūnus, duo, trēs*; to Greek *oinē* 'one-spot on a die,' *dyo, treis*; to Welsh *un, dau, tri*; to Gothic *ains, twai, *þreis*; and to Dutch *een, twee, drie*. Comparison of the forms designating the second digit indicates that non-Germanic (as in the Latin, Welsh, and Greek forms) *d* corresponds to Germanic (English, Gothic, Dutch) *t*. A similar comparison of the forms for the third digit indicates that non-Germanic *t* corresponds to Germanic *þ*, the initial sound of *three* and *þrir* in English and Icelandic. Allowing for later changes, as in the case of *þ*, which became *d* in German (*drei* 'three'),[22] as also in Dutch, and *t* in Danish, Norwegian, and Swedish (*tre*), these same correspondences come to light perfectly regularly in other cognates in which the consonants in question appear. We may safely assume, for reasons unnecessary to go into here, that the non-Germanic consonants are older than the Germanic ones. Hence we may accept with the greatest confidence (assuming a similar comparison of the vowel systems) the reconstructions **oinos, *dwo, *treies* as accurately representing the Indo-European forms from which the existing forms have developed. The comparative linguists have of course used all the Indo-European languages as a basis for their conclusions regarding correspondences, not just a few such as are cited here.

INDO-EUROPEAN CULTURE

On the basis of these cognates, which must not be confused with loan-words, we can infer a good deal about the state of culture attained by the Indo-Europeans before the various migrations began, probably during the third millennium B.C. or even somewhat earlier. This culture was not contemptible; it was in fact considerably more advanced than that of some groups of people living today. As we have seen, they had a clear sense of family relationship and hence of the family organization, and they could count. They made use of gold and perhaps silver as well; copper and iron were not to come until later. They drank a honey-flavored alcoholic beverage whose name has come down to us as *mead*. Some genius among them had thought up the principle of the wheel, as words corresponding to *wheel, axle,* and *yoke* testify;

[22] German has *t* from earlier *þ* in a very few words, for instance *tausend* 'thousand.'

and this was more than the American Indians had done by the nineteenth century. They were small farmers, not nomads, who worked their fields with plows, and they had domesticated animals and fowls. They had religious feeling of a sort, with a conception, not of God, but of gods. This much we can say on the basis of forms which were not actually recorded until long after Indo-European had ceased to be a more or less unified language.

THE INDO-EUROPEAN HOMELAND

Conjectures·differ as to the original Indo-European homeland—or at least the earliest for which we have any evidence. Plant and animal names are the principal clues, and the flora and fauna which these denote are northern European. The existence of cognates denoting trees which grow in northern Europe (*oak, birch, willow*), though they may grow elsewhere as well, coupled with the absence of such related words for Mediterranean or Asiatic trees (*olive, cypress, palm*); the similar occurrence of cognate words for *wolf, bear, turtle,* and *salmon,* but none for creatures indigenous to Asia—all this points to northern Europe as the predispersion home, just as the absence of a common word for *ocean* indicates, though it does not in itself prove, that this homeland was inland. Paul Thieme in his cogently reasoned *Die Heimat der indogermanischen Gemeinsprache* (Wiesbaden, 1954) and in the article cited above (n. 7) localizes the Indo-European homeland in the northern part of Central Europe, between the Vistula and the Elbe, on the basis of evidence adduced from the prehistoric geographical distribution of the beech, the turtle, and the salmon. Other Indo-Europeanists have argued from similar evidence for southern Russia, the Carpathians, Scandinavia, and southwestern Asia. The preponderance of scholarly opinion nowadays is in favor of a European center of dispersion—an opinion which implies that the earliest migrations were in a southeasterly direction.

THE MAIN DIVISIONS
OF THE INDO-EUROPEAN GROUP

Of some Indo-European languages—for example Phrygian, Scythian, Macedonian, and Illyrian—we possess only the scantiest remains. We may be certain that others have disappeared without leaving a trace. Members of the following subgroups survive as living tongues: Indo-Iranian, Balto-Slavic, Hellenic, Italic, Celtic, and Germanic. Albanian and Armenian are also Indo-European, but do not fit into any of these subgroups.

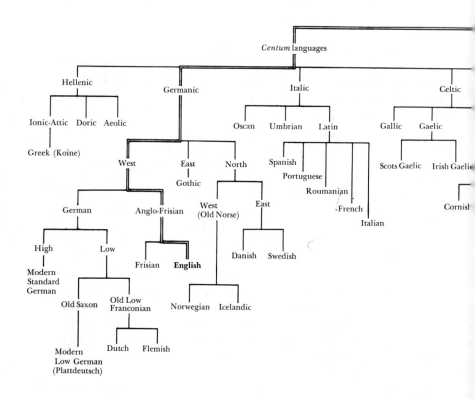

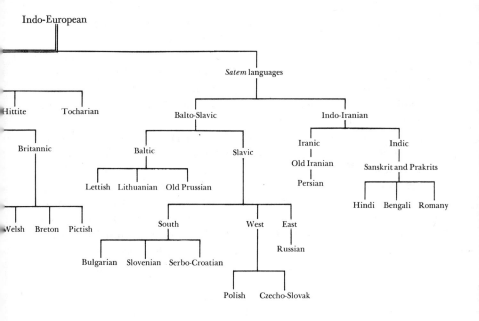

Indo-European

Hittite   Tocharian

Satem languages

Balto-Slavic   Indo-Iranian

Britannic

Baltic   Slavic

Iranic   Indic

Old Iranian

Sanskrit and Prakrits

Persian

Lettish   Lithuanian   Old Prussian

Welsh   Breton   Pictish

South   West   East

Hindi   Bengali   Romany

Russian

Bulgarian   Slovenian   Serbo-Croatian

Polish   Czecho-Slovak

INDO-EUROPEAN
AND THE
MORE IMPORTANT LANGUAGES
DEVELOPED FROM IT

The Indo-European languages have been conveniently classified into *satem* languages and *centum* languages, *satem* and *centum* being respectively the Avestan (a form of Old Persian) and Latin words corresponding to *hundred*. The classification is based on the development, in very ancient times, of Indo-European palatal *k*. In the *satem* languages—Indo-Iranian, Balto-Slavic, Armenian, and Albanian—this *k* sound became some sort of sibilant: for example Sanskrit (Indic) *śatam*, Lithuanian (Baltic) *šimtas*, Old Slavic *sŭto*.[23] In the other Indo-European languages the earlier *k* of Indo-European *kmtóm either remained or, in the Germanic group, shifted to *h* in the First Consonant Shift (Grimm's Law), as in Greek (Hellenic) *(he)katon*, Welsh (Celtic) *cant*, and Old English (Germanic) *hund*.[24]

The discovery of Tocharian, a *centum* language, early in our century was somewhat disturbing to the general supposition that this division according to the development of Indo-European palatal *k* represented a dialectal split in Indo-European, with those who migrated eastward coming to assibilate the sound. But the assumption of an earlier migration of Tocharians and Hittites, who also spoke a *centum* language, from Central Europe would account for the presence of *centum* languages in what was thought of as *satem* territory. It must be remembered, however, that this is only an inference.

THE INDO-IRANIAN LANGUAGES

The Indo-Iranian (*Iranian* is another form of *Aryan*) group is the oldest for which we have historical records. It is the usual opinion that the Vedic hymns, written in an early form of Sanskrit, date from about the middle of the second millennium B.C. Classical Sanskrit appears more than a thousand years later. It is much more systematized than

[23] Linguistic history often repeats itself: the prehistoric treatment of palatal *k* in the *satem* languages resulting ultimately in its becoming a sibilant was precisely the same thing which took place much later—perhaps about the third century of the Christian Era—in Latin *centum* (and in all other words in which the sound *k*, spelled with *c* in Latin, occurred before the palatal, or front, vowels *e* and *i*). This change is responsible for the occurrence of a sibilant in all the languages derived from Latin; for example the [č] in Italian *cento* and the [s] in French *cent*, Portuguese *cento*, and non-Castilian Spanish *ciento*.

[24] Modern English *hundred* is a compound, first occurring late in the Old English period. The *-red* is a development of what was once an independent word meaning 'number.'

Vedic Sanskrit, for it had been seized upon by a tribe of grammarians who formulated rules for writing it; even so, this was probably not until Sanskrit was ceasing to be widely spoken. The most remarkable of the Indian grammarians was Panini, who, at about the same time (fourth century B.C.) that the Greeks were indulging in more or less reckless speculations about language and in fantastic etymologizing,[25] wrote a grammar of Sanskrit which to this day holds the admiration of linguistic scholars. But there were yet others whose work, motivated as was Panini's by the importance of preserving unchanged the language of the old sacred literature, puts much of the grammatical writing of the Greeks and Romans to shame.

The written language was fixed by these grammarians, and Sanskrit is still written by Indian scholars according to their rules. It is in no sense dead as a written language; its status is roughly comparable to that of Latin in medieval and Renaissance Europe.

Indic dialects had developed, as we might expect, long before Sanskrit became an inflexible and learned language. These are known as Prakrits, and some of them—notably Pali, the religious language of Buddhism—achieved high literary status. From these Prakrits are indirectly derived the various non-Dravidian languages of India, the most widely known of which are Bengali, Hindi, Hindustani (a variety of Hindi, with mixed word stock), and Urdu, derived from Hindustani. Gypsy, or Romany,[26] is also an Indic dialect, with many loan-words from other languages acquired in the course of the Gypsies' wanderings. When they first appeared in Europe in the late Middle Ages, many people supposed them to be Egyptians—whence the name given them in English and some other languages. A long time passed before the study of their language was to indicate unmistakably that they had come originally from northwestern India.

Those Indo-Europeans who settled permanently in the Iranian Plateau developed a sacred language, Avestan, sometimes incorrectly

---

[25] The Romans later did no better, even deriving names of things from what they were *not*. Thus they fancied *bellum* 'war' was so named because it was not *bellus* 'beautiful.' The Middle Ages and the Renaissance failed to improve much on the Romans.

[26] *Romany* has nothing to do with *Rome*, *Romance*, *Romaic* (Modern Greek), or *Roumanian*, but is derived from Gypsy *rom* 'man,' ultimately Sanskrit. The *rye* of *Romany rye* (that is, 'Gypsy gentlemen') likewise has nothing to do with the cereal crop, but is a Gypsy word akin to Sanskrit *rājan* 'king,' as well as to Latin *rex* and German *Reich*.

called Zend,[27] preserved in the religious book the Avesta, after which the language is named. There are no modern descendants of Avestan, which is by some believed to be the language of the Medes, whose name is frequently coupled with that of the Persians, most notably in the phrase "the law of the Medes and Persians, which altereth not" (Daniel vi.8). Avestan was the language of the sage Zarathushtra—Zoroaster to the Greeks—many of whose followers fled to India at the time of the Mohammedan conquest of their country in the eighth century. These are the ancestors of the modern Parsees (that is, Persians) of Bombay. Persian is a different dialect from Avestan; it is the dialect of the district known to the Greeks as Persis, whose inhabitants under the leadership of the great Cyrus in the sixth century B.C. became the predominant tribe.

ARMENIAN AND ALBANIAN

Armenian and Albanian, as we have seen, do not fit into any subgroups. The first has in its word stock so many Persian loan-words that it was once supposed to belong to the Indo-Iranian group; there are also many borrowings from Greek and from Arabic and Syrian. Albanian also has a mixed vocabulary, with words from Italian, Slavic, Turkish, and Greek.

THE BALTO-SLAVIC LANGUAGES

The relationship between the Baltic and the Slavic languages is quite remote, yet so unmistakable that we must assume a common ancestor closer than Indo-European, called Balto-Slavic. The chief Baltic language is Lithuanian; the closely related Lettish is spoken in Latvia, to the north of Lithuania and like it now a part of the Soviet Union. Lithuanian is a notable example of a language which has changed little for thousands of years and hence, like Sanskrit and Greek, has preserved old forms lost in related languages. Still another Baltic language, Prussian, was spoken as late as the seventeenth century in what is now called East Prussia, which was considered outside of Germany until the early years of the nineteenth century. Prussia in time became the predominant state of the new German Empire. The Prussians, like the Lithuanians and the Letts, were heathens until the end of the Middle Ages, when they were converted at the point of the

[27] Actually the Middle Persian language of later commentaries on the Avesta.

sword by the Knights of the Teutonic Order—a military order which was an outcome of the Crusades. The aristocracy of the region (their descendants are the Prussian *Junkers*) came to be made up of members of this order, who, having saved the souls of the heathen Balts, proceeded to take over their lands.

Slavic falls into three main subdivisions: East Slavic includes Great Russian (or just Russian), the common and literary language of Russia; Little Russian (or Ruthenian), spoken in the Ukraine; and White Russian, spoken in western Russia north of the Ukraine. West Slavic includes Polish, Czech, the highly similar Slovak, and Sorbian (or Wendish), a language spoken by a small group of people in East Germany; these languages have lost many of the early forms preserved in East Slavic. The South Slavic languages are Bulgarian, Serbo-Croatian, and Slovenian. The oldest Slavic writing which we know is in Old Bulgarian, sometimes called Old Church Slavic (or Old Church Slavonic), which remained a liturgical language long after it ceased to be generally spoken.

THE DEVELOPMENT OF MODERN GREEK

In ancient times there were many Hellenic dialects, among them Aeolic, Doric, and Ionic, which included Attic. As in the course of history Athens came to assume tremendous prestige, its dialect, Attic— that of all the giants of the Age of Pericles—became the basis of a standard for the entire Greek world, a koine (that is, *koinē* [*dialektos*] 'common [dialect]') which was ultimately to drive out the other Hellenic dialects. The various local dialects spoken in Greece today, as well as the standard language, are thus all derived from Attic. With all their glorious ancient literature, the Greeks have not had a modern literary language until comparatively recently. This "purified" literary language makes considerable use of words revived from ancient Greek, as well as a number of ancient inflectional forms; it has become the ordinary language of the upper classes. A more natural development of the Attic koine is spoken by the masses and hence called *demotike*.

THE ITALIC LANGUAGES

As in the ancient Hellenic world, so also in ancient Italia there were a number of dialects, among them Oscan, Umbrian, and Latin, the speech of Latium, whose chief city was Rome. As Rome came to dominate the Italic world, spreading its influence into Gaul, Spain, and the

Illyrian and Danubian countries (and even into Britain, where it failed to displace Celtic), it became a koine as the dialect of Athens had done.

Spoken Latin, as has been noted, survives in the Romance languages. It was quite a different thing from the more or less artificial literary language of Cicero. All the Romance languages—such as Italian, Spanish, Catalan, Galician, Portuguese, French, Provençal, and Roumanian—are developments of the Vulgar Latin (so called because it was the speech of the *vulgus* 'common people') spoken in various parts of the Roman Empire in the early Middle Ages. Rhaeto-Romanic comprises a number of dialects spoken in the most easterly Swiss canton called the Grisons and in the Tyrol. In southern Belgium a dialect of French, called Walloon, is spoken. Other French dialects have included Norman—the source of the Anglo-Norman dialect spoken in England after the Norman Conquest—Picard, and the dialect of Paris and the surrounding regions (the Île-de-France), which for obvious reasons became Standard French.[28] For similar reasons the speech of the old kingdom of Castile, the largest and most important part of Spain, became Standard Spanish.[29] Because of the cultural pre-eminence of Tuscany during the Italian Renaissance, the speech of that region—and specifically of the city of Florence—became the standard of Italian speech. Both Dante and Petrarch wrote in this form of Italian; their use of it doubtless had much to do with its victory over other forms.

THE CELTIC LANGUAGES

Celtic shows such striking correspondences with Italic in certain parts of its verbal system and in inflectional endings as to indicate a relationship between them which is rather close, though not so close

---

[28] The highly similar varieties of French spoken in Quebec, Nova Scotia, New Brunswick, and Louisiana are developments of the dialects of northern France, and are no more to be regarded as "corruptions" of modern Standard French than American English is to be regarded as a corruption of the present British Standard. The "Cajuns" (that is, Acadians) of Louisiana are descendants of exiles from Nova Scotia, which was earlier a French colony called Acadia.

[29] The fact that Spanish America was settled in large part from Andalusia rather than from Castile accounts for the most important differences in pronunciation between Latin-American Spanish and the standard language of Spain.

as that between Indic and Iranian or Baltic and Slavic. Some scholars therefore group them together as developments of a language which they call Celto-Italic.

The Celts were spread over a huge territory in Europe long before the emergence in history of the Germanic peoples. Before the beginning of the Christian Era Celtic languages were spoken over the greater part of central and western Europe, and by the latter part of the third century b.c. even in Asia Minor, in the region called for them Galatia, to whose inhabitants Paul later addressed a famous letter. As the fortunes and the warlike vigor of the Celts declined, their languages were supplanted by those of their conquerors. Thus, the Celtic language spoken in Gaul (called Gallic or Gaulish) gave way completely to the Latin spoken by the Roman conquerors, which was to develop into French.

Roman rule seems to have had comparatively little effect on the continued use of their language by the British Celts. But they were ultimately to give it up after the Angles, Saxons, and Jutes arrived—though not altogether, for British (Brythonic, Britannic) Celtic still lives, if somewhat feebly, in Welsh (Cymric) and in Breton. Breton is the language of the descendants of those Britons who, around the time of the Anglo-Saxon invasion of their island and even somewhat before that time, crossed the Channel and settled in the Gaulish province of Armorica, naming their new home for their old one—Brittany. Breton is thus more closely related to Welsh than to long-extinct Gallic. There have been no native speakers of Cornish, another British language, since the early nineteenth century. Still another British language, Pictish, preserved in a few glosses and place-name elements, was spoken by the Picts in the northwestern part of Britain, in which many Gaelic Celts also settled. These Irishmen, or Scots (*Scotti*) as they were then called, named their new home Scotia, or Scotland.

The Celtic language which spread from Ireland, called Gaelic or Goidelic, was of a type somewhat different from that of the Britons. It was ultimately adopted by the Picts and survives in Scots Gaelic, sometimes called Erse, a word which is simply a variant of *Irish*. Scots Gaelic is spoken in the remoter parts of the Scottish highlands and in a somewhat different development on the Isle of Man (where it is called Manx). In Ireland, which was little affected by either the Roman or the later Anglo-Saxon invasions, Irish Gaelic survived until well into the nineteenth century, but ultimately gave way to English. It has fairly recently been revived for nationalistic reasons in Eire, but this resuscitation, roughly comparable to the official use of Hebrew in modern Israel, cannot be regarded as in any sense a natural development. It is taught, probably somewhat perfunctorily, in the schools.

THE GERMANIC LANGUAGES

The Germanic group merits a somewhat fuller treatment than has been given to any of the other groups because English belongs to it. In the course of many centuries certain radical developments occurred in the more or less unified language spoken by those Indo-European peoples living in Denmark and the regions thereabout—developments which differentiate it from all the other Indo-European languages more markedly than these are differentiated from Proto-Indo-European and hence from one another. The period during which these developments were in course of occurring we may refer to as Pre-Germanic. _Germanic_[30] is the usual term for the relatively unified language—distinctive in many of its sounds, its inflections, its accentual system, and its word stock—which resulted from these developments.

Unfortunately for us, those who spoke this particular development of Indo-European did not write. Germanic is to German, Dutch, the Scandinavian languages, and English as Latin is to Italian, French, and Spanish. But Germanic, which was probably being spoken shortly before the beginning of the Christian Era, must be reconstructed just like Indo-European. Latin, on the other hand, is amply recorded.

Spread over a large area as Germanic in time came to be, it was inevitable that more and more marked dialectal differences should have occurred, leading to a division into East Germanic, West Germanic, and North Germanic. The only East Germanic language of which we have any detailed knowledge is Gothic. The North Germanic languages are Icelandic, Norwegian, Faroese, Swedish, and Danish. The West Germanic languages are High German, Low German, Dutch, Flemish, Frisian, and English. Some scholars prefer to group Gothic with the North Germanic languages because of certain parallels which indicate that it was closer to Old Norse than to West Germanic. But,

---

[30] This term seems preferable to Teutonic or Gothonic. When the Romans referred to the Germanic nations (or to Germania), they included in the term Goths, Germans, Angles, Saxons, Frisians, and Scandinavians. Unfortunately _Germanic_ has acquired a more limited meaning in English, with nationalistic connotations, but there are equally important objections to the other terms used.

as E. Prokosch has pointed out, "these are hardly more important than the parallels between Gothic and West Germanic on the one hand, and Norse and West Germanic on the other," concluding that "none of these three groups of parallels is important enough to have any influence on the classification of the Germanic languages, and it seems best to consider the three groups independent branches."[31]

THE MAJOR CHANGES
FROM INDO-EUROPEAN TO GERMANIC

Germanic became differentiated from Indo-European principally in the following respects:

1. All Indo-European distinctions of tense and aspect[32] were lost in the verb save for the present and the preterit[33] tenses. This simplification of a more complex Indo-European verbal system (though it was not so complex as what developed in Latin, Greek, and Sanskrit) is reflected in all the languages which have developed out of Germanic—in English *bind–bound*, as well as in German *binden–band*, Old Norse *binda–band*, and all the rest. There is in no Germanic language anything comparable to such forms as those of the Latin future, perfect, pluperfect, and future perfect forms (for instance *laudābō, laudāvī, laudāveram, laudāverō*), which must be rendered in the Germanic languages by verb phrases (for instance English *I shall praise, I have praised, I had praised, I shall have praised*).

2. Germanic developed a preterit tense form with a dental suffix, that is, one containing *d* or *t*. All languages derived from Germanic thus have two types of verbs. Those which are distinctly Germanic—

---

[31] *A Comparative Germanic Grammar* (Philadelphia, 1939), p. 30.

[32] A modification of the form of verbs to indicate whether an action or state is viewed with regard to its beginning, duration, incompletion, completion, or repetition. Languages which lack inflectional forms to indicate such stages in action or being must employ phrases to express them, for instance *he is walking, he is being* (incompleted action or state), *he has walked, he has been* (completed action or state), and the like.

[33] From a historical and comparative point of view, *preterit* is a better term than *past*, which is good enough if our concern is only with the present state of the Germanic languages. *Preterit* designates the absolute past (*walked, was*) without reference to such aspects of past action or state as are expressed in *was walking, was being* (imperfect, or incompleted, action or state), *had eaten, had been* (perfect, or completed, action or state), or to any other stages of past action or state.

that is, those which employ the dental suffix—were called "weak" by Jacob Grimm because, being incapable of the type of internal change of *rise–rose* and *sing–sang* (which he called "strong"), they had to make do with suffixes (*"mit äusseren Mitteln"*), like *step–stepped* and *talk–talked*. Although Grimm's terminology is not very satisfactory, it has become traditional, and is at least as realistic as "regular" and "irregular." An overwhelming majority of our verbs add the dental suffix in the preterit—it is indeed the only living method of inflection for tense in English as in all the other Germanic languages[34]—and this method has thus been thought of as "regular." Historically speaking, however, the vowel gradation of the strong verbs is quite regular, and some of the weak verbs would probably seem quite irregular to the untrained observer. *Bring, think,* and *buy,* for instance, are weak verbs, as the dental suffix of *brought, thought,* and *bought* indicates; the vowel changes here are due not to Indo-European vowel gradation, but to special factors. The suffix is the real test. No attempt at explaining the origin of this suffix has been wholly satisfactory. Many have thought that it was originally an independent word meaning, and cognate with, *do*; but there are grave objections to this theory.

3. For adjectives, Germanic had a so-called weak declension, to be used chiefly when preceded by a pronoun (that is, a pronominal adjective, including the demonstrative pronoun which developed into the definite article). Thus in Old English, *þā geongan ceorlas* 'the young fellows (churls),' with the weak form of *geong,* but *geonge ceorlas* 'young fellows,' with the strong form; likewise in German, *die jungen Kerle,* but *junge Kerle.* This particular Germanic characteristic cannot be illustrated in Modern English, inasmuch as in the course of its development English has fortunately lost all such declension of the adjective.

4. The "free" accentual system of Indo-European, in which any syllable of a word might be accented, gave way to another type of accentuation in which the first syllable was regularly stressed in all words except compound verbs like modern *believe* and *forget*—that is, verbs in which the initial syllable was a prefix. None of the Germanic languages has anything comparable to the shifting accentuation of Latin *vírī* 'men,' *virórum* 'of the men' or of *hábeō,* 'I have,' *habémus* 'we

---

[34] For example, new verbs form their preterit so: *elbow–elbowed, televise–televised, rev–revved,* and so forth. Furthermore, as we shall see later, many verbs which were once strong have become weak.

have.' Compare the paradigms of the Greek and Old English developments of Indo-European *pətĕr 'father.'

GREEK

Singular nominative	patĕr
Singular genitive	patrós
Singular dative	patrí
Siŋgular accusative	patéra
Singular vocative	páter
Plural nominative	patéres (same for vocative)
Plural genitive	patérōn
Plural dative	patrási
Plural accusative	patéras

OLD ENGLISH

Singular nom., dat., acc.	fǽder
Singular genitive	fǽder(es)
Plural nom., acc.	fǽderas
Plural genitive	fǽdera
Plural dative	fǽderum

In these paradigms it will be noted that in the Greek forms the accent may occur on the suffix, the ending, or the root, unlike the Old English forms, which are representative of the Germanic accentual system in having their accent fixed on the root. Germanic accent is predominantly a matter of stress (loudness) rather than pitch (tone); Indo-European would seem to have had both types of accent at different stages of its development.

5. Indo-European vowels underwent Germanic modification. Indo-European *o*, retained in Latin, became *a* (compare Lat. *octo* 'eight,' Gothic *ahtau*); Indo-European *ā* became *ō* (Lat. *māter* 'mother,' OE *mōdor*); and there were other changes as well, which we shall not go into here.

6. The Indo-European stops *bh, dh, gh, p, t, k, b, d,* and *g*—that is, the *sounds* later symbolized by these letters—all underwent modification in what is called the First Sound Shift or, less happily, Grimm's Law. These modifications were gradual, extending over rather long periods of time. Rather than use reconstructed forms preceded by asterisks, we may illustrate this shift—really a series of shifts—by show-

ing correspondences between a non-Germanic language, usually Latin, and English.[35]

a. Indo-European *bh, dh, gh* became respectively Germanic *ƀ, ð, ӡ*,[36] and later, in initial position at least, *b, d, g*. Stated in phonetic terms, aspirated voiced stops became voiced fricatives and then unaspirated voiced stops. Sanskrit preserves Indo-European *bh* and *dh*, but not *gh*, which became *h* in that language. *Bh* appears in Latin as *f*, in Greek as φ (an aspirated *p*, later becoming [f]), written *ph* in Latin transcriptions of Greek, as we have seen in Chapter II. *Dh* also became *f* in Latin in initial position, but *d* medially; in Greek the Indo-European sound appears as θ (an aspirated *t*), the *th* of Latin transcriptions. *Gh* appears in Latin as *h*, in Greek as χ (an aspirated *k*), the *ch* of Latin transcriptions. Unless these non-Germanic changes are borne in mind, the examples to be cited below will not make sense. Except for initial *b*, the other stops are preserved in Latin and Greek. Correspondences may be noted in the following pairs of related words, in which the first member of each pair is Latin unless otherwise labeled:

INDO-EUROPEAN *bh* (LATIN *f*, GREEK *ph*)/GERMANIC *b*

fräter / brother	fundus (for **fudnus*) / bottom
fiber / beaver	fägus / beech
fläre / blow	(Gr.) phōgein 'to roast' / bake
fra(n)go / break	

INDO-EUROPEAN *dh* (LATIN *f*, GREEK *th*)/GERMANIC *d*

fi(n)gere 'to mold' / dough	(Gr.) thē- 'to place' / do
foris / door	(Gr.) thygatēr / daughter

[35] Derivatives of many of the Latin and Greek cognates to be cited below occur in English as loan-words, some having entered by way of French. Compare, for instance, such pairs as *fraternity–brotherhood, fragile–breakable, fundament–bottom, horticulture–gardening, paternal–fatherly, pyrotechnics–fireworks, pedal–foot, tenuous–thin, cornet–horn, cordial–hearty, canine–hound, gelid–cold*, and so forth.

[36] The *ƀ* symbolizes a bilabial fricative, the sound symbolized in Spanish by *b* or *v*. The *ð* stands for precisely the sound which it symbolizes in the alphabet of the International Phonetic Association, the initial consonant of *them*. The *ӡ* indicates the velar fricative plus voice, or resonance. Authorities identify it with the medial consonant of North German *sagen*; but, unless one has a North German handy, this is of little help. The symbol was used in the course of the Old English period with this value, as well as for [g] and [j].

INDO-EUROPEAN *gh* (LATIN *h*, GREEK *ch*)/GERMANIC *g*

hortus / garden	(Gr.) cholē (whence *cholera*) / gall
hostis / guest	(pre)he(n)dere 'to take' / get
homo / gome (obsolete)	hædus 'kid' / goat

b. Except when preceded by *s*, the Indo-European voiceless stops *p*, *t*, *k* became respectively the voiceless fricatives *f*, *þ*, *x*[37] (later *h* in initial position):

INDO-EUROPEAN *p*/ GERMANIC *f*

pater / father	per / for
piscis / fish	(Gr.) plinthos 'tile' / flint
pellis / fell 'animal hide'	ped- / foot
(Gr.) pyr / fire	pecu 'cattle' / fee
	(cf. Ger. *Vieh* 'cattle')

INDO-EUROPEAN *t*/ GERMANIC *þ*

trēs / three	tenuis / thin
torrēre 'to dry' / thirst	tumēre 'to swell' / thumb
	(that is, fat finger)
tu / thou	tonāre / thunder

INDO-EUROPEAN *k*/ GERMANIC *h*

cornū / horn	cent- / hund(red)
cord- / heart	celāre 'to hide' / hele
	(obsolete), hall, hell
quod / what (OE *hwæt*)	capere 'to take' / heave, have
cervus / hart	canis / hound

c. The Indo-European voiced stops *b*, *d*, *g* became respectively the voiceless stops *p*, *t*, *k*. Initial *b* was very infrequent in Indo-European. Rasmus Rask cites Greek *kannabis* and Old Norse *hampr* (English *hemp*) as showing the correspondence of *b* and *p*. Latin *turba* 'crowd'

---

[37] That is, the velar fricative and doubtless also its palatal allophone. The *x* is thus used here without brackets and similarly throughout this chapter with the value which it has in the alphabet of the International Phonetic Association. (IPA uses a different symbol, [ç], for the more forward variety.) It should not be confused with the letter *x* as used since Old English times to spell [ks]. By the time of the earliest writings the symbol used for [x], as well as for the aspirate which it had become initially, was *h*.

and English *thorp* 'town' (as in *Halethorp* and, with metathesis,[38] *Winthrop*) have also been cited. Other certain examples are impossible to find. The shifting of *d* and *g* is illustrated by the following cognates:

INDO-EUROPEAN *d*/ GERMANIC *t*

duo / two	(Gr.) drys 'oak' / tree
dentis / tooth	decem / ten (Gothic *taihun*)
domāre / tame	edere / eat

INDO-EUROPEAN *g*/ GERMANIC *k*

genu / knee (loss of [k-] is modern)	(Gr.) gynē 'woman' / queen, quean
ager 'field' / acre	grānum / corn
genus / kin	(g)noscere / know, can

Although we cannot be sure of the chronology of these consonant changes, it is certain that they stretched over centuries—perhaps as much as a millennium. Each set of shifts was completed before the next began; the First Sound Shift was no circular process. It is obvious, for instance, that the shift of Indo-European *b, d,* and *g* to Germanic *p, t,* and *k* must have occurred long after Indo-European *p, t,* and *k* had become Germanic *f, þ,* and *x*; otherwise, the Germanic *p, t,* and *k* from Indo-European *b, d,* and *g* would have gone on to become *f, þ,* and *x* also, and we should have no native words with *p, t,* and *k*.

FIRST SOUND SHIFT (GRIMM'S LAW)

IE **bh, dh, gh** ⟶ (respectively) Gmc **ƀ, ð, ȝ** ⟶ **b, d, g**
IE **p, t, k** ⟶ (respectively) Gmc **f, þ, x** (→ **h** initially)
IE **b, d, g** ⟶ (respectively) Gmc **p, t, k**

The First Sound Shift antedated the Stress Shift described above, for, at a time when the stress had not yet settled on the first syllables of all Germanic words, the voiceless fricatives *f, þ,* and *x* underwent a further modification in those words in which they were not immediately preceded by the stressed syllable: they were voiced, becoming respectively *ƀ, ð,* and *ȝ*.[39] Under the same circumstances, the voiceless fricative *s*, hitherto unchanged from Indo-European, became *z*. The

[38] A change in the position of sounds or syllables in a word, in this instance of [r].

[39] For a description of the sounds indicated by these symbols, see n. 36.

new ƀ, ð, and ȝ underwent the same later developments as the ƀ, ð, and ȝ which had resulted from the shifting of Indo-European *bh, dh,* and *gh.* In Old English, for instance, the ð appears as *d* (as in all other old West Germanic languages) and the ȝ as *g* (under certain circumstances as *w*). The *z* appears as *r*[40] in all recorded Germanic languages save Gothic.

These occurrences of voiced fricatives where according to Grimm's Law we should expect to find voiceless ones were explained by a Danish scholar named Karl Verner in 1875 as being due to the post-position of the stress before the Germanic shift to the first syllable. Hence voicing under such circumstances is said to be according to Verner's Law. Grimm, who recognized but failed to comprehend the reason for the voicing, called it "grammatical change" (*grammatischer Wechsel*). The phenomenon is most obvious in the preterit plural and the past participial forms of some Germanic strong verbs—forms in which the stress did not originally fall on the root: thus, in Old English, *sēaþ* '(I, he, she, it) seethed,' but *sudon* '(we, you, they) seethed' and *soden* (past participle). The *d* of the last two forms has developed from Germanic ð; in pre-Stress-Shift Germanic these forms did not have initial stress. It is similar with Old English *lēas* '(I, he, she, it) lost' contrasted with *luron* '(we, you, they) lost' and *loren* (past participle), in which the *s,* after being voiced to become *z* in those forms lacking initial stress, has been subsequently rhotacized.

One further illustration must suffice. Germanic developments of the Indo-European word meaning 'male parent' are evidenced in Gothic *faðar,* written *fadar* (but the *d* in this position indicated the voiced fricative), Icelandic *faðir,* and Old English *fæder* (in which the *d* is, as we have seen, a West Germanic development of earlier ð).[41] In all these forms we should ordinarily expect to find þ medially, since the Indo-European medial consonant was *t.* But examination of early

[40] This shift of *z* to *r,* known as *rhotacism* (that is, *r*-ing, from Gr. *rho,* the name of the letter) is by no means peculiar to Germanic: compare Latin *flōs* '*flower*,' which has *r* in all forms other than the nominative singular—for instance the genitive singular *flōris,* from earlier **flōz-,* the original *s* being here voiced because of its position between vowels.

[41] The fact that Modern English *father* has the same medial consonant as Proto-Germanic is sheer coincidence. The [ð] in this word, like that in *mother,* is comparatively recent—perhaps no older than the sixteenth century. Earlier [d] was "sometimes heard" in northern England and the lowlands of Scotland at the time of the publication of the relevant section of the *OED* (1895), and may still be.

cognate forms in non-Germanic languages reveals that the stressed syllable in this word followed rather than immediately preceded the *t*, as in Greek *patĕr*, Sanskrit *pitā́*. When the Germanic stress shifted to the first syllable, the reason for the voicing of the consonant was completely obscured. It required comparative linguistics (or comparative philology, as it was then called) to solve the puzzle presented by such apparent exceptions to the workings of the First Sound Shift—to demonstate that they were *only* apparent, and not real exceptions.

VERNER'S LAW

Later developments in the various Germanic languages which have obscured the workings of the shift are not indicated in the table below, where each of the consonants in question plus *a* stands for a syllable headed by that consonant, *o* standing for any preceding syllable; thus *otá* represents Indo-European *pətĕr* 'father,' *kmtóm* 'hundred,' and so forth:

IE opá ————→ Gmc ofá → obá → óba

IE otá ————→ Gmc oþá → oðá → óða (→ WGmc óda)

IE oká ————→ Gmc oxá → oȝá → óȝa

IE osá (remains) Gmc osá → ozá → óza → óra (except in Gothic).

---

7. Germanic has a large number of words which have no known cognates in other Indo-European languages. These could of course have existed in Indo-European and have been lost; it is also possible that they were taken from non-Indo-European languages originally spoken in the area occupied by the Germanic peoples. A few words which are apparently distinctively Germanic, given in their Modern English forms, are *rain, drink, drive, broad, hold,*[42] *wife, meat,* and *fowl.*

The earliest records in any Germanic language, aside from a few proper names recorded by classical authors, a few loan-words in Finnish, and some runic inscriptions found in Scandinavia, are those of Gothic.[43] For almost all our knowledge of Gothic we are indebted to

[42] These are all cited in their modern High German forms (*Regen, trinken, treiben, breit, halten*) by Robert Priebsch and W. E. Collinson, *The German Language*, 4th ed., rev. (London, 1958), pp. 281–82.

[43] *Gothic* was in the seventeenth and eighteenth centuries extended to mean 'Germanic,' even in the linguistic sense, but this meaning is now happily obsolete. It also came to mean 'romantically medieval'—a meaning which survives in the name of a fictional genre (*Gothic novel*) and of a style of architecture.

a translation of parts of the New Testament made in the fourth century by Wulfila (*Ulfilas* to the Greeks), bishop of the Visigoths, those
Goths who lived north of the Danube. There are also small fragments
of two other books of the Bible and of a commentary on the Gospel of
John. Late as they are in comparison with the literary records of
Sanskrit, Iranian, Greek, and Latin, these remains of Gothic provide
us with a clear picture of a Germanic language in an early stage of
development and hence are of tremendous importance to the student
of Germanic languages. Etymological dictionaries of English cite
Gothic cognates of English words (for instance *light–leihts, find–
finþan*) when the related Gothic form occurs in the literature cited
above. Gothic as a spoken tongue disappeared a long time ago without
leaving a trace. No modern Germanic languages are derived from it,
nor are there any Gothic loan-words in any of the Germanic languages.
Vandalic and Burgundian were apparently also East Germanic in
structure, but we know little more of them at first hand than a few
proper names.

   Certain differences between modern Standard German and the
other West Germanic languages are due to a second sound shift—the
so-called High German Shift—which occurred comparatively recently
as linguistic history goes. It was nearing its completion by the end of
the eighth century of our era. This shift began in the southern, moun-
tainous part of Germany and spread northward, stopping short of the
low-lying northern section of the country. The *high* in High German
(*Hochdeutsch*) and the *low* in Low German (*Plattdeutsch*) refer only
to relative distances above sea level. High German became in time
Standard German, relegating Low German to the status of a peasant
patois in Germany.

FROM GERMANIC TO ENGLISH

   The Continental home of the English was north of the area in which
the High German Shift occurred. But even if this had not been so, the
English language would have been unaffected by changes which had
not begun to occur at the time of the Anglo-Saxon migrations to
Britain, which began as early as the mid-fifth century. Consequently
English has the earlier consonantal characteristics of Germanic, which
among the West Germanic languages it shares with Low German,
Dutch, Flemish, and Frisian. We may illustrate the High German shift
in part by contrasting English and High German forms, as follows:
earlier Germanic *p* appears in High German as *pf* or, after vowels, as
ff (*pepper–Pfeffer*); earlier *t* appears as *ts* (spelled *z*) or, after vowels,

as *ss* (*tongue–Zunge*; *water–Wasser*); earlier *k* appears after vowels as *ch* (*break–brechen*); earlier *d* appears as *t* (*dance–tanzen*).

The German spoken by more or less simple folk in northern Germany is a development of Old Saxon, and it alone now bears the proper name Low German, though as we have seen it is only one type of low German. Dutch and the practically identical Flemish are the modern forms of Low Franconian, spoken respectively in Holland and, side by side with French, in Belgium. Formerly spoken in a much larger area, including the west coast of Schleswig, Frisian has survived principally in the northern Dutch province of Friesland and in some of the islands off the coast. English and Frisian share certain features not found elsewhere in the Germanic group to such an extent that some scholars regard them as developments of a relatively unified prehistoric language called Anglo-Frisian, a subgroup of West Germanic.

English, then, began its separate existence as a form of Germanic brought by pagan warrior-adventurers from the Continent to the then relatively obscure island which the Romans called Britannia and which had up until a short time before been part of their mighty empire. There, in the next five centuries or so, it was to develop into an independent language quite distinct from any Germanic language spoken on the Continent—a language sufficiently rich in its word stock, thanks largely to the impetus given to learning by the introduction of Christianity, that, as Kemp Malone so well puts it, "by the year 1000, this newcomer could measure swords with Latin in every department of expression, and was incomparably superior to the French speech that came in with William of Normandy."[44]

[44] *A Literary History of England,* ed. Albert C. Baugh (New York, 1948), p. 10.

CHAPTER V

The Old English Period (449–1100)

A CELTIC people had been in Britain for many centuries before Julius Caesar's invasion of that island in 55 B.C. The subsequent occupation, not really begun in earnest until the time of the Emperor Claudius almost a century later, was to make Britain, that is, Britannia, a part of the Roman Empire for a period somewhat longer than that intervening between the first permanent English settlement in America and our own day. It is not therefore surprising that there are so many Roman remains in modern England, some of them discovered quite recently in the very heart of London in the course of clearing away the rubble of World War II bombings. Despite the long occupation, the British Celts continued to speak their own language, though many of them, particularly those in the towns and cities who wanted to "get on," learned to speak and write the language of their Roman rulers. It was not until Britain became England that the survival of British Celtic was seriously threatened.

After the Roman legionaries were withdrawn from Britain in the early years of the fifth century, Picts from the north and Scots from the west savagely attacked the unprotected British Celts, who after generations of foreign domination had neither the heart nor the skill in weapons to put up much resistance. This was Celt eat Celt, for it should be remembered that the Picts were themselves British Celts, and the Scots—that is, Irishmen—were Gaelic Celts (see p. 87). These same Picts and Scots, as well as ferocious Germanic sea raiders whom the Romans called Saxons, had earlier been a very considerable nuisance to the Roman soldiers and their commanders during the latter half of the fourth century.

THE COMING OF THE ENGLISH

According to the Venerable Bede's account in his *Ecclesiastical History of the English Nation,* written in Latin and completed around

730, almost three centuries after the event, the Britons appealed to Rome for help. What relief they got, a single legion, was only temporarily effectual. When Rome could or would help no more, the wretched Britons—still according to Bede—ironically enough called the "Saxons" to their aid "from the parts beyond the sea." As a result of this appeal, shiploads of Germanic warrior-adventurers began to arrive. The date which Bede gives for the first landing—449—cannot be far out of the way, if at all. With it the Old English period begins. With it, too, we may in a sense begin thinking of Britain as England—the land of the Angles—for, even though the long ships carried Jutes,[1] Saxons, Frisians, and, doubtless, members of other tribes as well, their descendants a century and a half later were already beginning to think of themselves as Englishmen and of their speech as English. (They naturally had no suspicion that it was "Old" English.) The name of a single tribe was thus to be adopted as a national name (prehistoric Old English *Angli, becoming Engle), for what specific reasons we have no way of knowing.

These Germanic sea raiders, ancestors of the English, in short order gave the Pictish and Scottish aggressors what was coming to them. Then, with eyes ever on the main chance, a complete lack of any sense of international morality, and no fear whatever of being prosecuted as war criminals, they very unidealistically, though as it turned out sensibly, proceeded to subjugate and ultimately to dispossess the Britons whom they had come ostensibly to help. Word reached Continental kinsmen and friends of the cowardice of the Britons and the fertility of the island, and in the course of the next hundred years or so more and more of those whom Bede, our primary source for this period, calls Saxons, Angles, and Jutes arrived "from the three most powerful nations of Germania" to seek their fortunes in a new land.

About all that we can be certain of about the events of these exciting times is that the invading newcomers belonged to various Germanic tribes speaking a number of closely related and hence very similar regional types of Germanic, that they came from the great North German plain, including the southern part of the Jutland peninsula (the modern Schleswig-Holstein), and that by the time St. Augustine arrived to convert them to Christianity at the end of the sixth century they held in their possession practically all of what is now known as

[1] More properly Iuts or Euts. The I of Bede's Iuti and Iutae was confused with J so long ago that the error has become traditional.

England as far north as the Scottish highlands. As for the Britons, many fled to Wales and Cornwall, some crossed the Channel to Brittany, others were ultimately assimilated to the English by marriage or otherwise; many, we may be sure, lost their lives in the long-drawn-out fighting.

The Germanic tribesmen who came first—Bede's *Iutae, Iuti,* or "Jutes," led by the synonymously named brothers Hengest[2] and Horsa (both names mean 'horse')—settled principally in the southeastern part of the island, still called by its Celtic name of Kent. Subsequently Continental Saxons were to occupy the rest of the region south of the Thames, and Angles, stemming presumably from the hook-shaped peninsula in Schleswig known as Angeln, settled the large area stretching from the Thames northward to the Scottish highlands, except for the extreme southwestern portion (Wales).

The Germanic settlement comprised seven kingdoms, the Anglo-Saxon Heptarchy: Kent, Essex, Sussex, Wessex, East Anglia, Mercia, and Northumbria—the last, the land north of the Humber, being an amalgamation of two earlier kingdoms, Bernicia and Deira. Kent early became the chief center of culture and wealth, and by the end of the sixth century its King Ethelbert (Æðelberht) could lay claim to the hegemony over all the other kingdoms south of the Humber. Later, in the seventh and eighth centuries, this supremacy was to pass to Northumbria, with its great centers of learning at Lindisfarne, at Wear-

---

[2] He has been identified with the Hengest who plays a prominent role in the story of the fight at Finn's Borough, recounted in *Beowulf,* lines 1063–1159, and independently in a fragment of another Old English poem. This Hengest of Old English heroic poetry is the retainer of the Danish king Hnæf and, after Hnæf's fall in the treacherous sortie at Finn's Borough, makes peace of a sort with the victorious Finn, king of Frisia, whose subjects also included the Eote (the Old English equivalent of Bede's *Iuti*). The *Beowulf* poet tells us nothing of Hengest's subsequent career, but leaves him brooding vengeance for the death of his lord; he is mentioned only as a prominent Danish warrior in the fragment. Vengeance is later executed upon Finn by a Danish fleet, but what part, if any, Hengest took in it we are not told. The identification of this Hengest with the man mentioned by Bede presupposes that somehow after the death of Finn he, presumably a Dane, became king of the Jutes, at the same time acquiring an ancestry befitting an Anglo-Saxon monarch, for Bede tells us that Hengest and Horsa were the great-grandsons of Woden, the chief Germanic god. That the two Hengests were one and the same man seems on the whole unlikely, yet the possibility tantalizes.

mouth, and at Jarrow, Bede's own monastery; then to Mercia; and finally to Wessex, with its brilliant line of kings beginning with Egbert (Ecgberht), who overthrew the Mercian king in 825, and culminating in his grandson, the superlatively great Alfred, whose successors after his death in 899 took for themselves the title *Rex Anglorum* 'King of the English.'

The most important event in the history of Anglo-Saxon culture (which in its broadest sense includes American) occurred in 597, when Gregory I dispatched a band of missionaries to the Angles (*Angli*, as he called them, thereby departing from the usual Continental designation of them as *Saxones*), in accordance with a resolve he had made some years before. The leader of this band was, as everyone knows, St. Augustine—not to be confused with the African-born bishop of Hippo of the same name who wrote *The City of God* more than a century earlier. The apostle to the English and his fellow bringers of the Word, who landed on the Isle of Thanet in Kent, were received by King Ethelbert courteously, if at the beginning somewhat warily. Already somewhat ripe for conversion through his marriage to a Christian Frankish princess, Ethelbert was himself baptized in a matter of months. Four years later, in 601, Augustine was consecrated first Archbishop of Canterbury, and there was a church in England. Later, Irish missionaries who had come from Iona to found a monastery at Lindisfarne made many converts in Northumbria and Mercia. In the course of the seventh century the new faith spread rapidly,[3] and by the end of that century England had become a most important part of Christendom.

THE VIKING CONQUESTS

The Christian descendants of Germanic raiders who had looted, pillaged, and finally taken the land of Britain by force of arms were themselves to undergo harassment from other Germanic invaders, beginning in the latter years of the eighth century, in the course of which pagan Viking raiders sacked various churches and monasteries, including Lindisfarne and Bede's own beloved Jarrow. In the course of the first half of the following century there were other more or less disorganized but disastrous raids in the South. Then, in 865 a great and expertly organized army landed in East Anglia, led by the unforget-

[3] But not without some scandalous backsliding on the part of Ethelbert's own son Eadbald, who later fully repented. There was also a serious reversion to heathenism in Essex.

tably named Ivar the Boneless and his brother Halfdan, sons of Ragnar Lothbrok (*Loðbrók* 'Shaggy-pants'),[4] and during the course of the next fifteen years gained possession of practically the whole eastern part of England.[5]

In 870 began the attack upon Wessex, ruled by Ethelred (Æðelræd) with the able assistance of his brother Alfred, who was to succeed him in the year following. After years of discouragement, very few victories, and many crushing defeats, Alfred in 878 won a signal victory at Edington over Guthrum, the Danish king of East Anglia, who promised not only to depart from Wessex but also to be baptized. Alfred was godfather for him when the sacrament was later administered.

The troubles with the Danes, as they were called by the English, though there were Norwegians and later Swedes among them, were by no means over. There were further attacks, but these were so successfully repulsed by the English that ultimately, in the tenth century, Alfred's son and grandsons (three of whom became kings) were able to carry out his plans for the consolidation of England, which by this time had a sizable and peaceful Scandinavian population.

Then, in the latter years of the tenth century, trouble started again with the arrival of a fleet of warriors led by Olaf Tryggvason, later king of Norway, who was in a few years to be joined by the Danish king Svein Forkbeard. For more than twenty years there were repeated attacks, most of them crushing defeats for the English, beginning with the glorious if unsuccessful stand made by the men of Essex under the valiant Byrhtnoth in 991, celebrated in the fine Old English poem *The Battle of Maldon*. As a rule, however, the onslaughts of the later Northmen were not met with such vigorous resistance, for these were the bad days of the second Ethelred, known as *Unræd*, that is, 'unadvised,' but frequently misunderstood as 'unready.' After the deaths in 1016 of

---

[4] According to the legend, Ivar was born with gristle instead of bone because his father had refused his bewitched bride's plea for a deferment of the consummation of their marriage for three nights. Ragnar is said to have been put to death in a snake pit in York. On this occasion his wife, the lovely Kraka, who felt no resentment toward him, had furnished him with a magical snake-proof coat; but it was of no avail, for his executioners made him remove his outer garment. Ivar Ragnarsson's unique physique seems to have been no handicap to a brilliant if rascally career as warrior.

[5] The story of these bloodstained times is well and succinctly related in Chapter 2 of Peter Hunter Blair's *An Introduction to Anglo-Saxon England* (Cambridge, Eng., 1956).

Ethelred and his son Edmund Ironside, who survived his father by little more than half a year, Cnut, son of Svein Forkbeard, who himself was for a short time recognized as king of England, came to the throne. The line of Alfred was not to be restored until 1042, with the accession of Edward the Confessor, though Cnut in a sense allied himself with that line by marrying Ethelred's widow Emma of Normandy (the English preferred to call her Ælgifu),[6] who thus became the mother of two English kings by different fathers: by Ethelred, of Edward the Confessor, and by Cnut, of Harthacnut. (She was not the mother of Ethelred's son Edmund Ironside.)

As has been pointed out, those whom the English called Danes (*Dene*) were not all from Denmark. Linguistically, however, this fact is of little significance, for the various Scandinavian tongues were in those days little differentiated from one another. Furthermore, they were sufficiently like Old English as to make possible communication of a sort without great difficulty between the English and the Scandinavians. The English were perfectly aware of their racial as well as their linguistic kinship with the Scandinavians, many of whom had become their neighbors: the Old English poem *Beowulf* is exclusively concerned with events of Scandinavian legend and history, and approximately a century and a half after the composition of this great literary masterpiece, Alfred, who certainly had no reason to love the Danes, interpolated in his translation of the history of Orosius the first geographical account of the countries of the North, in the famous story of the voyages of Ohthere and Wulfstan.

THE SCANDINAVIANS BECOME ENGLISH

Despite the enmity and the bloodshed, then, there was a feeling among the English that when all was said and done the Northmen belonged to the same "family" as themselves—a feeling which their ancestors could never have experienced regarding the British Celts. Whereas the earlier raids had been dictated largely by the desire to pillage and to loot—even though a good deal of Scandinavian settlement resulted—the tenth-century and early eleventh-century invaders from the North seem to have been much more interested in colonization than their predecessors had been. This was successfully accomplished in East Anglia (Norfolk and Suffolk), Lincolnshire, Yorkshire, Westmorland, Cumberland, and Northumberland. The Danes set-

[6] As if to compound the confusion of these early times, Cnut's first wife or mistress, whom he set aside, was also named Ælgifu. She was the mother of King Harold Harefoot.

tled down peaceably enough in time, living side by side with English-men; Scandinavians were good colonizers, willing to assimilate them-selves to their new homes. As John Richard Green eloquently sums it up, "England still remained England; the conquerors sank quietly into the mass of those around them; and Woden yielded without a struggle to Christ."[7]

And what of the impact of this assimilation upon the English lan-guage, which is our main concern here? Old English and Old Norse had a whole host of frequently used words in common. Jespersen cites, among others, *man, wife, mother, folk, house, think, winter, summer, will, can, come, hear, see, think, ride, over, under, mine,* and *thine.*[8] In some instances where related words differed noticeably in form, the Scandinavian form has won out, for example *sister* (ON *systir;* OE *sweostor*). Scandinavian contributions to the English word stock will be discussed in more detail in a later chapter.

It has been supposed that other fundamental characteristics of Eng-lish may be due to Scandinavian influence. Jespersen, in the previ-ously cited work, thought it "probable" that the English use of relative clauses without pronouns (as in "The man the committee chose was unavailable") or without conjunctive *that* (as in "He thought the window was broken"), the use of *shall* and *will* as future auxiliaries, and the placing of the genitive before instead of after the noun may have been due to such influence (p. 70). But the fact is that all these constructions either occurred in Old English before the beginning of the Viking period or do not occur in Old Norse as we know it from runic inscriptions made before the beginning of that period.[9] There is thus no good reason to attribute these syntactical characteristics of English to Scandinavian influence.

THE OLD ENGLISH DIALECTS

Four principal dialects were spoken in Anglo-Saxon England: Kent-ish, the speech of the Jutes who settled in Kent; West Saxon, spoken in the region south of the Thames exclusive of Kent; Mercian, spoken from the Thames to the Humber exclusive of Wales; and Northum-brian, whose localization (north of the Humber) is adequately indi-

[7] *A Short History of England* (1874), cited in Otto Jespersen, *Growth and Structure of the English Language,* 9th ed. (Oxford, 1954), p. 58.

[8] *Growth and Structure,* p. 60. Jespersen is of course referring to older forms of these words.

[9] This has been pointed out by Max S. Kirch, "Scandinavian Influence on English Syntax," *PMLA,* LXXIV (1959), 503–10.

cated by its name. Mercian and Northumbrian have certain characteristics in common which distinguish them from West Saxon and
Kentish, and are sometimes grouped together as Anglian, since those
who spoke these north-of-the-Thames dialects were predominantly
Angles. There were presumably other dialects, but we possess no written remains of them. The records of Anglian and Kentish are scant,
but much West Saxon writing has come down to us, though probably
only a fraction of what once existed. It should be stressed that Old
English dialectal differences were slight as compared with those which
were later to develop and nowadays sharply differentiate the speech of
the lowland Scottish shepherd from that of his South-of-England
counterpart.

Hence, although Modern Standard English is in large part a descendant of the Mercian speech of the eastern section of the Midland
area, the dialect of Old English which will be described in this chapter
is West Saxon. During the time of Alfred and for a long time thereafter, Winchester, the capital of Wessex and therefore in a sense of all
England, was a center of English culture, thanks to the encouragement
given by Alfred himself to learning. Though London was at the same
time an important and thriving commercial city, it did not acquire its
cultural or even its political importance until later.

It is thus in West Saxon that most of the extant Old English manuscripts—all in fact which may be regarded as literature—are available
to us. Fortunately, however, we are at no great disadvantage when we
study the West Saxon dialect in relation to Modern English: because
dialectal differences were not great, the Old English forms cited in
what follows may usually be regarded without reference to the fact
that they occur in West Saxon rather than in Mercian writings. Occasionally a distinctive Mercian form (labeled Anglian if it happens to
be identical with the Northumbrian form) has been cited as more
obviously similar to the standard modern form than is the West Saxon
form, for instance Anglian *ald*, which regularly develops into Modern
English *old*. The West Saxon form was *eald*.

The Old English to be described here is of about the year 1000—
roughly that of the period during which Ælfric, the most representative writer of the late tenth and early eleventh centuries, was flourishing.[10] This development of English, which became the literary stand-

[10] It is the language of this period which is concisely treated by Kemp
Malone in the opening chapter of *A Literary History of England,* ed.
Albert C. Baugh (New York, 1948) and in detail by Randolph Quirk and
C. L. Wrenn in *An Old English Grammar* (London, 1955).

ard, is sometimes called classical Old English; that of the Age of Alfred, who reigned in the latter years of the ninth century, is usually included in what is called early West Saxon, though it is actually rather late early West Saxon. It is, however, about all that we know of the early West Saxon dialect from manuscript evidence.

The Old English period spans somewhat more than six centuries, the dates ascribed to it being more or less arbitrary. In a period of more than six hundred years many changes are bound to occur in sounds, in grammar, and in vocabulary. Some of these are evident from a comparison of the earliest writings with the later ones. (Written records of English are, incidentally, older than those of any other West Germanic language.) By a comparative study of all the Germanic languages and dialects, linguists are able to reconstruct prehistoric Old English and to infer changes which took place in that stage in the development of our language. With such early changes we shall be concerned here only incidentally.

THE PRONUNCIATION OF OLD ENGLISH

For the pronunciation of the Old English words cited in the following discussion, the reader will do well to review the treatment of Old English scribal practices in Chapter II, and to remember that our knowledge of the phonology of an older form of any language can be only approximate. The precise quality of any speech sound at any given period in the vast pre-tape-recording era stretching behind us in time cannot ever be determined with absolute certainty. It should further be borne in mind that in Old English times as today there were regional and individual differences, and doubtless social differences as well. A period in which all members of a given linguistic community speak exactly alike, let alone an entire nation, is inconceivable.

As regards stress in Old English, we are on rather certain ground. We have already seen in another connection (pp. 90–91) that Old English words of more than one syllable, like those in all other Germanic languages, were regularly stressed on their first syllables. Exceptions to this rule are verbs with prefixes, which were generally stressed on the first syllable of their second element: *wiðféohtan* 'to fight against,' *onbíndan* 'to unbind,' *ofdrǽdan*[11] 'to dread.' *Be-, for-,* and *ge-* were not stressed, regardless of whether or not they were used with verbs: *bebód* 'commandment,' *forsóð* 'forsooth,' *geháp* 'convenient.' Other

[11] The macron in Old English forms is editorial. Vowel quantity was not customarily indicated in Old English writing, for readers needed no such indication of what they unconsciously did in speaking their native language.

compounds had the customary Germanic stress on the first syllable; those consisting of two nouns or a noun and an adjective had secondary stress in their second elements: *lā́rhū̀s* 'school,' *hí̄ldedḕor* 'fierce in battle.' This heavy stressing of the first syllable of practically all words has had a far-reaching effect upon the development of English. Because of it, the vowels of final syllables began to be reduced to a uniform sound as early as the tenth century, as not infrequent interchanges of one letter for another in the texts indicate, though most scribes continued to spell according to tradition. In general the stress system of Old English was simple as compared to that of Modern English, with its many loan-words of non-Germanic origin, like *matérnal, vagáry, sublíme,* and *tabóo.*

As we have seen in Chapter III, the vowel symbols used in writing Old English, except for *æ*, had what are sometimes referred to as "Continental" values—approximately those of Italian, Spanish, German, and to some extent of French as well. In other words, the *a* of the Old English texts indicates a vowel of the quality of [ɑ] short or long; likewise, to long *e, i, o,* and *u* may be assigned the same values which these symbols have when written in square brackets in the system of phonetic transcription set forth on pp. 58–61. When short, they were approximately [ɛ], [ɪ], [ɔ], and [ʊ] respectively. Short *æ* was as in *mat;* long *æ* was approximately the same sound prolonged, but somewhat tenser. *Y,* used exclusively as a vowel symbol in Old English, indicated a rounded front vowel, long as in German *Bühne,* short as in *fünf.* Later losing its rounded quality, long and short *y* fell together with long and short *i.*

In the examples which follow, the Modern English form in parentheses, when its vowel differs in sound from that of the Old English form, illustrates a typical development of the Old English sound:

a as in *habban* (have)	*ī* as in *rīdan* (ride)
ā as in *hām* (home)	*o* as in *moððe* (moth)
æ as in *þæt* (that)	*ō* as in *fōda* (food)
ǣ as in *dǣl* (deal)	*u* as in *sundor* (sunder)
e as in *settan* (set)	*ū* as in *mūs* (mouse)
ē as in *fēdan* (feed)	*y* as in *fyllan* (fill)
i as in *sittan* (sit)	*ȳ* as in *mȳs* (mice)

Late West Saxon had two long diphthongs, *ēa* and *ēo,* to the first elements of which may be assigned respectively the values [æ:] and [e:]. The second elements of both, once differentiated, had been reduced to [ə], which in the course of the eleventh century was lost; to put it in another way, these diphthongs became monophthongs which continued to be differentiated until well into the Modern English period, but which ultimately fell together as [i:], as in *beat* from Old English *bēatan, creep* from *crēopan.* According to the traditional view, the writings *ea* and *eo* in such words as *seah*[12] 'saw,' *eoh* 'horse,' *eall* 'all,' *heard* 'hard,' *meolc* 'milk,' *weorc* 'work,' *ceaf* 'chaff,' and *geard* 'yard' stood for short diphthongs of the same quality as the corresponding long ones, approximately [æə] and [ɛə].[13]

The consonant symbols *b, d, l, m, n, k* (rarely used), *p, t, w* (that is, *ρ*), and *x* had in all positions the same values which these letters represent in Modern English. The doubling of consonant symbols between vowels indicated length; thus the *t*'s of *sittan* indicated the medial single consonant sound frequently heard in *hot tamale,* which is of longer duration than the medial consonant of Modern English *sitting*; similarly *ll* in *fyllan* indicated the lengthened medial *l* of *full-length,* in contrast to the short *l* of *holy*; *cc* as in *racca* 'part of a ship's rigging' was a long [k] as in *bookkeeper,* in contrast to *beekeeper,* and hence *racca* was distinguished from *raca* 'rake'; and so on.

The sound represented by *c* depended upon contiguous sounds. If these were back vowels, the letter indicated the velar stop [k] (*camp* 'battle,' *corn* 'corn,' *cūð* 'known,' *lūcan* 'to lock,' *acan* 'to ache,' *bōc* 'book'); if they were front (or had been in early Old English), the sound indicated was the affricate [č] (*cild* 'child,' *cēosan* 'to choose,' *ic* 'I,' *lǣce* 'physician,' *rīce* 'kingdom,' *mēce* 'sword'). In *cēpan* 'to keep,' *cynn* 'race, kin,' and a number of other words, the root vowels are mutated back vowels (Germanic **kopjan,* *kunjō); hence the palatalization of [k] resulting in Old English [č] did not occur.[14] In *bēc* 'books' from prehistoric Old English *bōci and *sēcan*[15] 'to seek' from prehistoric

---

[12] Old English verbs had the same form in the first and third persons of the preterit singular. This is the form here and hereafter cited as the preterit singular.

[13] Another more recent view holds that the *ea* and *eo* when short did not represent diphthongs at all, but (according to one interpretation) were merely spellings to indicate the nature of a contiguous consonant.

[14] For a discussion of mutation in a more appropriate place, see p. 115.

[15] For this word, Old English scribes frequently wrote *secean,* the extra *e* functioning merely as a diacritic to indicate that the preceding *c* was pronounced [č] rather than [k]. Compare the Italian use of *i* after *c* preceding *a, o,* or *u* to indicate precisely the same thing, as in *ciarlare* 'to prate,' *cioccolata* 'chocolate,' and *ciuffo* 'toupee.'

Old English *sōcjan, the immediately following i and j effected both palatalization of the original [k] (written c in the Old English reconstructions) and mutation of the original vowel. In swylc 'such,' ǣlc 'each,' and hwylc 'which,' an earlier ī before the c has been lost; but even without this information, we have a guide in the modern forms cited as definitions; similarly we may know from modern keep and kin that the Old English initial sound was [k].[16] Preconsonantal c was always [k], as in cnāwan 'to know,' crǣt 'cart,' and cwellan 'to kill.' The digraphs cg and sc were in post-Old English times replaced by dg and sh respectively—spellings which indicate to the modern reader exactly the sounds the older spellings represented, for example ecg 'edge,' scīr 'shire,' scacan 'to shake,' and fisc 'fish.'

The pronunciation of g (that is, ʒ) also depended upon neighboring sounds. The symbol indicated in late Old English the velar voiced stop [g] before consonants (gnēað 'niggardly,' glæd 'glad, gracious'), initially before back vowels (galan 'to sing,' gōs 'goose,' gūð 'war'), and initially before front vowels which had resulted from the mutation of back vowels (gēs 'geese' from prehistoric Old English *gōsi, gǣst 'goest' from *gāis). Medially or finally in the combination ng the letter indicated the same sound—that of Modern English linger as contrasted with ringer (bringan 'to bring,' hring 'ring'). The same symbol indicated [j] initially before e, i, and the y which was usual in late West Saxon for earlier ie (gecoren 'chosen,' gēar 'year,' giftian 'to give a woman in marriage,' gydd 'song'), medially between front vowels (slægen 'slain,' twēgen 'twain'), and finally when it followed a front vowel in either a word or a syllable (dæg 'day,' mægden 'maiden,' legde 'laid,' stigrāp 'stirrup,' manig 'many'). In practically all other circumstances g indicated the voiced velar fricative referred to above (p. 92, n. 36) as the earliest Germanic development of Indo-European gh—a sound difficult to describe for English-speaking people nowadays, nor is much gained by attempting to pronounce it except for professional purposes (dragan 'to draw,' lagu 'law,' hogu 'care,' folgian 'to follow,' sorgian 'to sorrow,' swelgan 'to swallow'). It later became [w], as in Middle English drawen, lawe, howe, and so on.

The symbols f, s, and þ (or ð, used more or less interchangeably with it)[17] indicated respectively voiceless fricatives except between voiced

---

[16] Unfortunately for easy tests, seek does not show palatalization (though beseech does) and the mutated plural of book has not survived.

[17] In words cited hereafter, þ will be used only initially; elsewhere ð will be used, in accordance with the preferred practice of many scribes in late Old English times. When Old English texts are cited, as on pp. 132

sounds; under the latter circumstances (that is, between vowels or between a vowel and a voiced consonant), they stood for the corresponding voiced fricatives [v], [z], [ð], as in *cnafa* 'boy,' *hæfde* 'had'; *lēosan*
'to lose,' *hūsl* 'Holy Communion'; and *brōðor* 'brother,' *fæðm* 'fathom.'
In a very few Latin loan-words which began with [v],[18] Old English
sometimes used *f* (which indeed indicated [v], as we have seen, under
certain circumstances), for example *fers* (Lat. *versus*) and *Firgilius*
(*Virgilius*). It is possible that the English actually pronounced [f] in
these words, in the Irish fashion. Occasionally *v* (written *u*, of course)
also occurs in such borrowings.

In initial position, *r* may have been a trill but preconsonantally and
finally it was in West Saxon probably the so-called retroflex *r* general
in American English except for eastern New England and the tidewater South. Initial *h* was about as in Modern English, but elsewhere
it stood for the fricative [x], the velar or palatal quality depending as
always upon the neighboring vowel, for example (with the *ach*-sound)
seah 'saw,' *þurh* 'through,' *þōhte* 'thought' (verb); (with the *ich*-sound)
syhð 'sees,' *miht* 'might,' *fēhð* 'takes.' Of the sequences *hl* (as in *hlāf*
'loaf'), *hn* (as in *hnitu* 'nit'), *hr* (as in *hræfn* 'raven'), and *hw* (as in
hwæl 'whale'), only the last[19] survives. The rare use of *z* with the value
[ts] has been previously referred to (p. 40).

OTHER DIFFERENCES
BETWEEN OLD ENGLISH AND MODERN ENGLISH

Aside from its pronunciation and its word stock, Old English differs
markedly from Modern English in having grammatical gender in contrast to the Modern English system of gender based on sex or sexless-
ness and in the degree of inflection of the noun, the adjective, and the
demonstrative and interrogative pronouns. The personal pronouns
have preserved much of their ancient complexity in Modern English.
The verb in Old English, except for the more extensive use of the
subjunctive, is only slightly more complex than in Modern English,
as we shall see, but Old English had a considerably larger number of
strong verbs than has Modern English.

The three genders of Indo-European were preserved in Germanic

and 133–36, the usage of the manuscripts will be exactly followed. Note
that, though ambiguous in Old English, ð is used in phonetic and phonemic
script for the voiced sound only.

[18] Late Latin [v] is a development of Classical Latin [w], the sound
usually taught nowadays in the schools.

[19] Later, and less accurately, spelled *wh-*.

and survived in English well into the Middle English period; they survive in German and Icelandic to this day. Doubtless the gender of a noun originally had nothing to do with sex, nor does it necessarily have sexual connotations in those languages which have retained grammatical (as opposed to "natural") gender. Old English *wīf* 'wife, woman' is neuter, as is its German cognate *Weib*; so is *mægden* 'maiden,' like German *Mädchen*. *Bridd* 'young bird' is masculine; *bearn* 'son, bairn' is neuter. *Brēost* 'breast' and *hēafod* 'head' are neuter, but *brū* 'eyebrow,' *wamb* 'belly,' and *eaxl* 'shoulder' are feminine. *Strengðu* 'strength' is feminine, *broc* 'affliction' is neuter, and *drēam* 'joy' is masculine.

Where sex was patently involved, however, this troublesome and to us illogical system was beginning to break down even in Old English times. It must have come to be difficult, for instance, to refer to one who was obviously a woman—that is, a *wīf*—with the pronoun *hit* 'it,' or to a *wīfmann*—a compound from which our word *woman* is derived —with *hē* 'he,' the compound being masculine because of its second element; and there are in fact a number of instances in Old English of the conflict of grammatical gender with the developing concept of natural gender.

Old English word order is somewhat less fixed than that of Modern English, but in general is about the same. Old English declarative sentences tend to fall into the subject-verb-complement order which is usual in Modern English, for example "Hē wæs swīðe spēdig man" ('He was a very successful man') and "Ēadwine eorl cōm mid landfyrde and drāf hine ūt" ('Earl Edwin came with a land army and drove him out'). Declarative sentences which do not conform to this pattern sometimes occur when the object of the verb is a pronoun ("Se hālga Andreas him andswarode," that is, 'The holy Andrew him answered') and usually when the sentence begins with *þā* 'then, when' or *ne* 'not' ("Þā sealde se cyning him sweord," that is, 'Then gave the king him a sword'; "Ne can ic nōht singan," that is, 'Cannot I nought sing [I cannot sing anything]'); in sentences of the first type the object may precede the verb, and in those of the second type the verb may precede the subject. In dependent clauses the verb usually comes last, as always in German ("God geseah þā þæt hit gōd wæs"—'God saw then that it good was'; "Sē micla here, þe wē gefyrn ymbe spræcon . . ."—'The great army, which we before about spoke . . .'). Interrogative sentences follow in Old English the same verb-subject-complement pattern as in Modern English ("Hæfst þū ænigne gefēran?" 'Hast thou any companions?').

Old English will inevitably seem to the modern reader a crabbed and difficult language full of needless complexities. Actually the inflection of the noun was somewhat less complex in Old English than it was in Germanic, Latin, and Greek and, naturally, considerably less so than in Indo-European, with its eight cases (nominative, accusative, genitive, dative, ablative, instrumental, locative, and vocative). No Old English noun had more than six forms; but even this number will seem exorbitant to the speaker of Modern English, who uses only two forms for all but a few nouns: a general form without ending and a form ending in -s.[20]

NOUNS

Almost half of the nouns frequently encountered in Old English are masculine,[21] and most of there are a-stems—the a being the sound with which the stem ended in Germanic. These correspond to the o-stems of Indo-European, as exemplified by nouns of the second declension (the numbering of declensions is traditional and purely arbitrary) in Latin and Greek: Greek *philos* 'friend,' Latin *servos* (later *servus*) 'slave.' The terminology is of significance only in a historical sense as far as Old English is concerned. For example Germanic *wulfaz* (nominative singular) and *wulfan* (accusative singular) appear in Old English simply as *wulf* 'wolf,' with both suffix and ending completely lost.

Such nouns (in which, because of change and loss of sounds in final syllables, the older distinctive nominative and accusative forms, as well as those for the dative and instrumental, had fallen together) show six different forms, for example *hund* 'dog':

SINGULAR		PLURAL	
Nom., acc.	hund	Nom., acc.	hundas
Gen.	hundes	Gen.	hunda
Dat., ins.[22]	hunde	Dat.	hundum

[20] The fact that the forms ending in -s are written differently is quite irrelevant; the apostrophe for the genitive is a fairly recent convention. As far as speech is concerned, *boys, boy's,* and *boys'* are the same.

[21] This and some subsequent statistical statements have been derived from Quirk and Wrenn, *An Old English Grammar,* p. 20.

[22] Hereafter the term *instrumental* will ordinarily be used only for distinctive forms, occurring in the masculine and neuter singular of the "strong" adjective declension and of the demonstrative pronouns, and in

More than a third of all commonly used nouns were inflected according to this pattern, which was in time to be extended to practically all nouns. The Modern English possessive singular and general plural form in -s comes directly from the Old English genitive singular and nominative-accusative plural forms—two different forms until very late Old English times, when they fell together because of the reduction of the vowel of unstressed -as, which came also to be written -es in Middle English times. New words invariably conform to what survives of the a-stem declension—for example *sputnik's, sputniks, sputniks'*— so that we may truly say that it is the only living declension.

Other masculine nouns—the so called *n*-stems—have only four forms, thus *oxa* 'ox':

SINGULAR		PLURAL	
Nom.	oxa	Nom., acc.	oxan
Acc., gen., dat.	oxan	Gen.	oxena
		Dat.	oxum

The Modern English plural *oxen* (from *oxan*) is the only "pure" survival of this declension, which is called the "weak" declension.[23]

A few other masculine nouns must be mentioned here because of the frequency of their occurrence—*fōt* 'foot,' *tōð* 'tooth,' *man(n)* 'man,' and the compound *wīfmann*, whose case endings were affixed to the final consonants of their roots. There are five different forms for each of these, thus:

SINGULAR	
Nom., acc.	fōt, tōð, man(n)
Gen.	fōtes, tōðes, mannes
Dat.	fēt, tēð, men(n)

PLURAL	
Nom., acc.	fēt, tēð, men(n)
Gen.	fōta, tōða, manna
Dat.	fōtum, tōðum, mannum

the neuter interrogative pronoun. Elsewhere the instrumental function (usually expressing 'by means of') was expressed by the dative form, as in Latin it was expressed by the ablative.

[23] Nouns whose stems had ended in vowels (like the a-stems) are traditionally referred to as belonging to "strong" declensions.

It will be noted that the dative singular and the nominative-accusative plural forms are identical. This is so because, although in prehistoric Old English the dative singular and the nominative plural forms had the same root vowel as the other forms, each had an *i* in the ending, thus: **fōti, *tōði, *manni*.

Anticipation of the *i*-sound caused mutation of the root vowel—a kind of assimilation, with the root vowel moving upward in its articulation in the direction of the *i*-sound, but stopping somewhat short of it. English *man–men*,[24] *foot–feet* show the same development as German *Mann–Männer, Fuss–Füsse*, though German has chosen to indicate the mutated vowel in writing by placing a dieresis over the same symbol used for the unmutated vowel, whereas English uses an altogether different letter. The process, which Grimm called *Umlaut*, occurred in different periods and in varying degrees in the various members of the Germanic group, in English beginning probably in the sixth century. The fourth-century Gothic recorded by Bishop Wulfila shows no evidence of it.

Somewhat fewer than a third of all commonly used nouns are feminine, most of them belonging to the so-called ō-declension (corresponding to the ā-stems, or first declension, of Latin). In the nominative singular, these had -u (sometimes -o) after a short syllable, as in *lufu* 'love' and no ending at all after a long syllable,[25] as in *lār* 'learning' and *wund* 'wound.' They were declined as follows:

SINGULAR		PLURAL	
Nom.	lufu	Nom., acc., gen.	lufa
Acc., gen., dat.	lufe	Dat.	lufum

There are a few feminine *n*-stems, most of them with -*e* in the nominative singular (*belle* 'bell,' *eorðe* 'earth') but otherwise precisely the same as the masculine *n*-stems; and there are also a few feminine nouns with mutation in the dative singular and the nominative-

[24] In *woman–women* the earlier vowel differentiation of the final syllables has been obscured by weakened stress. The modern differentiation between singular and plural depends entirely upon the pronunciation of the first syllable. Mutation has nothing to do with this modern differentiation.

[25] A long syllable is one whose vowel is long or is followed by a sequence of different consonants or a long single consonant (indicated in Old English writing by doubling letters).

accusative plural (sometimes in the genitive singular as well), for example *brōc* 'pants,' *cū* 'cow,' *mūs* 'mouse,' *lūs* 'louse,' and *gōs* 'goose.' The nominative-accusative plural forms of these are respectively *brēc* (whence *breech*, with *breeches* a double plural), *cȳ* (whence *kine*, in which the *n*-stem nominative-accusative plural ending has been added to make yet another double plural), *mȳs*, *lȳs*, and *gēs*.

About a quarter of the commonly used Old English nouns are neuter. Practically all of these are *a*-stems, differing from the masculine *a*-stems only in the nominative-accusative plural: this ends in *-u* after a short syllable, as in *gatu* 'gate(s),' and has no ending (except for an occasional analogical *-u*) after a long one. Under the latter circumstances the most frequently used singular and plural forms, the nominative and the accusative, are identical, for example *word* and *bān*. *Dēor* 'animal(s)' is a neuter *a*-stem which has retained its unchanged plural to this day as *deer*. There are two neuter *n*-stems, declined exactly like the masculine and feminine ones: *ēage* 'eye' and *ēare* 'ear.' A very few neuters had nominative-accusative plurals in *-ru*: these include *ǣg* 'egg,' *lamb* 'lamb,' *cealf* 'calf,' and *cild* 'child.' *Cild* frequently has an unchanged nominative-accusative form, but the form with *-r-* has acquired an additional plural ending in *-n* by analogy with the *n*-stems. *Children* is thus a double plural, but the "normal" development *childer* survives in the Northern dialects of English.

Some very frequently used words ending in *-r* and denoting family relationships—*fæder* 'father,' *brōðor* 'brother,' *mōdor* 'mother,' *dohtor* 'daughter,' and *sweostor* 'sister'—exhibit a number of peculiarities; for instance, all occur with uninflected genitive singulars, all have endingless datives, and all save *fæder* occur with unchanged nominative-accusative plurals. The singe form *sweostor* was used throughout the singular. Along with the unchanged nominative-accusative plurals, forms in *-ru* (alternating with *-ra* in the three feminine nouns), with loss of the unstressed *o* preceding the *r*, also occur, thus: *brōðru, mōdru, dohtru, sweostru*. *Mōdor, dohtor,* and *brōðor* had mutated vowels in their dative singular forms, thus: *mēder, dehter, brēðer*.[26] By analogy with the majority of masculine nouns, *fæder* always has a nominative-accusative singular in *-as* and very often a genitive singular in *-es* as well.

Another noun indicating family relationship, *sunu* 'son,' belonged

[26] The mutated form *brēðer* was later sometimes extended to the nominative-accusative plural and in early Middle English acquired an alternative ending *-en* (the later development of the *-an* of the *n*-stems); hence *brethren*.

to a minor declension containing not many but rather frequently used words, among them *lagu* 'sea,' *wudu* 'wood,' *medu* 'liquor,' and, with the -*u* lacking after long syllables and after disyllables, *feld* 'field,' *ford* 'ford,' *winter* 'winter,' *sumor* 'summer,' and a few others. These nouns, all masculine, might have only three different forms, thus for *sunu*:

SINGULAR		PLURAL	
Nom., acc.	sunu	Nom., acc., gen.	suna
Gen., dat.	suna	Dat.	sunum

The feminine *duru* 'door,' *nosu* 'nose,' *cinn* 'chin,' and *hand* 'hand' were originally treated in exactly the same way. But long-syllabled masculine nouns of this declension (for example *feld*) were for the most part declined like masculine *a*-stems, and long-syllabled feminine ones (for example *hand*) like feminine *ō*-stems.

It will be noted that in all declensions the genitive plural form ends in -*a* and the dative plural in -*m* (usually -*um*). The genitive plural -*a* survived as [ə] (written -*e*) in Middle English in the "genitive of measure" construction and continues to survive in Modern English (with loss of [ə]), in such phrases as *sixty-mile drive* and *six foot tall* (rather than *miles* and *feet*), though *feet* may more often occur in the latter construction; only *foot*, however, is idiomatic in *three-foot board* and *six-foot man*.[27] The dative plural survives in the antiquated form *whilom*, from Old English *hwīlum* 'at times,' and in the analogical *seldom* (earlier *seldan*). The dative singular in -*e* characteristic of the majority of Old English nouns survives in the word *alive*, from Old English *on līfe*; the Old English voiced *f* between vowels, later spelled *v*, is preserved in the Modern English form, though the final vowel is no longer pronounced. These are about the only traces left of the Old English declensional forms of the noun other than the genitive singular and the general plural forms in -*s* (along with a few mutated plurals); there are also a very few relics of Old English feminine genitives without -*s*, for instance *Lady Chapel*.[28]

---

[27] It will be remembered that the Old English form *fēt*, becoming Modern English *feet*, occurred in the plural only as the nominative and accusative form; the genitive plural, *fōta*, did not have the mutated vowel.

[28] For other instances of uninflected feminine genitives which survived into early Modern English, see p. 184. The *ō*-declension genitive, it will be remembered, had -*e*. This ending was completely lost in pronunciation by the end of the fourteenth century, along with all other final *e*'s of whatever origin.

One other observation before passing on to other matters: Old English had no device for indicating plurality alone—that is, unconnected with the concept of case. It was not until Middle English times that the plural nominative-accusative -es (from OE -as) drove out the other case forms of the plural (save for the comparatively rare genitive of measure construction discussed in the preceding paragraph). Even in the root consonant stems, the mutated forms were, as we have seen, not exclusively *plural* forms. They occurred also in the dative singular, as in *Beowulf*, lines 2283–85: "Ðā wæs . . . bēne getīðad fēasceaftum men" 'Then was [a] favor granted [the] wretched man.' The -en ending (from OE -an), surviving in *oxen*, likewise did not indicate plurality alone in earlier periods; in Old English, as a backward glance at the declension of *oxa* will show, the common non-nominative singular form had -an and was thus identical with the nominative-accusative plural form, *oxan*.

DEMONSTRATIVE PRONOUNS

Although it is usual to treat adjectives immediately after nouns, we shall here discuss the Old English demonstrative pronouns, on whose occurrence or nonoccurrence depends the use of one or the other Old English adjective declension (that is, the strong or the characteristic Germanic weak declension). There were two such demonstratives. The more frequently used was that which came to correspond in function to our definite article. The singular forms of this demonstrative were as follows:

MASCULINE		NEUTER		FEMININE	
Nom.	sē[29]	Nom., acc.	þæt	Nom.	sēo
Acc.	þone	(otherwise the		Acc.	þā
Gen.	þæs	same as the		Gen., dat.	þǣre
Dat.	þǣm	masculine)			
Ins.	þȳ, þon, þē				

It will be noted that, not including variants of the instrumental, we have here nine different forms, with distinct dative and instrumental forms in the masculine and neuter, though not in the feminine. In the plural there was no distinction of gender:

---

[29] This form had a short *e* when it was used without stress as a definite article.

Nom., acc.   þā
Gen.   þāra
Dat.   þǣm

Because of the analogy of all the other forms, sē̆ and sēo were in late
Old English superseded by the variants þē̆ and þēo. The other, less
frequently used demonstrative had the nominative singular forms þes
(masculine), þis (neuter, whence ModE this), and þēos (feminine). Like
sē, þæt, sēo, it had a distinctive singular instrumental form (þȳs) in the
masculine and neuter and common gender in the plural. Its nominative-accusative plural þās has developed into those. These is of Middle
English origin.

ADJECTIVES

The adjective in Old English agreed with the noun it modified in
gender, case, and number as in Latin; but Germanic, as we have seen,
had developed a distinctive adjective declension—the so-called weak
declension, used customarily after the two demonstrative pronouns
and frequently after possessive pronouns. In this declension -an predominates as an ending:

MASCULINE SINGULAR

Nom.	se dola cyning 'the foolish king'
Acc.	þone dolan cyning
Gen.	þæs dolan cyninges
Dat.	þǣm dolan cyninge
Ins.	þȳ dolan cyninge

MASCULINE PLURAL

Nom., acc.	þā dolan cyningas
Gen.	þāra dolra (or dolena) cyninga
Dat.	þǣm dolum cyningum

Modifying neuter nouns, the singular weak adjective forms were the
same as the masculine in the genitive, dative, and instrumental, but
both the nominative and accusative singular ended in -e (þæt dole
bearn 'the foolish child'). The feminine nominative adjective form
likewise ended in -e, but the other singular forms were the same as the
masculine, with -an (sēo dole ides 'the foolish woman,' but þā, þǣre

dolan idese). As with the pronouns, there was common gender in the plural, with nominative-accusative *-an*, genitive *-ra*, and dative-instrumental *-um*.

The so-called strong declension was used when the adjective was not preceded by a demonstrative or a possessive pronoun, or when it was predicative. Many of the endings are those characteristic of pronouns rather than of nouns, for instance the *-ne* of the masculine accusative singular (as in *hine, þone*), the *-re* of the feminine genitive-dative singular (as in *hire, þǣre*), the *-m* of the masculine and neuter dative singular (as in *him, þǣm*), and the *-ra* of the common-gender genitive plural (as in *hira, þāra*). Paradigms for the singular number, as above modifying appropriate nouns, follow:

MASCULINE

Nom.	dol cyning 'foolish king'
Acc.	dolne cyning
Gen.	doles cyninges
Dat.	dolum cyninge
Ins.	dole cyninge

NEUTER

Nom.	dol bearn 'foolish child'
Acc.	dol bearn
Gen.	doles bearnes
Dat.	dolum bearne
Ins.	dole bearne

FEMININE

Nom.	dolu[30] ides 'foolish woman'
Acc.	dole idese
Gen., dat.	dolre idese

The common-gender genitive and dative plural endings, respectively *-ra* and *-um*, are the same as those of the weak declension. The nominative-accusative plural strong forms are exemplified in *dole*

[30] After a long syllable no ending occurs in monosyllabic adjectives, for example *wīs ides* 'wise woman,' *geong ides* 'young woman.' The same is true of the neuter nominative-accusative plural. For what constitutes a long syllable, see n. 25.

cyningas (masculine), *dolu bearn* (neuter), and *dola idesa* (feminine).

The comparative of adjectives was regularly formed by suffixing *-ra,* as in *heardra* 'harder,' and the superlative by suffixing *-ost,* as in *heardost* 'hardest.' A few adjectives which had mutation by earlier *i* in alternative suffixes *-ira, -ist* in the comparative and superlative usually had *-est* in the superlative, for example *eald,* Anglian *ald* 'old'; *yldra,* Anglian *eldra* 'elder'; *yldest,* Anglian *eldest.* A very few others had comparative and superlative forms from a different root from that of the positive, among them *gōd* 'good,' *betra* 'better,' *betst* 'best' and *micel* 'great,' *māra* 'more,' *mǣst* 'most.'

Certain superlatives were originally formed with an alternative suffix *-(u)ma,* for example *forma* (formed from *fore* 'before'). When the ending with *m* ceased to be felt as having superlative force, these words and some others took by analogy the additional ending *-est.* Thus, double superlatives (though not recognized as such) like *formest, midmest, ūtemest,* and *innemest* came into being. The ending appeared to be *-mest* (rather than *-est*), which was even in late Old English times misunderstood as *mǣst,* Anglian *māst* 'most'; hence our Modern English forms *foremost,*[31] *midmost,* and *inmost,* in which the final syllable is and has long been equated with *most,* though it has no historical connection with it. Beginning thus as a blunder, this *-most* has subsequently been affixed to other words, for example *uppermost, furthermost,* and *topmost.*

ADVERBS

Old English adverbs give no particular trouble. Those formed from adjectives—the great majority—added the suffix *-e,* for example *wrāð* 'angry,' *wrāðe* 'angrily.' This *-e* was lost along with all other final *e*'s by the end of the fourteenth century, with the result that many Modern English adjectives and adverbs are identical in form, for instance *loud, deep,* and *slow,* though Modern English idiom sometimes requires adverbial forms with *-ly* ("He plunged deep into the ocean" but "He thought deeply about religious matters"; "Drive slow" but "He proceeded slowly"). Adverbs regularly formed the comparative with *-or* and the superlative with *-ost* or *-est* (*wrāðor* 'more angrily,' *wrāðost*

---

[31] Caxton writes (1483) the still common (and tautological) phrase *first and foremost* as *first and formest.*

'most angrily'). In addition, case forms of nouns and adjectives might be used adverbially, notably the genitive[32] and the dative.[33]

PERSONAL PRONOUNS

Except for the loss of the dual number and the old second person singular forms, the personal pronouns are almost as complex today as they were in Old English times. *I, me,* and *mine* correspond to the Old English nominative *ic,*[34] accusative-dative *mē,* and genitive *mīn.*

The first person dual forms (meaning 'I, me, or my plus some other person') were *wit* (nominative), *unc* (accusative-dative), and *uncer* (genitive). The second person dual forms (meaning 'singular you or your plus some other person') were *git* (nominative) *inc* (accusative-dative), and *incer* (genitive). Their history has been the same as that of the first person dual forms; they have disappeared completely—and a good thing too—though unquestionably their gradual disuse must have been regarded by many as evidence that the English language was going straight to the dogs. *Wit* and *git* took the ordinary plural verb forms.

Old English *wē* (nominative), *ūs* (accusative-dative), and *ūre* (genitive) correspond to the Modern English first person plural forms *we, us* (allowing for shortening due to lack of stress), and *our.* The Old English second person singular forms *þū* (nominative), *þē* (accusative-dative), and *þīn* correspond to early Modern English *thou, thee,* and *thine,* now archaic.

[32] As in *Beowulf,* lines 2267–69: "Swā giōmormōd . . . unblīðe hwearf dæges ond nihtes" ('So [the one] sad of mind . . . unblithe wandered [by] day and [by] night'). *Dæges* and *nihtes* are genitive singulars. The construction survives in "He worked nights" (labeled "dial[ect] and U.S." by the *OED*), sometimes rendered analytically as "He worked of a night." Nevertheless the usage is, as the *OED* says, "in later use prob[ably] apprehended as a plural," though historically, as we have seen, it is not so. The *-s* of *homewards* (OE *hāmweardes*), *towards* (*tōweardes*), *besides, betimes, needs* (as in *must needs be,* sometimes rendered analytically as *must of necessity be*) is from the genitive singular ending *-es.* The sibilant is merely written differently in *once, twice, thrice, hence,* and *since. Amongst, amidst, against,* and *whilst* have excrescent *t* after the genitive *s,* the same phenomenon occurring in frequent nonstandard pronunciations of *once* and *across.*

[33] As in (sg.) *elne* 'valiantly,' *wihte* 'at all'; (pl.) *hwīlum* 'at times, sometimes,' *þrymmum* 'mightily.'

[34] The final consonant was lost in Middle English because of lack of stress (see p. 145) . The resultant *i* was restressed as *ī,* which developed into the Modern English sound [aɪ] along with all other long *i*'s.

In the second person plural the forms were *gē* (nominative), *ēow* (accusative-dative), and *ēower* (genitive) corresponding to Modern English *ye*, *you*, and *your*, with *you* usurping by about 1600 all the nominative functions of *ye*, though this "misuse" began at least two and a half centuries earlier. When used as possessives, the genitives of the first and second persons were declined like the strong adjectives.

Gender appears only in the third person singular forms, exactly as in Modern English. Masculine *hē* (nominative), *him* (dative), and *his* (genitive) correspond to the modern forms which are identical with them in writing (and *him* in sound as well). A fourth form, the accusative *hine*, has survived only in Southwestern dialects of British English as [ən], as in "Didst thee zee un?" that is, "Did you see him?" (*OED*, s.v. *hin, hine*).

For the feminine pronoun, Old English had the following forms: nominative *hēo*, of which *she* is a development; genitive-dative *hi(e)re*; and accusative *hī(e)*, which has not survived.

The neuter pronoun likewise had three forms: nominative-accusative *hit*, surviving when stressed, notably at the beginning of a sentence, in some types of nonstandard Modern English;[35] and genitive *his* and dative *him*, which were identical with the masculine forms. *Its* is obviously not a development of the Old English form, but a new analogical form occurring first in Modern English.

The usual common-gender third person plural forms were nominative-accusative *hī(e)*, genitive *hira* (also often *heora*), and dative *him* (also *heom*). Of these only the dative form has survived; it is the regular spoken unstressed objective form in Modern English, with loss of *h-* as in the other *h-* pronouns, for example "I told 'em what to do." The Modern English stressed form, *them*, like *they* and *their*, is of Scandinavian origin.

INTERROGATIVE PRONOUNS

The interrogative pronoun *hwā* 'who' was declined only in the singular and had only masculine and neuter forms. The nominative-

[35] The loss of [h-] is due to lack of stress and is paralleled in the other *h-* pronouns when these are unstressed, as, for example "Give her his book," which in the natural speech of all cultural levels would show no trace of an [h]; compare also "rob his bank" and "Robbie's bank," "raise her up," and "razor up," "rub her gloves," and "rubber gloves," "tore his pants," and "Tory's pants." In the neuter, however, the older stressed form has in Standard English been completely lost, even in writing, whereas in the other *h-* pronouns we have two spoken forms but only one written form.

accusative neuter *hwæt* is the source of our *what*. The masculine accusative *hwone* did not survive beyond the Middle English period, its functions being taken over by the masculine and neuter dative *hwām* (or *hwǣm*), surviving in *whom*. *Whose* is from the masculine and neuter *hwæs*. The distinctive neuter instrumental *hwȳ* is obviously the source of our *why*. *Hwā, hwām*, and *hwæs* were exclusively interrogative in Old English. The particle *þe* was the usual relative in Old English. Since this had only a single form, it is a great pity that we ever lost it; it involved no choice such as that which we must make—in writing, at least—between *who* and *whom*, now that these have come to be used as relatives.

WEAK VERBS

To turn now to the verb, we may note at the outset that the Old English infinitive ended in *-an* or *-ian*, with only a handful of exceptions in which because of contraction the *a* of *-an* was lost, for example *sēon* 'to see' and *dōn* 'to do.' No trace of the Old English ending remains in Modern English.

The great majority of Old English verbs formed their preterits and past participles in the characteristically Germanic way,[36] by the addition of a suffix containing *d* or, immediately after voiceless consonants, *t*.[37]

Most of these dental-suffix, or "weak," verbs were derived from nouns, adjectives, or preterits of strong verbs by the addition of an infinitive suffix *-jan*, the *j* effecting mutation of the root vowel. Sometimes they were causative: thus *flȳman*, earlier *flieman* 'to cause to flee' from the noun *flēam* 'flight,' *fyllan* 'to cause to be full' (to fill) from the adjective *full*, and *settan* 'to cause to sit' (to set) from *sæt*, preterit singular of *sittan*—in pre-mutation form respectively **flēamjan*, **fulljan*, **sættjan*. A few more examples of Modern English survivals

[36] Though, as Quirk and Wrenn point out (p. 40), many of these occur rather infrequently, whereas the strong verbs occur very frequently.

[37] The same phenomenon occurs in Modern English when the infinitive of this type of verb ends in a voiceless consonant other than *t* (which requires an extra syllable to form its preterit and past participle, for example *heat* [hit], *heated* [hitɪd]). The first of each of the following pairs ends in [-t], the second in [-d]: *tacked–tagged, slapped–slabbed, luffed–loved, lunched–lunged, raced–razed, rushed–rouged, unearthed–bathed*. Old English scribes, who by and large wrote more phonetically than we do, very sensibly used *t* to indicate the voiceless dental when they heard it.

will suffice to illustrate the derivational relationship in both form and meaning: *food–feed, doom–deem, moot* (obsolete noun 'meeting')– *meet, drink–drench* (from **drankjan*), *fall–fell* 'to cause to fall,' *couth* (obsolete past participle 'known')–*kith* (obsolete 'to make known'), *lust* (in OE 'pleasure')–*list* 'to desire,' *lie–lay, sit–set.*

A certain number of weak verbs had in the preterit both vowel differentiation and dental suffix. The difference in vowel was not due to anything remotely like the gradation of the "strong" verbs, but to lack of mutation in the preterit. Modern English survivals are *tell–told* (*tellan* 'to count'–*talde*), *sell–sold* (*sellan* 'to give'–*salde*),[38] *seek–sought* (*sēcan–sōhte*), *buy–bought* (*bycgan–bohte*), *think–thought* (*þencan–þōhte*),[39] and *work–wrought* (*wyrcan–worhte*). The real test in all these verbs is not the vowel differentiation, but the presence of the dental suffix in the preterit.

Quite irregular but very frequently used verbs with dental-suffix preterits are *willan* 'to wish, will'–*wolde, dōn* 'to do'–*dyde, habban* 'to have'–*hæfde, libban* 'to live'–*lifde, secgan* 'to say'–*sǣde, hycgan* 'to think'–*hog(o)de,* and *gān* 'to go'–*ēode,* the preterit form of the last being from an entirely different verb.

STRONG VERBS

Most other Old English verbs—all others, in fact, except for a few very frequently used ones to be discussed later—formed their preterits by a vowel change called gradation (Grimm's *Ablaut*), due to Indo-European variations in pitch and stress. Gradation is by no means confined to these strong verbs,[40] but it is best illustrated by them. Grada-

---

[38] The Old English preterit forms from which *told* and *sold* come are Anglian, with late lengthening of the vowel before *-ld* (see p. 150). The West Saxon forms *tealde, sealde* will be more familiar to students of Old English literature.

[39] *þencan* 'think' and *þyncan* 'seem' (pret. *þūhte*) were early confused and ultimately fell together. Archaic *methinks* '(it) seems to me' is thus not to be interpreted as 'I think,' but as '[it] seems to me.'

[40] Simeon Potter, *Modern Linguistics* (London, 1957), pp. 80–81, interestingly demonstrates the gradational relationship of *sit, sat, seat, soot* 'what sits in the chimney,' and *nest. Nest* goes back ultimately to Indo-European **nisdos* 'sitting-down place,' in which the prefix *ni-* (related to *nether*) means 'down' and the *-sd-* corresponds to Germanic *-st-*, the loss of the vowel being due to lack of stress in Indo-European. Compare also *strike, streak, stroke, strick(en).*

tion should never be confused with mutation (umlaut), which, as we have seen (p. 115), is the approximation of a vowel in a stressed syllable to another vowel (or semivowel) in a following syllable. Although there are roughly similar phenomena in other languages, the type of mutation we have been concerned with is confined to Germanic languages. Gradation, which is much more ancient, is an Indo-European phenomenon common to all the languages derived from Indo-European.[41] The vowel differences reflected in Modern English *ride–rode–ridden, choose–chose, bind–bound, come–came, eat–ate, shake–shook* are thus an Indo-European inheritance.

Like Germanic, Old English had seven classes of strong verbs. The first of these—the numerical order is merely traditional—had the root vowels *ī, ā, i, i* in the present, the preterit singular first and third persons, the preterit plural, and the past participle respectively:[42]

rīdan 'to ride'	rād	ridon	(ge)riden[43]

Had the number distinction in the preterit survived into present-day English, we should be saying *I rode* but *we rid*—the form *rid* being what would survive of *ridon* after loss of final inflectional *-n* and of the unstressed *o*, reduced to [ə] by late Old English times. In the course of the development of this particular verb the preterit singular form of the first and third persons[44] has been generalized for both numbers, though not without some wavering until fairly recently, as we shall see in the detailed treatment of Modern English verbs in Chapter VII. The development of *drīfan* 'to drive,' *wrītan* 'to write,' *smītan* 'to smite,' and *rīsan* 'to rise' has been identical with that of *rīdan*.

Old English strong verbs of Class II had the gradation *ēo (ū), ēa, u, o*, for example:

crēopan 'to creep'	crēap	crupon	cropen
sprūtan 'to sprout'	sprēat	spruton	sproten

Grammatical change (Verner's Law) is responsible for the consonantal

[41] There are parallelisms in the Semitic and the Finno-Ugric languages.

[42] For all strong verbs it is necessary to give four principal parts, that is, forms from which the entire conjugation can be constructed. The singular-plural distinction in the preterit has survived in Modern English only in *was–were*.

[43] Hereafter past participles will be cited without the prefix *ge-*, concerning which see p. 133.

[44] For the form of the second person, see p. 131.

shifts in the last two principal parts of *lēosan* 'to lose' (*luron, loren*), *cēosan* 'to choose' (*curon, coren*), *frēosan* 'to freeze' (*fruron, froren*), and *sēoðan* 'to seethe' (*sudon, soden*).

Old English strong verbs of Class III comprise (1) those with root vowel followed by *m* or *n* plus another consonant (or long *m* or *n*, written *-mm-* and *-nn-*), with the gradation *i, a, u;* (2) those with root vowel followed by *l* plus a consonant other than *c*, or by long *l* (written *-ll-*), with the gradation *e, ea, u, o;* and (3) those with *lc* or with *r* or *h* plus another consonant, which differed from those immediately preceding only in having *eo* in the infinitive. An example of each follows:

1. findan 'to find'	fand	fundon	funden
2. helpan 'to help'	healp	hulpon	holpen
3. weorpan 'to throw'	wearp	wurpon	worpen

In two Class III verbs, *byrnan* (*birnan*) 'to burn' and *yrnan* (*irnan*) 'to run,' the older root vowel and *r* have undergone metathesis; consequently the preterit forms are respectively *barn, burnon, burnen* and *arn, urnon, urnen.* Two other verbs of this class had *u* in their infinitives (*murnan* 'to mourn' and *spurnan* 'to spurn'), but otherwise followed the pattern of *weorpan.* A few verbs of Class III had consonants after the root vowel other than those specified. Those which have survived are *bregdan* 'to pull' (whence *braid*), *þerscan* 'to thresh' and *berstan* 'to burst,' the last two of which are metathetic forms of **þrescan* and **brestan;* they have *æ* in their preterit singular forms. In late Old English times originally short vowels followed by the consonant sequences *-nd, -mb,* and *-ld* were lengthened if no third consonant followed. This lengthening explains the development of glides in *find, found* (ME *finden, fōunden*)[45] and the like, in contrast to the short vowels in *sing, sang, sink, sunk, spin, spun,* and other verbs lacking these sequences.

Class IV comprised a small number of verbs that had single *l, m,* or *r* after the root vowel. Those with *l* and *r* had the gradation *e, æ, ǣ, o,* for example:

teran 'to tear'	tær	tǣron	toren

Niman 'to seize' and *cuman* 'to come' are the only verbs with single *m*

[45] As we have seen (p. 43), *ū* came to be written *ou* in Middle English because of French influence.

following the root vowel, and *cuman*, the only one of these to survive, was irregular even in Old English times, with the preterit forms *cōm*, *cōmon*, and the past participle *cumen*. *Brecan* 'to break,' as we should expect from the fact that its root vowel is not followed by any of the consonants specified, did not originally belong to Class IV, but formed its past participle as *brocen* (instead of **brecen*, the expected form) by analogy with verbs of Class IV.

Class V, also rather small, comprises verbs whose root vowel is followed by a single consonant other than *m, n, l,* or *r,* with the characteristic gradation e, æ, ǣ, for example:

metan 'to mete'   mæt   mǣton   meten

After *g,* the *e* of the infinitive became *ie,* which in turn became late West Saxon *y* or *i,* and *ǣ* in the same situation became *ĕa,* for example:

gyfan (gifan) 'to give'   geaf   gēafon   gifen

The preterit forms of *wesan* 'to be' (indicative *wæs, wǣron;* subjunctive *wǣre, wǣren*) were used, and still are, as the preterit forms of an entirely different verb, *bēon* 'to be.' The *s–r* alternation is due to grammatical change and is preserved in *was–were.*

Class VI verbs typically have *a* in the infinitive and the past participle, and *ō* in the two preterit forms, for example:

faran 'to go, fare'   fōr   fōron   faren

Standan 'to stand' has an *n*-infix in its infinitive and its past participle (*standen*), but not in its preterit forms, *stōd* and *stōdon;* hence *stand* and *stood.*

The verbs of Class VII lack the comparative regularity of the other six classes. Called "reduplicating" for reasons inappropriate to go into here, they "present one of the most difficult problems of Germanic grammar," according to an authority whose conclusion regarding them can be taken as representative.[46] It is sufficient here to point out that in the verbs of this class the infinitive forms show considerable variety, though the vowel (or diphthong) of the infinitive is always repeated in the past participle. The preterit vowels, identical in singular and plural, are always either *ē* or *ēo,* for example:

[46] E. Prokosch, *A Comparative Germanic Grammar* (Philadelphia, 1939), p. 176.

feallan 'to fall'	fēoll	fēollon	feallen
cnāwan 'to know'	cnēow	cnēowon	cnāwen
hatan 'to be called'	hēt	hēton	haten
slǣpan 'to sleep'	slēp	slēpon	slǣpen
flōwan 'to flow'	flēow	flēowon	flōwen

PRETERIT-PRESENT VERBS

Āgan 'to possess,' cunnan 'to know how,' magan 'to be able,' sculan 'to be obliged,' *mōtan (the infinitive happens not to be recorded) 'to be allowed,' and a few other verbs had in their present indicative forms the vowels of old strong preterits, but formed their preterits by means of a dental suffix, for example sceal 'shall,' sceolde 'should,' which are respectively the singular present indicative (first and third persons) and preterit indicative of sculan. Verbs of this type, which were and are of very frequent occurrence, are customarily called preterit-present verbs. They survive in modern speech in such forms as the aforementioned shall–should, (from cunnan) can–could–(un)couth,[47] (from āgan) owe–ought (OE āhte), (from magan) may–might (OE mæg, mihte), and (from *mōtan) archaic mote–must (OE mōt, mōste).

ANOMALOUS VERBS

It is not really surprising that very commonly used verbs should have developed irregularities. Bēon 'to be' was in Old English, as its modern descendant still is, to some extent a badly mixed-up verb, with alternative present indicative forms from several different roots, as follows (with appropriate pronouns):

ic eom, bēo 'I am'
þū eart, bist 'thou art'
hē, hēo, hit is, bið 'he, she, it is'

wē sind(on),[48] sint, bēoð 'we are'
gē sind(on), sint, bēoð 'you are'
hī sind(on), sint, bēoð 'they are'

[47] For the l of could, see p. 164. Couth 'known' is current only in the negative form uncouth. It is the past participial form cūð. It is obvious from its pronunciation that it got into modern Standard English as a Northern dialect word, inasmuch as Old and Middle English ū remained in the North. The mouse and the louse which Robert Burns celebrated in song were to him a "moose" and a "loose."

[48] The forms with s- are from the same root as eom and is. In Indo-European the root was *es-. Eom 'am' is cognate with Sanskrit as-mi,

The Modern English plural form *are* is an Anglian form. The present subjunctive likewise had alternative forms. The preterit indicative and subjunctive forms were from yet another verb, whose infinitive in Old English was *wesan*, from Class V (see p. 128). Also highly irregular were *dōn* 'to do,' *gān* 'to go,' and *willan* 'to will, want.'

It is notable that *to be* alone has preserved distinctive singular and plural preterit forms (*was, were*) in modern Standard English, though it is highly doubtful that the distinction would have been so preserved if the leveling which is characteristic of all other preterits had been well established in this verb before the beginning of public education. As far as *to be* is concerned, the folk have carried through the tendency which has reduced the preterit forms of all other verbs to a single form, and they get along very nicely with *you was, we was,* and *they was,* which are certainly no more inherently "bad" than *you sang, we sang,* and *they sang*—for *sung* in the plural would be the historically "correct" development of Old English *gē, wē, hī sungon.*

INDICATIVE FORMS OF VERBS

The Old English present indicative singular of verbs typically had the personal endings *-e, -st, -ð,* as in *cēpan* 'to keep,' cited here with the appropriate pronouns:

> ic cēpe 'I keep'
> þū cēp(e)st 'thou keepest'
> hē, hēo, hit cēp(e)ð 'he, she, it keepeth'

The *-t* of the second person singular is not a part of the original ending; it comes from the frequent use of *þū* as an enclitic, that is following the verb and spoken without stress as if it were a part of it, for

---

Latin *s-um,* and Greek *em-mi* (later *eimi*); all are developments of Indo-European **es-mi.* Similarly *is,* Sanskrit *as-ti,* Latin *es-t,* and Greek *es-ti* are all from an Indo-European form identical with the Greek form *esti* just cited. Old English *s-ind, s-int,* Sanskrit *s-anti,* and Latin *s-unt* are likewise all from Indo-European **s-enti.* The relationship of the forms cited should be apparent even to the nakedest eye. In some (like *sint, sunt*) the vowel before the *s* is missing; in others the *s* itself has disappeared as the result of assimilation to the following *m*—notably in Greek *emmi* and in the Germanic forms (Gothic *im,* OE *eom,* ON *em*). The form with *-r-* (*eart*) is from another root and the forms with *b-* are from still another, cognate with Latin *fuī.*

example *beres þū* becoming *berespu* becoming *berestu*,[49] with later loss of the unstressed *-u*. The *-e-* of the second and third persons singular is usually missing in West Saxon, resulting in various changes of one sort or another when the root ended in *d, s, t, ð,* or *s* (and sometimes in *g*); for example *-dst* becomes *-tst*, *-dð* and *-tð* become *-t(t)*, *-ðst* becomes *-tst* or *-st*, and *sð* becomes *-st*.

All persons of the present indicative plural of practically all verbs ended in *-að*, exceptions being the verbs with infinitives in *-n*, which had *-ð* alone, and for obvious reasons the preterit-present verbs:

wē, gē, hī cēpað 'we, you (ye), they keep'

Strong verbs had mutation, if their root vowels were capable of it— in general, if they were other than front vowels—in the second and third persons of the present indicative because of their earlier endings *-ist* and *-ið*, for example with *faran* (Class VI) 'to fare, go':

ic fare 'I fare'
þū fær(e)st 'thou farest'
hē, hēo, hit fær(e)ð 'he, she, it fareth'

The first and third persons preterit indicative singular of all weak verbs ended in *e*, the second in *(e)st*, for example with *þancian* 'to thank,' a weak verb of a class which had *-o-* in the preterit:

ic þancode 'I thanked'
þū þancodest 'thou thankedest'
hē, hēo, hit þancode 'he, she, it thanked'

The first and third persons singular preterit indicative of the strong verb were endingless, for example with *singan* (Class III) 'to sing':

ic sang 'I sang'
hē, hēo, hit sang 'he, she, it sang'

But the second person singular strong preterit indicative had the same vowel as the preterit plural with the ending *e*, thus *þū sunge*. In addition, if grammatical change had been operative, the shifted consonant

---

[49] Cited by A. Campbell, *Old English Grammar* (Oxford, 1959), p. 193.

also occurred, for example in *cēosan* (Class II) 'to choose' and *snīðan* (Class I) 'to cut':

ic cēas	ic snāð
þū cure	þū snide
hē, hēo, hit cēas	hē, hēo, hit snāð

The preterit plural indicative of all verbs used the single ending *on* for all persons, for example:

> (weak) wē, gē, hī þancodon 'we, you (ye), they thanked'
> (strong) wē, gē, hī sungon 'we, you (ye), they sang'

SUBJUNCTIVE AND IMPERATIVE FORMS

The subjunctive, used much more extensively than in Modern English, did not indicate person, but only tense and number. The endings were (singular) *-e,* (plural) *-en* in both tenses,[50] the present singular subjunctive form of all verbs thus being identical with the first person forms of the indicative. The preterit subjunctive of strong verbs had in both singular and plural the root of the preterit indicative plural; hence the preterit singular subjunctive form was identical with the second person singular of the preterit indicative. Thus, in *Beowulf,* line 2818, ". . . ǣr hē bǣl cure . . . ," that is, 'ere he chose the pyre.'

The imperative singular of all verbs ended in *-e, -a,* or was endingless, all three types being illustrated in the following passage from *Beowulf,* lines 658–660:

> Hafa nū ond geheald hūsa sēlest,
> gemyne mǣrþo, mægen-ellen cȳð,
> waca wið wrāþum!

> *Have now and hold (of) houses the best,*
> *remember fame, mighty valor make known,*
> *watch against (the) hostile (one)!*

The imperative plural ended in *-(a)ð.*

---

[50] Except for the small group of contracted verbs, which had no *-e* in either their present singular subjunctive or their first person present indicative. In these verbs the present plural subjunctive was identical with the infinitive, for example *fōn* 'to seize,' *flēon* 'to flee,' and *slēan* 'to slay, strike.'

NONFINITE FORMS

The present participle of both weak and strong verbs ended in -ende (-nde in those verbs in which the -a- of the infinitive was missing). The past participle of strong verbs ended, as must have been observed, in -en, which has survived in many strong verbs to the present day. The prefix ge- was fairly general for past participles, but occurs sometimes as a prefix in all forms. It survives in the past participle throughout the Middle English period as y- (or i-), and is familiar to us in Milton's archaic use in "L'Allegro": "In heaven ycleped Euphrosyne . . ." (from OE geclypod 'called').

OLD ENGLISH ILLUSTRATED

The following passage in late West Saxon is the beginning of a sermon by Ælfric, the greatest prose writer of the Old English period, recounting the martyrdom of a group of Christian soldiers in Asia Minor. Abbreviations (for instance Þ, always used for þæt; 7, always used for and; and the line over vowels frequently used to indicate a following m) have been expanded. Macrons have been placed over long vowels. The capitalization and punctuation of the manuscript are retained—the latter consisting solely of slightly raised points serving to set off grammatical units and hence indicating pauses in oral delivery.

WĒ	WYLLAÐ	ĒOW[51]	GERECCAN	ÞǢRA	fēowertigra
We	*want*	*[to] you*	*to tell*	*of the*	*forty*

cempena	ðrōwunge	þæt	ēower	gelēafa	þē	trumre
soldiers	*[the] suffering,*	*that*	*your*	*belief*	*the*	*firmer*

sȳ·	þonne	gē	gehȳrað	hū	þegenlice	hī	þrōwodon
may be,	*when*	*ye*	*hear*	*how*	*thanelike*	*they*	*suffered*

for	crīste·	On	þæs	cāseres	dagum	þe	wæs	gehāten
for	*Christ.*	*In*	*that*	*Caesar's*	*days*	*who*	*was*	*called*

licinius	wearð	āstyred	mycel	ēhtnys	ofer	þā
Licinius	*was*	*stirred up*	*much*	*persecution*	*over*	*the*

[51] The indirect object of *gereccan* 'to tell'; the direct object is *ðrōwunge* 'suffering.'

crīstenan·	swā	þæt	ǣlc	crīsten	mann	sceolde	be
Christians,	so	that	each	Christian	man	should[52]	by

his	āgenum	fēore	þām	hǣlende	wiðsacan	and	tō
his	own	life	the	Saviour	deny	and	to

hǣðenscype	gebūgan·	and	þām	dēofolgyldum	drihtnes
heathenship	bow,	and	to the	idols	[the] Lord's

wurþmynt	gebēodan·	Þā	wæs	geset	sum	wælhrēowa
honor	submit.	Then	was	set	some[53]	bloodthirsty

dēma	agricolaus	gecīged·	on	ānre	byrig	sebastia	gehāten·
judge	Agricolaus	called	in	a	city	Sebastia	called,

on	þām	lande	armenia·	Se	foresǣde	dēma	wæs	swīðe
in	the	land	Armenia.	The	aforesaid	judge	was	very

ārlēas·	crīstenra	manna	ēhtere	and	arod	tō
merciless,	[of] Christian	men	[a] persecutor	and	ready	to

dēofles	willan·	Þā	hēt	se	cwellere	þæs
[the] devil's	will.	Then	ordered	the	murderer	the

cāseres	cempan	ealle	geoffrian·	heora	lāc	þām
Caesar's	soldiers	all	to offer	their	sacrifices	to the

godum·	Þā	wǣron	on	þām	campdōme	cappadonisce
gods.	Then	were	in	the	military service	Cappadocian

cempan·	fēowertig	crīstenra	unforhte	on	mōde·
soldiers,	forty	[of] Christians	unafraid	in	spirit,

ǣwfastlice	libbende	æfter	godes	lāre·	Þās	gelǣhte	se
devoutly	living	after[54]	God's	lore.	Those	seized	the

52 That is, 'had to.'
53 That is, 'a certain.'
54 That is, 'according to.'

dēma	and	gelǣdde	hī	tō	þām	dēofolgyldum·	and
judge[55]	*and*	*led*	*them*	*to*	*the*	*idols*	*and*

cwæð	mid	ōlecunge·	þæt	hī	æþele	cempan	wǣron·
said	*with*	*flattery*	*that*	*they*	*noble*	*soldiers*	*were*

and	on	ælcum	gefeohte	fæstrǣde	him	betwȳnan·	and
and	*in*	*each*	*fight*	*loyal*	*them*	*between,*[56]	*and*

symle	sigefæste	on	swiþlicum	gewinne·	ætēowiað	nū
ever	*victorious*	*in*	*violent*	*battle:*	*"Show*	*now*

forðī	ēowre	ānrǣdnysse·	and	ēow sylfe	underþēodað
therefore	*your*	*loyalty,*	*and*	*yourselves*	*submit to*

þǣra	cyninga	gesetnyssum·	and	geoffriað	þām	godum
the	*kings'*	*decrees,*	*and*	*offer*	*to the*	*gods*

ǣr þām þe	gē	bēon	getintregode·	Þā	cwǣdon	þā
ere	*ye*	*be*	*tortured."*	*Then*	*said*	*the*

crīstenan·	tō	ðām	cwellere	þus·	Oft	wē	oferswīðdon
Christians	*to*	*the*	*murderer*	*thus:*	*"Oft*	*we*	*overcame,*

swā swā	þū	sylf	wistest	ūre	wiðerwinnan	on
as	*thou*	*[thy]self*	*knowest,*	*our*	*adversaries*	*in*

gehwylcum	gewinne·	þā þā	wē	fuhton	for	ðām	dēadlicum
each	*battle*	*when*	*we*	*fought*	*for*	*the*	*mortal*

kynincge·	ac	ūs	gedafenað	swȳðor	mid	geswince	tō
king,	*but*	*us*	*it befits*	*rather*	*with*	*labor*	*to*

[55] In Modern English this must be expressed as "The judge seized those." No ambiguity is involved in the Old English structure, for, although *þās* might be either nominative or accusative, both *se* and *dēma* (a weak, or *n*-stem, noun) are distinctively nominative in form.

[56] That is, 'to one another.' Note this use of *between* (OE *betwȳnan*) for more than two.

campigenne·   for   þām   undēadlicum   cynincge   and   þē
do battle   *for*   *the*   *immortal*   *king*   *and*   *thee*

oferswīðan·   Þā   cwæð   se   dēma   þæt   hī   ōþer
to overcome."   *Then*   *said*   *the*   *judge*   *that*   *they*   *other*[57]

þǣra   dydon·[58]   swā   hī   þām   godum
of these   *should do:*   *either*   *they*   *to the*   *gods*

geoffrodon   and   ārwurðnysse   hæfdon·   swā   hī
should offer   *and*   *honor*   *should have,*   *or*   *they*

ðā   offrunge   forsāwon   and   gescynde   wurdon·
the   *offering*   *might neglect*   *and*   *confounded*   *be:*

smēageð   nū   ic   bidde   hwæt   ēow   betst   fremige·   Ða
"Consider   *now,*   *I*   *bid,*   *what*   *you*   *best*   *profits."*   *The*

hālgan   andwyrdon   þām   hæðenan   cwellere·   Drihten
saints   *answered*   *the*   *heathen*   *murderer,*   *"[The] Lord*

forescēawað·   hwæt   ūs   fremige·
foreshoweth   *what*   *us*   *profits."*

The homily goes on to tell of the bloodcurdling and bone-chilling punishment meted out to the Christian soldiers, who were, among other indignities, shoved into a lake which froze to such an extent that they were completely encased in ice, causing their flesh to break open. The sublinear translation given above furnishes a poor idea indeed of Ælfric's style, which is better indicated by a freer translation of the entire homily included in the most recent edition of "The Forty Soldiers."[59]

THE ENGLISH GOLDEN AGE

It is frequently supposed by those whose knowledge of it is more or less limited to the story of King Alfred and the cakes—and their num-

---

[57] That is, 'one of two.'

[58] *Dydon* and the following *geoffrodon, hæfdon, forsāwon,* and *wurdon* are preterit subjunctives, with *-on* where we would expect *-en.*

[59] John Thomas Algeo, "Ælfric's 'The Forty Soldiers': An Edition" (unpublished dissertation, University of Florida, 1960), pp. 68–79.

ber includes many otherwise well-educated people—that the Old English period was somehow gray, dull, and crude.[60] Nothing could be further from the truth. England after its conversion to Christianity at the end of the sixth century became a veritable beehive of scholarly activity. The famous monasteries at Canterbury, Glastonbury, Wearmouth, Lindisfarne, Jarrow, and York were great centers of learning where men such as Aldhelm, Benedict Biscop, Bede, and Alcuin pursued their studies. The great scholarly movement to which Bede belonged is largely responsible for the preservation of classical culture for us. It was to the famous cathedral school at York founded by one of Bede's pupils that Charles the Great (Charlemagne) turned for leadership in his Carolingian Renaissance, and especially to the illustrious English scholar Alcuin (Ealhwine), born in the year of Bede's death and educated at York. A Devonshire man, Wynfrith, later known as Boniface, led the band of English missionaries who brought the Christian faith and Christian culture to Germany. Earlier in a brilliant career which ended in his martyrdom by a band of heathen fanatics, Boniface had assisted Willibrord, the English-born and English-educated bishop of Utrecht, in his missionary labors in Frisia (Friesland).

The culture of the North of England in the seventh and eighth centuries was to spread over the entire country, despite the decline which it suffered as a result of the hammering onslaughts of the Danes. Luckily, because of the tremendous energy and ability of Alfred the Great, it was not lost; and Alfred's able successors of the royal house of Wessex down to the time of the second Ethelred consolidated the cultural and political contributions made by their most distinguished ancestor.

With English culture more advanced than any other in western

[60] Those who think so are advised to examine the marvelous Sutton Hoo treasure the next time they visit the British Museum. This collection of finely wrought gold jewelry, weapons and armor, and luxurious household furnishings, dating from the seventh century, was discovered in Suffolk in 1939. It is the subject of Chapter 5 of D. Elizabeth Martin-Clarke's *Culture in Early Anglo-Saxon England* (Baltimore, 1947), which contains illustrations. *The Sutton Hoo Ship Burial,* published by the Trustees of the British Museum (London, 1947), has a full description of the finds, with many illustrations. The issue of *Life* for July 16, 1951, pp. 81–85, has some excellent pictures in color. For the benefit of Americans, and doubtless of many Englishmen as well, *Hoo* is a topographical term, from Old English *hōh* 'spur of land.'

Europe, the Norman Conquest amounted to a crushing defeat of a superior culture by an inferior one, as the Normans themselves were in time to have the good sense to realize—for they, like the Scandinavian invaders who had preceded them, were ultimately to become Englishmen. As for the English language, which is our main concern here, it was certainly one of the most highly developed vernacular tongues in Europe—for French did not become a literary language until well after the period of the Conquest—with a word stock capable of expressing subtleties of thought elsewhere reserved for Latin. This word stock will be dealt with in some detail in a later chapter.

CHAPTER VI

The Middle English Period (1100–1500)

THE dates for the beginning and end of the Middle English period are conventional and more or less arbitrary. By 1100 certain changes, which had begun long before, were sufficiently well established to justify our use of the adjective *middle* to designate the language in what was actually a period of transition from the English of the early Middle Ages—Old English—to that of the earliest printed books, which, despite certain superficial differences, is essentially the same as our own.

The changes which occurred during this transitional, or "middle," period may be noted in every aspect of the language: in its sounds, in its grammatical structure, in the meanings of its words, and in the nature of its word stock, where many Old English words were replaced by French ones. As we proceed, we shall examine these developments in some detail.

THE BACKGROUND OF THE NORMAN CONQUEST

Almost at the end of the Old English period the great catastrophe of the Norman Conquest befell the English people—a catastrophe more far-reaching in its effects on English culture than the earlier harassment by the Scandinavians who had subsequently become one with them. The Norman Conquest—fortunately for Anglo-American culture and civilization, the last invasion of England—was also carried out by Northmen, who under the leadership of William the Conqueror, the seventh duke of Normandy, defeated the English under the hapless King Harold II at the battle of Hastings in 1066. Harold was killed by an arrow which pierced his eye, and the English, deprived of his effective leadership and that of his two brothers, who also fell in the battle, were ignominiously defeated.

After the death without issue of Edward the Confessor, the last king in the direct male line of descent from Alfred the Great, Harold, son of the powerful Earl Godwin, was elected to the kingship. Almost immediately his possession of the crown was challenged by Duke William of Normandy, who was distantly related to Edward the Confessor and who felt that he had a better claim to the throne for a number of reasons unnecessary to go into here.

William and the Northmen whose *dux* he was came not immediately from Scandinavia, but from France, a region of whose northern coast their not-very-remote Viking ancestors had invaded and settled as recently as the ninth and tenth centuries, beginning at about the same time that other pagan Vikings were making trouble for Alfred the Great in England. Those Scandinavians who settled in France are commonly designated by an Old French form of *Northmen,* that is, *Normans,* and that section of France which they settled and governed was called Normandy.

The Conqueror was a bastard son of Robert the Devil, who took such pains in the early part of his life to earn his surname—among other things, he was accused, doubtless justly, of poisoning the brother whom he succeeded as duke of Normandy—that he became a figure of legend. So great was his capacity for rascality that he was also called Robert the Magnificent. Ironically, he died in the course of a holy pilgrimage to Jerusalem.

Robert's great-great-grandfather was Rollo (*Hrólfr*), a Danish chieftain who was created first duke of Normandy after coming to terms satisfactory to himself with King Charles the Simple of France. In the five generations intervening between Duke Rollo and Duke William, the Normans had become Frenchmen culturally and linguistically, at least superficially—though we must always remember that in those days the French had no learning, art, or literature comparable to what was flourishing in England, nor had they ever seen anything comparable, as they themselves were willing to admit, to the products of English artisans and craftsmen: carving, jewelry, tapestry, metalwork, and the like.[1]

---

[1] These facts have been frequently pointed out, notably by R. W. Chambers, *On the Continuity of English Prose from Alfred to More and His School* (New York, 1932). See numerous quotations from Chambers and others in Kemp Malone's "Earliest England," *Emory University Quarterly,* V (1949), especially 142–46.

THE LINGUISTIC INFLUENCE
OF THE CONQUEST

The impact of the Norman Conquest on the English language, like that made by the earlier Norse-speaking invaders, is to a large extent confined to the word stock, though Middle English shows some instances of the influence of French idiom. A huge body of French words were ultimately to become part of the English vocabulary, many of them replacing English words which would have done for us just as well. This older French element (in contrast with newer borrowings like *chef, tête-à-tête,* and *café*) will be discussed in a later chapter dealing specifically with loan-words in English. Suffice it to point out here merely that English acquired as it were a new look. Compare the following passages from two different translations of the parable of the prodigal son, the first from the West Saxon Gospels of *ca.* 1000 and the second from John Wyclif's translation in the latter fourteenth century:

> Luke xv.12:
> Fæder, syle mē mīnne dǣl mīnre ǣhte þe mē tō gebyreþ.
> Fadir, ʒyve me a porcioun of þe substance[2] þat falliþ me.

> Luke xv.25:
> ... and þā hē þām hūse genēalǣhte, hē gehȳrde þone sweg and þæt weryd.
> ... and whanne he cam and was nyʒ þe hous, he herde a symphonie and oþer noise of mynstralcye.[3]

Where the Old English translator renders "uni civium regionis illius" as "ānum burhsittendan men þæs rīces" (that is, '[to] a borough-dwelling man of that kingdom'), Wyclif has "oon of þe citizeins of þat contré." Other correspondences of Old English and French in the two versions of the parable are *gewilnode–coveitide* 'coveted,' *forwurðe–perishe, mildheortnesse–mercy, onfēng–resceyved* 'received,' *hālne* 'whole'–*saaf* 'safe,' *biddan–preie* 'to pray,' *bebod–mandement* 'command,' *gǣlsan–lecherie.*

THE RISE OF A LONDON STANDARD

Inasmuch as there is writing in all dialects, it is necessary to take some account of the dialectal diversity of Middle English. The North-

---

[2] The Vulgate, the Latin version of the Bible used by both translators, has "Pater, da mihi portionem substantiae, quae me contingit."

[3] Vulgate: ". . . audivit symphoniam et chorum."

ern dialect corresponds roughly to Old English Northumbrian, its southernmost eastern boundary being also the Humber. Likewise, the Midland dialects, subdivided into East Midland and West Midland, correspond roughly to Old English Mercian. The Southern dialect, spoken south of the Thames, similarly corresponds roughly to West Saxon, with Kentish a subdivision.

It is not surprising that a type of speech—that of London—essentially East Midlandish in its characteristics, though showing Northern and to a less extent Southern influences, should in time have become a standard for all of England. London had for centuries been a large (by medieval standards), prosperous, and hence important city.

Until the late fifteenth century, however, authors wrote in the dialect of their native regions—the authors of *Sir Gawain and the Green Knight* and of *Piers Plowman* in the West Midland dialect; the authors of *The Owl and the Nightingale,* of the *Ancrene Riwle,* and of the *Ayenbite of Inwit* in the Southern dialect (including Kentish); the author of the *Bruce* in the Northern dialect; and John Gower and Geoffrey Chaucer in the East Midland dialect, specifically the London variety of East Midland. Modern Standard English—American, however indirectly, as well as British—is a development of the speech of London. To this type of speech people of consequence and those who aspired to be people of consequence or to be the ancestors of people of consequence were endeavoring to conform long before the settlement of America by English-speaking people in the early part of the seventeenth century, though many of those who migrated to the New World obviously retained traces of their regional origins in their pronunciation, their vocabulary, and to a lesser degree in their grammar. Rather than speaking local dialects, most used a type of speech which had been tremendously influenced by the London Standard. In effect, their speech was essentially that of London, with regional shadings.

Thus it comes about that the language of Chaucer and of Gower is so much easier for us to comprehend at first sight than, say, the Northern speech (specifically lowland Scots) of their contemporary John Barbour, author of the *Bruce.* In the following lines from Chaucer's *House of Fame,* for instance, an erudite eagle explains to Chaucer what speech really is:

> Soune ys noght but eyre ybroken
> And every spech that ys yspoken,
> Lowde or pryvee, foule or faire,
> In his substaunce ys but aire;

For as flaumbe ys but lyghted smoke,
Ryght soo soune ys aire y-broke.
But this may be in many wyse,
Of which I wil the twoo devyse:
Of soune that cometh of pipe or harpe.
For whan a pipe is blowen sharpe
The aire ys twyst with violence
And rent. Loo, thys ys my sentence.
Eke, whan men harpe strynges smyte,
Whether hyt be moche or lyte,
Loo, with the stroke the ayre to-breketh:
Thus wost thou wel what thinge is speche.[4]

Now compare Chaucer's English, so like our own, with that of the following excerpt from the *Bruce*:

Þan wist he weill þai wald him sla,
And for he wald his lord succour
He put his lif in aventur
And stud intill a busk lurkand
Quhill þat þe hund com at his hand,
And with ane arrow soyn hym slew
And throu the wod syne hym withdrew.[5]

Distinctively Northern forms in this passage are *sla* (corresponding to East Midland *slee*), *wald* (E. Midl. *wolde[n]*), *stud* (E. Midl. *sto[o]d*); *weill*, in which the *i* indicates length of the preceding *e*;[6] *lurkand*

---

[4] Except for modernization of the use of *u* and *v*, this passage is in the spelling of Fairfax MS 16 (Bodleian Library) as reproduced in *A Parallel-Text Edition of Chaucer's Minor Poems*, Part II, ed. Frederick J. Furnivall for the Chaucer Society (London, 1878), pp. 201–02. Inconsistent spellings (for instance *eyre–ayre–aire, is–ys, thinge–thynge, lowde–ʒoule*) did not bother medieval scribes overmuch. The notion that there was one, and only one, "right" way to spell a word was a long time in developing.

[5] Then he knew well they wished to slay him,
And because he wished to succor his lord
He put his life in fortune's hands
And stood lurking in a bush
While the hound came to his hand,
And with one arrow immediately slew him
And through the wood afterward withdrew himself.

[6] This Northern form with long *e* survives in *ne'er-do-weel*, a Northern variant of *ne'er-do-well*. The phrase is of Northern English and Scots origin.

(E. Midl. *lurking*), *quhīll* (E. Midl. *whȳl*), *āne* (E. Midl. *ǫnⁿ*[7]), *intill* (E. Midl. *intō*), and *syne* (E. Midl. *sith*). *Soyn* 'soon, immediately' is merely a matter of spelling: the *y*, like the *i* in *weill*, merely indicates length in the preceding vowel, and not a pronunciation of the vowel different from that indicated by the usual East Midland spelling *sone*. The nominative form of the third person plural pronoun, *þai* 'they,' was adopted in the North from Scandinavian and gradually spread into the other dialects. The oblique forms *their* and *them* were not used in London English or in the Midland and South generally at this time, though common enough in the North. Chaucer uses *they* for the nominative, but retains the native forms *here* (or *hire*) and *hem* as oblique forms. A Northern characteristic not illustrated in the passage cited is the *-es* ending of the third person singular and all plural forms of the present indicative. Also Northern, but not occurring in the passage, is the frequent correspondence of *k* to the *ch* of the other dialects, as in *birk–birch, kirk–chirche, mikel* 'much'–*michel*, and *ilk* 'each'–*ęch*.

THE PRINCIPAL CONSONANTAL CHANGES

Throughout the history of English the consonants have remained relatively stable, as compared with the notable vowel changes which have occurred. The Old English consonant sounds written *b, c* (in both its values in late Old English, [k] and [č]), *d, f* (in both its values [f] and [v]), *ʒ* (in two of its values [g] and [j]), *h* (as [h-] and as [x]), *k, l, m, n, p, r, s, t, þ (ð), ƿ*, and *x* (that is, [ks]) remained unchanged in Middle English. Important spelling differences occur, however, most of them due to Anglo-Norman influence. These have been rather fully discussed in Chapter II. In accordance with later Middle English spelling practices, the *ȝ*, the modified form of *ʒ* which was long used in early Middle English for [x], will be represented as *gh*, even though such spelling of a few words may not be actually attested. The same symbol will be represented by *y* when it has the value of [j]—also in accord with later Middle English practice. *Th* will hereafter regularly be used for *þ* and the less frequently occurring *ð* in citations of Middle English words.

The more important consonantal changes, other than the part

---

[7] The editorial hook under the *ǫ* indicates the "open *o*" sound [ɔ:]. Likewise, *ę* indicates "open *ē*," that is, [ɛ:]. For the development of these sounds, see pp. 146–48.

played by *g* in the formations of new diphthongs (see p. 149), may be summarized as follows:[8]

1. The Old English sequences *hl, hn,* and *hr* (as in *hlēapan* 'to leap,' *hnutu* 'nut,' and *hraðor* 'sooner') were simplified to *l, n,* and *r* (as in *lẹ̄pen, nute,* and *rather*). To some extent *hw,* written *wh* in Middle English, was also frequently so reduced to *w,* at least in the Southern dialect. In the North, however, the *h* in this sequence was vigorously sounded, as the spellings *gn* and *quh* used for it in Northern texts indicate.

2. The Old English voiced velar fricative *g* after *l* or *r* became *w* (and subsequently [ʊ]), as in *halwen* 'to hallow' (OE *halgian*) and *morwe(n)* 'morrow' (OE *morgen*).

3. After consonants, particularly *s* and *t,* and before back vowels, *w* was lost, as in *sọ̄* (OE *swā*) and *tọ̄* 'two' (OE *twā*). Since Old English times it had been lost in various negative contractions regardless of what vowel followed, as in Middle English *nil(le)* from *ne wil(le), nọt* from *ne wọt, nas* from *ne was,* and *niste* from *ne wiste* (in which the *w* was postconsonantal because of elision of the *e* of *ne*). *Nille* survives in *willy-nilly.* A number of spellings with "silent *w*" continue to occur, for example *two, sword,* and *answer* (early ME *andswarien*).

4. In unstressed syllables, *-ch* was lost in late Middle English, as in *-ly* (OE *-lic*). The form *ī* for the first person nominative singular pronoun represents a restressing of the *i* which alone remained of *ich* (OE *ic*) after this loss.

5. Before a consonant, though an *e* might intervene, *v* was lost in a few words like *hẹ̄d* (by way of *hẹ̄vd, hẹ̄ved,* from OE *hēafod*), *lọ̄rd* (*lọ̄verd,* OE *hlāford*), *hast, hath,* and *had* (OE *hæfst, hæfð,* and *hæfde*).

6. The Old English prefix *ge-* became *i-* (*y-*) as in *iwis* 'certain' (OE *gewiss*) and *ilimpen* 'to happen' (OE *gelimpan*).

7. In the Southern dialect, including Kentish, initial *f, s,* and doubtless *þ* as well, were voiced. This characteristic is reflected in spelling in the use of *v* for *f* and *z* for *s.* It was noted as current in some of the Southern counties of England by Joseph Wright in his *English Dialect*

---

[8] For a more detailed treatment, see Joseph Wright and Elizabeth Mary Wright, *An Elementary Middle English Grammar,* 2nd ed. (London, 1928), pp. 107–14. Clear examples of some of the phenomena treated are somewhat limited, hence many of the forms cited by the Wrights are used here, as also in other works.

Grammar (Oxford, 1905), and is reflected in such Standard English words of Southern provenience as *vixen* 'she-fox' and *vat*.

8. Final inflectional *n* was gradually lost,[9] as was also the final *n* of the unstressed possessive pronouns *mīn* and *þīn* and of the indefinite article before a consonant: compare Old English *mīn fæder* 'my father' with Middle English *mȳ fader* (but *mȳn eye* 'my eye'). This loss of *-n* has resulted in such doublets as *an–a, none–no* (OE *nān* from *ne ān* 'not one').

THE MIDDLE ENGLISH VOWELS

The Old English vowels *ē, ī, ō*, and *ū* remained unchanged in Middle English, as in Old English *fēt*—Middle English *fēt, feet*[10] 'feet'; Old English *rīdan*—Middle English *rīden, rȳden*[11] 'to ride'; Old English *fōda*—Middle English *fo(o)de*; Old English *hūs*—Middle English *hōūs*[12] 'house.' Old English *ȳ* was unrounded to [i:] in the Northern and the East Midland areas. It remained unchanged, though written *u* or *ui*, in the greater part of the West Midland and all of the Southwest until the latter years of the fourteenth century, when it was unrounded and hence fell together with the Northern and East Midland development. In Kent and elsewhere in the Southeast the Old English sound became [e:]. Hence Old English *hȳdan* 'to hide' is reflected in Middle English in such dialectal variants as *hiden, hūden,* and *hēden*.

Old English *ā* remained only in the North (*hām* 'home,' *rāp* 'rope,' *stān* 'stone'), becoming [e:], as in *hame, rape,* and *stane,* in Modern Scots; everywhere south of the Humber it became [ɔ:], and was spelled *o* or *oo* exactly like the [o:] which remained from Old English, as in

[9] Infinitives will nevertheless henceforth be cited with *-n,* though as often as not in late Middle English times they occur without it.

[10] Doubling *e* and *o* to indicate length became usual in late Middle English times, though encountered much earlier. Such spelling practices have been discussed above, pp. 42–43. Double *a* and double *i* are much less general, and have not survived. Henceforth double *e* and double *o* forms will sometimes be cited, particularly if they are Chaucerian. They require no macrons.

[11] For the Middle English interchange of *i* and *y*, see p. 44. It is reflected in such variants as American *tire* (for a wheel)–British *tyre,* with the preference reversed in American *gypsy*–British *gipsy*.

[12] This French spelling, alongside *ow,* for [u:] has been discussed on p. 43.

fo(o)de. One can tell certainly how to pronounce a Middle English word so spelled by referring to its Old English form; thus, if the *o(o)* corresponds to Old English *ā* (*stǫn–OE stān*), the Middle English sound is [ɔ:]; if the Old English word has *ō* (*mōne–OE mōna, roote–OE rōt*), the Middle English sound is the same. But there is an easier way for, say, the beginning student of Middle English literature, who may not be familiar with Old English, and it is fairly certain: if the modern sound is [o:], spelled *o* with "silent *e*" (as in *roe, rode*), *oa* (as in *road*), sometimes *ow* (as in *snow*), but never *oo*, then the Middle English sound is [ɔ:].[13] If the Modern English sound is [u:], [ʊ], or [ʌ], spelled *oo*, the Middle English sound is [o:], as in, respectively, Modern English *food, foot,* and *flood*,[14] going back to Middle English [fo:də], [fo:t], and [flo:d].

West Saxon Old English *ǣ* had two quite distinct sources. It might be either a development of West Germanic **ā* (compare the unchanged vowel of Ger. *Schlāf* 'sleep' with the shifted one of WS *slǣp*), corresponding to non-West Saxon (that is, Kentish, Mercian, and Northumbrian) *ē*; or the result of *i*-mutation of prehistoric Old English *ā*, a development of West Germanic **ai*, as in *dǣl* 'part, deal,' from prehistoric Old English **dāli*.

But in non-West Saxon dialects these sounds were differentiated by the raising of the first *ǣ* (from W. Gmc. **ā*) to *ē* [e:] early in the Old English period. On the other hand, the Old English *ǣ* resulting from *i*-mutation remained in the Anglian dialects as well as in West Saxon. It corresponds to [ɛ:] in the Northern and (what is our principal concern) much of the Midland area. Unfortunately for the novice, both [e:] and [ɛ:] were written *e* or *ee* in Middle English regardless of their sources, which include also West Germanic *ē* for [e:] and the *e* which

[13] Exceptions are *gold* and *Rome*, which had [o:] in Middle English and [u:] in early Modern English. Compare the proper name form *Gould* and early rimes of *Rome* with *doom, room,* and so forth, in the poetry of the early Modern period—for example that of Pope and Dryden. The earlier pronunciation of *Rome* is indicated by Shakespeare's pun in *Julius Caesar* I.ii.156: "Now is it Rome indeed, and room enough . . . ," which he repeats elsewhere. The change back to [ro:m] and [go:ld] has occurred in fairly recent times.

[14] *Brooch* [bro:č] is an exceptional instance of *oo* as a spelling for [o:] from Middle English [ɔ:]. A spelling pronunciation [bru:č] is occasionally heard from naïve speakers.

was lengthened in open syllables to [ɛ:] (p. 150) in the early thirteenth century.[15]

In early Modern English times *ea* was adopted as a spelling for most of those words which in the Middle English dialects spoken north of the Thames had [ɛ:] from whatever source, whereas those words which had in the same dialects [e:] from whatever source usually continued the Middle English *e(e)* spelling (p. 42). This difference in spelling is a great blessing to the beginning student of Chaucer. By reference to it he may ascertain that *swete breeth* in the fifth line of the General Prologue to the *Canterbury Tales* is to be read ['swe:tə brɛ:θ]. The Modern English spellings *sweet* and *breath* here, as often, provide the clue to the Middle English pronunciation.

Except for Old English *æ* and *y*, the short vowels of those Old English stressed syllables which remained short were unchanged in most Middle English speech (unless otherwise qualified, *Middle English* will refer to the speech of the East Midland area), for example Old English *wascan* 'to wash'–Middle English *washen, helpan* 'to help'– *helpen, sittan* 'to sit'–*sitten, hoppian* 'to hop'–*hoppen*, and *hungrig* 'hungry'–*hungry* ['huŋgrɪ]. Old English short *æ* came to be written *a* in Middle English: Old English *glæd*–Middle English *glad*. In Southwest Midland and in Kentish, however, words which in Old English had short *æ* were written with *e* (for instance *gled*) in early Middle English times—a writing which probably indicated little change from the Old English sound in those areas. In the Northern and East Midland areas Old English *y* was unrounded to *i*, exactly as *ȳ* was unrounded to *ī* in the same areas (see p. 146). In the Southeast it became *e*, but remained as [y], written *u*, in the West Midland and the Southwest until late Middle English times, when it was unrounded along with [y:].

CHANGES IN DIPHTHONGS

The Old English long diphthongs *ēa* and *ēo* were "smoothed," or monophthongized, in late Old English times (eleventh century), occurring in the twelfth century as [ɛ:] and (in the greater part of England) [e:] respectively, their subsequent Modern English development coinciding with that of [ɛ:] and [e:] from other origins. Because of this, post-eleventh-century Middle English *lēɛf* 'leaf' [lɛ:f] develops out of

[15] Thus West Saxon Old English *slǣp* and *dǣl* correspond to Northern and Midland Middle English *sleep* [sle:p] and *dēɛl* [dɛ:l]; *mētan* 'to meet' and *etan* 'to eat' to *mēten* ['me:tən] and *ēten* ['ɛ:tən].

Old English *lēaf* and *seen* 'to see' [se:n] out of Old English *sēon*. The short diphthongs *ea* and *eo*[16] became by the twelfth century respectively *a* and *e*, as in Middle English *yaf* 'gave' from Old English *geaf*, *herte* 'heart' from Old English *heorte*.

New diphthongs appear in Middle English, though their development began in late Old English times, from the vocalization of *g* to *i* after front vowels (OE *sægde* 'said'—ME *saide*) and later of *g* (the voiced velar fricative) to *u* after back vowels (OE *boga* 'bow'—ME *bowe*). Before Old English *h*, which other than initially stood for a voiceless velar fricative, an *i*-glide developed after a front vowel (late OE *ehta* 'eight'—ME *eighte*) and a *u*-glide after a back vowel (OE *āht* 'aught'—ME *aught*). *W* after a vowel became a *u*-glide, for instance Old English *grōwan* 'to grow'—Middle English *grōwen*, the *w* continuing to be written. The diphthong [ɔi], spelled *oi, oy,* is of French origin, as in *joie* 'joy,' *cloistre* 'cloister,' as is [ui], usually also written *oi, oy,* as in *boilen* 'to boil,' *poisen* 'to poison,' and *joinen* 'to join.'[17] The off-glides [i] and [u] merely lengthened *i* and *u* respectively (OE *lige* 'falsehood'—ME *līe*; OE *fugol* 'fowl'—ME *fōul*). It should be noted that diphthongization often involved a new conception of syllabic division, for example Old English *cnāwan* ['knɑ:-wɑn]—Middle English *knowen* ['knɔu-ən].

Other diphthongal developments are taken up in specialized grammars of Middle English. Before passing on to other matters, it is significant that we note here by way of summarization that as the Old English diphthongs were smoothed into monophthongs, new diphthongs developed in Middle English. These have in turn undergone smoothing in Modern English (for instance *drawen* ['drauən]—*draw* [drɔ:]), new glides have developed (for instance *rīden* ['ri:dən]—*ride* [raɪd], *hous* [hu:s]—house [haʊs]), and others are even now in the course of developing. Some inland Southern American speakers lack off-glides in [aɪ] and [aʊ], so that "My wife is in the house" comes out as something very like [ma waf ɪz ɪn ðə has]; the off-glide may also be lost in *oil, boil,* and the like, as also occasionally in *ruin*. Comparatively new *u* and *i* off-glides may occur in *boat, bait,* and the like, which, as we have seen, some phoneticians and most phonemicists

---

[16] Diphthongs according to the traditional view, but see p. 109, n. 13 for another interpretation of these digraphs.

[17] Words containing this diphthong have [ʌɪ] in early Modern English, pronunciations which are reflected in nonstandard *bile, pizen,* and *jine*. See p. 173.

nowadays transcribe as diphthongs. As E. E. Wardale aptly puts it, "The constant loss of old and formation of new diphthongs illustrate in a striking manner the life and movement inherent in any spoken language."[18]

THE LENGTHENING AND SHORTENING OF VOWELS

As we have seen, in late Old English times originally short vowels were lengthened before *m, n, l,* or *r* followed by another single consonant. This lengthening frequently failed to maintain itself, and by the end of the Middle English period is to be found only in *i* and *o* before *-mb* (*clīmben* 'to climb,' *cǫmb* 'comb'); in *i* and *u* before *-nd* (*bīnden* 'to bind,' *boūnden* 'bound'); and generally before *-ld* (*mīlde* 'mild,' *yēlden* 'to pay, yield,' *ǫld* 'old,' *gōld* 'gold'). Reshortening even under these circumstances has occurred, however, in some words, for instance *wind* (noun), *held, send, friend*; compare *wind* (verb), *field, fiend,* in which the lengthening survives. If another consonant followed any of the sequences mentioned, lengthening did not occur; this fact explains Modern English *child, children* (OE nominative-accusative plural *cildru*).

Considerably later than the lengthenings due to the consonant sequences just discussed, short *a, e,* and *o* were lengthened when they were in open syllables, that is, in syllables in which they were final, for instance *bā-ken* 'to bake' (OE *bacan*). To put it somewhat differently, these vowels were lengthened when followed by a single consonant plus another vowel. In Old English short vowels frequently occurred in such syllables, for example *nama* 'name,' *stelan* 'to steal,' *þrote* 'throat,' which became in Middle English respectively *nāme, stęlen, thrǫte*. This lengthening is interestingly reflected in *staff* (from ME *staf,* going back to OE *stæf*) and its plural *staves* (from ME *stāves,* going back to OE *stafas*). Short *i* (*y*) and *u* were likewise lengthened in open syllables, beginning in the fourteenth century in the North, but these vowels underwent a qualitative change also: *i* (*y*) became *ē,* and *u* became *ō,* for example Old English *wicu* 'week,' *yvel* 'evil,' *wudu* 'wood,' which became respectively *wēke, ēvel, wōde*.

This lengthening in open syllables was a new principle in English. It has prevailed ever since Middle English times, though the distinc-

---

[18] *An Introduction to Middle English* (London, 1937), p. 55.

tion between open and closed syllables became largely historical except as a matter of spelling. When final unstressed *e* ceased to be pronounced (see pp. 156–57), the letter was often used after a consonant to indicate that the preceding vowel was long. This -*e* indicates in Modern English the difference between *win* and *wine* (see pp. 42–43), though the vowels of both words appear in closed syllables ([wɪn], [waɪn]); as far as modern practice is concerned, this final *e* serves only as a diacritic—the equivalent of a macron over the preceding vowel. This use of -*e*, beginning in Middle English times, was greatly extended in the sixteenth century.

Conversely, beginning in the Old English period, originally long vowels in closed syllables—that is, followed by consonant sequences, including lengthened (doubled) consonants—were shortened, except when followed by those consonantal sequences which caused lengthening, for example *hidde* 'hid' (OE *hȳdde*), *kepte* 'kept' (OE *cēpte*),[19] *fifty* (OE *fīftig*), *fiftēne* (OE *fīftȳne*)[20] *twenty* (OE *twēntig*), *shepherde, wisdom*. It made no difference whether the consonant sequence was in the word originally (as in OE *sōfte*–ME *softe*), was the result of adding an inflectional ending (as in *hidde*), or was the result of compounding (as in OE *wīsdōm* [that is, *wīs* plus *dōm*]–ME *wisdom*). Reduced stress accounts for the shortening of the second syllable of the last cited word—a general tendency which also operated in words which were not normally stressed within the sentence, as in *an*, the indefinite article (OE *ān* 'one'), *but* (OE *būtan*), *not* (OE *nāwiht*). There was considerable wavering in vowel length before the sequence -*st*, as indicated by such Modern English forms as *fist–Christ, lost–ghost, breast–least*. Before two unstressed syllables shortening regularly occurred, as reflected in *wilderness* (*wild*), *Christendom* (*Christ*), and *holiday* (*holy*).

THE LEVELING OF UNSTRESSED VOWELS

As far as the structure of English is concerned, the most significant of all developments in the language occurred with the Middle English falling together of *a, o,* and *u* with *e* in unstressed syllables, all ultimately becoming [ə], for example:

[19] The alternation of long-voweled infinitives with short-voweled preterits is reflected in Modern English *hide–hid, keep–kept,* and a number of other weak verbs.

[20] Reflected in Modern English *fifty, fifteen,* contrasted with *five*.

OLD ENGLISH	MIDDLE ENGLISH
lama 'lame'	lāme
faran 'to fare,' faren (past part.)	fāren
stānes 'stone's,' stānas 'stones'	stǫnes
feallað 'falleth'	falleth
nacod 'naked'	nāked
macodon 'made' (pl.)	mākeden
sicor 'sure'	sēker
lengðo 'length'	lengthe
medu 'liquor'	mẹde

This phenomenon has already been alluded to (p. 108), for it began well before the end of the Old English period. The *Beowulf* manuscript (*ca.* A.D. 1000), for instance, has occurrences of *-as* for the genitive singular *-es* ending, *-an* for the preterit plural ending *-on* and the dative plural ending *-um*[21] (and conversely *-on* for the infinitive ending *-an*), *-o* for the genitive plural ending *-a* and for the neuter nominative plural ending *-u*, among a number of such interchanges pointing to identical vowel quality in such syllables.

THE REDUCTION OF INFLECTIONS

As a result of this merging of unstressed vowels into a single sound, the number of forms in English was drastically reduced. Middle English became a language with few inflectional distinctions, whereas Old English, as we have seen, was relatively highly inflected, though less so than Germanic, which was about as fully inflected as Latin. This reduction of inflections was thus responsible for a structural change of the greatest importance.

In the adjective, for instance, the Old English weak forms—those used after the demonstrative pronouns—ending in *-a* (masculine nominative) and in *-e* (neuter nominative-accusative and feminine nominative) fell together in a single form in *-e*. Thus an indication of gender distinguishing the masculine form was lost. Middle English *the ǫlde man* corresponds to Old English *se ealda man*, the ending of the adjective being identical with that used for the *ǫlde tāle* (OE feminine *sēo ealde talu*) and *the ǫlde sword* (OE neuter *þæt ealde swurd*). The Old English weak adjective endings *-an* and *-um* similarly fell together as *-en* and, with the loss of final *-n* (see p. 146), these also came to have

---

[21] The *-m* in *-um* became *n* late in the Old English period.

only -e. The Old English genitive plural forms of the weak adjective in -ena and -ra, after first becoming -ene and -re, were made to conform to the predominant weak adjective form in -e, though there are a very few late survivals of the Old English genitive plural in -ra as Middle English -er, notably in aller (OE ealra) and related forms. Thus the five singular and plural forms of the Old English weak adjective declension (-a, -e, -an, -ena, and -um) are reduced to a single form ending in -e, with gender as well as number distinctions completely obliterated. For the strong function the endingless form of the Old English nominative singular was used throughout the singular, with a generalized plural form (identical with the plural of the weak adjective declension) in -e: thus (strong singular) with grēęt solempnytee 'with great solemnity,' (generalized plural) grēęte lordes 'great lords.'

To describe the situation more simply, Middle English monosyllabic adjectives ending in consonants had a single inflection, -e, used to modify singular nouns in the weak function and all plural nouns. Other adjectives—for example frē (or free) and all disyllables—were uninflected. This simple grammatical situation can hardly be inferred from many of the manuscripts, whose scribes frequently wrote final e's where they did not belong.

Changes resulting from this new identity of vowel in unstressed syllables were considerably more far-reaching than what has been shown in the declension of the adjective. For instance, the older endings -an (infinitives, most of the oblique, or non-nominative, forms of n-stem nouns), -on (indicative preterit plurals), and -en (subjunctive preterit plurals, past participles of strong verbs) all fell together as -en. With the later loss of final inflectional -n in some of these forms, only -e [-ə] was left, and this was in time also to go. This fact accounts for endingless infinitives, preterit plurals, and some past participles of strong verbs in Modern English, for instance:

OLD ENGLISH	MIDDLE ENGLISH	MODERN ENGLISH
findan (inf.)	finden	find
fundon (pret. pl.)	foūnde(n)	found
funden (past part.)	foūnde(n)	found

It was similar, as we have seen from the examples cited (p. 152), with the nominative-accusative plural of the most important declension (-as) which became a pattern for the plural of most nouns, and the genitive singular of the same declension (-es); and with the noun end-

ings -eð, and -að (OE hæleð 'fighting-man,' mōnað 'month') and the
same endings as they occurred in verbs (OE findeð 'he, she, it finds,'
findað 'we, you, they find')—all ending up as Middle English -eth.[22]
Also similarly, the -ast of many Old English weak verbs fell together
with the -est of strong verbs (and the largest group of weak verbs as
well).

THE LOSS OF GRAMMATICAL GENDER

One of the important results of the leveling of unstressed vowels was
the loss of grammatical gender—a loss which, like many others in language, was really a tremendous gain. We have seen how this occurred
with the adjective. We have also seen that grammatical gender, for
psychological reasons rather than phonological ones, had begun to
break down in Old English times as far as the choice of pronouns was
concerned (see pp. 111–12), as when the English translator of Bede's
Latin Ecclesiastical History refers to Bertha, the wife of King Ethelbert of Kent as hēo 'she' rather than hit, though she is in the same
sentence designated as þæt (neuter demonstrative used as definite article) wīf rather than sēo wīf, which would still have been impossible.

In Old English, gender was readily distinguishable in most nouns:
a-stem masculine nominative-accusative plurals, for instance, ended
in -as, feminines in -a, and short-stemmed neuters in -u. In Middle
English all but a handful of nouns acquired the masculine nominative-
accusative plural ending -es (OE -as). This important development,
coupled with the invariable the which supplanted the Old English
masculine se, the neuter þæt, and the feminine sēo with all their
oblique forms (see p. 118), left grammatical gender without a leg to
stand on. Subsequent generations of speakers may well say good rid-
dance to it.

THE INFLECTION OF NOUNS

It should be obvious that the structure of English was profoundly
affected in all departments by the leveling of unstressed vowels.
Among the nouns, to cite some further instances, the Old English
distinctive feminine nominative singular form in -u fell together with
the nominative plural form in -a, that is, singular denu 'valley' and
plural dena 'valleys' became for a while Middle English dẹne. It was
similar with the neuter nominative-accusative plurals in -u and the

[22] A present indicative plural form only in the Southern dialect of Middle
English.

genitive plurals in *-a*: all came to have the same *-e* ending. What further happened with *dēne* happened to most other nouns which had not formed their nominative-accusative plurals in *-as* in Old English, and has been alluded to before: namely, the *-es* which was the Middle English reduced form of this ending was made to serve as a general plural ending for such words: thus, singular nongenitive *dēne*, general plural *dēnes*. In like fashion, the genitive singular ending *-es* was extended to nouns which had belonged to declensions lacking this ending; thus the genitive singular and the general plural forms of most nouns fell together, and have remained that way ever since: Old English genitive singular *speres* and nominative plural *speru* become Middle English *spēres*, Modern English *spear's, spears*; Old English genitive singular *tale* and nominative plural *tala* become Middle English *tāles*, Modern English *tale's, tales*.

A few *s*-less genitives—feminine nouns and the family-relationship nouns ending in *-r*—remained throughout the period (as in Chaucer's "In hope to stonden in his lady grace" and "by my fader kyn") and survived into early Modern English, along with a few nouns from the Old English "weak" declension.[23] Sometimes the genitive *-s* was left off a noun which ended in *s*[24] or which was followed by a word beginning with *s*.[25]

The few nouns which did not conform to the pattern of forming the plural by suffixing *-es*[26] nevertheless followed the pattern of using the nominative-accusative plural as a general plural form. In Old English the mutated forms *fēt, men, tēð, gēs, lȳs, mȳs* were dative singular as well as nominative-accusative plural forms, whereas the genitive and dative plural forms had unmutated vowels. Mutation in itself thus, as

[23] In this declension the Old English genitive ended in *-an*, which, as we have seen, became Middle English *-en*, then *-e*.

[24] For the same phonological reason that accounts for the occasional modern loss of the genitive *-s* in "Keats' poems, Dickens' novels," assuming that these are not merely matters of writing.

[25] Solely a matter of writing. Compare the occasional modern writing "for pity sake," which indicates the same pronunciation as "for pity's sake."

[26] They include those which lack *-s* plurals today, for example *ox, deer, foot*. There were also in Middle English a number of survivals of weak-declension plurals in *-(e)n* which have subsequently disappeared (for example *eyen* 'eyes,' *fǭn* 'foes'). The *-(e)n* was even extended to a few nouns which belonged to the *a*-stem strong declension in Old English, for example *shoon* 'shoes' (OE *scōs*).

we have seen, was in Old English no sign of the plural, nor did lack of it indicate the singular. From Middle English times onward, however, the mutated vowel in what had been merely the most commonly occurring plural form came to be regarded as a sign of the plural; hence the Modern English plural forms *feet, men, teeth, geese, lice, mice.* This development was precisely parallel to what happened to the Old English nominative-accusative plural *-es* when it became in Middle English simply the plural *-es,* and for that matter to the surviving weak nouns, in which the Old English singular accusative-genitive-dative form in *-n* was made to conform to the nominative without *-n,* whereas the same ending occurring in the nominative-accusative plural was retained as the general plural form; thus *-n* became a sign of the plural. A few long-syllabled words which had been neuters in Old English occurred with unchanged plural forms, especially animal names like *sheep, deer,* and *hors.*

During the Middle English period, then, practically all nouns were reduced to two forms, just as in Modern English—one without *-s* used as a general nongenitive singular form, and one with *-s* used as a genitive singular and general plural form. The English language thus acquired a device for indicating plurality without consideration of case—the *-s* ending, which had been in Old English only one of three plural endings in the strong masculine declension. It also lost all trace of any case distinctions except for the genitive, identical in form with the plural. English had come to depend upon particles—mainly prepositions and conjunctions—and word order to express grammatical relations which had previously been expressed by inflection. No longer could one say, as Ælfric had done, "Þās gelæhte se dēma," (p. 135, n. 55) and expect the sentence to be properly understood as 'The judge seized those.' To say this in Middle English, it is necessary that the subject precede the verb: "The dēme ilaghte thǫs."

THE LOSS OF SCHWA IN FINAL SYLLABLES

The leveled final *e* was gradually lost[27] in the North in the course of the thirteenth century and in the Midlands and the South somewhat later. Many words, however, continued to be spelled with *-e,* which had also been extended by analogy to a number of words in which it was not historical, for example *brīde,* from Old English *brȳd* 'bride.' This inorganic *-e,* as it is sometimes called, underwent the

---

[27] The loss of a final sound is called *apocope.*

same development as other final *e*'s—that is, it had ceased to be pronounced by the end of the Middle English period.

Nonfinal unstressed *e* (written *i, y,* and *u* in some dialects) was ultimately lost in the inflectional ending *-es,*[28] except of course after [s],
[z], [š], [č], and [ǰ]. This loss was a comparatively late development,
beginning in the North in the early fourteenth century. It did not
occur in the Midlands and the South until somewhat later. In the West
Saxon and Kentish dialects of Old English the ending *-eð* for the third
person singular of the present indicative of verbs was usually syncopated (p. 131). It is hence not surprising to find syncope in this ending
in the Southern dialect of Middle English and, after long syllables, in
the Midland dialects as well, for example *mākth,* 'maketh,' *bę̄rth*
'beareth,' as also sometimes after short syllables, for example *comth.*
Chaucer uses both syncopated and unsyncopated forms of this ending;
sometimes the syncopation is not indicated by the spelling, but is
dictated by the meter. Syncope did not occur in *-ed* until the fifteenth
century.[29]

PERSONAL PRONOUNS: LOSS OF THE DUAL NUMBER

As we have noted, simplification occurred in other categories as
well. Only the pronouns retained, and for that matter still do retain,
a considerable degree of the complexity which characterized them in
Old English. These words alone preserved distinctive subject and
object case forms, except for the neuter pronouns *(h)it, that, this,* and
what, which even in Old English had not differentiated the nominative and accusative. With the virtual disappearance of the dual number in Middle English,[30] the objective forms of the personal pronouns
surviving from Old English are *mē* (nominative *ich, Ī,* Northern *ik*),
ūs (nominative *wē*), *thee* (nominative *thōu*), and *yōu* (nominative *yē*).
The third person masculine accusative *hine* survived into Middle

[28] The loss of a sound within a word is called *syncope.*

[29] It has not yet done so in the forms *aged, blessed,* and *learned* when
these are used as adjectives. Compare *learnëd man, the blessëd Lord,
agëd woman* with "The man learned his lesson," "The Lord blessed the
multitude," "The woman aged rapidly." There is of course no syncope of
-ed after *t* or *d.*

[30] Such a phrase as *git būtū,* that is 'you two both,' occurring in late Old
English, indicates that the form *git* had lost much of its idea of twoness and
needed the reinforcement of *būtū* 'both.'

English only in the South; elsewhere *him* took over. The Old English feminine accusative *hī* likewise survived for a while in the same region, but in the latter thirteenth century was supplanted by the *hir(e)* or *her(e)* current elsewhere.

The feminine pronoun had a variety of subject forms, one of them identical with the corresponding masculine form—certainly a well-nigh intolerable state of affairs, forcing the lovesick author of the lyric "Alysoun" to refer to his sweetheart as *he*,[31] the same form she would have used in referring to him. This and the various other forms (among them *hō, hyō, hyē, hī, chō,* and *shē*) had a fairly well defined dialectal distribution, with *shē* the predominant form in East Midland speech.

The native third person nominative-accusative plural forms in *h-*, which remained current in the Southern dialect, were also varied. In the North and Midlands the Scandinavian-derived nominative forms *they, thei* (or *thay, thai*) prevailed. The Midlands and the South, however, continued to use the native *hem* (or *heom*) as an objective form. This is in perfect accord with Chaucer's usage (see p. 144). Ultimately the Scandinavian objective form *them* (*thaim, thame, theim*) current in the Northern dialect was also to prevail; in the generation following Chaucer it everywhere displaced the English forms save for unstressed *hem*.

The genitive forms of the personal pronouns came in Middle English to be used exclusively as possessives. Such a construction as Old English *nǣniġ hira* could be rendered in Middle English only by *of* plus the objective form *hem*, or *them*, precisely as in Modern English *none of them*. The variant forms of the genitive first and second persons singular—*mīn–mī, thīn–thī*—preceding a noun were in exactly the same type of distribution as the forms *an* and *a*, that is, the *n* was lost before a consonant (see p. 146). Following a noun, the forms with *-n* were invariable (as in the rare construction *baby mine*, as also when the possessives were used as in Modern English "That book is mine," "Mine is that book," and *that book of mine*).[32] The possessive of the neuter third person singular *(h)it* was *his*, the same as the masculine. In the same person the feminine possessive form was *hir(e)* or

[31] For example, "Bote he me wolle to hire take" means 'Unless she will take me to her.'

[32] By analogy with this unvarying use of the forms in *-n* as pronouns, *hisen, heren, ōuren, yōuren,* and *theiren* arose. From the beginning their status seems to have been much the same as that of their Modern English descendants *hisn, hern, yourn,* and *theirn*.

her(e). The first, second, and third person plural possessives were respectively *ōur(e)*, *yōur(e)*, and *her(e)*, to cite the most usual East Midland spellings. The form *their(e)*, Scandinavian like *they* and *them*, was almost exclusively Northern in Middle English times, and *her* for the third person plural possessive survives as an occasional form well into the Modern English period.[33] The personal pronouns in *-r* developed new analogical genitive forms in *-es* rather late in Middle English: *hires, ōures, yōures, heres* (Northern *theires*). These *-es* forms were used precisely like Modern English *hers, ours, yours,* and *theirs*—predicatively, as in "The books on the table are hers (ours, yours, theirs)" and when a word modified by the *s*-less forms was to be inferred, as in "Hers (ours, and so forth) are on the table."

DEMONSTRATIVE PRONOUNS

Old English *se, þæt,* and *sēo,* with their various oblique forms, were ultimately reduced to *the, that,* and plural *thō*; however, inflected forms derived from the Old English declensions continued to be used in some dialects, though not in East Midland, until the thirteenth century. The *the* which at first replaced only the masculine nominative *se* came to be used as an invariable definite article. *That* and *thǫ*, which were used both as articles and as demonstratives in Old English (as *þæt* and *þā*), were thus restricted to the demonstrative function. Another *the*, from the Old English masculine and neuter instrumental *þē* has had continuous adverbial use in English, as in "The sooner the better" and "He did not feel the worse for the experience."

In Old English *þes, þis,* and *þēos,* with their various inflectional forms, were exclusively demonstrative. They remained so in Middle English. By the thirteenth century, when gender distinction and some traces of inflection which had survived up to that time were lost, the singular nominative-accusative neuter *this* was used for all singular functions, and a new plural form, *thise* or *thēse,* the ending *-e* as in the plural of adjectives, appeared. These developments have resulted in Modern English *that–those* and *this–these*; the distinction between the singular forms seems currently in process of breaking down, with "This was right" displacing "That was right."

Thǫ ultimately gave way to *thǫs* (ModE *those*), from Old English *þās,* though the form with *-s* did not begin to become common in the

---

[33] Otto Jespersen, *A Modern English Grammar on Historical Principles* (Copenhagen, 1949), VII, 306–07, cites three instances in Shakespeare: *Othello* III.iii.66; *1 Henry VI* I.i.83; and *Lucrece,* l. 1588. For the first two of these, modern texts have *their*.

Midlands and the South until the late fifteenth century. Chaucer, for instance, uses only *thǫ* where we would use *those*. In the North *thās*, the form corresponding to *thǫs* elsewhere, began to appear in writing more than a century earlier.

INTERROGATIVE PRONOUNS

The Old English masculine-feminine interrogative pronoun *hwā* became in Middle English *whǫ*, and the neuter form *hwæt* became *what*. As with the other pronouns, the dative drove out the accusative (OE *hwone*) of the first of these, the dative *whǫm* (OE *hwām, hwæm*) being used in any objective function. *Hwæt* had the same dative form as *hwā* in Old English, but, as with other neuters, this was given up. The genitive of both *hwā* and *hwæt* was *hwæs*; in Middle English this took by analogy the vowel of *whǫ* and *whǫm*: thus *whǫs*.

It should be noted that *whǫ* was in Middle English customarily used only as an interrogative pronoun or an indefinite relative meaning 'whoever,' as in "Who steals my purse steals trash," a usage that occurs first in the thirteenth century. The simple relative use of *who* was not really widespread until the sixteenth century, though there are occasional instances of it as early as the late thirteenth century. The oblique forms *whǫs* and *whǫm*, however, were used as relatives in late Middle English, at about the same time that another interrogative pronoun, *which* (OE *hwylc*), also began to be so used, in reference to either persons or things. Sometimes *which* was followed by *that*, as in Chaucer's "Criseyde, which that felt hire thus i-take" that is 'Criseyde, who felt herself thus taken.'

RELATIVE PRONOUNS

The most frequently used relative pronoun in Middle English is indeclinable *that*. It is of course still so used, though modern literary style limits it to restrictive clauses: "The man that I saw was Jones," but "This man, who never did anyone any real harm, was nevertheless punished severely." A relative particle *þe* usually regarded as a survival of the Old English indeclinable relative-of-all-work occurs in early Middle English side by side with *that* (or *þat,* as it would have been written early in the period).

COMPARATIVE AND SUPERLATIVE FORMS

In the general leveling to *e* of unstressed vowels the Old English comparative ending -*ra* became -*re*, later -*er*, and the superlative suffixes -ost and -est fell together as -est. If the root vowel of an adjective was long, it was shortened before these endings, for example swēte, swetter, swettest, though the analogy of the positive form, as in the example cited, frequently caused the original length to be restored in the comparative and superlative forms; the doublets latter and later show respectively shortness and length of vowel. As in Old English, ēvel (and its Middle English synonym badde, of uncertain origin), gōd, muchel (mikel), and lītel had comparative and superlative forms unrelated to them etymologically: werse–werst, bettre, better–best, mǫre–mǫst, lesse, lasse–lęste. Some of the adjectives which in Old English had mutation in their comparative and superlative forms retained the mutated vowel in Middle English, for instance long–lengre, lenger–lengest, ǫld–eldre, elder–eldest. The simplification of the Old English adjective declensions has been already discussed in another connection (see pp. 152–53).

VERBS

Verbs continued to conform to the Germanic division into strong and weak, as they still do. Although the vowels of endings were leveled, the gradational distinctions expressed in the root vowels of the strong verbs were fully preserved. The tendency to use exclusively one or the other of the preterit vowel grades, however, had begun, though there was little consistency: the vowel of the older plural might be used in the singular, or vice versa. The older distinction (as in I sang, we sungen) was more likely to be retained in the Midlands and the South than in the North.[34]

In strong verbs of the first class, the vowel gradation was ī–ǫ–i–i: rīde(n) (infinitive)–rǫd (preterit singular)–riden (preterit plural)–(i)ride(n) (past participle), with perfectly regular development from Old English rīdan–rād–riden–(ge)riden. Examples of the other classes follow,[35] which should be compared with the Old English forms (see pp. 125–29):

[34] It should be remembered that in Old English the vowel of the first and third person singular of the preterit of strong verbs differed from that of the second person and of all plural forms: thus ic, hē sang, but þū sunge, wē, gē, hī sungon. See pp. 126 and 131.

[35] The forms cited are for the most part those which are the regular developments of the Old English forms. All are attested, but many other "irregular" ones are to be encountered in Middle English writings.

   II. crēpen–crẹ̄p–crupen–crǫpen[36]
  III. fīnden–fǫnd–foūnden–foūnden
      helpen–halp–hulpen–holpen
      fighten–faught–foughten–foughten
  IV. tẹ̄ren–tar–tēren–tǫren
   V. mẹ̄ten–mat–mēten–mẹ̄ten[37]
  VI. fāren–fōr–fōren–fāren
 VII. fallen–fẹ̄l–fēlen–fallen
     hǫten–hēt–hēten–hǫten

By analogy with the considerably larger group of weak verbs, a good many strong verbs in the course of the Middle English period acquired, side by side with their strong forms, dental-suffix preterits and past participles. These include (to take a single example from each class of strong verbs) glīden 'to glide,' crēpen 'to creep,' helpen 'to help,' shẹ̄ren 'to shear,' mẹ̄ten 'to mete,' āken 'to ache,' and wēpen 'to weep.' Ultimately the strong forms were lost altogether in these and other verbs.

THE PERSONAL ENDINGS

When the Old English endings -ast and -að which were characteristic of the second and third persons of the present indicative of those weak verbs which had infinitives in -ian not preceded by r (thus lufian, lufast, lufað) fell together with the endings -est and -eð of verbs with infinitives in -an, a historical distinction of form which was not worth making in the first place was broken down. When the Old English present indicative plural ending -að likewise became -eth, the distinction between plural and third person singular was also obliterated: Old English bereð and berað both end up as bẹ̄reth, a single form which continued to do double duty in the South of England. The Midland dialects,[38] however, substituted the -en of the plural sub-

---

[36] For the sake of consistency, infinitives and past participles will be cited with the -n which was ultimately lost in all infinitives, though retained in the past participial forms of some strong verbs. The initial i (y) of past participles is omitted, though its use in many parts of the country was, as in Old English, more or less general. See p. 164.

[37] Some verbs belonging originally to the fifth class moved up into the fourth by acquiring participles with ǭ, for example brẹ̄ken (OE brecan), spẹ̄ken (OE specan), wẹ̄ven (OE wefan).

[38] The forms were differentiated in the Southern dialects in those verbs which had -ien (OE -ian) in the infinitive: these retained the i of Old English -iað in the plural: thus singular -eth, plural -ieth.

junctive for the plural *-eth,* and thereby achieved a formal distinction in number at the expense of one in mood. In the Northumbrian dialect of Old English *-as* was somewhat more frequent as the present indicative plural ending, at least in the extant texts.[39] The development of this ending, *-es* (sometimes spelled *-is*), is characteristic of the Northern dialect of Middle English: thus *wē, yē, thai bēres* 'we, you, they bear.' The same ending is a Northern characteristic in the present indicative third person singular; this ending was in Modern English times to drive out the *-eth.* In Middle English times it had spread from the North into the Midland dialects, which show both *-es* and *-eth* in the third person and *-es* and *-e(n)* in the plural. Thus with *finden* 'to find' (strong) and *thanken* 'to thank' (weak) as models, the indicative forms were as follows in the Midland dialects:

PRESENT SINGULAR	PRESENT PLURAL (ALL PERSONS)
1. fīnde, thanke	fīnde(n)(-s), thanke(n)(-s)
2. fīndest, thankest	
3. fīndeth(-es), thanketh(-es)	

PRETERIT SINGULAR	PRETERIT PLURAL (ALL PERSONS)
1. 3. fǫnd, thanked(e)	fōunde(n), thanked(e)(n)
2. fōunde, thankedest	

The verbs *been* 'to be' (OE *bēon*), *doon* 'to do' (OE *dōn*), *willen* 'to want, will' (OE *willan*), and *gǫǫn* 'to go' (OE *gān*) remained highly irregular in Middle English. Typical Midland indicative forms of *been* and *willen* follow:

been: PRESENT SINGULAR	PRESENT PLURAL (ALL PERSONS)
1. am	bee(n), beeth, sinden, ār(e)n[40]
2. art, beest	
3. is, beeth	

PRETERIT SINGULAR	PRETERIT PLURAL (ALL PERSONS)
1. 3. was	wēre(n)
2. wast, wēre	

[39] A. Campbell, *Old English Grammar* (Oxford, 1959), p. 302.

[40] This form is comparatively rare in Middle English save in the North and in the West Midland. Chaucer seldom uses it.

willen: PRESENT SINGULAR	PRESENT PLURAL (ALL PERSONS)
1. 3. wil(le), wol(le)[41]	wilen, wol(n)
2. wilt, wolt	

PRETERIT SINGULAR	PRETERIT PLURAL (ALL PERSONS)
1. 3. wolde	wolde(n)
2. woldest	

Developments of the following Middle English forms of the preterit present verbs are still in frequent use: *o(u)ghte* 'owed, was under obligation to,' *can* 'knows how to, is able,' *cōūde* (ModE *could*)[42] 'knew how to, was able,' *shal* 'must,' *mōst(e)* (ModE *must*) 'was able to, must,' *may* 'am able to, may,' *mighte* (preterit of the preceding), *dar* (ModE *dare*), and *durst* (preterit of the preceding).

PARTICIPLES

The ending of the present participle varied from dialect to dialect, with *-and(e)* in the North, *-ende, -ing(e)* in the Midlands, and *-inde, -ing(e)* in the South. The *-ing* ending, which has prevailed in Modern English, is from the old verbal noun ending *-ung*, as in Old English *leornung* 'learning' (that is, knowledge), *bodung* 'preaching' (that is, sermon) from *leornian* 'to learn' and *bodian* 'to announce, preach.' Past participles might or might not have the initial inflection *i-* (*y-*), from Old English *ge-*; the prefix was lost in many parts of England, including the East Midland, but frequently occurred in the speech of London as this is reflected in the writings of Chaucer.

WORD ORDER

Although all possible variations in the order of subject, verb, and complement occur in extant Middle English literature, as in Old English literature, it must be remembered that much of this is verse, in which even today variations (inversions) of what is thought of as "normal" word order may occur. The prose of the Middle English period has much the same word order as Modern English prose. Sometimes a pronoun as object might precede the verb ("Yef þou me

---

[41] This late Midland form, with the vowel of the preterit, survives in *won't,* that is, *wol not.*

[42] The preterit of *can* (infinitive *cunnen*), this word later acquired an unetymological *l* by analogy with *would.*

zayst, 'How me hit ssel lyerny?' ich hit wyle þe zigge an haste . . . ,"
that is, word for word, 'If thou [to] me sayest, "How one it shall learn?"
I it will [to] thee say in haste . . . ,' or, in Modern English order, 'If
thou sayest to me, "How shall one learn it?" I will say it to thee in
haste . . .'). In subordinate clauses nouns used as objects might also
precede verbs ("And we, þet . . . habbeþ Cristendom underfonge . . . ,"
that is, 'And we, that have Christian salvation received . . .'). In the
frequently occurring impersonal constructions of Middle English the
indirect object regularly preceded the verb: *me mette* '(it) to me
dreamed,' that is, 'I dreamed'; *me thoughte* '(it) to me seemed.' *If you
please* is very likely a survival of this construction,[43] though the *you* is
now taken as nominative. Other than these, there are very few inversions that would be inconceivable in Modern English. Strange as parts
of the following passage in the Northern dialect may look to modern
eyes, it is possible to put it word for word into Modern English:[44]

Twa	lyves	þar	er	þat	cristen	men	lyfes:	ane	es
Two	*lives*	*there*	*are*	*that*	*Christian*	*men*	*live:*	*one*	*is*

called	actyve	lyfe,	for	it	es	mare	bodili	warke;
called	*active*	*life,*	*for*	*it*	*is*	*more*	*bodily*	*work;*

another,	contemplatyve	lyfe,	for	it	es	in	mare	swetnes
another,	*contemplative*	*life,*	*for*	*it*	*is*	*in*	*more*	*sweetness*

gastely.	Actife	lyfe	es	mykel	owteward	and	in	mare
spiritually.	*Active*	*life*	*is*	*much*	*outward*	*and*	*in*	*more*

travel,	and	in	mare	peryle	for	þe	temptacions	þat
travail,	*and*	*in*	*more*	*peril*	*for*	*the*	*temptations*	*that*

er	in	þe	worlde.	Contemplatyfe	lyfe	es	mykel	inwarde,
are	*in*	*the*	*world.*	*Contemplative*	*life*	*is*	*much*	*inward,*

and	forþi	it	es	lastandar	and	sykerar,
and	*therefore*	*it*	*is*	*more lasting*	*and*	*more secure,*

[43] Parallel to French *s'il vous plaît* and German *wenn es Ihnen gefällt,*
that is, 'if it please(s) you.'

[44] The passage is from *The Form of Living,* by Richard Rolle of Ham-
pole, a gentle mystic and an excellent prose writer, who died in 1349.

restfuller,   delitabiler,   luflyer, and mare
more restful, more delightful, lovelier, and more

medeful,   for it hase joy in goddes lufe and
full of reward, for it has joy in God's love and

savowre in þe lyf þat lastes ay   in þis present
savor in the life that lasts forever in this present

tyme if it be right   ledde. And þat   felyng of joy
time if it be rightly led.   And that feeling of joy

in þe lufe of Jhesu passes   al other merites in
in the love of Jesus surpasses all other merits on

erth, for it es swa harde to com to for þe freelte
earth, for it is so hard to come to for the frailty

of oure flesch and þe many temptacions þat we er
of our flesh and the many temptations that we are

umsett with þat lettes us nyght and day. Al other
set about with that hinder us night and day. All other

thynges er lyght at com to in regarde þarof, for
things are easy to come to in regard thereof, for

þat may na man deserve, bot anely it es gifen of
that may no man deserve, but only it is given of

goddes godenes til þam þat verrayli gifes þam
God's goodness to them that verily give them(selves)

to contemplacion and til quiete for cristes luf.
to contemplation and to quiet for Christ's love.

THE DECLINE OF FRENCH IN ENGLAND

It should be pointed out in closing that although for a long time after the Norman Conquest French was the language of the governing classes in England, there was never any period during which the majority of the country's population did not speak English. The loss of Normandy in 1204 by King John, a descendant of the Conqueror, removed an important tie with France, and subsequent events were to loosen those which remained. The Hundred Years' War, beginning in 1337, saw England and France bitter enemies in a long-drawn-out conflict—though it actually fell somewhat short of a hundred years—which gave the death blow to the already moribund use of French in England.[45] Those whose ancestors were Normans had come to think of themselves as Englishmen.

[45] For an admirable treatment of this whole state of affairs, see Albert C. Baugh, *A History of the English Language,* 2nd ed. (New York, 1957), Chapter 5, "The Norman Conquest and the Subjection of English, 1066–1200," and Chapter 6, "The Re-establishment of English, 1200–1500."

CHAPTER VII

The Modern English Period to 1800
Sounds and Spellings

THE fifteenth century, following the death of Chaucer, marks a turning point in the history of English, for during this period the language underwent greater, more important phonological changes than in any other century before or since. Despite these radical changes in pronunciation, the old spelling was maintained and, as it were, stereotyped. (This has already been pointed out: see pp. 41–42.) William Caxton, who died in 1491, and the printers who followed him based their spelling norm not on the pronunciation current in their day, but on the usage of the medieval manuscripts. Hence, though the quality of every single one of the long vowels had changed, the graphic representation of the newer values remained the same as it had been for the Middle English ones: for instance, though the [e:] of Middle English *feet, see, three,* and so forth, had been raised to [i:], all such words went on being written as if no change had taken place.

The influence of printers and that of men of learning—misguided though they frequently were—has been greater than any other on English spelling. The first are responsible for a further normalization of the older scribal practices. While it is true that early printed works exhibit a good many inconsistencies, they are nevertheless quite orderly as compared with the everyday writing·of the time.

A SPECIMEN OF ENGLISH IN 1525

The following paragraph is the chapter "Rosemary" from Banckes's *Herball,* a hodgepodge of botanical and medical lore and a good deal of sheer superstition thrown together and "imprynted by me Richard Banckes, dwellynge in London, a lytel fro yᵉ Stockes in yᵉ Pultry, yᵉ .xxv. day of Marche. The yere of our lorde .M.CCCCC. & xxv." The only known copies of this old "doctor book" are one in the British Museum and one in the Huntington Library in California. What became of the many other copies of the work, which went through at least fifteen editions, no man can say. It will be noted that *the* is sometimes printed yᵉ (actually, as was often the case, the *e,* considerably smaller than the *y,* is placed directly above it), sometimes *the.* The spelling yᵉ is also used three times for the form of the second person singular objective pronoun, *thee,* for which *the* is the usual spelling. The second person plural nominative form, if it occurred, would have been written *ye;* when the *e* was above the line, the *y* was always a makeshift for þ (see p. 31), and never to be interpreted as *y.* A line over a vowel (Banckes and a good many other printers actually used a tilde-like diacritic) indicates omission of a following *n* or *m,* as in *thē* for *them* and *thā* for *than.* This device is very ancient. Modern commas are used for the virgules of the original. As was the custom (see p. 33), *v* is used initially (*venymous, vnder*) and *u* elsewhere (*hurte, euyll*), regardless of whether consonant or vowel was to be indicated. Some of the final *e*'s are used for "justifying" lines of type—that is, making even right-hand margins—a most useful expedient before the days of the lintotype machine, when type had to be set by hand. The long *s,* used everywhere in the original save in final position, is not here represented.

ROSEMARY.

This herbe is hote and dry, take the flowres and put them in a lynen clothe, & so boyle them in fayre clene water to yᵉ halfe & coole it & drynke it, for it is moche worth agaynst all euylles in the body. Also take the flowres & make powder therof and bynde it to the ryght arme in a lynen clothe, and it shall make the lyght and mery. Also ete the flowres with hony fastynge with sowre breed and there shall ryse in the none euyll swellynges. Also take the flowres and put them in a chest amonge youre clothes or amonge bokes and moughtes [moths] shall not hurte them. Also boyle the flowres in gotes mylke & than let them stande all a nyght vnder the ayer fayre couered, after that gyue hym to drynke therof that hath the tysyke [phthisic] and it shall delyuer hym. Also boyle the leues in whyte wyne & wasshe thy face therwith, thy berde & thy browes and there shall no cornes growe out, but thou shall haue a fayre face. Also put the leues vnder thy beddes heed, & thou shalbe delyuered of all euyll dremes. Also breke yᵉ leues small to powder & laye them on a Canker & it shall slee it. Also take the leues & put thē into a vessel of wyne and it shall preserue yᵉ wyne fro tartnesse & euyl sauour, and yf thou sell that wyne, thou shall haue good lucke & spede [success] in the sale. Also yf thou be feble with vnkyndly [unnatural] swette, take and boyle the leues in clene water, & whan yᵉ water is colde do [put] therto as moche of whyte wyne, & than make therin soppes & ete thou well therof, & thou shal recouer appetyte. Also yf thou haue the flux boyle yᵉ leues in stronge Aysell [vinegar] & than bynde them in a lynē [c]lothe and bynde it to thy wombe [belly] & anone the flux shal withdrawe. Also yf thy legges be blowen with the goute, boyle the leues in water, & than take the leues & bynde them in a lynen clothe aboute thy legges, & it shall do yᵉ moche good. Also take the leues and boyle them in stronge Aysell & bynde them in a clothe to thy stomake, & it shall delyuer yᵉ of all euylles. Also yf thou haue the coughe, drynke the water of the leues boyled in whyte wyne, & thou shalbe hole. Also take the rynde of Rosemary & make powder therof and drynke it for the pose [cold in the head], & thou shalbe delyuered therof. Also take the tymbre therof & brūne [burn] it to coles & make powder therof & thā put it into a lynen cloth and rubbe thy tethe therwith, & yf there be ony wormes therin it shall slee them & kepe thy tethe from all euyls. Also make the a box of the wood and smell to it and it shall preserne[1] thy youthe. Also put therof in thy doores or in thy howse & thou shalbe without daunger of Adders and other venymous serpentes. Also make the a barell therof & drynke thou of the drynke that standeth therin & thou nedes to fere no poyson that shall hurte yᵉ, and yf thou set it in thy garden kepe it honestly [decently] for it is moche profytable. Also yf a mā haue lost his smellynge of the ayre or-elles he maye not drawe his brethe, make a fyre of the wood & bake his breed therwith & gyue it hym to ete & he shalbe hole.

THE GREAT VOWEL SHIFT

Comparison of the modern developments in parentheses in the chapter on Old English (p. 108) shows sufficiently clearly what are the modern representatives of the Old English long vowels. As has been pointed out, these changed only slightly in Middle English: [ɑ:], in Old English written *a*, as in *stān*, was rounded except in the Northern dialect to [ɔ:], in Middle English written *o(o)*, as in *stoon*. But this was really the only particularly noteworthy change in quality.[2] But by the end of what we think of as the Middle English period, or by the beginning of the Modern English period, all these long vowels had shifted:

[1] The printer has inadvertently turned the *u* which was in his copy, to make an *n*.

[2] There were, as we have seen, important changes in quantity when vowels in open syllables or before certain consonant combinations were lengthened. Two of these involved changes in quality. See p. 150.

ē, as in *sweete* 'sweet,' had already acquired the value [i:] which it currently has, and the others were well on their way to acquiring the values which they have in current English. In phonological terms, Middle English *ā, ę̄, ē, ǭ,* and *ō* were raised and fronted in their articulation, and the two highest front and back vowels, *ī* and *ū* respectively, became sounds traditionally referred to as diphthongs and in this book represented by two symbols as if they were indeed the same as diphthongs. The change, known as the Great Vowel Shift, has been alluded to on pp. 42–43.

Long *i*, as in Middle English *riden* 'to ride,' at first became [ii], and then went through successive slight changes, becoming in the fifteenth century [əi],[3] then [ʌɪ], with initial stress, in the course of the following century. This pronunciation survives in certain types of speech, particularly before voiceless consonants. It went on in most types of English to become at approximately the end of the eighteenth century [aɪ], though there are variations in pronunciation.

It was similar with Middle English *ū* as in *hous* 'house': it first became [ʊu], then [əu], then, with initial stress in the course of the sixteenth century, [ʌu]. This [ʌu], surviving in eastern Virginia and in some types of Canadian English, became [aʊ] at about the same time as [ʌɪ] became [aɪ].

Middle English [o:] as in *ro(o)te* 'root,' became [u:]. Shortening of this [u:] to [ʊ] has occurred in *foot, good, book, look, took,* and other words; in *flood* and *blood* there has been unrounding in addition to shortening, resulting in [ʌ] in these two words. The chronology of these subsequent shortenings and unroundings is difficult to establish, as is the distribution of the various developments. As Helge Kökeritz points out,[4] Shakespeare's riming of words which had Middle English long close *o* gives no clue to his pronunciation, for he rimes *food* with *good* and *flood, mood* with *blood, reprove* with *love* and *dove.* If these are not merely traditional rimes, we must conclude that the distribution of [u:], [ʊ], and [ʌ] was not in early Modern English the same as it is in current English, and there is indeed ample evidence that colloquial English did vacillate a good deal. This fact is not particularly surprising when we remember that there is at the present time a certain amount of wavering between [u:] and [ʊ] in

[3] [ii] and [əi] are to be interpreted as having stress on their final elements.

[4] *Shakespeare's Pronunciation* (New Haven, Conn., 1953), p. 236. For a most useful index of Shakespeare's rimes, see Appendix 3 of this work, pp. 399–495.

such words as *roof, broom, room,* and a few others. Pronunciation of *root* with the shortened vowel is fairly common in some types of American English. The development of Middle English [ɔ:] as in *hǫ(ǫ)m* 'home' presents no problem: the sound shifted to [o:] except for a few words in which it underwent very early shortening, for instance *hot* (ME *hǫ(ǫ)t*).

Late Middle English *ā* as in *name* and *ai* as in *nail* had been leveled as [a:] and subsequently went through the stages [æ:], [ɛ:], [e:]. The [e:] became normal in Standard English probably in the early years of the eighteenth century.[5]

Middle English [ɛ:] as in *heeth* 'heath' must have been retained by many speakers well into the seventeenth century, as Falstaff's *reason-raisin* pun of 1598 (*1 Henry IV* II.iv.264), cited on pp. 179–180, and many others indicate.[6] But there is also convincing evidence that [i:], the usual present English value, existed in words which in Middle English usually had [ɛ:] presupposing an early shift from [ɛ:] to [e:] in certain types of speech. Chaucer very occasionally rimes older close *ē* and open *ę̄*, indicating at least his familiarity with a pre-1400 raising of the open vowel. The usual early Modern vowel after about 1600 of words which typically had [ɛ:] in Middle English was [e:], which survives to the present day in *break, steak, great,* and a few others. Many rimes from the seventeenth and eighteenth centuries testify to this [e:] pronunciation in words which today have [i:], for instance Swift's "You'd swear that so divine a creature/Felt no necessities of nature" ("Strephon and Chloe"), in which the riming words are to be pronounced ['kre:tər] and ['ne:tər], and "You spoke a word began with H,/And I know whom you meant to teach" ("The Journal of a Modern Lady"), in which the riming words are [e:č] and [te:č].

The short vowels have remained relatively stable throughout the history of English. The most obvious changes affect Middle English

---

[5] It should always be borne in mind that all these pronunciations may have existed side by side, just as "retarded" and "advanced" pronunciations may and do exist in current English. Sound-changes occur gradually and more or less imperceptibly; and some speakers retain characteristics which, if they are noticed at all, are considered old-fashioned by younger-generation speakers (like *forehead* as ['fɑrid] in contrast to ['fɔrˌhɛd]; furthermore, developments proceed at different paces in different dialects.

[6] For example *abased–a beast, grace–grease–grass.* The fullest treatment of Shakespeare's puns is in Part II of Kökeritz' *Shakespeare's Pronunciation.*

short *a*, which shifted by way of [a] to [æ], and Middle English short *u*, which was unrounded from [ʊ] to [ʌ], though the older quality survives in a good many words in which the vowel was preceded by a labial consonant, especially if it was followed by *l*, for instance *bull*, *full*, *put* (but compare the variant *putt*), *pull*, and *bush*. It is evident that there was an unrounding of *o* [ɔ] to [ɑ], reflected in late sixteenth and in seventeenth-century spellings,[7] and in the most widespread American pronunciation of words which had short [ɔ] in Middle English (*God*, *stop*, *clock*, and so forth). This unrounding did not affect the language as a whole, but such doublets as *strop–strap* and *god–gad* remain to testify to its having occurred.[8] Short *e* has not changed, except occasionally before [ŋ], as in *string* and *wing* from Middle English *streng* and *wenge*, and short *i* remains what it has been since Germanic times.

The first element [ʊ] of a Middle English diphthong written *oi* (for *ui*), as in *poison, join,* and *boil,*[9] and occurring almost exclusively in words of French origin, underwent unrounding to [ʌ] along with other short *u*'s. The diphthong thus fell together with the development of Middle English *ī* as [ʌɪ], both subsequently becoming [aɪ], so that the verb *boil*, from Old French *boillir* (ultimately Lat. *bullīre*) and the etymologically quite distinct noun meaning 'inflamed, infected sore,' which is of native English origin (OE *bȳl*, occurring in Middle English as *bȳle* or *bīle*), have both become current nonstandard [baɪl]. Many rimes in our older poetry testify to this identity in pronunciation of the reflexes of Middle English *ī* and *ui*, for instance Pope's couplet "While expletives their feeble aid do join;/And ten low words oft creep in one dull line." The current Standard pronunciation of words spelled with *oi* for etymological *ui* is based upon the spelling. The folk, however, preserve the pronunciation with [aɪ].[10] The quite different Middle English diphthong spelled *oi* and pronounced [ɔɪ] is, as we have seen (p. 149), also of French origin, going

---

[7] H. C. Wyld, *A History of Modern Colloquial English*, 3rd ed. (New York, 1937), pp. 240–41, cites a number of examples of *a* for *o* in spellings, including Queen Elizabeth I's "I pray you stap the mouthes."

[8] The unrounded vowel was later advanced to [æ] in these words.

[9] As we have seen (p. 43), *o* was a symbol for *u* in Middle English.

[10] For the distribution of [aɪ] in *oi*-words in the eastern United States, see Hans Kurath and Raven I. McDavid, Jr., *The Pronunciation of English in the Atlantic States* (Ann Arbor, Mich., 1961), pp. 167–68 and maps No. 143–46.

back to Latin *au,* as in *joie* (ultimately Lat. *gaudia*) and *cloistre* (Lat. *claustrum*).

Similar Middle English diphthongs written *eu, ew, iu, iw,* and *u* (depending to some extent upon when they were written) merged into [ju:], which has tended to be reduced to [u:] in such words as *duty, Tuesday, music,* and *news.* The [j] has been retained after *b* (*beauty* as distinct from *booty*), *p* (*pew* as distinct from *pooh*), *m* (*mute* as distinct from *moot*), *g* (the second syllable of *argue* as distinct from *goo*), *k* (*c*) (*cute* as distinct from *coot*), *v* (*view* as distinct from the first syllable of *voodoo*), and *f* (*few* as distinct from *foo*). After [z] this [j] gave rise to a new single sound [ž] in *azure, pleasure,* and the like. Similarly the earlier medial and initial [sj] in *pressure, nation, sure,* and the like has become [š], though this was not a new sound, having occurred under other circumstances in Old English.

The shift of vowels, or in the case of some of the short vowels the shiftlessness, may be indicated thus in tabular and hence somewhat oversimplified form, with the current pronunciations shown being those most widespread in Standard English (the unrounded [ɑ] from Middle English *o* is not included) and with no indication of such changes as most speakers are not particularly conscious of, for instance the recently developed off-glides in words like *bait* and *boat,* which in early Modern English had simple [e:] and [o:]:

LATE MIDDLE ENGLISH	EARLY MODERN ENGLISH (after *ca.* 1500)	LATER ENGLISH (after *ca.* 1700)
a as in *that* [θat] ⟶	[æ]	
ā as in *name* ['na:mə] ⟶	[æ:] > [ɛ:] ⟶	[e:]
e as in *bed* [bɛd]		
ē as in *sweete* ['swe:tə] ⟶	[i:]	
ę̄ as in *greet* 'great' [grɛ:t] ⟶ (*ca.* 1600) [e:]		
i as in *in* [ɪn]		
ī as in *ride* ['ri:də] ⟶	[ʌɪ] ⟶	[aɪ]
o as in *on* [ɔn]		
ō as in *boote* 'boot' ['bo:tə] ⟶	[u:]	
ǭ as in *boot* 'boat' [bɔ:t] ⟶	[o:]	
u as in *but* [bʊt] ⟶	[ʌ]	
ū as in *hous* [hu:s] ⟶	[ʌʊ] ⟶	[aʊ]

The loss of final *e* [-ə] at the end of words is as widespread a change as the Great Vowel Shift. As we have seen, however, this wholesale apocopation had occurred by the end of the fourteenth century and hence can hardly be regarded as a modern change, though it is frequently so regarded, just as the leveling of all final vowels in inflectional syllables, frequently regarded as a Middle English change, actually began long before the date which is traditionally given for the beginning of the Middle English period (see pp. 108 and 151). From early Modern spellings, as well as from poetic meter, this tendency to lose an unstressed *-e* seems also to have affected *the*, as in *th'earth* and the like.

THE EARLY MODERN ENGLISH CONSONANTS

The consonants of English, like the short vowels, have been rather stable, though certain losses have occurred within the Modern English period. The velar fricative [x] spelled *gh* disappeared or under certain circumstances became [f] as early as the fifteenth century in all England south of the Humber, though there is evidence that as late as the latter part of the sixteenth century old-fashioned speakers and a few pedants still retained the sound,[11] or thought that it ought to be retained. In the final sequence *-mb*, the *b* had disappeared in pronunciation before the beginning of the Modern English period, so that it could be added after final *m* where it did not etymologically belong, for instance in *limb*. There was a similar tendency to reduce final *-nd*, as in *lawn*, from Middle English *laund*; confusion seems to have arisen, and a nonetymological *-d* has been added in *sound*[12] and *lend* (ME *soun* and *lene*), though in the latter word the excrescent *d* occurred long before the Modern English period. The *l* of Middle English preconsonantal *al* was lost after first becoming a vowel: thus Middle English *al* and *au* fell together as *au*, ultimately becoming [ɔ:] (as in *talk, walk*) except before *f, v,* and *m,* where it became [æ:] in such words as *half, salve,* and *psalm*. The *l* retained in the spelling of the cited words and others[13] has led to spelling pronunciations, particularly when it occurs before *m*; many speakers now pronounce the *l* except before *f,* and seem to more traditional speakers to be making a special effort to do so: a certain motor car known as the *Falcon* is everywhere, because of the pseudoliteracy upon which the present age

[11] Kökeritz, p. 306.

[12] The noun and verb; the adjective is quite another word, from Old English *gesund*.

[13] It has been restored from the Latin etymon in *falcon* (ME *faucon*, from Old French, in which the vocalization to [u] also occurred).

prides itself, called ['fælkən], though the spelling has as yet had little if any effect upon the pronunciation of the name of the American writer William Faulkner. Perhaps if the name had been written *Falconer*, which amounts to the same thing, the spelling pronunciation might in time have come to prevail. The *l* of *ol* was similarly lost before certain consonants by vocalization, as in *folk, yolk, Holmes,* and the like. As we have seen (p. 45), the *l* in *fault* and *vault* has been inserted. The older pronunciation of the first of these words is indicated by Swift's "O, let him not debase your thoughts,/Or name him but to tell his faults" ("Directions for Making a Birth-Day Song"). In French loan-words, *h,* because it is in the spelling, has gradually come to be pronounced (p. 35). Medieval spelling habits are, as we have seen, responsible for the *h* in *author, throne,* and other words which have been cited (p. 36). There was an early loss of [r] before sibilants, not to be confused with the much later loss (not really normal before the nineteenth century) before any consonant or before a pause: older *barse* 'fish' by such loss became *bass,* as *arse* became *ass* and *bust, nuss, fust* develop from *burst, nurse, first*; this was not, however, a widespread change. An early loss of [r] before *l* is indicated by such a word as *palsy* (ME *parlesie,* a variant of *paralisie* 'paralysis'). Just as *l* occasionally generates a svarabhakti vowel, as in *elm* ['ɛləm], *film* ['fɪləm], and *athlete* ['æθəlit], *r* has done likewise in the old form *alarum,* a variant of *alarm.* The final unstressed syllable *-ure* was pronounced [-ər], with preceding *t, d,* and *s* having the values [t], [d], and [s] or intervocalically [z], for instance in *nature* [-tər], *verdure* [-dər], *censure* [-sər], and *leisure* [-zər], until the nineteenth century, though Noah Webster's use of such pronunciations was considered rustic and old-fashioned by his more elegant contemporaries.[14] The older pronunciation is indicated by many rimes: to mine Dean Swift once more, "If this to clouds and stars will venture,/That creeps as far to reach the centre" ("Verses on Two Celebrated Modern Poets"). Webster was also opposed to assibilation in *fortune, virtue,* and the like, which he seems to have associated with fast living; he also equated *value* and *valley, tenure* and *tenor.* But these, like many of the pronunciations which he prescribed, were scorned by the proper Bostonians of his day. The initial sequences *gn-* (as in *gnaw*) and *kn-* (as in *know*) had lost their first elements by the early seventeenth century, as evidenced

---

[14] In his *Elementary Spelling Book* of 1843 he gave *gesture* and *jester* as homophones.

by the Shakespearean puns *knack–neck, knight–night,* and others cited by Kökeritz (p. 305). Final *-ing,* except in monosyllables like *sing* and *thing,* had long been practically universally pronounced [-ɪn]. According to H. C. Wyld, "this habit obtains in practically all Regional dialects of the South and South Midlands, and among large sections of speakers of Received Standard English."[15] The velarization of the *n* to [ŋ] began as a hypercorrect pronunciation in the first quarter of the nineteenth century and, still according to Wyld, "has now a vogue among the educated at least as wide as the more conservative one with *-n.*" Long before Wyld wrote these words, which would need some revision for British English today, the [-ɪn] pronunciation had come to be considered substandard in American speech, largely due to the crusade which teachers had conducted against it, though it continues to occur rather widely in unselfconscious speech on all social levels. Many spellings and rimes in our older literature testify to the orthodoxy of what is popularly called "dropping the *g,*"[16] for instance Swift's couplets "See then what mortals place their bliss in!/Next morn betimes the bride was missing" ("Phyllis") and the delicate "His jordan [chamber pot] stood in manner fitting/Between his legs, to spew or spit in"("Cassinus and Peter"). Inverse spellings such as Shakespeare's *cushings (cushions), javelings (javelins),* and *napking (napkin)*[17] tell the same story.

Quantitative changes in the Modern English period have been previously alluded to, such as the lengthening of an originally short vowel before a voiceless fricative (of [æ] as in *staff, glass,* and *path,* the resultant [æ:] in the late eighteenth century coming to be replaced by [ɑ:] in Standard British English; of [ɔ] as in *soft, lost,* and *cloth*) and before voiced velar stops, as in *dog* and *sag.*[18] The earlier shortening of [u:] to [ʊ] in *hood, good,* and so forth, has already been referred to in connection with the development of [o:] in the Great Vowel Shift. In *mother, brother, other,* and *smother,* all having originally long vowels, the shortening (with subsequent unrounding to [ʌ]) seems to be due to their disyllabicism, though disyllabic *father* and *rather,* with originally short vowels, have undergone lengthening, for what reason we

[15] *History of Modern Colloquial English,* p. 289.

[16] In phonological terms, using the dental [n] instead of the velar [ŋ], for there is of course no [g].

[17] Cited in Kökeritz, p. 314.

[18] Compare *dock* and *sack* with voiceless velar stops, where the lengthening has not occurred.

cannot be sure—quite contrary to the shortening which occurred in *lather* and *gather.*

STRESS

A good many words in early Modern English were stressed otherwise than they are in current speech. *Character, illustrate, concentrate, contemplate* were all stressed on their second syllables, and most polysyllabic words in *-able* and *-ible* had initial stress, frequently with secondary stress on their penultimate syllables, as in " 'Tis sweet and cómmendàble in your Nature Hamlet" (*Hamlet* I.ii.87). *Antique,* like *complete* and other words which now have final stress, had initial stress. But it is not always possible to come to a firm conclusion on the basis of verse, as the many instances of variant stress in Shakespeare's lines indicate.[19] It is likely that most of these variant stressings occurred in actual speech; it would be surprising if they had not, considering the variations which occur in current English.

PRONUNCIATION OF EARLY
MODERN ENGLISH

Our knowledge of early Modern English pronunciation comes from many sources. Fortunately not all gentlefolk knew how to spell in earlier days, which is to say that they did not know what have become in our own day conventional spellings, and were pretty much so even then, thanks to the printers. So they spelled phonetically, according to their lights. What is by modern standards a "misspelling," like *coat* for *court* or *crick* for *creek,* may tell us a good deal about the writer's pronunciation. A good many such writings have come down to us. H. C. Wyld in his *History of Modern Colloquial English* has used many memoirs, letters, diaries, and documents from this period as the basis for his conclusions concerning the pronunciation of early Modern English. Kökeritz relies somewhat more than Wyld on the grammars and spelling books that began to appear around the middle of the sixteenth century, which he considers "our most important sources of information" (p. 17) on the pronunciation of the English of Shakespeare's day—works such as John Hart's *An Orthographie* (1569) and *A Methode or Comfortable Beginning for All Unlearned* (1570), William Bullokar's *Booke at Large* (1580) and *Bref Grammar for English* (1586), Richard Mulcaster's *The First Part of the Elementarie*

---

[19] See Kökeritz, Appendix 2, pp. 392–98.

(1582), and, in the following century, Alexander Gill's *Logonomia Anglica* (1619; 2nd ed., 1621) and Charles Butler's *English Grammar* (1633; 2nd ed., 1634), which has a list of homophones in its "Index of Words Like and Unlike." These same works, with others, provide the basis for E. J. Dobson's two-volume *English Pronunciation: 1500–1700* (Oxford, 1957). There are special studies of these early Modern writers on language by Otto Jespersen (on Hart), Bror Danielsson (Hart), Helge Kökeritz (Hart and Gill), R. E. Zachrisson (Bullokar), along with general studies of early Modern English by Wilhelm Horn (*Historische neuenglische Grammatik*, 1908),[20] Eilert Ekwall (*Historische neuenglische Laut- und Formenlehre*, 3rd ed. [Berlin, 1956]), and Karl Luick (*Historische Grammatik der englischen Sprache* [Leipzig, 1914–40]). The first volume of Jespersen's *Modern English Grammar on Historical Principles* (Copenhagen, 1909) deals with early Modern English phonology and orthography. The use of word-play and rime has already been alluded to a number of times. Kökeritz makes extensive and most effective use of these in *Shakespeare's Pronunciation*, a work which has been cited a number of times heretofore. There is no dearth of evidence, though frequently what we have is difficult of interpretation.

The following passage from Shakespeare's *1 Henry IV* (II.iv.257–64) indicates in phonetic transcription a somewhat conservative pronunciation which was in all probability current in the south of England in the late sixteenth and early seventeenth centuries; the Prince, Poins, and Falstaff, who has just told a whopping lie, are speaking:

Prin[ce]	Why,	how	could'st	thou	know	these
	[(h)wʌɪ	hʌu	kuːdst	ðʌu	noː	ðiːz
	men	in	Kendall	Greene,	when	it	was
	mɛn	ɪn	'kɛndəl	griːn	(h)wɛn	ɪt	wæz
	so	darke,	thou	could'st	not	see	thy
	soː	dærk	ðʌu	kuːdst	nɔt	siː	ðʌɪ
	Hand?	Come,	tell	us	your	reason:	what
	hænd	kʊm	tɛl	ʊs	jʊr	'rɛːzən	(h)wæt

[20] Reissued as *Laut und Leben. Englische Lautgeschichte der neueren Zeit (1400–1950)*, rev. and ed. Martin Lehnert, 2 vols. (Berlin, 1954).

    say'st thou to this?
    sɛ:st ðʌu tə ðɪs

Poin[s]   Come, your reason Jack, your reason.
    kʊm jʊr 'rɛ:zən ǰæk jʊr 'rɛ:zən

Falst[aff]   What, upon compulsion? No: were I
    (h)wæt ə'pɔn kʊm'pʊlsɪən no: wɛr ʌɪ

    at the Strappado, or all the Racks in
    æt ðə stræ'pædo: ɔr ɔl ðə ræks ɪn

    the World, I would not tell you on
    ðə wʊrld ʌɪ wu:(l)d nɔt tɛl ju: ɔn

    compulsion.... If Reasons were as plentie
    kʊm'pʊlsɪən ɪf 'rɛ:zənz wɛr æz 'plɛntɪ

    as Black-berries, I would give no man
    æz 'blæk˳bɛrɪz ʌɪ wu:(l)d gɪv no: mæn

    a reason upon compulsion, I.
    ə 'rɛ:zən ə'pɔn kʊm'pʊlsɪən ʌɪ]

CHAPTER **VIII**

The Modern English
Period to 1800
Forms and Syntax

INFLECTIONAL and syntactical developments in early Modern English are important, if somewhat less spectacular than those which occurred in the sound system. As we have seen, by the end of the Middle English period *-es* had been extended to practically all nouns as a genitive singular and caseless plural suffix. The handful of mutated-vowel plurals for the most part resisted the analogical principle, so that *geese, feet, teeth, mice, lice, men,* and *women*[1] have survived to the present and show no tendency to give way to plurals in *-s*. A few plurals in *-n* remained in early Modern English, including *eyen* 'eyes,' *shoon* 'shoes,' *kine* 'cows' (with mutation plus analogical *-n*), *oxen, children,* and *brethren.* Of these, *kine* continues to eke out a precarious existence as an archaic poetic word, and *brethren* has a very limited currency, being confined in serious use to certain religious groups. As with *kine,* the *n* is an accretion in *brethren*[2] and *children,* added by analogy with other plurals in *-n.* The regularly developed *ky* and *childer,* going back respectively to Old English *cȳ* and *cildru,* are current in dialect speech, or were so until fairly recently, in the North of England and in Scotland. *Oxen* is thus the only "pure" survival of the Old English weak declension, which formed its nominative-accusative plural (as well as all non-nominative forms of the singular) with the suffix *-an* (see p. 114).

[1] But see p. 115, n. 24, concerning this word.

[2] The development of this form is too complex to go into here, but it should be pointed out again that the mutated vowel did not occur in the Old English plural (*brōðor* or *brōðru* in the nominative-accusative) any more than did the *n.*

Unchanged plurals survive from Old and Middle English times to the present in *deer, sheep, swine, folk,* and *kind.* Analogical *folks* occurred very early in the Modern English period. Despite the precedent of its use by many distinguished writers in "these (those, all) kind of,"[3] *kind* has acquired a new plural in *-s* because of the feeling that the older construction was a "grammatical error." Its synonym *sort,* which is not of Old English origin, acquired as early as the sixteenth century by analogy with *kind* an unchanged plural, as in "these (those, all) sort of,"[4] but this construction also is frowned upon by most writers of school grammars. Doubtless by analogy with singular-plural *deer, sheep,* and the like,[5] the names of other creatures which had *-s* plurals in earlier times came to have unchanged plurals, for example *fish* and *fowl,* particularly when these are regarded as game.[6] The unchanged plural may be extended to the names of quite un-English beasts, like *buffalo* ("a herd of buffalo") and *antelope.*[7]

THE HIS-*GENITIVE*

The use of *his* (and presumably of *her* as well) as a sign of the genitive began in Old English times, but had its widest currency in the sixteenth and seventeenth centuries, as in Shakespeare's "And art not thou Poines, his Brother?" (*2 Henry IV* II.iv.308) and, in the "Prayer for All Conditions of Men" in the 1662 Book of Common

---

[3] Including Shakespeare, Sidney, Dryden, Swift, Goldsmith, and Jane Austen.

[4] Jespersen (*A Modern English Grammar on Historical Principles* [Copenhagen, 1914], II, 68) cites its occurrence in the writings of Swift, Fielding, Austen, Dickens, Trollope, Meredith, Wells, and others. There are additional examples in the *OED.*

[5] *Horse* retained its historical unchanged plural, as in Chaucer's "His hors were goode . . ." (*Canterbury Tales,* General Prologue, line 74) and Shakespeare's "Come on, then, horse and chariots let us have" (*Titus Andronicus* II.ii.18), surviving until the seventeenth century, though the analogical plural *horses* had begun to occur as early as the thirteenth.

[6] The barnyard creatures take the *-s* (*fowls, ducks, pigs,* and so forth), and Jesus Christ, it will be remembered, distributed to the multitude "a few little *fishes*" (Matt. xv.34). But one shoots (wild) *fowl* and (wild) *duck,* hunts *pig* (that is, wild boars), and catches *fish.*

[7] Jespersen, *Modern English Grammar,* II, 53, quotes from a newspaper dispatch of 1906 as follows: "The gift by the Government of Nepal . . . consists of two *nilgai,* . . . three *sambhar,* two *ogrial,* . . . three *bhurrel,* two *thar.* . . ."

Prayer, "And this we beg for Jesus Christ his sake." The historical genitive ending in *-s* was doubtless regarded by many as having originated in, or as being a corruption of, *his*. H. C. Wyld's explanation of the *his*-genitive as being due to the confusion of the unstressed form of *his*—that is, without [h], as in "He lost 'is hat"—with the *-is, -ys*[8] endings of the genitive in Middle English is very attractive,[9] though one is troubled by the fact that *her* in this construction occurs in writing about a century before *his*, which of course does not necessarily mean that it is of prior origin. The phonetic explanation will not serve for *her* (OE *hire*), though if we assume that *his* did actually occur first in the construction *her* could well be an extension of the *his*-genitive.[10] *Their* in the same construction would seem almost unquestionably to be an extension of *his* and *her*, as in Pepys's reference to "The House of Lords their proceedings in petitioning the King" (*OED* citation). It should be said that *his* (*is, ys*) has been much more common than *her* in this construction, being often used after feminine nouns: Wyld cites "her Grace is requeste" (that is, 'her Grace's request') and "My moder ys sake" ('my mother's sake') among other instances of the feminine use (p. 315). The construction has survived in printed bookplates: "John Smith His Book."

THE GROUP-GENITIVE

The group-genitive construction, as in "King Priam of Troy's son" and "The Wife of Bath's Tale," is a development of the early Modern English period. Though there are sporadic occurrences in Middle English, the usual older idiom is illustrated by Chaucer's "the kyng Priamus sone of Troye" and "The Wyves Tale of Bathe." What has happened is that a word group—usually, as in these examples, two nouns connected by a preposition—has come to be regarded as a unit; the sign of the genitive is thus affixed to the last word of what is in fact a phrase. The construction also occurs with a pronoun plus *else*, as in *everybody else's*, and with nouns connected by a coordinating conjunction, as in "Kenyon and Knott's *Pronouncing Dictionary*" and

---

[8] Northern variants of *-es*.

[9] *A History of Modern Colloquial English*, 3rd ed. (New York, 1937), pp. 314–15. See also Jespersen's *Modern English Grammar*, VI, 301–02.

[10] It is also possible that the sentence from King Alfred's translation of Orosius, cited in the *OED*, is to be regarded as a nonce usage: "Nilus seo ea hire æwielme is neh þæm clife," that is, 'Nile the river her source is near the cliff.'

an hour or two's time. There are comparatively few literary examples of clauses so treated, but in everyday speech such constructions as *the little boy that lives down the street's dog* do occur.[11]

THE UNINFLECTED GENITIVE

In early Modern English uninflected genitives occur in some nouns which were feminine in Old English, in nouns in *-r* denoting family relationships (see pp. 115–16), and occasionally in nouns ending in [-s] or preceding words beginning in [s-], for example *for conscience sake* and *for God sake.* A few uninflected genitives, though not generally recognized as such, survive to the present day in reference to the Virgin Mary, for example *Lady Day* (that is, Our Lady's Day 'Feast of the Annunciation'), *Lady Chapel* (Our Lady's Chapel), and *lady-bird* (Our Lady's bird).

ADJECTIVES AND ADVERBS

As for the adjective, with general loss of [-ə] in pronunciation, though the letter *e* which symbolized it might be retained in spelling as "silent *e*"[12] and even extended to words which in Middle English did not have it, the distinction between strong and weak adjective forms, already greatly simplified by the Middle English loss of final *n*, was completely lost. The Modern English adjective thus came to be invariable in form regardless of number or of what preceded it.[13]

Adjectives and adverbs continued to form comparatives in *-er* and superlatives in *-est*, along with the analytical formations with *mo, more,* and *most* which had occurred as early as Old English times. The present stylistic objection to affixing the endings to polysyllables had somewhat less force in the early Modern English period, when forms like *eminenter, impudentest,* and *beautifullest* are not particu-

---

[11] "He is the woman who is the best friend this club has ever had's husband" is an extreme example which I seem to have heard from Gracie Allen; at any rate, it is perfectly in keeping with the lovable birdbrained character which she created professionally.

[12] It should always be borne in mind that, whereas in Middle English *-e* after a single consonant indicated length, with the shifting of all the long vowels in Modern English it came to indicate the quality rather than the quantity of the preceding vowel, as in *mad* and *made.* It may sometimes perform the same function after a consonant sequence, as in *past* and *paste.*

[13] For the situation in Middle English, see pp. 152–53.

larly hard to find, nor, for that matter, are monosyllables with *more* and *most*, like *more near, more fast, most poor,* and *most foul.* As was true in earlier times also, a good many instances of double constructions like *more fitter, more better, more fairer, most worst, most stillest,* and (probably the best-known example) *most unkindest* occur in early Modern English.

Many adverbs which now must end in *-ly* did not require the inflection in early Modern English times. The works of Shakespeare furnish many typical examples: *grievous sick, indifferent cold, wondrous strange,* and *passing* ['surpassingly'] *fair.* Note also the use of *sure* in the following citations, which would nowadays be condemned as "bad English" in the schools: "If she come in, shee'l sure speake to my wife" (*Othello* V.ii.96); "And sure deare friends my thankes are too deare a halfepeny" (*Hamlet* II.ii.282); "Sure the Gods doe this yeere connive at us" (*Winter's Tale* IV.iv.692).

PERSONAL PRONOUNS

Rather important changes are to be noted in the pronouns. In the personal ones the historical forms of the first person remained as *I,*[14] *me,* and *mine* and *my,* with the old distinction between the *n*-less form of the possessive and the older form with *n* being for a long time maintained as it had been in Middle English from the thirteenth century on—that is, *mine* before a vowel or *h,* and *my* before consonants. This distinction continued to be made down to the eighteenth century, when *my* came to be the only regular first person possessive modifier. The Fool's *nuncle* in *King Lear* is due to his misunderstanding of *mine uncle* as *my nuncle,* and it is likely that *Ned, Nelly,* and *Noll* (a nickname usually associated with Oliver Goldsmith) have the same origin from *mine Edward, mine Eleanor, mine Oliver.*[15] The form with *n* has continued in use as a predicate adjective, in the *of*-possessive construction, and when the word which it modifies is not stated but must be inferred—in other words, precisely as the "double possessives"

[14] Capitalized not through any egotism, but only because lower-case *i* standing alone looks so utterly insignificant.

[15] Similarly with *a newt* (ME *an ewte*) and *a nickname* (ME *an ekename* 'an also-name'), where the *n* of the indefinite article has attached itself to a following word. In *umpire* (ME *noumpere*), *adder* (ME *nadder,* compare Ger. *Natter* 'snake'), *auger* (ME *nauger*), and *apron* (ME *napron,* compare *napkin, napery*) just the opposite has happened: the *n* of the noun has attached itself to the article.

hers, ours, yours, and *theirs* have been used since late Middle English times (see p. 159).

The second person singular forms were nominative *thou,* objective *thee,* and possessive *thine* and *thy.* The situation with the possessive forms was precisely the same as that which has been described for *mine* and *my.* As early as the late thirteenth century, the second person plural forms (*ye, you, your*) began to be used with singular meaning in the so-called polite plural, though it might be better to call the construction a "polite singular."[16] In imitation of the French use of *tu* and *vous,* the English historical plural forms were used in addressing a superior, whether by virtue of social status or age, and in upper-class circles among equals, though high-born lovers might slip into the *th*-forms in situations of intimacy. In losing this distinction English has obviously lost a useful literary device. Even when the two forms were available for choosing, however, the English did not always use them as consistently as the French. There is frequently no apparent reason for their interchange, as in the dialogue between two servants in *The Taming of the Shrew* IV.i.101–04:

> Cur[*tis*]   Doe you heare ho? you must meete my maister to
>   countenance my mistris.
> Gru[*mio*] Why she hath a face of her owne.
> Cur[*tis*]   Who knowes not that?
> Gru[*mio*] Thou it seemes. . . .

Frequently, however, our older writers use the forms with artistic discrimination, as in *Hamlet* III.iv.9–21:

> Qu[*een*]   Hamlet, thou hast thy Father much offended.
> Ham[*let*] Mother, you have my Father much offended.
> Qu[*een*]   Come, come, you answer with an idle tongue.
>
>   .   .   .   .   .
>
> Qu[*een*]   What wilt thou do? thou wilt not murther me?

This passage is cited by W. Franz,[17] who points out that the Queen's *thou* in "What wilt thou do?" is an expression of strong emotion. In addition, it might be pointed out that her first "Hamlet, thou hast

---

[16] The distinction is retained in other languages, which may even have a verb meaning 'to use the singular form,' for example French *tutoyer,* Spanish *tutear,* Italian *tuizzare,* German *dutzen.* Late Middle English had *thoute,* with the same meaning.

[17] *Shakespeare-Grammatik,* 2nd ed. (Heidelberg, 1909), p. 256.

thy Father much offended" is tender and affectionate. Hamlet's "Mother, you have . . ." is indicative of an attitude of cold dignity; there is even more than a hint of a rebuff in his choice of the more formal pronoun, and the Queen accepts it in effect by her "Come, come, your answer. . . ." It is similar with her passionate "Oh Hamlet, thou hast cleft my heart in twaine" and Hamlet's consistent use of *you* in his response: "Assume a Vertue, if you have it not. . . . Ile blessing begge of you." Elsewhere also Shakespeare chooses the *y*-forms and the *th*-forms with artistic care.

The *th*-forms of the second person singular, which had become quite rare in upper-class speech by the sixteenth century, were completely lost in Standard English in the eighteenth, though they lingered on in the dialects. Our familiarity with them today is largely due to their occurrence in poetry, in the King James Bible, and in the Book of Common Prayer. When people pray extempore, however, God is usually addressed and referred to by these forms. But for a mere mortal, the *y*-form must be used; grammatically, he must be regarded as if he were two or more mortals. A few elderly Quakers doubtless still use *thee* for both the nominative and the objective functions.

The third person singular masculine pronoun has been relatively stable since late Old English times, when the dative *him* took over all objective functions. The unstressed form of *he* was often written *a*, as in "Now might I doe it, but now a is a-praying,/And now Ile doo't, and so a goes to heauen" from the Second Quarto of *Hamlet* III.iii. 73–74 (the Folio has *he* in both instances). In the feminine, *she* and *her(s)* show no change since Middle English times. In the neuter, however, an important change took place in the latter part of the sixteenth century, when the new possessive form *its* arose. The predominant subject form was the restressed *it*,[18] and, by analogy with other genitives in *'s* the newer form (at first written *it's*, as many unstylish people still write it) began to be used instead of *his*, which nevertheless remained the usual form in the early years of the seventeenth century, as in Shakespeare's *Troilus and Cressida* II.ii. 53–54: "But value dwels not in particular will,/It holds his estimate and dignitie. . . ." The *OED* cites an interesting American example from 1634: "Boston is two miles North-east from Roxberry: His situation is very pleasant."

---

[18] That is, older *hit* lost its *h-* when unstressed; then the *h*-less form came to be used in stressed as well as unstressed positions—though, as has already been pointed out, *hit,* the form preferred by Queen Elizabeth I, remains in nonstandard speech as a stressed form.

Perhaps because of its ambiguity, *his* was nevertheless to some extent avoided as a neuter possessive even in Middle English times: an uninflected *it* occurs from the fourteenth to the seventeenth century, and to this day in British dialectal usage. The latest citation by the *OED* of its occurrence in Standard English is from 1622: "Each part as faire doth show/In it kind, as white in Snow." *Its* is quite rare in Shakespeare and occurs only twice in Milton's *Paradise Lost*[19]; but by the end of the seventeenth century *its* had become the usual form, completely displacing *his* and the less frequent *it* as a neuter possessive.

Similar to the use of the second person plural form to refer to a single person is the "regal *we*," except that here a sense of one's own importance rather than that of someone else is implied. It is still used in proclamations by a sovereign, and in earlier times, if we can judge by the older drama, it was even used in conversation. The usage is very ancient. Queen Victoria is said to have been the last monarch in Europe to employ it as a spoken form, as in her famous, but doubtless apocryphal reproof to one of her maids of honour who had told a mildly improper story: "We are not amused." The "editorial *we*" dates from Old English times. It is sometimes used by one who is a member of a staff of writers who are assumed to share the opinions he is expressing. It may also be used to include one's readers in such phrases as "as we have seen."

In the second person plural, which became singular also, as we have just seen, by the gradual loss of the *th-* singular forms, the old distinction between the nominative *ye* and the objective *you*, though still maintained in the King James Bible,[20] was generally lost during the sixteenth century. Some writers make the distinction, some do not.[21] In time it was the objective form which prevailed to such an extent as to drive *ye* from Standard English. Nonstandard speech distinguishes singular and plural *you* in a number of ways, for example, the analogical *youse* of the "underprivileged" city dweller (also cur-

[19] Jespersen, *Modern English Grammar,* VII, 308.

[20] For example: "The Lord deal kindly with you, as ye have dealt with the dead, and with me. The Lord grant you that ye may find rest. . . ." (Ruth i.8–9)

[21] According to Wyld, *History of Modern Colloquial English,* p. 330, the two forms are carefully distinguished by Sir Thomas More and Lord Berners, whereas Bishop Latimer, Ascham, Cavendish, and Lyly (in *Euphues*) "use both forms indifferently for the Nom[inative]," and Queen Elizabeth I seems to have employed only *you* for both functions.

rent in Irish English) and the *you-all* and *you-uns* (that is, you ones) which probably stem from Scots English. From the latter seventeenth century and throughout the eighteenth many speakers made a distinction between singular *you was* and plural *you were*. James Boswell uses singular *you was* throughout his *London Journal* (1762–63),[22] and even reports it as coming from the lips of Dr. Johnson: "Indeed, when you was in the irreligious way, I should not have been pleased with you" (July 28, 1763).[23] *You was* was very common in cultivated American usage also: George Philip Krapp cites its use by John Adams in a letter of condolence to a friend whose house had burned down: "You regret your loss; but why? Was you fond of seeing or thinking that others saw and admired so stately a pile?"[24] The construction became unfashionable in the early nineteenth century, but Noah Webster continued to defend it.[25]

In the third person plural the native *h*-forms had become all but archaic by the end of the fifteenth century, in the course of which the *th*-forms current in present English gradually took over. The only *h*-form to survive is that earlier written *hem*, and it survives only as an unstressed form; when it is written at all nowadays, it is written *'em*. The plural possessives in *h*- (*here, her, hir*) occurred only very rarely after the beginning of the sixteenth century (but see p. 159).

RELATIVE AND INTERROGATIVE PRONOUNS

We have noted that the usual Old English relative particle was *þe*, which, since it had only one form, would have continued to do very well. It is rather a pity that it was ever lost. Middle English adapted

[22] But in the second edition of his *Life of Johnson* he changed over to *you were* for both singular and plural.

[23] He also reports it from Lord Eglinton and the Honourable Andrew Erskine, who must be presumed to have spoken Standard English. See Esther K. Sheldon, "On Boswell's English in the *London Journal*," *PMLA*, LXXI (1956), 1072, for a review of the status of the construction in Boswell's day: Bishop Lowth (see pp. 14 and 214–16) in his very influential *Short Introduction to English Grammar* (1762) had condemned it in no uncertain terms as "an enormous Solecism," but George Campbell testified in his *Philosophy of Rhetoric* (1776) that "it is ten times oftener heard."

[24] *The English Language in America* (New York, 1925), II, 261.

[25] There were two reasons why Webster should have approved *you was*: it was no longer much used by people of fashion, who merited his hatred by having rejected him as a belligerent though "learned" bumpkin; and it appealed to his sense of logic, order, and reason—for he was essentially a child of the Age of Reason—to have distinctive singular and plural forms.

the neuter demonstrative pronoun *that*, without inflection, for the same relative function, later adding the previously interrogative *which*, sometimes preceded by *the*, and likewise uninflected. It was not until the sixteenth century that the originally interrogative *who* (OE *hwā*), which had already been put to use as an indefinite relative,[26] came to be at all commonly used as a simple relative to refer to persons. The King James Bible, which we should expect to be in its grammar a little behind the times,[27] has *which* where we should today use *who*, as in "The kingdom of heaven is likened unto a man which sowed good seed in his field" (Matt. xiii.24) and, as everyone knows, in "Our Father which art in heaven." Shakespeare, who with all his daring as a coiner and user of words was essentially conservative in his grammar, also uses *which* in the older fashion to refer to persons and things alike, as in "he which hath your Noble Father slaine" (*Hamlet* IV.vii.4).

THE INFLUENCE OF THE SCHOOLMASTER

In the freewheeling aristocratic usage of earlier days—as in that of the learned and the literary men who looked to a courtly society for their standards—there was not so much concern as now with what are conceived to be "proper" choices of case forms. English had to wait until the latter years of the seventeenth century for the rise of the schoolmaster's attitude towards language which was to become predominant in the eighteenth century and is still so—a relatively new thing, be it noted, which has given us a codified set of rules, some of them based on an arbitrary appeal to logic and "reason," but having very little relevance to older usage. After a coordinating conjunction, for instance, the subjective form tended to occur invariably, as indeed it yet does,[28] whether it is object of verb or preposition or second

[26] That is, as the equivalent of present *who(m)ever*, as in Shakespeare's "Who tels me true, though in his Tale lye death,/I heare him as he flatter'd" (*Antony and Cleopatra* I.ii.102–03) and Lord Byron's "Whom the gods love die young" (*Don Juan*, IV,12).

[27] It was the work of almost fifty theological scholars designated by James I, and afterwards reviewed by the bishops and other eminent scholars. It is not surprising that these men should have been little given to anything that smacked of innovation.

[28] See the queen's "for my husband and I" and former President Eisenhower's "for Mrs. Eisenhower and I," p. 231, n. 34. The difference between former times and now is that when uttered publicly or printed (as it rarely would be), the construction nowadays invariably gives rise to disapproving comment of the "What is the English language coming to?" variety.

element of a compound subject. H. C. Wyld cites "with you and I" from a letter by Sir John Suckling, as well as two seventeenth-century occurrences of "between you and I,"[29] to which may be added Shakespeare's "all debts are cleerd betweene you and I" (Merchant of Venice III.ii.321). Jespersen cites the usage in question (that is, after between) from Congreve, Defoe, and Fielding, along with a few examples from our own day.[30] There is of course no doubt that at the present time the desire to be "correct" causes many speakers who may have been reproved as children for saying "Mary and me went downtown" to use "Mary and I" under all circumstances; but "hypercorrectness" is hardly a satisfactory explanation for the phenomenon as it occurs in the writings of well-bred people from the sixteenth to the early eighteenth centuries, a period during which people of consequence talked pretty much as they pleased and others less fortunately placed followed their example. After other prepositions Jespersen cites equally distinguished precedent for I, as well as for its use as object, direct or indirect, of a verb. It is not only the first person, however, for which the nominative form occurs after and regardless of school grammar; there seems to be a widespread preference for the nominative form of any personal pronoun after this conjunction, though in the nature of things the first person would be most likely to occur.

School grammar requires the nominative form after as and than in such sentences as "Is she as tall as me?" (Antony and Cleopatra III.iii.14). Boswell, who wrote in a period in which men of strong minds and characters were attempting to "regularize" the English language, shows no particular pattern of consistency in this construction. In the entry in his London Journal for June 5, 1763, he writes "I was much stronger than her," but elsewhere used the nominative form in the same construction.[31]

In early Modern English the historical nominative and objective

---

[29] History of Modern Colloquial English, p. 332.

[30] Modern English Grammar, VII, 273.

[31] As Esther K. Sheldon points out in the article cited above in n. 23, the grammarians of Boswell's day were not in agreement on this particular matter: some demanded the "same case [after than and as] as before"; others wanted than and as regarded as prepositions, and would thus require the objective form of the pronoun to be used consistently; still others thought the choice of case form should be determined by expanding the construction, as in "I was much stronger than she (is strong)"; "You do not know him as well as (you know) me." The last is the rule laid down by present-day prescriptive grammarians.

forms of the personal pronouns, particularly of the first person singular, tend to occur more or less indiscriminately after the verb *be*. In *Twelfth Night*, for instance, Sir Andrew Aguecheek, who, though a fool, is yet a gentleman, uses both forms within a few lines: "That's mee I warrant you. . . . I knew 'twas I" (II.v.87–89). The generally inconsistent state of things before the prescriptive grammarians took over is exemplified by Shakespeare's usage elsewhere with other pronouns: "I am not thee" (*Timon of Athens* IV.iii.277); "you are not he" (*Love's Labour's Lost* V.ii.550); "And damn'd be him, that first cries hold, enough"[32] (*Macbeth* V.viii.34); "you are she" (*Twelfth Night* V.i.334). Instances of *her, us,* and *them* in this construction are infrequent in early Modern English writings. "Here's them" occurs in *Pericles* II.i.67, but the speaker is a fisherman.

Today also the objective form of personal pronouns continues to occur after *be*, though not without bringing down upon the head of the user the thunder of those who regard themselves as guardians of the language. There are nevertheless a great many speakers of Standard English who do not care and who would say "It's me" if there were occasion to do so[33] despite the school doctrine that "the verb *to be* can never take an object." There is little point in labeling the construction colloquial or informal as contrasted with a supposedly formal "It is I," inasmuch as the utterance would not be likely to occur in any but a conversational environment.

The tendency to use an objective pronominal form after a verb and a subjective form before one is of course due to the structure of Modern English. Every native speaker has a certain "feel" for the subject-verb-complement word order which characterizes most of our statements, the complement usually being an object rather than a so-called predicate nominative. The tendency to frame our utterances in this order is indeed so powerful that when for stylistic reasons we choose to put before the verb a pronoun which is its object—as in "Him I detest"—it goes a little against the grain: despite our con-

---

[32] Pope and other later editors emend this to "damn'd be he." *He* is usual after *be*. Jespersen believes that *damn'd be* is here the equivalent of a single word and governs the same case as (*God*)*damn* (*Progress in Language, with Special Reference to English*, 2nd ed., London, 1909, p. 239).

[33] There seldom is, for one would usually say one's name rather than use a pronoun. As for the uncontracted form "It is me (I)," frequently cited in handbooks, it is difficult to imagine any circumstances in which it would be likely to occur.

sciousness of the principles governing case, we feel a "pull" toward *he* in this position. "Ham I detest" presents no such problem.

The "proper" choice between *who* and *whom*, whether interrogative or relative, frequently involves an intellectual chore that many speakers from about 1500 on have been little concerned with. The interrogative pronoun, coming as it usually does before the verb, tended in early Modern English to be invariably *who,* as it still does in unself-conscious speech. One could cite from the most distinguished writers scores[34] of examples of *who* as the object of a verb or of a preposition (particularly if the preposition is placed last) from the Middle English period on, though because of the emphasis of the schools on the supposed importance of using *whom* in these functions, current printed examples are harder to find than early Modern English ones. Jespersen cites interrogative *who* as object before the verb from Marlowe, Greene, Ben Jonson, the old *Spectator* of Addison and Steele, Goldsmith, and Sheridan, with later examples from Thackeray, Mrs. Humphrey Ward, and Shaw. Schmidt's *Shakespeare-Lexicon* furnishes fifteen quotations for interrogative *who* in this construction, and then adds an *etc.,* though, as Jespersen points out, "Most modern editors and reprinters add the -*m* everywhere in accordance with the rules of 'orthodox' grammar."[35]

Relative *who* as object of verb or preposition is hardly less frequent. For Shakespeare, Schmidt uses the label *etc.* after citing a dozen instances, and Jespersen cites from a few other authors. The *OED,* along with its statement that *whom* is no longer current in natural colloquial speech, cites Lord Berners and Edmund Spenser, among others. It should be noted, however, that there are a good many instances of *whom* for the nominative, especially where the relative may be taken as the object of the verb of the principal clause, as in Matthew xvi.13: "Whom do men say that I the Son of man am?"[36]

[34] Jespersen (*Modern English Grammar,* VII, 241) is probably not exaggerating when he says "hundreds."

[35] *Modern English Grammar,* VII, 242. Compare his earlier and somewhat bitter statement that they show thereby "that they hold in greater awe the schoolmasters of their own childhood than the poet of all the ages" (*Progress in Language,* p. 216). It is an amusing irony that *whom*-sleuths, imagining that they are great traditionalists, are actually adhering to a fairly recent standard as far as the period from the fifteenth century on is concerned. In view of the facts, such a sentence as "Who are you waiting for?" can hardly be considered untraditional.

[36] Also in verse 15: "But whom say ye that I am?" Both the Tindale

Shakespeare's "Whom in constancie you thinke stands so safe" (*Cymbeline* I.iv.138) and "Yong Ferdinand (whom they suppose is droun'd)" (*Tempest* III.iii.92) would be condemned by all prescriptive grammarians nowadays; but in Shakespeare's usage, which may in this respect as in all others be taken as representative of early Modern English, such constructions stand side by side with "I should do Brutus wrong, and Cassius wrong:/who (you all know) are Honourable men" (*Julius Caesar* III.ii.128–29) and others which employ the "approved" form in the same construction.[37] The fact is, however, that this use of *whom* (or "misuse," according to one's point of view and one's teaching) occurs very frequently during the whole Modern English period. Jespersen, whose *Modern English Grammar* is a storehouse of illustrative material upon which apparently few writers of school grammars have drawn, has many examples ranging from Chaucer to the present day (III, 198–99), and Sir Ernest Gowers cites contemporary instances from E. M. Forster, Lord David Cecil, *The Times,* and Somerset Maugham, all of which might be presumed to be Standard English.[38] What has been said of *who* and *whom* applies also to *who(so)ever* and *whom(so)ever*, as in "The slaves of the lamp . . . render faithful service to whomsoever holds the talisman"[39] and, to give a less eloquent example, "I am beginning to despair of whomever it is that writes the Foreign Secretary's speeches."[40] Examples from early Modern English, as well as two from Middle English, may be found in the *OED*.

VERBS

Throughout the history of English the strong verbs, always a minority, have fought a losing battle, having either joined the ranks of the weak verbs or been lost altogether. Comparatively few which have

---

(1526) and the King James versions have this *whom.* Accusative *hwæne* occurs in the Anglo-Saxon Gospels. As the *OED* points out, the English construction is sometimes doubtless due to confusion with the Latin accusative and infinitive construction, as in the Vulgate "Quem dicunt homines esse Filium hominis?" (13) and "Vos autem quem me esse dicitis?" (15). The Revised Version (1881) changes to *who* in both verses.

[37] Note the double use of the single form *who* in "the blood o' th' Prince, my Sonne,/ (Who I doe thinke is mine, and love as mine)" (*Winter's Tale* I.ii.330–31).

[38] *Plain Words: Their ABC* (New York, 1954), p. 228.

[39] Sir Winston Churchill, cited in Gowers, pp. 227–28.

[40] "Taper" [Bernard Levin], *Spectator*, May 1, 1959, p. 606.

survived can be said to show what could be called in any way a regular development. A number of factors, which will be dealt with as occasion requires, have brought about such changes that, except for most of the surviving Class I verbs and some from Class III, the orderly arrangement into classes which prevailed in the older periods has now no more than a historical relevance.

Class I is still rather clearly defined, with *write, smite, stride, ride, rise,* and *drive* showing regular development from the Old English preterit singulars *wrāt, smāt, strād, rād, rās,* and *drāf* in Modern English *wrote, smote, strode, rode, rose,* and *drove*; similarly in their past participles, from Old English *writen, smiten, striden,* and so forth. A Northern form, *drave*,[41] sometimes occurs as the preterit of *drive* in early Modern English, for instance, "And I delivered you out of the hand of the Egyptians . . . and drave them out from before you . . ." (Judges vi.9). *Bite* and *slide* now have in their preterits the short *i* of the past participle and the old preterit plural, but *bote* and *slode* both occur in literary early Modern English and survive in present British dialectal usage. Until fairly recently there has been wavering in Standard English between *writ* and *wrote, rid*[42] and *rode,* and *ris*[43] and *rose. Dive,* historically a weak verb, has acquired by analogy with Class I verbs a strong preterit *dove,* dialectal in British English but by no means confined to uneducated use in America,[44] where the form seems to be gaining ground rapidly. *Thrive,* of Scandinavian origin, and *strive,* borrowed from Old French (though ultimately Germanic), acquired strong inflection in Middle English times, though *strived* is more common than strong *striven* as a participial form. *Strike* shows the regular preterit development *stroke* (OE *strāc*) until the seventeenth century,[45] when *struck* began to occur, it may

[41] Old English *ā*, it will be remembered, remained *ā* in the Northern dialect of Middle English and, along with the Middle English long *a* which resulted from lengthening of vowels in open syllables, shifted to Modern English [e:].
[42] The *OED* cites this form from Byron and Thackeray.
[43] Still current in eastern New England *ris bread* 'homemade white bread.'
[44] E. Bagby Atwood, *A Survey of Verb Forms in the Eastern United States* (Ann Arbor, Mich., 1953), p. 9. Atwood records *div* and *duv* also, though these were not used by educated speakers. The first is by analogy with *bit* and *slid.*
[45] *Strick, strake,* and *strook* were also current to some extent in earlier times as preterits, as were weak forms *striked* and *stryckt.*

be by analogy with *stuck*. The historical participle *stricken* survives in such figurative uses as "stricken in years" and "stricken from the record," but various other forms, including *stroke* and *struck(en)*, occurred in early Modern English. In *abide* and *shine* the old preterit singular forms are used as past participles. *Abide* may also have dental-suffix forms ("He abided by the laws"), as may *shine* when used causatively ("He shined his shoes"). *Hide* and *chide*, originally weak verbs, acquired in the early Modern period the participial forms in -*en* characteristic of strong verbs; their preterits with shortened vowels are the normal development of Old English *hȳdde* and *cīdde*, but could quite naturally be felt as analogical with the strong preterits *bit* and *slid*.[46]

Participial forms of verbs of this class frequently occur without -*en* in the seventeenth and eighteenth centuries, for example, *rid, writ, bit, smit*. Furthermore, the preterit forms *(a)rose, drove, rode, shone, smote, strove,* and *wrote* were all used as participles and remained current as such in literary English as late as the eighteenth century, for example, Boswell's "I imagined that your father had wrote in such a way . . ." (*London Journal,* December 30, 1762).

Other verbs of this class have become weak, for example *glide, gripe, spew,* and *writhe*. Still others have disappeared altogether from the language.

The verbs of Class II have likewise undergone many changes in the course of their development into their present forms. Some of these could hardly have been predicted, for instance, the vowels of *choose* (OE *cēosan,* ME *chēsen*) and *lose* (OE *lēosan,* ME *lēsen*), as contrasted with *creep* (OE *crēopan,* ME *crēpen*). The present English forms are to be explained by a shifting of stress in the Old English diphthong, *cĕosan* and *lĕosan* thereby becoming *ceósan* and *leósan*, which would in turn become Middle English *chōsen* and *lōsen* and thus yield the Modern forms with *o(o)*.[47] The expected forms *che(e)se* and *le(e)se*, however, survived into the fifteenth and seventeenth centuries respectively. *Leese* occurs both in the King James Bible, later printings of which change it to *lose*, and in Shakespeare.[48] Middle English had both strong and weak preterits of *leese*, the weak forms appearing as

[46] Analogical *chode* also occurs, as in the King James Bible: "And the people chode with Moses . . ." (Num. xx.3).

[47] Another form, *chuse*, was common until well into the nineteenth century.

[48] As in Sonnet 5: "But flowers distill'd, though they with winter meet, Leese but their show, their substance still lives sweet."

early as the thirteenth century. Weak forms of *choose, cheese,* and *chuse* also occur as late as the eighteenth century. Both these verbs have lost the *-r-* in their past participles which was the result of grammatical change, though Old English *loren* survives in *lorn* and the compounds *forlorn* and *lovelorn.*

In addition to *choose,* verbs of this class which have retained strong inflection are *fly* (though the preterit *flew* is not regularly derived from Old English *flēah*) and *freeze* (with the vowel of preterit *froze* coming from the participle and the [-z] from the infinitive).[49] E. Bagby Atwood reports from the eastern United States the following variant preterit forms of *freeze: friz, frez, freezen, frozen,* and, with dental suffix, *freezed, frozed,* and *frazed*—all "distinctly older forms [which] are no doubt receding rapidly" (p. 15). *Cleave* is usually weak in Modern English (*cleaved, cleft*[50]), but a strong preterit *clove* is still to some extent current, as is the strong participle in *cloven hoof* (but *cleft palate*). A variant strong preterit form, *clave,* is familiar from the King James Bible, as in "And Abraham rose up early in the morning . . . and clave the wood for the burnt offering" (Gen. xxii.3). The Old English weak verb *cleofian* 'stick' fell together with strong *clēofan* 'split' in Middle English *cle(e)ven,* so that it came to acquire the same strong preterit forms. *Clave* thus occurs in the sense 'stuck' also: "Certain men clave to Paul" (Acts xvii.34). Participles of *choose* and *freeze* without *-n* are common in early Modern English, as in Shakespeare's "O what a time have you chose out brave Caius/To weare a Kerchiefe" (*Julius Caesar* II.i.314–15) and "This word (Rebellion) it had froze them up" (*2 Henry IV* I.i.199), as indeed they still are in folk speech. *Flew* occurs as a participle in the seventeenth and eighteenth centuries; it too is still current among those who continue to use the *n*-less participles just cited.

In addition to *lose* and *cleave,* the following surviving verbs of

---

[49] This verb, it may be remembered, showed grammatical change in Old English: infinitive *frēosan*–preterit singular *frēas*–preterit plural *fruron*–past participle *froren. Frore,* with loss of *-n,* occurs occasionally as an archaism, as in Shelley's "Snow-fed streams now seen athwart frore vapours," which the *OED* suggests is, like other nineteenth-century occurrences of the rhotacized form, a reflection of Milton's "The parching Air Burns frore" (*Paradise Lost,* II,594–95).

[50] The vowel differentiation in this preterit form is of course not a matter of gradation, but merely a matter of shortening. The same phenomenon is responsible for the short-voweled preterits of *weep, sleep, sweep, keep,* and a few other verbs.

Class II are now weak: *creep, chew, brew, rue, lie* 'prevaricate,' *reek, seethe, flee, bow* 'bend,' *crowd, shove, sprout,* and *suck. Sodden,* the old strong participle (with grammatical change) of *seethe,* is still sometimes used as an adjective. *Crope,* a strong preterit of *creep,* occurs in formal English as late as the eighteenth century and in folk speech to the present day.

Practically all verbs of Class III with nasal consonants which have survived from Old English have retained their strong inflection. Some of those in *-n* (OE *-nn-*), *-m* (OE *-mm-*), *-nk* (OE *-nc-*), or *-ng* preserve in current Standard English the Old English form of the preterit singular, following the pattern *i* (infinitive), *a* (preterit), *u* (past participle), for example *spring, sing, ring, drink, sink, shrink, stink, swim,* and *begin.* But there has been in these verbs since early Modern English times considerable wavering between the historical preterit and participial forms, with *u* for the preterit strongly predominating in the eighteenth century. Preterit *drunk* is still fairly common in New England and the Middle Atlantic states, acccording to Atwood's survey, and *shrunk* "strongly predominates among all types [cultured and uncultured, old and young] in all areas [of the eastern United States]" (p. 21). Only about half of his cultured New England informants and a third of those in the Middle Atlantic states used the standard combination *drank—drunk* as preterit and past participle respectively. The great majority of those who did not do so used one form or the other for both functions. Participial forms of these verbs, and especially of *drink,* with *a* were by no means uncommon in cultivated usage in earlier days. Jespersen cites *drank* as participle from Scott, Byron, Shelley, Keats, Dickens, Trollope, Kingsley, and, from our own day, Robert Graves.[51] The older participial forms *drunken* and *shrunken* occur as adjectives. In *run* (ME *rinnen*) the vowel of the participle was in early Modern English extended into the present tense. An unchanged preterit *run,* coming from early Modern English times, is common in folk speech. The use of *ran* as a participle is equally old.

Other Class III verbs with nasal consonants have in current English the pattern *i, u(o), u(o),* as in *win, spin, cling, swing, wring, sting,* and *slink,* though these had preterits with *a* also in early Modern English, as in the familiar lines "When Adam dolve and Evë span/

[51] VI, 54. Boswell also uses it in his *London Journal*: ". . . he told me that he had once drank a bottle of sherry. . . (May 11, 1763); "Mr. Johnson and I had formerly drank the health of Sir David Dalrymple" (July 14, 1763).

Who was then the gentleman?" A few verbs entering the language after Old English times have conformed to this pattern, for example, *fling, sling,* and *string* (from the noun). By the same sort of analogy the weak verb *bring* has acquired in nonstandard speech the strong preterit and participial form *brung.* Though lacking the nasal, *dig* (not of Old English origin) and *stick,* having at first weak inflection, have taken on the same pattern.[52] The preterit *dug* is first recorded in the eighteenth century;[53] as participle the form is much older. Class III verbs in *-nd,* for example *find, bind, grind,* and *wind,* have in their preterits and participles the modern development [aʊ] of the lengthened *u* (spelled *ou*) of the old preterit plural and past participle.

Except for *fight,* the development of whose Modern English preterit and participle presents certain difficulties which we need not go into here,[54] all other surviving verbs of this class have become weak, some in Middle English times: *climb, bark, burn, braid, carve, help, starve, delve,*[55] *mourn, spurn, yield, yell, yelp, melt, swallow,* and *swell.* The old participial forms *molten* and *swollen* are still used, but only as adjectives. *Holp,* an old strong preterit of *help,* was common until the seventeenth century and survives in current nonstandard usage.[56] The old participial form *holpen* is doubtless familiar to many from its use in the King James Bible, for instance in Luke i.54 ("He hath holpen his servant Israel"), Psalms lxxxvi.17, Isaiah xxxi.3, and Daniel xi.34. Both *holp* and *holpen* have been used by poets as conscious archaisms; the *OED* has citations from Tennyson and Mrs. Browning, among others. The older forms *clum, clam, clim, cloom,* and *clome* survive dialectally as strong preterits of *climb.*[57] The last of these, sometimes written *clomb* or *clombe,* occurs probably as a conscious archaism

[52] *Stack, stake,* and *stoke* also occur in early Modern English as preterits of *stick.*

[53] Note the seventeenth-century and earlier preterit in the King James Bible, for example in the parable of the talents: "But he that had received one went and digged in the earth, and hid his lord's money" (Matt. xxv.18).

[54] The expected form [faʊt] is current in American folk speech, particularly in parts of the South (Atwood, p. 14). *Fit,* presumably analogical with *bit,* is also fairly common, both in British and American folk usage.

[55] But note the older strong form *dolve* in the quotation in the preceding paragraph.

[56] See Atwood, pp. 16–17. Those who use this form pronounce it, and usually *help* as well, without *l.*

[57] For their distribution in eastern American English, see Atwood, pp. 8–9 and Figure 5.

in Spenser and those other Elizabethan writers who affected old-fashioned forms; it also occurs in the writings of Dryden, Wordsworth, Coleridge, Scott, and Tennyson, doubtless as a reflection of its Elizabethan use. *Burst* has only a single form in current Standard English, though *brast* is common as a preterit in the early Modern period. A weak preterit *bursted* and its variant *busted*, with loss of *r*, frequently occur in nonstandard speech.

The principal surviving verbs of Class IV are *bear, break, shear, steal, tear*, and *come*. All these have remained strong, and all save the last have the inflectional pattern *ea, o, o*, from earlier *ea, a, o* (OE *e, æ, o*). The *o* of the modern preterit is from the past participle. In Middle English times a number of verbs from other classes took over the inflectional system of Class IV: *speak, weave*, and *tread* from Class V; *heave* and *swear* from Class VI; *get*, the Scandinavian word replacing Old English *-gitan*, which, like *tread*, has a short root vowel in all its parts; and the weak verb *wear*.[58] In early Modern English there was considerable variation between preterits in *a* and *o*, for instance *spoke–spake, tore–tare, got–gat, bore–bare, broke–brake*.[59] In time the *o*-preterits came to predominate and ultimately to drive out altogether the forms with *a*. Participial forms of these verbs without *-n* are frequent in the seventeenth and eighteenth centuries; that of *get* has remained in British English, but *gotten* is still very much alive in American English. *Come* frequently occurs as a preterit in early Modern English,[60] as it continues to do in folk speech. *Shear* may have either weak or strong inflection. Analogical *roke* occurs in the deep South as a past participle (and presumably a preterit as well)

[58] Class V earlier had *e* in the participle and Class VI, *a*. *Get* conformed to Class V inflection like its Old English cognate *-gitan*, with participle with *e* (*geten, gete, i-gete*) up to near the end of the sixteenth century. But *gotten*, with root vowel *o* from Class IV participles, occurs as early as the thirteenth century.

[59] The *a*-forms are familiar from their use in the King James Bible, as in "When I was a child, I spake as a child . . ." (1 Cor. xiii.11). Compare also "And when he went forth to land, there met him . . . a certain man, which had devils long time, and ware no clothes . . ." (Luke viii.27); "And when he had taken the five loaves and the two fishes, he looked up to heaven, and blessed, and brake the loaves . . ." (Mark vi.41); "And they brought him unto him; and when he saw him, straightway the spirit tare him . . ." (Mark ix.20).

[60] For example, in Pepys's *Diary*: "Creed come and dined with me . . ." (June 15, 1666) and elsewhere, though Pepys also uses *came*.

of *rake* in the usage of colored folk, and doubtless of poor whites also, as in the common solicitation "Do you want your yard roke?"

Verbs of Class V have all diverged in one way or another from what might be considered regular development. *Speak* and *tread*, as we have just seen, ultimately took on the characteristics of Class IV verbs. For the preterit of *eat*, early Modern English for a while had *at*, but *ate*, with lengthened vowel, and *eat*, pronounced [ɛt], also occur—the last probably by analogy with preterit *read* [rɛd]. The pronunciation today indicated by the spelling *ate* (that is, [et]) is the only one current in educated American speech. The same spelling has, however, long prevailed in British English, though *et* would better indicate the usual pronunciation. The same spoken form [ɛt], written *eat*, was commonly used as a participle in early Modern English and continues to occur as late as the early nineteenth century. Jespersen cites examples from Jane Austen, Lamb, and Shelley (VI, 69). The preterit *(for)bad* is regularly developed from Old English *bæd*; the form *bade*, with lengthened vowel, begins to occur in Middle English times. Since the sixteenth century *bid*, from the participle *bidden*, has also been used as a preterit form. The *i* (instead of *e*) of the participle has been variously explained; it occurs first in Middle English times.[61] The preterit *gave* has predominated since early Modern times, though preterit *give*[62] and participial *gave*[63] also occur fairly frequently. *Sit* had in early Modern English the preterit forms *sat, sate,* and (occasionally) *sit,* the participial forms *sitten, sit, sat,* and *sate. Sit* and *set* were confused as early as the fourteenth century, and continue to be.[64] A nonstandard form *sot* occurs as preterit and participle of both verbs. The confusion of *lie*[65] and *lay* is as old as that of *sit* and *set*. The intransi-

---

[61] See Eilert Ekwall, *Historische neuenglische Laut- und Formenlehre,* 3rd ed., rev. (Berlin, 1956), pp. 128–29, and H. C. Wyld, *A Short History of English,* 3rd ed. (New York, 1927), p. 276.

[62] As in Pepys's "This day I sent my cozen Roger a tierce of claret, which I give him" (August 21, 1667).

[63] As in Shakespeare's *Venus and Adonis,* line 571: "When he did frown, O, had she then gave over. . . ."

[64] Of the situation in current eastern American English, Atwood states, "In the entire area south of Pa., outside of the larger cities, *sit* is rather uncommon except in cultured speech" (p. 21).

[65] Old English *licgan,* Middle English *liggen.* The expected modern form would be **lidge,* but the infinitive has been re-formed by analogy with the present indicative singular forms, Old English *ligest, ligeþ,* Middle

tive use of *lay*, according to the *OED*, "was not app[arently] regarded as a solecism" in the seventeenth and eighteenth centuries. It has been so used by some very important writers, including Francis Bacon. Everyone is familiar with Lord Byron's "There let him lay" in Canto IV of *Childe Harold's Pilgrimage* (line 1620). The brothers H. W. and F. G. Fowler cite with apparently delighted disapproval "I suspected him of having laid in wait for the purpose"[66] from the writing of Richard Grant White, the eminent nineteenth-century American purist—for purists love above all to catch other purists out in some supposed sin against English grammar. Better writers than White have committed the same "error," however: George H. McKnight cites the usage from William Morris, Fiona Macleod, George Moore, Joseph Conrad, and Lytton Strachey.[67] Old English *cweðan* 'say' survives only in *bequeath*, which has weak inflection. *Quod* and *quoth* occur as early Modern English preterits of the simple form. H. C. Wyld suggests that the *o*, which is found also in the participle—the regular development would be **quath*—is due to the analogy of the participles of Class IV.[68] The form *quotha* is for *quoth he* (see p. 187). The preterit *saw* predominates all through the Modern period, though *see*, still common as a preterit in folk speech, also occurs. A weak form *seed* is likewise confined to folk speech, as is *seen*, from the participle. Other surviving Class V verbs have become weak: *mete, knead, reap, scrape, wreak, fret*, and *weigh*.

Some verbs from Class VI show regular development with *a, oo, a*, for example, *shake, forsake*, and the Scandinavian *take* which ultimately ousted its Old English synonym *niman* from the language. Early Modern English frequently uses the preterit form of these verbs as participle.[69] *Stand* (and the compound *understand*) has lost its old participle *standen*; the preterit form has served as participle since the sixteenth century, though not exclusively. *Stand* also occurs as par-

---

English *lyest, lyeth*. Preterit *lay* and participial *lain* are regular developments of Old English *læg* and *legen*. *Lien*, or *lyen*, with the vowel of the infinitive, sometimes occurs as a participial form from the fourteenth century on.

[66] *The King's English*, 2nd ed. (Oxford, 1906), p. 40.

[67] *Modern English in the Making* (New York, 1928), p. 534.

[68] *A Short History of English*, p. 279.

[69] As in Shakespeare's "Save what is had or must from you be took" (Sonnet 75), "Have from the forests shook three summers' pride" (Sonnet 104), and "Hath she forsooke so many Noble Matches?" (*Othello* IV.ii.125).

ticiple, as does a weak form *standed*.[70] *Slay* (OE *slēan*) was newly formed in late Middle English from the participle *slayn* (OE *slagen*), though *slea* and *slee*[71] continued in use until the seventeenth century. The preterit *slew* supplanted the older form *slow*, apparently by analogy with Class VII preterits like *knew* and *blew*; the same explanation doubtless holds for *drew* (older *drow*). *Quake* is likewise peculiar among Class VI verbs in having *o* rather than *oo* in its preterit; it also has weak inflection. Other surviving verbs of this class have become weak: *fare, gnaw, (en)grave, flay, heave, lade, laugh, shave, step, wade,* and *wash,* though strong participial forms *laden* and *shaven* survive as adjectives, and *heave* has an alternative strong preterit *hove*.

Surviving Class VII verbs which remain strong include *blow, grow, know, fall, hang,* and *hold.* The present and preterit of *beat* have been leveled, but the verb retains its strong participle in *-en. Crow* sometimes has a strong preterit *crew,* but its participle is always *crowed.* The old participle of *hold* survives in the somewhat old-fashioned *beholden. Hang* is frequently weak when used in reference to capital punishment—at least, the books on usage tell us that it ought to be, though no less imposing a personage than a British Lord Chief Justice (Lord Goddard) chose to use the strong form in this connection: "Your lordships can be assured that the only people hung are those guilty of cruel, deliberate murder without mitigation." In reporting this statement, the London *Daily Express* made a point of commenting, "It was noted that the Lord Chief Justice speaks regularly of a man being 'hung.' He does not say 'hanged'" (July 11, 1956, p. 2). In the seventeenth century *fell* was frequent as a participial form, as in Shakespeare's "have with one Winters brush / Fell from their boughes" (*Timon of Athens* IV.iii.264–65). (He also uses *fallen.*) Weak *blowed* and *growed* occur rather often in early Modern English and survive in nonstandard speech.[72]

The following verbs surviving from this group have become weak, the first two acquiring weak preterit forms as early as Old English times: *read* (OE preterit *rædde*), *sleep* (OE preterit *slēpte*), *dread,*

[70] As in "a tongue not understanded of the people" in the fourteenth Article of Religion of the Anglican Communion.

[71] See the chapter "Rosemary" from Banckes's *Herball* cited on p. 169: ". . . laye them on a Canker & it shall slee it."

[72] For their distribution in eastern American English, see Atwood, pp. 6 and 15–16.

weep, leap, span 'join,' *mow, hew, fold, sow, flow, walk, wax* 'grow,' and *row.* Strong participial forms *sown, mown,* and *hewn* survive, mainly as adjectives. *Let* is the single form to survive from Old English *lǣtan.*

With the loss of Middle English *-e* as ending for the first person singular present indicative, the endingless form became identical with the infinitive, which had lost first its final *-n* and then its *-e.* The early Modern English second person singular present indicative had *-(e)st,* sometimes *-(e)s,* and the third person varied between *-(e)s* and *-(e)th.* From the beginning of the seventeenth century the *-s* form of the third person was to prevail, though for a while the two forms might be used interchangeably, particularly in verse, for example Shakespeare's "Sometime she driveth ore a Souldiers necke, & then dreames he of cutting Forraine throats" (*Romeo and Juliet* I.iv.82–83). But *doth* and *hath* went on until well into the eighteenth century. The King James Bible uses only *-th* forms, as does the Book of Common Prayer, but, as H. C. Wyld points out, "Evidently the translators of the Authorized Version of the Bible regarded *-s* as belonging only to familiar speech, but the exclusive use of *-eth* here, and in every edition of the Prayer Book, may be partly due to the tradition set by the earlier Biblical translations and the early editions of the Prayer Book respectively."[73] The *-s* forms of the third person singular present indicative are usually attributed to Northern dialectal influence. In the present indicative plural the endings *-eth* of the Southern dialects and *-en* of the Midland were lost as early as the fourteenth century, resulting in the current endingless forms, though forms in *-eth,* *-ith* survived into the sixteenth century. Third person plural forms in *-s,* of Northern provenience, occur also, as in "Where lo, two lamps, burnt out, in darkness lies" (*Venus and Adonis,* line 1128) and else-where in Shakespeare and other Elizabethan writers; these should not of course be regarded as "ungrammatical" uses of the third person singular for the plural form. Wyld believes that this plural form in *-s* is due to analogy with the singular, however, rather than to Northern influence, inasmuch as to this day "certain sections of the people inflect all Persons of both Sing. and Pl. with *-s* after the pattern of the 3rd Pers. Sing., while others drop the suffix even in the 3rd Sing. and the Pl. of all Persons" (p. 340). The extension of the *-s* to the first and second persons is indeed particularly noticeable in current speech

---

[73] *History of Modern Colloquial English,* p. 334.

in the usage of naïve raconteurs, with their "I says" and "says I," and is the source of the rude expression of disbelief "Sez you!"

The early Modern English preterit had no personal endings save for the second person singular *-(e)st*, which began to be lost in the sixteenth century.

In the verb *to be* the early Modern indicative singular forms were (1) *am*, (2) *art*, (3) *is*. In the plural either *be* or *are* might occur,[74] the first being widely current as late as the seventeenth century. The preterit indicative second person singular was *were* until the sixteenth century, when the forms *wast, werst,* and *wert* began to occur, the last remaining current in literature throughout the eighteenth century. Nineteenth-century poets were also very fond of it ("Bird thou never wert"); it gave a certain archaically spiritual tone to their writing which they presumably considered desirable. *Wast* and *wert* are by analogy with present *art*. In *werst*, the *s* of *wast* has apparently been extended. *Wert* was also used in the second person of the preterit subjunctive. The locution *you was* has been discussed earlier (p. 189).

Of the other highly irregular verbs little need be said. *Could,* the preterit of *can*, acquired its unetymological *l* in the sixteenth century by analogy with *would* and *should*. Early Modern forms which differ from those now current are *durst*, preterit of *dare*, which otherwise had become weak; *mought*, a variant of *might*; and *mowe*, an occasionally occurring present plural form of *may*. *Will* has early Modern forms with *u* and *o*.

Before it was supplanted by *not* (a form of *nought*) in the sixteenth century, *ne* was frequently joined to a following verb if this began with *h* or *w* or with a vowel, for example Old English *nabban* 'not to have,' *neom* 'am not,' *nat* 'know(s) not,' *nyllan* 'be unwilling,' corresponding to Middle English *nave, nam, no(o)t, nille*.[75]

CONTRACTED NEGATIVE FORMS

Most of our current contracted negative forms in *-n't* first occur in writing in the seventeenth century. It is likely that all were actually used long before ever getting written down, for contractions are in their very nature colloquial and thus would have been considered un-

---

[74] Ekwall cites "The powers that be" as a survival of the *be* form (p. 139).

[75] As in *willy-nilly* 'will I (ye, he), won't I (ye, he).' Not only verbs but other words as well underwent this contraction, for example Old English *nān* (*none*), *nǣnig* 'not any,' *nǣfre* (*never*).

suitable for writing, as most people still consider them. *Won't* is from *wol(l) not* (see p. 164, n. 41), and *don't*, the vowel of which presents an annoying problem,[76] may be from either *do* or, in the third person singular, from *does not*, with loss of [-z-]. The *OED* derives third person *don't* from *he (she, it) do,* and cites a number of instances of *do* in the third person from the sixteenth and seventeenth centuries, including Pepys's "Sir Arthur Haselrigge do not yet appear in the House" (March 2, 1660). Karl W. Dykema, who believes that the most likely explanation of third person *don't* is the principle of morphological analogy—the same tendency which has reduced the various preterit forms of the strong verbs to a single form—has found an occurrence of it in 1697, but none for *doesn't* before 1818, though it is likely, as he admits, that there are some earlier occurrences of the latter form. As far as the evidence goes, however, *doesn't* first occurs one hundred and twenty-one years later than the earliest known occurrence of third-person *don't.*[77] Elsewhere Dykema concludes that "Such variants as *don't* and *doesn't* in the third person are considered by speakers of Standard English as the recent innovation and the original contraction respectively, whereas it is probably more nearly the case that *don't* is the older form!"[78]

An't (early ModE [ænt]) for *am (are, is) not* is apparently of late seventeenth-century origin; the variant *ain't* occurs about a century later. With the eighteenth-century British English shifting of [æ:] to [ɑ:] as in *ask, path, dance,* and the like, and the loss of preconsonantal *r*, the pronunciation of this word shifted to [ɑ:nt], and *aren't* was thus a perfectly good spelling for it, suitable alike in *aren't I?* and *aren't you?* This spelling has been grievously misinterpreted by those, including most Americans, who pronounce *r* before a consonant. Of *ain't*, which has fallen victim to a series of schoolteachers' crusades, Dean Alford testified that in his day "It ain't certain" and "I ain't

---

[76] That is, one would expect [du:nt] for all forms save the third singular, for which [dʌnt] would be the expected form. It has been suggested that the [o:] of *don't* is analogical with that of *won't* (Jespersen, *Modern English Grammar,* V, 431).

[77] "An Example of Prescriptive Linguistic Change: 'Don't' to 'Doesn't,' " *English Journal,* XXXVI (1947), 372.

[78] "How Fast Is Standard English Changing?" *American Speech,* XXXI (1956), 90: reprinted in Harold B. Allen's *Readings in Applied English Linguistics* (New York, 1958), pp. 222–28.

going" were "very frequently used, even by highly educated persons."[79] Frederick James Furnivall (1825–1910), an early editor of the *OED* and founder of the Chaucer Society and the Early English Text Society, is said to have used the form *ain't* habitually.[80] Though he may not have used it himself, the late Monsignor Ronald Arbuthnott Knox, Oxford don and Roman Catholic chaplain at that university, puts it into the mouth of the expensively educated hero of his detective stories.[81]

Contractions of auxiliary verbs occur somewhat earlier, though they must be about equally old. *It's* as a written form is from the seventeenth century, and ultimately drove out *'tis,* in which the pronoun rather than the verb is reduced. There is no current contraction of *it was* to replace older *'twas,* and, in the light of the practical disappearance of the subjunctive, it is not surprising that there is none for *it were. It'll* has replaced older *'twill; will* similarly is contracted after other pronouns and, in speech, after other words as well. In older times *'ll,* usually written *le* (as in *Ile, youle*), occurred only after vowels and was hence not syllabic, as it must be after consonants. *Would* is contracted as early as the late sixteenth century as *'ld,* later becoming *'d,* which came in the eighteenth century to be used for *had* also. The contraction of *have* written *'ve* likewise seems to have occurred first in the eighteenth century. After a consonant this contraction is identical in pronunciation with unstressed *of,*[82] hence such uneducated spellings as *would of* and *should of,* frequently written in dialogue to indicate that the speaker is unschooled; the point seems to be "This is

---

[79] *The Queen's English,* 8th ed. (London, 1889), first published 1863, cited in Jespersen, *Modern English Grammar,* V, 434. Henry Alford (1810–71), dean of Canterbury from 1857 until his death, was a Cambridge scholar who edited the New Testament in Greek (a monumental work in four volumes) and was first editor of the *Contemporary Review.* He was the author of a number of well-known hymns.

[80] Jespersen, *Modern English Grammar,* V, 434.

[81] "Yes, but it ain't such plain sailing as all that," *Still Dead* (London, 1952; first published 1934), p. 38, and again on p. 41: ". . . as you justly observe, that ain't much." With a similar disregard for *petit-bourgeois* grammar, the heir to the "Laird of Dorn" in the same novel uses *he don't,* as does the young, charming, and cultured wife of Miles Bredon in these spare-time literary productions of an English gentleman and priest.

[82] Compare "The wood of the tree" and "He would've done it."

the way the speaker would write *have* if he had occasion to do so." As indicative of pronunciation the spelling is pointless.[83]

EXPANDED VERB FORMS

Expanded verb forms consisting of a form of *to be* plus a present participle ("I am working"), sometimes called "progressive," occur occasionally in Old English, but do not begin to be used with any frequency until the fifteenth century; even so, they remain relatively infrequent until the seventeenth century. The expanded passive form, the so-called progressive passive, as in "He is being punished," does not occur until the latter part of the eighteenth century. Samuel Pepys, for instance, writes ". . . I met a dead corps of the plague, in the narrow ally just bringing down a little pair of stairs"[84] (August 15, 1665), where we should use the newer construction "being brought down"; and ". . . to Hales's the painter, thinking to have found Harris sitting there for his picture, which is drawing for me" (April 26, 1668), where we should use "is being drawn."

Do is frequently used as a verbal auxiliary in the early Modern period, though it is used somewhat differently from the way it is used today, for example "I do wonder, his insolence can brooke to be commanded" (*Coriolanus* I.i.265–266) and "The Serpent that did sting thy Fathers life/ Now weares his Crowne" (*Hamlet* I.v.39–40), where current English would not use it at all. Compare with these instances "A Nun of winters sisterhood kisses not more religiouslie" (*As You Like It* III.iv.17), where we should say *does not kiss*. In such negative expressions, however, the *do*-forms current today were in use

---

[83] This to some extent characterizing device of using distorted spellings which indicate pronunciations not differing from standard ones is called *eye dialect,* in contrast to spellings which actually tell us something of a speaker's regional provenience (like *minny* for *many*) or his cultural status (like *intregal* for *integral* or *nucular* for *nuclear*). Compare also *doncha, cuppa, lotta,* and *wuz,* which indicate the way everyone, educated and uneducated alike, is likely in unself-conscious speech to pronounce *don't you, cup of, lot of,* and unstressed *was.* The old favorites *wimmen* and *likker* merely indicate that the speaker is an ignoramus, a comic, or both. The actual misspellings used are phonetically better representations of the pronunciations of words which all people pronounce alike than are conventional *women* and *liquor.*

[84] "Pair of stairs," "pair of beads" (as in Chaucer's description of the Prioress), and a few other phrases in which *pair* denotes more than two are still current in folk speech.

in early Modern English side by side with such locutions, now archaic, as *forbid them not* and *I doubt not*.

OTHER VERBAL CONSTRUCTIONS

Impersonal and reflexive constructions are fairly frequent in early Modern English, as they were to a much greater extent in Middle English. Shakespeare has, for instance, "it dislikes [displeases] me," "methinks," "it yearns [grieves] me," "I complain me," "how dost thou feel thyself now?" "I doubt me," "I repent me," and "give me leave to retire myself." Some verbs now intransitive were used transitively, as in "despair [of] thy charm," "give me leave to speak [of] him," and "Smile you [at] my speeches." Verbs of motion frequently have a form of *be* instead of *have* in their expanded perfect forms: "is risen," "are entered in the Roman territories," "were safe arrived."[85]

SHALL *AND* WILL

In Old and Middle English times *shall* (OE present indicative *sceal*, second person *scealt*) and *will* (OE *wille, wilt*) were sometimes used to express simple futurity, though as a rule they implied respectively obligation and volition. The present prescribed use of these words, the bane of many an American and North British schoolchild, stems ultimately from the seventeenth century, the "rules" having first been drawn up by John Wallis, an eminent professor of geometry at Oxford who wrote in Latin a grammar of the English language.[86] His successors were also men of considerable prestige who have elaborated upon Wallis's prescription and have been to a great extent successful in imposing his idea of a desirable distinction in the use of *shall* and *will* upon a large part of the English-speaking world. Despite the crusade in behalf of the distinction, the rules for making it are not very clear.

Charles Carpenter Fries has pointed out that in the many vigorous discussions concerning *shall* and *will* in recent times, one cannot help "being impressed by the wide diversity of the points of view and the definite conflict of the opinions and conclusions thus brought together."[87] The fact seems to be that, when Fries began to investigate

---

[85] Practically all these examples have been cited by Franz, *Shakespeare-Grammatik*, pp. 503–07.

[86] *Grammatica Linguae Anglicanae*, 1653.

[87] *American English Grammar* (New York, 1940), p. 151. See also his "The Periphrastic Future with *Shall* and *Will* in Modern English," *PMLA*, XL (1925), 963–1024, and "The Expression of the Future," *Language*, III (1927), 87-95.

the use of *shall* and *will*, there were "after more than a century of discussion . . . no accepted views of what the actual usage of these two words is, of the meaning and trend of the development of that usage, and of the causes that gave rise to it." In any case, the conventional rules, differing as they do from "authority" to "authority," neither describe pre-eighteenth-century usage nor usage as it was at the time when the eighteenth-century grammars which gave them currency were written. Fries's own investigations indicate that there has been no great change in the use of *shall* and *will* with the first person from the middle of the sixteenth century to the present, *will* greatly predominating; with the second person the situation existing in the sixteenth century, when *shall* predominated, has been completely reversed; similarly with the third person, *will* has come to predominate over *shall*.[88]

THE IMPORTANCE OF PREPOSITIONS

With the Middle English loss of all distinctive inflectional endings in the noun save for the *-s* of the genitive and the plural, prepositions acquired an importance greater than they had ever had in Old English. There was in fact need for more of them in the early Modern period to indicate grammatical relationships more precisely than these had ever been indicated by the inflectional endings of earlier times. *During*, apparently first used by Chaucer ca. 1385,[89] *concerning*, *except* (*Piers Plowman, ca.* 1377), and *because*, itself originally a prepositional phrase (*be* being an unstressed form of *by*) all appear first either in the fourteenth or the fifteenth century. Changes in the uses of certain prepositions are illustrated by the practice of Shakespeare, who in this respect as in most others is representative of the early Modern period: "And what delight shall she have to looke on [at] the divell?" (*Othello* II.i.229); "He came of [on] an errand to mee" (*Merry Wives* I.iv.80); "But thou wilt be aveng'd on [for] my misdeeds" (*Richard III* I.iv.70); " 'Twas from [against] the Cannon [canon]" (*Coriolanus* III.i.90); ". . . we are such stuffe/As dreames are

---

[88] *American English Grammar*, pp. 154–55, preceding a discussion of *shall* and *will* in questions, where there has been no shift in usage comparable to that which occurred with the second and third persons in independent statements: here *shall* predominated throughout the Modern English period with the first person, *will* with the second and third persons.

[89] According to the *OED*, it is derived from the Latin ablative absolute construction, as in *vita durante* 'while life lasts (or lasted).'

made on [of]" (*Tempest* IV.i.156–57); "Then speake the truth by [of] her" (*Two Gentlemen* II.iv.151); ". . . that our armies joyn not in [on] a hot day" (*2 Henry IV* I.ii.234).

Even in Old English times *on* was sometimes reduced in compound words like *abūtan* (now *about*), a variant of *on būtan* 'on the outside of.' The contracted form was usually written *a*,[90] for instance, *aboard, afield, abed, asleep,* and, with verbal nouns in *-ing, a-hunting, a-bleeding, a-praying,*[91] and the like. The *a* of "twice a day" and other such expressions[92] has the same origin. *In* was sometimes contracted to *i'*, as in Shakespeare's "i' the head," "i' God's name," and so forth. This particular contraction was much later fondly affected by Robert Browning, who doubtless thought it singularly archaic, for example "would not sink i' the scale" and "This rage was right i' the main" ("Rabbi Ben Ezra," lines 42 and 100).

THE EARLY DICTIONARIES

The first dictionaries appear in the period under discussion. If one had to set up a line of development for these, one would start with the Old and Middle English interlinear glosses in Latin and French texts, then proceed through the bilingual vocabularies produced by schoolmasters and designed for those studying foreign languages, specifically Latin, French, Italian, and Spanish. But the first work designed expressly for listing and defining English words for English-speaking people was the schoolmaster Robert Cawdrey's *A Table Alphabeticall* (1604) ("conteyning and teaching the true writing, and vnderstanding of hard vsuall English wordes, borrowed from the Hebrew, Greeke, Latine, or French. &c.") Other dictionaries followed in the same tradition of explicating "hard words," for instance that of J[ohn] B[ullokar], Doctor of Physick, *An English Expositour* (1616), Henry Cockeram's *English Dictionarie* (1623), Thomas Blount's *Glossographia* (1656), Edward Phillips's *New World of English Words* (1658), Edward Cocker's *English Dictionary* (1704),[93] and Nathan

[90] Less frequently *o'*, which might also be a contraction of *of* (as in *o'clock*).

[91] As in Hamlet's *a-praying,* cited on p. 187.

[92] For a Middle English example, note Chaucer's, "ful ofte a day" in the *Knight's Tale,* Part II, line 2.

[93] Cocker died in 1676, but was a person of such importance—not as a lexicographer, but as a teacher of handwriting and arithmetic—that "according to Cocker" became a proverbial phrase, like "according to Hoyle,"

Bailey's *Universal Etymological English Dictionary* (1721), with a second volume that was really a supplement appearing in 1727. In 1730, Bailey (and others) produced the *Dictionarium Britannicum*, with about 48,000 items (more words than Johnson included), which provided the basis for Johnson's great work. In 1755 appeared both the Scott-Bailey *New Universal Etymological English Dictionary*[94] and Samuel Johnson's two-volume *Dictionary*. For the history of dictionaries up to Johnson's, the best study is that of DeWitt T. Starnes and Gertrude E. Noyes, *The English Dictionary from Cawdrey to Johnson, 1604–1755* (Chapel Hill, N.C., 1946), on which the foregoing summary is based. For Johnson's dictionary, the best study is that of James Sledd and Gwin J. Kolb, *Dr. Johnson's Dictionary: Essays in the Biography of a Book* (Chicago, 1955).

The publication of Johnson's *Dictionary* was certainly the most important linguistic event of the eighteenth century, not to say the entire period under discussion, for it to a large extent "fixed" English spelling and it established a standard for the use of words. Johnson did indeed attempt to exercise a directive function. It would have been strange had he not done so at that time, and we cannot censure him very harshly in view of the fact that most people in our own day expect dictionaries to do so. For most people it is apparently not sufficient even today for the lexicographer simply to record and define the words of the language, and to indicate the way in which they are pronounced by those who use them; he is also supposed to have some God given power of determining which are "good" words and which are "bad" ones, and to know how they "ought" to be pronounced. But Johnson had the good sense usually to recognize the prior claims of usage over the arbitrary appeals to logic, analogy, Latin grammar, and sheer prejudice so often made by his contemporaries, even if he did at times settle matters by appeals to his own taste, which was fortunately good taste. Though the son of a bookseller in Lichfield, Johnson had a tremendous admiration for those who were his social

---

though Cocker may have had little or nothing to do with the works ascribed to him: only copybooks by him were published during his lifetime, though the eighteenth century regarded him most highly as a mathematician.

[94] Joseph Nicol Scott, designated as editor (for Bailey died in 1742), was a very big wig at the time. He apparently did little beyond lending the prestige of his name to a volume designed by the booksellers to compete with Johnson's.

betters: he was a Tory both by denomination and conviction. Hence, along with his typical eighteenth-century desire to "fix" the language went a great deal of respect for upper-class usage. He can thus be said truly to have consolidated a standard of usage which was not altogether of his own making. His use of illustrative quotations, literally by the thousands, was an innovation; but his own definitions show the most discriminating judgment. The quirky definitions, like that for oats—"a grain which in England is generally given to horses, but in Scotland supports the people"—are well known, so well known that some people must have got the utterly false impression that there are very many others not so well known. It is in a way unfortunate that these have been "played up" for their sheer amusement value as much as they have been, for they are actually few in number.

EIGHTEENTH-CENTURY ATTITUDES TOWARD LANGUAGE

What has already been implied more than once in the course of this book should be stressed at this point: there have been, and are, plenty of purists in England, where the "rules" originated, for the puristic attitude towards language is above all a matter of temperament. Purists have undoubtedly existed in all times and in all places. By no means all of them are schoolteachers. Moreover, the English variety are about as ill-informed and as inconsistent as their American counterparts. Modern purism is to some extent based on the notions— prominent in the eighteenth century—that language is of divine origin and hence was perfect in its beginnings but is constantly in danger of corruption and decay unless it is diligently kept in line by wise men who are able to get themselves accepted as authorities, for instance, men who write dictionaries and grammars. Along with this notion of the divine origin of language went the concept of a universal grammar whose principles governed, or ought to govern, all known languages. Latin was regarded as having retained much of its original "perfection." No one seems to have been very much aware that it was the culmination of a long development and had undergone many changes of the sort which were deplored in English. Hence when English grammars came to be written, they were based on Latin grammar, even down to the terminology.

These misconceptions regarding language, and specifically the English language, are still widely current—even, one is tempted to declare, predominant. It is likely that everyone between the Cockney and the earl,[95] between Jeeter Lester and a Back Bay Bostonian—which is to say, most of us—pays lip-service to the mossy precepts of the prescriptive grammarians of the eighteenth century.

The most influential of these was Robert Lowth (1710–87), theologian, Hebraist, professor of poetry at Oxford from 1741 to 1753, later bishop of Oxford, then of London, and dean of the Chapel Royal, who four years before his death was offered the archbishopric of Canterbury, which he turned down. In the Preface to his *Short Introduction to English Grammar* (1762), Lowth agreed with Dean Swift's charge, made in 1712 in his *Proposal for Correcting, Improving, and Ascertaining* [that is, fixing, making certain] *the English Tongue*,[96] that "our language is extremely imperfect," "that it offends against every part of grammar," and that most of the "best authors of our age" commit "many gross improprieties, which . . . ought to be discarded." Lowth was able to find many of the most egregious blunders in the works of our most eminent writers; his footnotes are filled with them. It apparently never occurred to any of his contemporaries to doubt that so famous and successful a man had inside information about an ideal state of the English language. Perhaps they thought he got it straight from a linguistic Jahveh.

In any case, Lowth set out in all earnestness in the midst of a busy life to do something constructive about the deplorable English written by the masters of English literature. Like most men of his time, he believed in "universal grammar"—and this is strange in view of the fact that he was well acquainted with a non-Indo-European language —and consequently he believed that English was "easily reducible to a System of rules." Among many other things, he gave wide currency, probably because of his high position in the Establishment, to those rules for *shall* and *will* as they had been cooked up by John Wallis in his *Grammatica Linguae Anglicanae*.

In actual practice, as we have seen, the "rules," which everybody continues to think are inflexibly right, have been honored more in the breach than in the observance. This is to say that most people,

[95] It is to be doubted that dukes, marquesses, and earls bother themselves overmuch. The last dukedom (except for the royal dukedoms of Windsor and Edinburgh) was created in 1874, and new creations of marquesses and earldoms are also rather rare. Newly created barons and viscounts would doubtless be considerably less secure.

[96] In this, a letter written to the Lord Treasurer, Swift urges the formation of an academy to regulate usage.

only dimly comprehending their complexities, seem to think that they should observe them more conscientiously than they have actually done. But because of the deference which has been paid to these supposedly omniscient law-givers of the eighteenth century—even though the names of many may have been long forgotten[97]—it is probably safe to say that the most important eighteenth-century development in the English language—as the publication of Johnson's *Dictionary* may be said to have been the most important single event—has been its conscious regulation by those who were not really qualified for the job but who managed to acquire authority as linguistic mahatmas.

Yet it must not be thought that the men who promulgated the rules were contemptible. Bishop Lowth was certainly not and, heaven knows, Dean Swift, one of the glories of English literature, was certainly not. Nor was Joseph Priestley, who, in addition to writing *The Rudiments of English Grammar* (1761), was the discoverer of oxygen, a prominent nonconformist preacher, and a voluminous writer on subjects theological, scientific, political, and philosophical. Like George Campbell, who in his *Philosophy of Rhetoric* (1776) went so far as to call language "purely a species of fashion," Priestley recognized the superior force of usage; he also shared Campbell's belief that there was need for some form of control of language other than that furnished by custom. Being children of the Age of Reason, both would have had recourse to the principle of analogy to settle questions of divided usage, though admitting that it was not always possible to do so. All these men were indeed rather typical of their time, and it was in most respects a good time in which they lived; and they were honest men according to their lights, which in other respects were quite bright indeed. We cannot blame them very harshly for not having information which was not available in their day. And, despite the tremendous advances of linguistic science in the nineteenth and twentieth centuries, attitudes toward language have actually changed very little since Bishop Lowth and Lindley Murray were laying down the law. Their precepts were largely based on what they supposed to be logical and reasonable, for they believed that the laws of language were rooted in the natural order, and this was of course "reasonable." To cite an example, they outlawed, as far as the educated are con-

[97] Lowth was of course not the only one. For a discussion of the contributions of George Campbell, Joseph Priestley, the Philadelphia-born Lindley Murray, and others, see Sterling A. Leonard, *The Doctrine of Correctness in English Usage, 1700–1800* (Madison, Wis., 1929).

cerned, the emphatic and still very viable double negative construction on the grounds stated by Lowth that "two Negatives in English destroy one another, or are equivalent to an Affirmative"—in English, that is to say, just as in mathematics, though the analogy implicit in the appeal to logic was quite false. Many very reasonable men before them had spoken and written sentences with two or even more negatives: Chaucer has four in ". . . Forwhy to tellen nas [ne was] nat his entente/ To nevere no man, for whom that he so ferde,"[98] and it certainly never occurred to him that these would cancel out and thus reverse his meaning.

Modern linguistic studies have made very little headway in convincing those who have not made a special study of language that language is a living thing, the possession and the servant of man rather than an ideal towards which we should all fecklessly and hopelessly aspire. Many schoolroom grammars and handbooks of English usage widely used at the present day perpetuate the tradition of Bishop Lowth's *Short Introduction to English Grammar.* Indeed, the very word *grammar* means to many highly literate people not the study of language, but merely so simple a thing as making the "proper" choice between *shall* and *will, between* and *among, different from* and *different than, who* and *whom* and the avoidance of terminal prepositions, of *ain't,* and of *it's me.* In the following chapter we shall among other matters examine in more detail the later developments of this comparatively recent tradition in England and America.

[98] *Troilus and Criseyde,* I,738–39. There are also four in his description of the Knight in the General Prologue to the *Canterbury Tales:* "He nevere yet no vileynye ne sayde/In al his lyf unto no maner wight" (lines 70–71).

CHAPTER IX

Recent British
and American English

"THE American language," despite the distinguished precedent of H. L. Mencken's use of the term,[1] is as much of a misnomer for the English spoken by Americans as would be "the Mexican language" for the Spanish spoken by Mexicans. Though educated Continental Europeans must certainly be aware of this fact, they are by and large so overconscious of the differences between it and the way they as schoolchildren were taught to speak English that one suspects they regard these differences as somewhat comparable to those which make Icelandic and Norwegian, or Swedish and Danish, separate languages.[2]

One suspects indeed that Europeans, including the English themselves,[3] really prefer to think that the speech of Americans is a corrupt and degraded variety of current Standard British English, which has

[1] He was not the first to use it. Noah Webster and others had already done so.

[2] According to an Associated Press item in the Jacksonville *Florida Times-Union* (October 4, 1957, p. 2), the shortwave broadcast service from West Germany "beams German language courses to the outside world in French, Spanish, Portuguese, English and Amerikanisch."

[3] Whoever wrote the blurb on the front flap of the dust cover of the London (1954) edition of my *Words and Ways of American English* (first pub. New York, 1952) is an honorable exception. He or she was quite aware of the necessity of informing the prospective English reader, whose name was certainly not Legion, that "the American-English [*sic*] language . . . has, *after all,* as much claim to the name English as our own tongue" (italics added). The point of view of Isabel Quigly, the cinema critic for the *Spectator,* is much more representative: she writes in a review of *Ben Hur* that the director had "a cunning idea" regarding the speech of the players, for "Romans speak English, the rest speak American" (December 18, 1959, p. 909).

presumably remained unchanged, hence "pure," at least since the early years of the seventeenth century, at which time what must have been an inferior brand of Englishmen, unable for one reason or another to make their way in their own land, began to settle the North American continent.

Such notions of course fly in the face of the facts, but they have the virtue, dubious though it is, of fortifying prejudice. It would be just as well if Americans tried to understand this prejudice.

Painful though it is to have to admit it, the course of early American history was not particularly glorious from a cultivated European point of view—despite a spurious sort of admiration for our Old Hickories, our Honest Abes, and our Davy Crocketts. And it is perhaps a bit unreasonable for Americans to expect to be loved—and being loved seems very important to us, to the tune of many millions of dollars—for those aspects of what we are pleased to call the "American way of life" which we take such pride in and insist upon publicizing. There is in fact nothing universally lovable about the dour, hard-working, plain-living, hymn-shouting men and women who supposedly made up the bulk of our early population. Those who must struggle hard all their lives against an uncharitable environment in order merely to survive can have little concern with the blessings of civilization. What is remarkable is that many of these, and their descendants as well, came to prefer the harshness of the simple rustic life to the richness of their European heritage, thus making some sort of virtue—the "American dream" it is sometimes called—out of necessity. It is equally unreasonable to expect others not to perceive the shoddiness and the hypocrisy behind the homespun idealism, the wooden-nutmeg know-how, and the apparently irrelevant concept of "gracious living" upon which we have come to pride ourselves. Yet we must not here oversimplify, for it is certainly true that the European man in the street has avidly adopted many of the least prepossessing features of what Americans are pleased to call their civilization—rock 'n' roll, evangelism, cowboys in form-fitting pants, and cola drinks, for instance.

The fact remains, however, that most cultured Europeans have no great admiration for American speech, regardless of how much they may be awed by the softer aspects of our present "way of life" as this is represented to them by those who write our advertising copy—certainly not great enough for them to have any desire to use it or to substitute it for the British Standard now taught in their schools. British speech continues to have far more prestige, and few Continental Europeans—not to mention the English themselves—have any desire or inclination to speak any other variety. As a German candidate for the doctorate in English once remarked to me in an unusual outburst of frankness, American speech simply lacked *Eleganz*. And when I thought of the speech of some of my countrymen prominent in public life at that time and contrasted them with their English counterparts, I suspect that I got the point of the remark all too well.

For it is true that most American speech does lack this most undemocratic quality of elegance, which still means much to the cultured European. In a classless society—even in one which is only theoretically so—elegance cannot thrive. The very word becomes a smear. In the countries of the Old World, on the other hand, the standard of speech has to a large extent risen out of the usage of a privileged leisure caste, though it has certainly been molded to some extent by men of learning. Americans are proud to suppose that they have no such caste in their society, and that the most horny-handed bumpkin, if he follows the proper precepts, may sit in the seats of the mighty.

Elegance cannot be instilled or inculcated. Even if it were agreed to be a desirable characteristic of speech, who would provide the standards? It is, indeed, a rather casual quality, as such phrases as "well-bred ease" and "careless elegance" would indicate. It is a product of *dolce far niente*, for which democracy has no use. It is quite a different thing from the tortured precision, the "good grammar," which has been our national ideal and which is theoretically within the reach of every man. It must be understood that we are here neither recommending elegance in American speech nor condemning its absence; we are concerned only with a state of things. We are not even attempting to define so intangible a quality, which is as much a matter of an attitude toward life as of articulation and intonation. It is a matter of style, moreover, not an inherent quality of any language or any form of any language: there were certainly tasteless, sloppy speakers of Classical Latin, and one would be very much surprised not to find at least a few elegant speakers of Hottentot. We are here merely pointing out that British English has greater prestige than American English and suggesting a reason for it.

THE PRESTIGE
OF THE MODERN BRITISH STANDARD

The English have, at least since the latter part of the eighteenth century, cooked up a form of speech based on that of London that kept the darker-skinned natives of the Empire in check for a good many years. Even now, when it seems to be losing some of its former political efficacy, it retains its prestige value: the English-educated African chieftains speak it, often with considerable elegance, and doubtless regard American English with a certain scorn, much as Europeans are likely to do. That the British themselves are not uniformly sympathetic toward it is indicated by the following, from the *Spectator*: "Effusive thanks also to the BBC for the documentary film *Our School*, an absolute cracker with a dozen moments of sheer delight, including one in which a (Scottish) English teacher blew his top over his (English) pupils' obsession with 'posh accents'" (May 4, 1962, p. 587). The writer (Clifford Hanley) goes on to say: "This has always baffled me too. If we get a United States of Europe, will solemn English codgers have to teach themselves to identify the Right Type of Frenchman by the way he pronounces *merde?*" The cream of the jest is that even Americans, though they may be slightly put off by "posh accents" at times, are impressed by them and hence likely to suppose that Standard British English is somehow "better" English than what they speak. From a purely linguistic point of view, this is of course nonsense; but it is a safe bet that it will long survive any conceivable loss of British influence in world affairs.

THE CONSERVATISM
OF AMERICAN ENGLISH

The fact remains that no form of any language is impugnable by any objective standards; only those who speak may be so impugned. Since language undergoes no changes as a result of crossing an ocean, the first English-speaking colonists in America continued to speak precisely as they had done in England. But people isolated from their mother country tend always to be conservative, linguistically as well as in other ways, and the English spoken in America at the present day has retained a good many characteristics of earlier British English which do not survive in present British English, much as Icelandic has retained characteristics of older Scandinavian which have been lost in the other Scandinavian languages.

Thus to regard American English as inferior to British English is to impugn earlier Standard British English as well, for there was doubtless little difference at the time of the Revolution. There is a strong likelihood, for instance, that George III and Lord Cornwallis pronounced *ask, after, path, glass, dance,* and the like exactly the same as did George Washington and John Hancock—that is, as the overwhelming majority of Americans do to this day. It was similar with the treatment of postvocalic *r*, whose loss under certain circumstances did not occur in the speech of the London area until about the time of the Revolution.

Other supposed characteristics of American English are also to be found in pre-Revolutionary British English, and there is very good reason indeed for the conclusion of the eminent Swedish Anglicist Eilert Ekwall that from the time of the Revolution on, "American pronunciation has been on the whole independent of British; the result has been that American pronunciation has not come to share the development undergone later by Standard British, but remains at about the stage it had reached by the time of the Revolution."[4] Ekwall's concern is exclusively with pronunciation, but the principle implied holds good also for many lexical items, some morphological characteristics, and probably to some degree for intonation as well.

American retention of *gotten* is an example of conservatism, though it was of course not consciously preserved. This form, the usual past participle of *get* in older British English, survives in present Standard British English mainly in the phrase "ill-gotten gains"; but it is very much alive in American English, being the usual past participial form of the verb except in the senses 'to have' and 'to be obliged to.'[5] Similarly, American English has kept *fall* for the season[6] and *deck* for a pack of cards (though American English also uses *pack*); and it has retained certain phonological characteristics of earlier British English to be discussed later in some detail.

VOCABULARY CHANGES
IN AMERICAN ENGLISH

It works both ways, however; for American English has lost certain features—mostly vocabulary items—which have survived in British English, for example *waistcoat* (the name for a garment which Americans call a *vest*, a word which in England usually means 'undershirt'), *fortnight*, a useful term completely lost to American English, and a number of topographical terms which Americans had no need for—

[4] *American and British Pronunciation* (Upsala, 1946), pp. 32–33.

[5] For instance "He has gotten permission to go" and "He would have gotten there sooner if he had left earlier" as contrasted with "He hasn't got the nerve to do it" and "He has got to do it."

[6] *Autumn* was first used in English by Geoffrey Chaucer, according to the *OED*.

words like *fen, wold, spinney, copse, dell, heath,* and *moor.* Americans, on the other hand, desperately needed terms to designate topographical features different from any known in the Old World. To remedy the deficiency, they used new compounds of English words like *backwoods, watergap,* and *underbrush*; they adapted English words to new uses, like *creek,* in British English 'a small arm of the sea,' which in American English may mean 'any small stream,' and they adopted foreign words like *prairie* (ultimately derived from Fr. *pré* 'field'), *canyon* (Sp. *cañón* 'tube'), and *mesa* (likewise Spanish).

It was similar with the naming of flora and fauna strange to the colonists. When they saw a bird that somewhat resembled the English robin, they simply called it a robin, though it was not the same bird at all. When they saw an animal that was totally unlike anything that they had ever seen before, they might call it by its Indian name, if they could find out what this was, for example *raccoon* and *woodchuck.* It was similar with the names of plants: *catalpa* and its variant *catawba* are of Muskhogean origin; *Johnny-jump-up* was inspired by a crude kind of fancy; *sweet potato* might have originated just as well in England as in America except for the fact that this particular variety of potato did not exist in England.

American English is, as we have said, essentially a development of seventeenth-century British English. Except in vocabulary, there are probably few significant characteristics of American English which are not traceable to British English. There are also some American English characteristics which were doubtless dialectal British English in the seventeenth century, for there were certainly dialect speakers among the earliest settlers, though they would seem to have had little influence. A literary standard had arisen in London long before, as we have seen, which had greatly influenced the various regional types of common speech of England—the speech of the majority of those Englishmen to settle permanently in the New World, for these were not illiterate bumpkins but ambitious and industrious members of the upper-lower and lower-middle classes, with a sprinkling of educated men—clergymen, lawyers, and even a few younger sons of the aristocracy. It is likely that there was a cultured nucleus in all of the early American communities. Such facts as these explain why American English resembles present Standard British English more closely than it resembles any other British type of speech.

In American English there are three main regional types—Northern, Midland, and Southern—with a good many different blendings of these as one travels westward. There are also a number of subtypes on the Atlantic Coast, such as the speech of the New York and Boston areas in the North and the Charleston-Savannah area in the South. All types of American English have grown out of the regional modifications of the British Standard—with some coloring from the British dialects—as it existed in the seventeenth century, when it was much less rigid than it is today.

Boston failed to maintain its early pre-eminence as the hub of American culture, such as it was. Had it not done so, America might well have had a geographical and ultimately a caste standard based upon the speech of Boston. As things have turned out, an American may use with complete social impunity any of the types of speech to which we have referred or practically any modifications thereof. So long as it is obvious from his bearing and from what he talks about that he is an educated man (in the American sense of the term), his speech will pass muster, that is, be socially acceptable in any part of the country despite occasional references to a "harsh Midwestern *r*" and a "lazy Southern drawl." It should be stressed at this point that, compared with British English, French, Italian, Spanish, German, and other European languages, American speech is quite homogeneous: there is no type of American English which is not readily understood—though regional prejudice may cause an occasional eyebrow to lift—in all parts of the country, with the exception of Gullah, spoken by about 100,000 Negroes who live along the coastal region of South Carolina and Georgia, and who have lived there in cultural isolation for many generations.[7] A Texas oil magnate speaks in one way; a Back Bay Bostonian in a slightly different way; and a landed Virginian in a yet slightly different way. But as long as they all speak like "educated" men, they all speak "good" American English. The Chicagoan is just as proud of pronouncing his *r*'s—provided that he ever gives a thought to the matter—as the Charlestonian is of losing them. Neither practice is ordinarily regarded as either superior or inferior; they are merely regarded as somewhat different, and the difference is not always noticed, though it usually is.

A CASE OF MUTUAL INTOLERANCE

Since about 1930 Americans have become increasingly tolerant of British English. Even its most posh variety doubtless offends them less—if indeed it offends them at all—than it does those younger-

[7] The best treatment of Gullah—actually the only authoritative one—is that of Lorenzo Dow Turner, *Africanisms in the Gullah Dialect* (Chicago, 1949).

generation Englishmen who lack it by tradition and have been unable, or in some cases unwilling, to acquire it—the so-called angry young men. For one thing, Americans have become quite familiar with it by way of the radio, the talking films, and television; most now take it pretty much in their stride. But it has not always been so. When Matthew Arnold visited the United States in 1884, he was anything but beloved in Chicago, where it was reported that "he has harsh features, supercilious manners, parts his hair down the middle, wears a single eye-glass and ill-fitting clothes."[8] It is nevertheless likely that even these un-American shortcomings would have been forgiven him had it not been that, according to his American agent, his accent was baffling to his audiences. Other derogatory comments indicate little more than that Arnold spoke the "toniest" type of British English current in his day; he obviously had a posh accent. It should be added that New York seems to have received him a little more graciously. It is impossible to conceive of such comments being made nowadays about the speech of Queen Elizabeth II, Sir Winston Churchill, or Lord Avon (best known to Americans as Anthony Eden), not to mention the actor-knights Alec Guinness, John Gielgud, Laurence Olivier, Michael Redgrave, and Ralph Richardson,[9] all of whom have a considerable following in the United States.

The English are considerably less tolerant of American speech, which, as has been pointed out, they tend to regard as a corruption of their own rather than as an independent development of earlier British English. When I inadvertently used the term *British English* in conversation with a neighbor in London, she asked in her most fluting upper-class tones (but, in justice it must be said, with some good-natured amusement), "Why, whatever other kind is there?" The answer, which was easy enough, was not given on this occasion, for feelings about language run so high as to make it a subject unsuitable for social intercourse: there are, of course, in addition to American English, Australian English, Canadian English, South African English, Indian English, among others—all as legitimately English as that form of the language which happens to be spoken in the mother coun-

[8] Cited in Allan Nevins, *American Social History* (New York, 1923), p. 501.

[9] Perhaps it is unfair to bring actors into the picture, for American actors of an older school were in fact trained to use a type of artificial stage speech which, though by no means British, had a number of British characteristics.

try. Appearing on an American television program, the late Gilbert Harding grumpily pretended misunderstanding a reference to his "English accent." "How could I have an English accent?" he asked; "I *am* English."

AMERICAN INFILTRATION
OF THE BRITISH WORD STOCK

Because in the course of recent history Americans have acquired greater commercial, technical, and perhaps even political prestige than any other English-speaking group, it is perhaps not unnatural that the English and others should take a somewhat high-handed attitude toward American speech. The fact is that the English have done so at least since 1735, when one Francis Moore, describing for English readers the then infant city of Savannah, said, "It stands upon the flat of a Hill; the Bank of the River (which they in barbarous English call a *bluff*) is steep. . . ."[10] Mencken treats the subject of British attitudes toward American speech fully and with characteristic zest in the first chapter of his *American Language* and also in the first supplement to that wonderful work (pp. 1–100).

But the truth is that, as far as vocabulary is concerned—and most people, when they think of language, think of it in terms of vocabulary items—British English has been rather constantly infiltrated by American usage, as the frequent objurgations of English writers indicate. Cyril Ray is particularly vocal on the subject in the "Postscript" which he used to contribute to the London *Spectator*; he makes many disapproving references to "the continuing Americanisation [*sic*] of English usage since the war,"[11] deploring the fact that in a short story by Ian Fleming a "very senior" British official tells the secret-service hero that there will be an "FO pouch" for him. Says Ray, "I have never met *any* Foreign Office official, senior or otherwise, who referred to anything but 'the bag,' which has been English diplomatic usage for generations: 'pouch' is pure American." As a result of the present prominence of America in international affairs, American *Top Secret* is now being used in England for what used to be merely *Secret*; *high-ranking officer* (an "ugly and otiose American neologism . . . unknown

[10] Cited in H. L. Mencken, *The American Language,* 4th ed. (New York, 1936), p. 3, from Moore's *Voyage to Georgia, Begun in the Year 1735* (London, 1744), p. 24.

[11] February 9, 1962, p. 190. It has, as we shall see, been continuing for a much longer time than this.

here until the last war . . ."[12]) for what used to be *general, flag, field,* or, more loosely, *senior officer*; and *career diplomat* (along with the "horrid hybrid" *career diplomatist*) for what used to be *professional diplomatist.* Mr. Ray's own profession of journalism is by no means immune from American corruption, for he alludes to a reference in "a very stylish English newspaper" to the *wire services,* meaning 'news agencies.' Two years earlier, Mr. Ray, whom one can grow very fond of as a writer, asked plaintively why, in some of the new Lyons eating establishments "we have to call chips—an English form of food—by the longer and inaccurate American name of French Fried?" remarking quite understandably that "it seems stupid to me."[13] Elsewhere this same custodian of the purity of British English deplores the fact that even the august *Times* has taken to calling adolescents *teenagers,* right on its "leader-page" (*Americanice* "editorial page"),[14] and to referring to the American Civil War *centennial,*[15] though "it seems a pity to substitute yet another unnecessary Americanism for the perfectly good English word, 'centenary.' "

[12] July 8, 1960, p. 78. It is interesting to note that *The New English Bible: New Testament,* published jointly by the Oxford University Press and the Cambridge University Press (1961) has "high-ranking officers" for the Authorized Version's "chief captains" in Acts xxv.23. One English reviewer has suggested "top brass" as an alternative.

[13] March 4, 1960, p. 334. In British English, as can be inferred, *chips* are (or were) what in American English are called *French fries.* What Americans call *potato chips* are *crisps* in England. Thus the famous English "fish and chips" is the same as American "fish and French fried potatoes." But the distinction in terminology seems to be breaking down, and it is not Americans who are changing over, distressing as the fact may seem to all good Englishmen. The same is true of the old shibboleth distinction between American *can* and British *tin* (both as noun and verb), according to a half-page advertisement in the "posh Sundays" (conservative Sunday newspapers): "So that when your husband returns from his hard day at the office, he finds you waiting like the dedicated wife you are, cool, calm and competent, all ready to open him a can of beer, while a canned steak pie browns in the oven, and canned fruit and cream wait on the sideboard," of which the writer for the *Spectator* comments, "Must have been quite a strong-minded copywriter to resist writing, 'So that when your husband returns canned from his hard day at the office, he finds you waiting like the dedicated wife you are, cool, competent, and canned. . . .' " (December 8, 1961, p. 882).

[14] June 9, 1961, p. 859.

[15] March 17, 1961, p. 382.

Americanisms—words and phrases peculiar to the United States, though they may have occurred in earlier English—have indeed made their way into British English in large numbers. The transfer began quite a while ago, long before talking films, radio, and television were ever thought of, let alone World War II, which Mr. Ray considers a main corrupting influence. Sir William Craigie, the eminent editor of the *Dictionary of American English on Historical Principles*,[16] pointed out in 1927[17] that although "for some two centuries . . . the passage of new words or senses across the Atlantic was regularly westwards . . . with the nineteenth century . . . the contrary current begins to set in, bearing with it many a piece of drift-wood to the shores of Britain, there to be picked up and incorporated in the structure of the language," citing such Americanisms in British English as *backwoods, blizzard, prairie, swamp, bunkum, caucus, belittle*,[18] *cloudburst*, and a good many others which have long been completely acclimatized.

Recent years have seen the introduction of many other Americanisms into British usage: *cafeteria, electrocute* (both in reference to the distinctively American mode of capital punishment and in the extended sense 'to kill accidentally by electric shock'[19]), *highbrow* (and

[16] This four-volume work was published by the University of Chicago Press (1938–44). For some years unobtainable, it has recently been reissued. It should not be confused with M. M. Mathews' *Dictionary of Americanisms*, published by the same press in 1951.

[17] *The Study of American English*, S. P. E. Tract No. XXVII (Oxford), p. 208.

[18] Apparently first used by Thomas Jefferson in his *Notes on the State of Virginia*, written in 1782 and published in 1787, this word brought forth shocked cries from English commentators. See Mencken, *American Language*, p. 14, for an amusing example from the *European Magazine and London Review*, ending with the plaintive appeal, "O spare, we beseech you, our mother-tongue."

[19] Thus Edward Marjoribanks in *For the Defence* (New York, 1937), p. 458, first published in London in 1929: "A young collier went ratting with some friends; and, although their dogs passed unscathed through the 'live' wires, when the boy came against it he was electrocuted." The *OED* Supplement of 1933 has British citations with this meaning from 1909 and 1913. Mathews' *Dictionary of Americanisms* does not include this later meaning, in which the connotation of purely accidental death has been added and which may indeed have originated in England, where the word, coined in America to designate a new-fangled, ultrascientific way of putting criminals to death, may have lacked some of the immediate horror that it connoted in the United States.

more recently *egghead*), *lowbrow, cocktail, filling station, fan* 'sports
devotee,' and, of course, the ubiquitous *O.K.*, to cite only a handful.
American *radio* has practically superseded British *wireless*, and *TV*
will doubtless crowd out the somewhat nurseryish *telly. O.K.* is, if anything, of more frequent occurrence nowadays in England than in the
land of its birth, and may occur in quite formal situations such as, for
example, on many legal documents to indicate the correctness of details
therein.[20] These and other Americanisms have slithered into British
English in the most unobtrusive way, so that their American origin is
hardly regarded at all save by a few crusted older-generation speakers:
since they are used by Englishmen, they are "English," and that is all
there is to it. Woe be to the American who tries to convince a run-of-
the-mill Englishman to the contrary!

Brian Foster, an Englishman who is anything but run-of-the-mill,
has written knowingly of the "enormous impact of American idiom on
the standard British usage," though "by a strange paradox few people,
even among specialists, are conscious of the extent of its influence,
and some . . . virtually deny its existence."[21] Foster cites as firmly

[20] Since the publication of my summarizing account of this most wide-
spread of all Americanisms (in *Words and Ways of American English* [New
York, 1952], pp. 158–65), Ralph T. Eubanks in "The Basic Derivation of
'O.K.,' " published in *American Speech* for October 1960 (XXXV, 188–
92), cited an occurrence about a month earlier (February 24, 1840) than
that hitherto thought to be the earliest, which had been cited by Allen
Walker Read from the New York *New Era* of March 23, 1840, in "The
Evidence on 'O.K.,' " *Saturday Review of Literature*, XXIV (July 19, 1941),
3–4, 10–11. Read found another occurrence of the word, appearing four
days later in the same paper as the slogan of a political club made up of
supporters of Martin Van Buren and explained as being from the initials
of *Old Kinderhook,* the birthplace of Van Buren. Read is now able to cite
a number of earlier occurrences, including Eubanks' find and those set
forth by Woodford A. Heflin in " 'O.K.' and Its Incorrect Etymology,"
American Speech, XXXVII (1962), 243–48. The new material is presented
and summarized by Read in "The First Stage in the History of 'O.K.' "
and "The Second Stage in the History of 'O.K.' " in the same journal,
XXXVIII (1963), 5–27 and 83–102. By a strange coincidence, the first occurrence now known is exactly a year earlier than the occurrence discovered in
1941 by Read; it is from the Boston *Morning Post* of March 23, 1839, and is
an acronym of *oll korrect.*

[21] "Recent American Influence on Standard English," *Anglia*, LXXIII
(1956), 328–57. Compare this view with the less realistic one of Eric Part-

established in Standard British English *show business, to build up* (by advertising), *of all time* 'ever,'[22] *star* 'popular performer' (also as verb), *disk-jockey* (the more usual British spelling has *disc-*), *bobby-soxer, natural* 'brilliant but untrained performer,'[23] *to put* (something) *over, to get* (something) *across, stooge, double-talk,* and *ballyhoo*—all originally from the usage of the world of entertainment, enormously important in modern America, and all, with the possible exception of *of all time*, more or less nonliterary. But the following Americanisms, while they may be offensive in varying degrees to those who, whatever their national ties, have a rarefied and sophisticated sense of style, appear in the formal utterances of V.I.P.'s,[24] as well as in the writings of some quite respectable writers on both sides of the Atlantic:[25] *way of life*,[26] *alibi* 'excuse,' *breakdown* 'analysis,' *blurb*

---

ridge, who writes that "the Americanization has, in the main, affected only cant, slang, colloquialisms and catch-phrases; indeed, the Americanization of Standard English has been amazingly slight" in *British and American English Since 1900*, in collaboration with John W. Clark (New York, 1951), p. 180.

[22] As in "the greatest film of all time," at first regarded as a "typical example of the American love of grandiloquence."

[23] Later 'something very suitable,' as in the British advertisement for face powder sold in three varieties, cited by Foster: "One of these is a natural for you" (p. 332).

[24] Another Americanism which is now a part of the British vocabulary. It has been used in all seriousness on the floor of the House of Commons, and without any need to define it. Foster, who was puzzled by the term when he first heard it in 1946, reports its use by a clergyman in a B.B.C. religious broadcast as follows: "They [children] are V.I.P.'s to Him" (p. 334). Certainly American taste has never sunk lower.

[25] The words to be cited, except for *blurb*, are obviously not of American origin; it is the meanings and in some instances the combinations which have developed in the United States.

[26] Originally in the sentiment-charged phrase "American way of life," denoting freedom, equality, gracious living, super-salesmanship, baseball, and heaven only knows what else, *way of life* shortly petered out to mean nothing more than 'life,' 'living,' or even 'regimen' (as in the statement of a Federal judge in Miami, Florida, in sentencing a vegetarian who evaded the draft on the grounds that his vegetarianism was a religion: "There was . . . evidence that his . . . vegetarianism was regarded by other vegetarians as a philosophy and dietary way of life, rather than a religion" [International News Service item, April 11, 1958]).

("now used quite solemnly as an indispensable item in the jargon of literary critics and booklovers"), *quit* (previously regarded as archaic except in a few stock phrases), *maybe*,[27] *crash* 'collide,' *allergy* 'aversion' (and *allergic* 'averse from'), *angle* 'viewpoint,' *sales-resistance, to slip up, to stand up to, to go back on, know-how. Fortnight* 'two consecutive weeks,' a stock Britishism to most Americans who know the word at all (as all those who read books do), "seems to appear rarely in the speech of the younger generation," who increasingly are using American *two weeks*.[28]

As has been pointed out, words and usages are frequently borrowed from American English quite unconsciously. Where this is not so, the fact that they are of transatlantic provenience is soon forgotten. H. W. Horwill testifies that a good many Americanisms which he wrote down during a residence in the United States between 1900 and 1905 would not have been recognized by him as of American origin in 1935 if he had trusted to his memory alone, for "usages that to-day are peculiar to America are to-morrow adopted by English writers and speakers, frequently without the least suspicion of their transatlantic origin."[29] He cites *cut* in the sense 'reduction' as an Americanism that became widely used in England during the financial crisis of 1931. By 1935 there was no consciousness of its American provenience; it was thoroughly naturalized, though for a time it was written within quotation marks (which Horwill calls by the frequent British variant, *inverted commas*).

The convenient use of noun as verb in *to contact*, meaning 'to see, call, meet, or in any other way to get in touch with,' seems to have originated in America,[30] though it might just as well have done so in

[27] *Maybe,* labeled archaic and dialectal by the *OED,* has always been common in Northern England, but, as Foster says, "It can hardly be doubted that the revival of this word [in Standard, or Southern, British English] is due to the American example" (p. 336).

[28] Complete loss of this word will blur a distinction previously possible to make in British English, though American English has got on very well without it—that between, to cite Foster's example, "Last year I spent a fortnight at London" and "Last year I spent two weeks (i.e. two separate weeks) at London" (p. 336). (Note British *at* where American English would invariably use *in*.)

[29] *A Dictionary of Modern American Usage* (Oxford, 1935), Preface.

[30] Both the *Dictionary of Americanisms* and the *OED* Supplement cite the same American occurrence as the earliest in this sense. Mathews in the former work labels the word as slang, though there is nothing particularly slangy about its use in any of his citations.

England, since there is nothing un-English about such a conversion: scores of other nouns have undergone the same functional shift, as we shall see (p. 299). The fact is that this particular conversion had occurred earlier in British English, but the new verb was confined to technical writing: the *OED* cites "The spark and the gunpowder contacted" from 1834, but calls such use rare. We may thus regard the occurrence in 1929 as to all intents and purposes a new American creation. The verb began to catch on in England around the mid-1940's, though many persons there as well as in the United States objected to it vociferously.[31] No one gets much disturbed over it nowadays. The mandarin attitude of Nigel Strangeways, the aristocratic detective hero of Nicholas Blake (a novel-writing pseudonym of the poet C. Day Lewis), though still faintly persistent on both sides of the Atlantic, is no longer widespread; the speaker is a police inspector who has not had the advantages of Nigel's expensive education: "I've not contacted him yet, sir" (Nigel shuddered inwardly at the word), "but I'm expecting a report. . . ."[32] Crane Brinton, in a review of H. C. Allen's *Great Britain and the United States*[33] cites "Lord North despatched an emissary to contact Benjamin Franklin," written "apparently without a qualm" by the author, an Oxford don. The reviewer concludes that this one word *contact* "carries high symbolic importance. . . . Mr. Mencken was wrong—there will be no American language, for the simple reason that, apart from deviations in ephemeral slang and regional dialects . . . the Queen's English and the President's English grow together."[34]

[31] To Sir Alan Herbert it was a "loathsome" word, according to Sir Ernest Gowers, *Plain Words: Their ABC* (New York, 1954), p. 53. Ivor Brown, as cited by Gowers, was considerably more tolerant in his judgment that "there is no word which covers approach by telephone, letter and speech, and *contact* is self-explanatory and concise."

[32] *There's Trouble Brewing* (London, 1956), p. 75. The novel was first published some years previous to 1956, when shuddering at the word was more indicative of one's fine-drawn sense of style than it has now come to be.

[33] New York *Herald-Tribune Book Review*, May 1, 1955, p. 3.

[34] It is probably just as well not to take the phrase "President's English" too literally. The President of the United States in 1955 was Dwight David Eisenhower, the most graceless speaker to occupy the White House since Warren Gamaliel Harding. But our concern is primarily with language, not with style, and the then President's English, like that of all native speakers, was certainly basically the same as the Queen's, even to the common, if unorthodox, preference for invariable *I* after *and*, as follows: *Queen* (on returning from her tour of the colonies in 1954): "It is a wonderful moment

Actually, though, they were never so far apart as it has been pleasing to American patriotism (which has sometimes manifested itself un-pleasingly in a prideful "mucker pose")[35] and British insularity (which has sometimes equally unpleasingly manifested itself in an overweening assumption of superiority) to pretend. "How quaint of the British to call a muffler a silencer!"[36] "How boorish of the Americans to call an egg-whisk an egg beater!" The most striking of such presumably amusing differences, however, will not be very important, for they almost inevitably occur on a rather superficial level—in the specialized vocabularies of travel, sports, schools, government, and various trades.

NATIONAL DIFFERENCES IN WORD CHOICE

There are many lists of British and American equivalents,[37] but these must not be taken too seriously. On the American side of the

---

for my husband and I after nearly six months away to be met and escorted by ships of the Home Fleet" (*Illustrated London News*, May 22, 1954, p. 824). *President* (on returning from Denver, where he suffered an illness): "I am deeply honored that so many of you should have come down to welcome Mrs. Eisenhower and I back to Washington" (*Time*, November 21, 1955, p. 17).

[35] For instance the following, from a review in the *Saturday Review* (May 12, 1962, p. 28): "It [the book] is sometimes too much the author's own, larded with Briticisms as obscure for most of us over here as those uproariously blank jokes in jolly old *Punch.* . . ." One cannot but suspect a trace of inverted snobbery in such a linguistically chauvinistic attitude. If the *Saturday Review* is read in England, the pretense of American provincialism quoted here has done American prestige no good. The English are of course guilty of exactly the same sort of prideful provincialism, as has been indicated by a good many previous citations. As for "jolly old *Punch,*" many Americans—even some who have borne arms in defense of their country—find it quite amusing; the English by and large like the *New Yorker* in a grudging sort of way, and some of them even prefer it to jolly old *Punch*.

[36] The American motoring term is apparently that used by the Swedes when they have occasion to use English. "London Day by Day," a column in the London *Daily Telegraph*, has referred to "the astonishing statement" in a summary of Swedish traffic regulations, printed in English, that "driving without a muffler is forbidden" (September 1, 1956, p. 6). The columnist has chosen to misunderstand *muffler* as a heavy scarf for the neck, a meaning which is also widely current in American English.

[37] For instance, those prepared by Mencken in *The American Language*, pp. 233–37 and in *Supplement I* (New York, 1945), pp. 457–87.

page will be found many locutions perfectly well understood, many of them in use, Britain[38]—for instance, *automobile,* represented as the American equivalent of *car* or *motor car,* is practically a formal word in America, the ordinary term being the supposedly British *car;* whereas the supposedly American word occurs in the names of two English motoring organizations, the Royal Automobile Club and the Automobile Association. And on the British side will be found many locutions perfectly well known and frequently used in America—for instance, *postman* (as in James M. Cain's very American novel *The Postman Always Rings Twice*) and *railway* (as in *Railway Express* and the *Southern Railway*), though it is certain that *mailman* (or *letter carrier*) and *railroad* do occur more frequently in American speech. Similarly, one usually finds *baggage* as the American equivalent of British *luggage,* though *luggage* has come to be very commonly used in American English, perhaps because of its frequent occurrence in "prestige" advertising. Mencken lists *drawers* (men's) as the American equivalent of British *pants.* It is doubtful that this was true even in 1936 (the date of the fourth edition of Mencken's great work), but one can say with confidence that *drawers* has now become archaic for the nether undergarments of either sex—imagine asking to buy a pair in either a men's furnishings or a lingerie shop! The usual American term is *shorts,* which may also designate outer garments; *pants* for the undergarment has become increasingly feminine, though usually in the diminutive form *panties.*

Other hardy perennials of such lists include[39] *mad–angry,* though Americans use *angry* in formal contexts, often under the impression that *mad* as a synonym is "incorrect," and though many speakers of British English use *mad* in the sense 'angry'[40] as it was frequently

[38] Randolph Quirk, an English observer of American speech, put the matter well in the New York *Times* Weekly Review, International Edition (December 2, 1956, p. 7): "The long and imposing lists of so-called distinctively British and American words and usages are 75 per cent misleading; it turns out either that both the words so neatly separated are used in one or the other country, or that both are found in both countries but are used in slightly different contexts or in different proportions." There is usually no question of influence from one side or the other.

[39] The supposedly American term is given first in these pairs.

[40] Note the following striking use of the synonyms in consecutive sentences, from *Speak Justly of the Dead* (Garden City, N.Y., 1953), an English detective story by the highly literate E. C. R. Lorac (a pseudonym of Edith Caroline Rivett, born 1894): "It's no use getting angry, Venner. I know you feel mad with me. . . ." (p. 115). The speaker is a doctor.

used in older English, for example in the Authorized (King James) Version of 1611, Acts xxvi.11: ". . . being exceedingly mad against them, I persecuted them even unto strange cities";[41] *sick–ill,* though *sick,* supposed to mean only 'nauseated' in England, is frequently used in the older sense, that which is supposed to be American, in British English: in "A Book for Christmas," a short article printed in *Books of the Month,* an organ of the British Book Centre, Sir Ralph Richardson writes, "I was often sick as a child, and so often lonely, and I remember when I was in hospital a kindly visitor giving me a book. . . ." (November–December 1952, p. 15), in which only the phrase "in hospital" instead of American "in the hospital" indicates the writer's Englishness,[42] except possibly for *visitor* where many Americans, under the impression that the "subject of a gerund" *must* be possessive, would have written *visitor's; letter-box*[43]–*pillar-box,* though the English use *letter-box* for any receptacle for mailing (that is, posting)[44] letters in, other than the actual low pillar with a slit for putting the letters through, which is called a pillar-box because that is precisely what it is; *package–parcel,* though the supposedly British word is perfectly well known to all Americans, who have for a long time sent packages by Parcel Post (not Package Mail); *stairway–staircase,* though Mary Roberts Rinehart's best seller of the early years of the present century was entitled *The Circular Staircase,* though *stairs* is the usual term in both countries, and though *stairway* is recorded in British dictionaries with no notation that it is confined to American usage; and *window-shade–blind,* though *blind(s)* is the usual term throughout a thickly populated section of the eastern United States,[45] including the city of Baltimore. There are many other equally weak sisters; these have been chosen almost at random.

This is not to say that there are not many genuine instances of

---

[41] The *New English Bible: New Testament* has ". . . my fury rose to such a pitch that I extended my persecution to foreign cities," which does not improve what did not need improvement in the first place.

[42] The new specialized senses 'insane' ("He's a sick man" may mean, depending upon context, "He's a paranoiac, a schizophrenic, or a victim of some other form of 'mental illness' ") and 'morbid, macabre' (as in *sick jokes*) may ultimately come to prevail in all types of English.

[43] The form cited by Mencken as American, though it seems to me much less usual than *mailbox.*

[44] The use of *mail* and *post* as verbs is a legitimate difference.

[45] Hans Kurath, *A Word Geography of the Eastern United States* (Ann Arbor, Mich., 1949), pp. 28, 52.

differences in word choice, though most of these would not cause any serious confusion on either side. Testimony is, however, frequently contradictory, because where choice of words is concerned, many other factors—age, social station, and esthetic predilections, to name three—are bound to obtrude themselves. For instance, regarding *filling station*, of American origin but not really synonymous in American English with *garage*, having taken over only part of its semantic content, a then mid-fiftyish titled gentleman wrote me in 1954 as follows: "I deny that this is really used in British English. A few pretentious garages (one in fifty perhaps) may call themselves filling stations, but no motoring Englishman, of whatever age or class, would dream of saying 'Our petrol is low, let's stop at the next filling station.'" Within a few days of my receiving this communication, I heard from a lecturer in an English university, then in his early thirties, as follows: "*Filling station* is obviously ousting *garage* in the specific sense [which is precisely what had already happened in American English], being less ambiguous. An amusing incident here illustrates the importance of 'youth and age' in these matters. A German lady asked the English word for *Tankstelle*. The professor of German replied 'garage' and simultaneously his assistant said 'filling station.'"

No American has ever said *pram* (or the full form *perambulator*, either) for *baby carriage*,[46] *compère* for *M.C.* (or *emcee*, less frequently *master of ceremonies*) in a theatrical or television entertainment, *mental*[47] for *insane*, *petrol* for *gas(oline)*, *lorry* for *truck*, *coach* for *bus* (interurban),[48] *treacle* for *molasses*, *first floor* (or *storey* [*sic*]) for *second floor* (or *story*),[49] or called an *intermission* (between divisions of an entertainment) an *interval*, an *orchestra seat* a *seat in the stalls*, a *trillion* a *billion*,[50] or referred to a *raise* (in salary) as a *rise*. But most

---

[46] Regional variants are *baby buggy*, *baby coach*, and the somewhat rare *baby cab*. For their geographical distribution, see Kurath, p. 77 and Fig. 147.

[47] An unaristocratic (non-U) euphemism, according to the Hon. Nancy Mitford, "The English Aristocracy," reprinted from *Encounter* in her *Noblesse Oblige* (London, 1956), pp. 39–61.

[48] The English bus carries passengers from one part of a city or town to another, but motor transportation from, say, London to Brighton is by coach.

[49] In England, as on the Continent, the *first floor* is immediately above the *ground floor* (also used in American English, but as a synonym of *first floor*).

[50] In British English a billion is a million millions, whereas in American English it is what the British call a *milliard*—a mere thousand millions.

sophisticated Americans are quite aware of the British equivalents. Unfortunately America is sometimes judged abroad by small-town magnificos, neatly barbered and bedizened with diamond-encrusted lodge emblems, who make the "grand tour" and who complain loudly of the plumbing and ask in loud tones, when their sightseeing buses pass Trafalgar Square, "Just who in heck was this Nelson?" They are doubtless the salt of the earth, but they are, it is hoped, hardly representative of American culture.

Certainly the average, garden-variety American is not to be unduly censured as if he were some sort of crude hillbilly for not immediately understanding such a sentence as "On one stand, a white-coated mechanic was leaning into the bonnet [American *hood*] of a saloon [American *sedan*] carefully dusting the engine with a piece of rag,"[51] so long as his lack of comprehension has in it no tinge of superiority or of the arrogance that frequently goes hand in hand with provincial ignorance. Nor is there any great sin in not knowing that "an old geyser [if pronounced *geezer*, as it often is] in the bath" refers, not to an eccentric old gentleman in a tub, but to an antiquated gas water-heater in the bathroom. Many educated Americans are, however, quite aware that an English *clerk* is a bookkeeper, unless he happens to be a barrister's (lawyer's) clerk or a parish clerk, whose duties are far less well known. When they read that Charles Lamb was a clerk in the East India House, they do not picture the gentle Elia selling Hindus over the counter of a retail establishment. For many Americans have sufficient acquaintance with, and interest in, the Mother Country to be aware of differences in usage so widely publicized as these, and are likely to feel that their intelligence and sophistication are being traduced when English acquaintances painstakingly and, it is regrettable to have to report, frequently condescendingly "explain" these terms.

The American may equip himself with what are sometimes advertised in his own country as *braces* to hold up the trousers without cuffs (in British English, without turn-ups) that he wears with his tailcoat (if he owns one) or his dinner jacket (not all Americans call it a *tuxedo*, though most probably do),[52] but he never calls them anything

---

[51] *Spectator*, October 9, 1959, p. 496.

[52] In some men's clothing establishments in the United States, only the white coat worn in the summer is called a dinner jacket. The traditional black (or less traditional "midnight blue") garment is the *tuxedo* in such commercial usage.

but *suspenders*.[53] *Suspenders*, the word for what were earlier intended for the suspension of trousers in British English, came to be used (the first *OED* citation is from 1895) for the device for holding up women's stockings or men's socks.[54] The word is now almost exclusively feminine in British English, as *garters* is in American English, inasmuch as nowadays men's socks frequently have "built-in" elastic tops and hence do not require suspension. Similarly, because of a change in fashion the older distinction between American *boot* 'covering for foot and leg extending at least to a little below the knee' and the same word in British English, meaning 'foot covering extending to a little above the ankle,' corresponding to American *high(-topped) shoe*, has been largely obliterated. Only weak-ankled old gentlemen and those whose work requires a great deal of walking out of doors now wear *boots* in the English sense; all others, English and American alike, ordinarily wear *shoes*, as Americans had done for a long time without as a rule making any distinction in nomenclature between the under-the-ankle and the over-the-ankle variety. By a strange perversity, these may now be bought in a "boot shop."

There remain valid differences in the use of words other than those which have been mentioned, but, as far as everyday speech is concerned, these are not really very numerous or very significant. The well-known *pitcher–jug* difference continues to hold: what Americans call a pitcher (for cream, milk, cider, and the like) is a jug in England, where a pitcher is something considerably larger, some such receptacle as Rebecca carried to the well; to Americans a jug is ordinarily somewhat larger, with a narrow neck which need have no spout or lip. An

---

[53] Rural *galluses* (that is, *gallowses*) is probably obsolete in American English by now. Brian Foster informs me (in a private communication) that it is still the colloquial term in the county of Durham in northern England, from which region (or from Scotland) it was doubtless brought to America in the beginning—assuming that it was not a general English term at the time. *Suspenders* in the present American sense occurred in nineteenth-century British English (*OED* citations from 1830 and 1841). The fact that the earliest citation of the word is American does not necessarily, or in this case even probably, indicate an American origin; the word is not one which would be expected to occur frequently in the printed works quoted in the *OED*. The earliest citation for *braces* in the same sense is from 1816.

[54] The English limit the meaning of *garter* to the elastic band worn around the leg.

English *spool* is for wire, typewriter ribbons, or film; cotton or other thread comes on a *reel*. What Americans call a *trailer* is in England a *caravan*; a *prep(aratory) school* is a *public school*; a *public school* is a *council school*; *installment buying* is *hire purchase*; *chain stores* are usually *multiple stores*; *sneakers* 'canvas rubber-soled shoes' are *plimsolls* (sometimes capitalized); and, in addition to being a policeman, a *copper* is a large vat made of copper for boiling clothes in a laundry.[55]

SYNTACTICAL AND MORPHOLOGICAL DIFFERENCES

Syntactical and morphological differences are quite as trivial as those in word choice. In regard to collective nouns, for instance, the English are much more likely than Americans to use a plural verb form, like "the public are. . . ." I have collected from a single page of the London *Evening News* (July 16, 1956, p. 10) these three specimens of nouns which, because they lack the plural *-s*, would require singular verbs in American usage: "England Await Chance to Mop Up" (a headline, the reference being to England's cricket team, then engaged in a test match with Australia); "Wimbledon Are Fancied for Double" (also a headline); and "Middlesex were in a strong position when they continued their innings at Gloucester. . . ." This usage is not confined to sports pages: witness "The village are livid";[56] "The U.S. Government are believed to favour . . .";[57] "Eton College break up for the summer holidays to-day . . .";[58] "The Savoy [Hotel] have them [that is, lavatories that work straight off the mains]—but the Savoy have their own water supply . . .";[59] and, from a single page of the *Spectator*, "The Government regard . . ." and "Scotland Yard are. . . ."[60]

The following locutions, all from contemporary British writings,

---

[55] The last two terms, along with *Jeyes Fluid* 'an antiseptic and odor-killing liquid' were the only words explained in footnotes by the American editor of Ludovic Kennedy's *Ten Rillington Place* (New York, 1961). The English editor of a work by the present writer needed help with only two words—*campus*, which he thought meant 'playing field,' and *bleachers*, the meaning of which he had no notion of.

[56] "Strix," "Posh Lingo," in *Noblesse Oblige*, ed. Nancy Mitford, p. 59.

[57] London *Star*, September 7, 1956, p. 1.

[58] London *Daily Telegraph and Morning Post*, August 1, 1956, p. 6.

[59] *Spectator*, February 26, 1960, p. 301.

[60] January 27, 1961, p. 103.

would have been phrased as indicated within square brackets by American writers; yet as they stand they would not puzzle an American reader in the least:

> Thus Mgr. [Monsignor] Knox is faced by a word, which, if translated by its English equivalent, will give a meaning possibly very different to [from, than] its sense. (Letter to the editor of the *Spectator* by Quentin de la Bedoyere)[61]
>
> When he found his body on Hampstead Heath, the only handkerchief was a clean one which had certainly not got [certainly did not have] any eucalyptus on it. (Michael Underwood)
>
> She'd got [she had] plenty of reason . . . for supposing that she would count in her father's will. (Ronald Knox)
>
> He hadn't got [didn't have] any relatives . . . except a sister . . . in Canada or somewhere. (Macdonald Hastings)
>
> You don't think . . . that he did confide in any person?—Unlikely. I think he would have done [would have] if Galbraith alone had been involved. (Edmund Crispin [Bruce Montgomery])
>
> I'll tell it you [to you]. (Philip MacDonald)
>
> Are you quite sure you could not give it me [give it to me, give me it] yourself? (Josephine Bell)
>
> In the morning, I was woken [waked] up at eight by a housemaid. (Nancy Mitford)

Although the constructions cited are not to be heard in American English, their bracketed equivalents are, or have been in the case of *different than*, common as British variants.

There are certain differences other than *different to* in the choice of prepositions: for instance, the English householder lives *in* a street, the American lives *on* it; the English tradesman caters *for* a particular

---

[61] *Different to* is well established in British English, "found in writers of all ages" (*OED*). Even H. W. Fowler approves it (*A Dictionary of Modern English Usage* [Oxford, 1926]), calling the objection to it one of a number of "mere pedantries." He goes on to say, however, that *different from*, far from being wrong, is more usual; "but it is only so owing to the dead set made against *different to* by mistaken critics." (See C. S. Forester's "dead set," below, p. 244, n. 70.) *Different than* has been the target of as much abuse in this country as *different to* in England, but it is equally well established in American usage, as it also was in older British usage; the *OED* cites examples of it from Goldsmith and Cardinal Newman and states that it is also found in Coleridge, Southey, De Quincey, Carlyle, and Thackeray, among others.

clientele, the American caters *to* it; and there are still other variations, equally inconsequential. A recent proliferation of redundant prepositions in English may well have received its impetus from American usage, but the tendency is by no means new or native to America. In 1957 Henry George Strauss, first Baron Conesford of Chelsea, attacked American "pretentious illiteracy" in a speech before the Authors' Club of London on these grounds; but the use of prepositions which seem redundant to Lord Conesford really began a long time ago. It is, in fact, a tendency inherent in the Germanic languages, but it does seem frequently to have gone haywire in American English, where it is not enough merely to visit someone—one must visit *with* them; or to refer to something, when one can refer *back* to it; or to head, say, a committee, when one can head it *up*; or even to continue, when it sounds so much more impressive to continue *on*. Nowadays we plan *on* doing something or other rather than merely plan doing it; we cancel *out*, when just canceling would be sufficient;[62] we check *up on* rather than merely check; and we face *up to* something when it might have been in earlier times considered sufficient merely to face it.

NATIONAL DIFFERENCES IN IDIOM

In general it may be said that, perhaps because America lacks a "caste" dialect comparable to Standard British English, American attitudes toward language lay somewhat greater stress on a more easily acquired "correctness" based on what is conceived to be the proper position of *only*, which the English tend to put where it comes more or less naturally to all of us, before the verb.[63] Likewise it becomes a matter of tremendous importance—practically a moral obligation—in-

[62] This usage, if it is really of American provenience, has made the Atlantic crossing with the greatest of ease. Note the reference by Gilbert Phelps in the *Spectator* (January 13, 1961, p. 50) to "diffidence that goes a long way to cancelling out the worst of one's first impressions."

[63] As in A. S. C. Ross's "U and Non-U: An Essay in Sociological Linguistics," in *Noblesse Oblige,* ed. Nancy Mitford: "At all events I have only come across one case of it" (p. 33, n. 2). Ross is Professor of English Language in the University of Birmingham (England). It must not be supposed, however, that *only*-snoopers, to use Sir Ernest Gowers' apt term for those who engage in "the sport of pillorying [what they conceive to be] misplaced *onlys*" (*Plain Words*, p. 185), are all American. Gowers was, it must be remembered, writing primarily for English readers. But the English are far more tolerant toward the "illogical" but idiomatic preverbal position of the adverb. Even the frequently crotchety H. W. Fowler was of the very sensible opinion that "when perspicuity is not in danger, it is

variably to use *whom* where what is thought of as good grammar seems
to call for it;[64] to eschew *can* in asking or giving permission[65] and *like*
as a conjunction;[66] to choose forms of personal pronouns strictly in

---

needless to submit to an inconvenient restriction" as to the position of *only*
(*Modern English Usage*). It is yet likely that educated American speakers—
more particularly writers, and even more particularly teachers and editors
—concern themselves more with the matter than do their English counterparts.

[64] The "Who are you with?" (that is, what newspaper do you work
for?) addressed by Queen Elizabeth II to various newspapermen at a re-
ception given for her by the press in Washington (*Time*, October 28, 1957,
p. 53) would certainly not pass muster in most educated circles in America.
Compare also the following single specimen from my rather voluminous
collection of instances of this "error" from the writings of highly literate
writers: "He did not need to look round to know who it came from, but he
looked round none the less." The sentence, not in dialogue but in the
author's exposition, occurs in Cyril Hare's *With a Bare Bodkin* (London,
1954; first pub. 1946), p. 49. Cyril Hare is the novel-writing pseudonym
of Judge Alfred Alexander Gordon Clark, educated at Rugby and New
College, Oxford.

George H. McKnight, *Modern English in the Making* (New York, 1928)
has citations of objective *who* from Steele, Smollett, Lamb, Jane Austen,
Sheila Kaye-Smith, Rose Macaulay, James Stephens, Joseph Conrad,
Laurence Housman, George Meredith, Rudyard Kipling, and others (pp.
531–32).

[65] Even small children are frequently corrected when they use the supposedly "ungrammatical" *can* in asking permission: "Mother dear, can I
go out to swim?" "Yes, my darling daughter, you *can*—but you *may* not."
Compare with this the easygoing "Babs, dear, can I see you for a few
moments, please?" from a note written by Sir Richard Cherrington to a
young acquaintance in Dilwyn Rees's *The Cambridge Murders* (London,
1952; first pub. 1945), p. 67. Sir Richard Cherrington is Vice-President of
"Fisher" College, Cambridge, and Professor of Prehistory in the University.
Dilwyn Rees is the pseudonym of Glyn E. Daniel, Fellow and Steward of
St. John's College, Cambridge, and a lecturer in archaeology in the university. In view of the similarity in backgrounds, it is probably safe to
assume that Sir Richard's grammar is that of his creator. It is doubtful
that either Sir Richard or Daniel would pass American College Board
Examinations, for Sir Richard also says "prevent him getting back next
term" (p. 11) and "Who are you going to shoot?" (p. 15).

[66] This usage, as in Clive Barnes's "These Russians dance like the
Italians sing and the Spaniards fight bulls" (*Spectator*, July 1, 1960, p. 21),
has been current in self-assured, cultivated English since the early sixteenth
century (*OED* s.v. *like, a., adv.* [*conj.*], and *sb.*[2], B6a), but has been banned

accordance with what is conceived to be their proper case;[67] to refer to *everyone, everybody, someone, somebody, no one,* and *nobody* with a personal pronoun singular in form (that is, *he, she, it,* or any of their oblique forms);[68] and, not to make too long a story of it, to observe

---

in more recent times, for purely arbitrary reasons as far as one can determine. The current prejudice is well illustrated by Wolcott Gibbs in a review of a play, *Three by Thurber,* published in the *New Yorker* (March 19, 1955, p. 66), in which he takes to task the adapters of James Thurber's material for "a great deal of text that is far inferior to Thurber's work in wit, style, and even, I'm sorry to say, the simple, correct use of the English language," going on to say, "I have complained too often before of the conjunctional 'like.' "

[67] As in Ben Ray Redman's review (*Saturday Review,* February 22, 1958, p. 19) of *The Conscience of the Rich,* by C. P. (Sir Charles) Snow, who is a novelist, a physicist, a literary critic, a Cambridge don, and a knight, among other distinctions: ". . . as he has before, Sir Charles does more than his bit towards making misused pronouns one of England's most notable exports." A few examples of this alleged linguistic sin follow: "No one had eyes or thought for anyone but he as he got slowly to his feet. . . ." (Edgar Lustgarten, *Defender's Triumph,* [London, 1957], p. 108); ". . . respectable people like you and I. . ." (Sir Winston Churchill, quoted by Sir John Slessor in *The Central Blue;* from the review in *Time,* April 1, 1957, p. 55); ". . . it would not be right for either you or I to be where we planned to be on D-Day" (King George VI, quoted in Churchill's War Memoirs in *Life,* October 29, 1951, p. 83); ". . . a good deal older than me" (Somerset Maugham, *The Vagrant Mood,* quoted with a disapproving *sic* by the American reviewer in the New York *Herald Tribune Book Review,* April 5, 1953, p. 5); ". . . I imagined . . . that there was only one 'you' in the world and that was me" (Sarah, heroine of Graham Greene's *The End of the Affair* [New York, 1955], p. 12; first pub. 1951).

[68] Note the following infractions from Standard British English: "Everybody seemed to be particularly on their best front parlour behaviour" (Stephen Potter, as television Guest Critic, London *Evening Standard,* June 5, 1956, p. 6); "No one, when they saw her, could believe . . ." (William Roughead, "To Meet Miss Madeleine Smith," reprinted in *The Pocket Book of True Crime Stories,* New York, 1943, p. 151); "Everyone felt uncomfortable and fidgeted in their chairs" (C. S. Forester, *Plain Murder,* London, 1951, p. 127).

McKnight, *Modern English in the Making,* has specimens of this "solecism" from Jane Austen, James Stephens, Thomas De Quincey, Lord Dunsany, Cardinal Newman, Samuel Butler, and George Moore, along with some older examples (pp. 528–29). Concerning the construction, "established not only by long tradition but by current practice," McKnight

the whole set of fairly simple rules and regulations designed for the timorous—prescriptions and proscriptions which those who are secure have never given much thought to.

The examples cited in the footnotes have been chosen almost at random from the many specimens in my "usage" files. American examples, like General Eisenhower's "to welcome Mrs. Eisenhower and I" (p. 231, n. 34), are much harder to find in print. Eisenhower was of course speaking extemporaneously into a microphone. The construction in question would never have occurred in a formal speech, for such speeches by great Americans are nowadays always carefully edited. (Some of them, we are told, are even written in the first place by "ghost writers," but this is almost too shocking for belief.) In any event, the use of *I* after *and* in an objective construction, familiar though it is to all of us, brought forth a flurry of letters-to-the-editor of the "what-is-the-English-language-coming-to?" variety from newspaper readers and television viewers all over the country, and there was no doubt some editorial comment as well. In England the "non-U" use of "Mrs. Eisenhower" instead of "my wife" (it will be noted in the parallel citation that the Queen referred to her husband simply and frankly as "my husband") would be more likely to occasion disapproval.

The paucity of American printed examples of such locutions (other than those which occasionally occur in small-town newspapers) may be due to some extent to the greater care given to such details by American editors, which has given rise to a functional variety known as "edited English"—a type of speech which would not necessarily reflect in all details the actual usage of professional writers. Even so, it is likely that most American writers themselves, because of the widespread American concept of a mechanical sort of correctness supposed to be characteristic of cultivated usage, would more or less habitually employ the forms of speech prescribed as standard for American usage, which are certainly not those which have been cited above from English printed works.

BRITISH AND AMERICAN PURISM

It is not to be inferred that the British citations necessarily illustrate constructions which occur most of the time in British English, but only that, despite the feelings of horror which they evince from

---

concludes: "The awkward necessity, so often met with in American speech of using the double pronoun, 'his or her,' is obviated by the 'misuse' of *their*."

most educated speakers of American English, they *do* actually occur within the framework of Standard British English.[69] What has already been strongly implied must be strongly stressed at this point, namely, that there are plenty of purists in England, where the "rules" originated. There are plenty everywhere else, for that matter, for the puristic attitude toward language is above all a matter of temperament. By no means are all of them teachers, either. Moreover, the English variety are about as ill-informed and as inconsistent as their American counterparts.[70]

It is in fact likely that everyone between the cockney and the peer pays lip-service[71] to the mossy precepts of the eighteenth-century prescriptive grammarians who formulated most of the "rules" which constitute "grammar" in the lay mind. But in actual practice, as we have just seen, English purists—with the possible exception of the late H. W. Fowler, whose pleasantly magisterial *Dictionary of Modern English Usage* enjoys considerable prestige in England as in America,

[69] If a number of my specimens come from "whodunits," it is only because stories of murder and its detection have been in the past a means of escape from a more or less cloistered and hence uneventful life. It will be noted, however, that all the works cited from this *genre,* which has a considerably higher status abroad than in the United States, are highly literate ones, for the most part written by distinguished writers.

[70] For instance, C. S. Forester in *Plain Murder* (London, 1951) writes of a copy writer, characterized as a vulgar fellow, that "split infinitives and 'different to's' meant nothing to him as long as they did not detract from the appeal of advertisement to the class of person to whom it was addressed" (p. 102). But note that Forester frequently offends against schoolroom standards of "correctness," as when he writes "cannot help but" (p. 124) and "why his voice changed was because he was not at all sure that it [his decision] was a wise one" (p. 151), whereas prescriptive grammar calls for *that* instead of *because.* His use of *everyone . . . their* has already been cited in another connection (p. 242, n. 68). Purists, who should not be expected to be scholars also, are frequently "pure" only in regard to a few stigmatized constructions of which they happen to be especially aware (terminal prepositions and split infinitives are favorite bugaboos with them), and quite unconscious of others which have been just as arbitrarily stigmatized.

[71] For instance, C. Day Lewis (using the pseudonym Nicholas Blake) in *There's Trouble Brewing* (London, 1956; first pub. 1937), has a doctor, an old Oxonian, apologize for his natural speech as follows: "Besides, if the remains were not Bunnett, yet are dressed up to make us believe that they are him—I'm getting ungrammatical—the deduction would be that it was Bunnett who did the murder" (p. 62).

perhaps because it makes such beguiling reading—have not been accorded the deference enjoyed by the American variety.[72] Standard British English is still essentially the speech of those who are expected to speak Standard British English. With the new distinction acquired by a good many "angry young men" from the "red-brick universities" north of the Thames, like the unbrushed young D. H. Lawrence of a generation or so ago—young men who have had little or no acquaintance with the "language of well-bred ease"—all this may change. Many of these new men have an emotional bias against Southern, that is, Standard British, pronunciation which is somewhat like the ambivalent attitude of many Americans toward it. So long as they remain angry, they will doubtless retain this bias, tinged though it is with envy. But success and prosperity go a long way in mollifying ire, and it may well be that they will want their sons and daughters to acquire the speech as well as the social deportment of the Establishment which they now affect to despise. For there is no snob like a self-made man— a statement which is not in the least irrelevant when we are considering linguistic usages. It will be most interesting to observe developments in Standard British English a generation hence.

Katharine Whitehorn, an English journalistic writer who is quite familiar with America, has put the matter very well: "In America, where it is grammar, not accent, that places you, anyone can learn the grammar; maybe Bostonians don't accept it, but Bostonians only impress other Bostonians."[73] The "American way" in language has been to make gentility accessible to all not by laying the stress on anything so subtle, let alone aristocratic, as "accent," but by basing "good usage" wholly upon certain morphological and syntactical shibboleths —the avoidance of *ain't, he don't, it's me,* terminal prepositions, split infinitives, dangling participles, and the like. These are rather easy for all to learn, even though not all bother to do so. Those who do not conform to the supposedly inflexible rules are thought to speak "bad English," even though they may be persons of considerable consequence in the national life; it is as simple as all that.

[72] Enjoyed, it should be said in all justice, for a very good reason: in the absence of a type of speech stemming from an aristocratic society, they have kept in circulation a set of easy precepts, the conscientious observance of which enables, or is supposed to enable, any man to speak as well as any other man. Most of these precepts are based on logically and analogically sound principles, and some of them have even been drawn from the actual observation of usage.

[73] "What Makyth Manners?" *Spectator,* March 9, 1962, p. 317.

By *accent* Miss Whitehorn means, or certainly ought to mean, those intonational characteristics—risings and fallings in pitch—plus to an unrealized extent timbre of voice which distinguish British English from American English far more than pronunciations of individual words, for, as we shall see, there is actually only a handful of words for which all speakers of Standard British English use pronunciations which are not current in any part of America. Voice quality in this connection has not been much investigated, and most statements about it are impressionistic; but there can be little doubt of its significance. Even if he were to learn British intonation, the American (say, a Bostonian) whose treatment of *r* and of the vowel of *ask, path,* and the like agreed with that of Standard British English would never in the world pass among English people for an Englishman. Almost before he could finish saying "A packet of Players, please," he would be spotted as a "Yank" by practically any tobacconist in the British Isles. Precision in the description of nationally characteristic voice qualities must, however, be left for future investigators.

In regard to intonation, the differences are most noticeable in questions and requests. Contrast the intonational patterns of the following sentences, very roughly indicated as they are, as they would customarily be spoken in Standard British English and American English:[74]

SBE: Where are you going to be?

AE: Where are you going to be?

SBE: Are you sure?

AE: Are you sure?

SBE: Let me know where you're going to be.

AE: Let me know where you're going to be.

SBE: Don't tell me that you're sure.

AE: Don't tell me that you're sure.

[74] Standard works on British English intonation are those of Harold E. Palmer, *English Intonation* (Cambridge, Eng., 1922) and Lilias E. Armstrong and Ida C. Ward, *A Handbook of English Intonation,* 2nd ed.

It should be noted that it is usually difficult or impossible to tell whether a singer is English or American, for the intonational patterns in singing are those of the composer.

It is most unlikely that tempo plays any part in the identification of a British or an American "accent." To Americans unaccustomed to hearing it, British speech frequently seems to be running on at a great rate, but this impression of speed is doubtless also experienced by those English people who have not come into contact with American television shows, movies, and tourists, if there be any such remaining, in regard to American English. Some people speak slowly, some rapidly, regardless of nationality; moreover, the same individual is likely to speak more rapidly when he knows what he is talking about than when he must "make conversation."

NATIONAL DIFFERENCES IN PRONUNCIATION

As for the pronunciation of individual words, much the same situation holds true as for word choices: the differences are really inconsequential. The pronunciation of a given word which is most widely current in American English may occur in Standard British English as a less frequently used variant; for instance, for *either* and *neither* an overwhelming majority of Americans have [i] in the stressed syllable, though some—largely from the Atlantic coastal cities—quite naturally acquired [aɪ] when they were learning to talk, and others all over the country have doubtless affected this pronunciation because they have supposed it to have social prestige. In any case, the [aɪ] pronunciation cannot be said to be exclusively British; and it may come as a surprise to some Americans to learn that the [i] pronunciation occurs in Standard British English, probably much more frequently than the [aɪ] pronunciation occurs in American English. Pronunciation with [i] is in fact listed first in the *OED*, which notes, however, that the pronunciation ['aɪðə] "is in London somewhat more prevalent in educated speech" than ['iðə].[75] All dictionaries of British English, in fact, list the supposedly "American" pronunciation as a variant.

The prevalent Standard British English pronunciation of each of

---

(Cambridge, Eng., 1931). The most thorough study of American intonation is that of Kenneth L. Pike, *The Intonation of American English* (Ann Arbor, Mich., 1945).

[75] It should be remembered that the *E–Every* section of the *OED* was published in 1891. For *neither* also the [i] pronunciation is given first (1906).

the following words differs from the usual or only pronunciation in American English: *ate* [ɛt], *again* [ə'gen], *been* [bin], *evolution* [ˌivə'lušn], *fragile* ['fræjaɪl], *medicine* ['mɛdsɪn], *nephew* ['nɛvju], *patriot* ['pætrɪət], *patron* ['pætrən], *process* ['prosɛs], *profile* ['profil], *quandary* [kwɔn'dɛrɪ], *trait* [tre], *tryst* [traɪst], *valet* ['vælɪt], *zenith* ['zɛnɪθ]. But it is a fact that the prevalent American pronunciation of each (allowing for an interchange of [ɔ] and [ɑ] in *process* and *quandary*) occurs also in Standard British English, thus, [et] [ə'gen], [bɪn], [ˌevə'lušn], ['fræjɪl], ['nɛfju], ['petrɪət], ['petrən], ['prosɛs], ['profaɪl], ['kwandərɪ], [tret], [trɪst], ['væle],[76] ['zinɪθ]. The pronunciation [ɛt] for *ate* occurs in American speech, but is regarded as substandard. For *nephew*, ['nɛvju] is current in America according to Hans Kurath and Raven I. McDavid, Jr., "both in folk speech and in cultivated speech, in Eastern New England, in Chesapeake Bay, and especially in South Carolina, rarely elsewhere."[77]

The prevalent American pronunciations of the following words do not occur in Standard British English: *figure* ['fɪgjər], *leisure* ['ližər], *quinine* ['kwaɪnaɪn], *squirrel* ['skwɜrəl] (also *syrup* and *stirrup* with the same stressed vowel), *tomato* [tə'meto], *vase* [ves].[78] But the prevalent British pronunciations of all of them are current, though indeed not widespread, in American English, that is, ['fɪgə(r)], ['ležə(r)], [kwɪ'nin], ['skwɪrəl], [tə'mato], [vɑz], though the first of these, for *figure*, is regarded as substandard. (The British have [-j-] in *figurative*, *figuration*, *figurant*, and *figurine*.)

The British English pronunciation of *lieutenant* as [lɛf'tɛnənt] when it refers to the army subaltern[79] is now never heard in American English, though it was usual until [lu'tɛnənt] was recommended for Americans by Noah Webster in his *American Dictionary of the English Language* (1828). As we have seen in another connection (see

[76] It is more usual in American English to stress the final syllable of this and other French words (for example, *café, ballet, Calais*), or even words thought to be French.

[77] *The Pronunciation of English in the Atlantic States* (Ann Arbor, Mich., 1961), p. 176.

[78] For the American distribution of some of these, see Kurath and McDavid, p. 127 (*squirrel, syrup, stirrup*), p. 151 (*tomato*), p. 166 (*quinine*), and p. 177 (*vase*).

[79] The naval rank is, however, pronounced without the [f], either precisely as in American English or as [lɛ'tɛnənt], [lə'tɛnənt], or ['lutnənt].

p. 38), Webster also recommended *schedule* with [sk-].[80] It is likely, however, that the historical pronunciation with [s-] was that most widely used in both England and America in 1828.

Other pronunciations which are nationally distinctive include (with the American pronunciation given first) [šəˈgrɪn]/[ˈšægrɪn] for *chagrin*, [ˈkɔrəˌlɛrɪ] or [ˈkɑrəˌlɛrɪ]/[kəˈrɔlərɪ] for *corollary*, [ˈdaɪnəstɪ]/ [ˈdɪnəstɪ] for *dynasty*, [prɪˈmɪr]/[ˈprɛmjə] for *premier*, [klɜrk]/[klɑk] for *clerk*, [ˈmɪsəˌlenɪ]/[mɪˈsɛlənɪ] for *miscellany*, [swɑv]/[swev] for *suave*, [frʌnˈtɪr]/[ˈfrʌntjə] for *frontier*, and [ˈlæbrəˈtɔrɪ]/[ləˈbɔrət(ə)rɪ] or [ˈlæbrət(ə)rɪ] for *laboratory*.[81] American *carburetor* [ˈkɑrbəˌretər] and British *carburettor* [ˈkɑbjuˌretə] are, in addition to being pronounced differently, variant written forms, as are *alúminum* (again, old Noah Webster's choice) and *alumìnium*. The American pronunciation of *carburetor*, in which one would expect [-ˌitər], is apparently due to the analogy of the many nouns of agency in *-ator*.

A few more items might be added to the differentiae cited above, but actually not very many. As for more sweeping differences, what strikes most American ears most strongly (for the differences in intonation and voice quality are rather too subtle for ready identification) is the modern Standard British shift of the older lengthened [æ], which survives in American English except before *r* (as in *far*), *lm* (as in *calm*), and in *father* (and to some extent in *rather*), to [ɑ] in a number of very frequently used words.[82] Up to the very end of the eighteenth century [ɑ] in these and the other words affected was considered vulgar. This shift cannot, however, be regarded as exclusively British, inasmuch as its effect is evident in the speech of eastern New England and to some extent in the tidewater South. Present American usage in

---

[80] Webster's choice was not unknown in England in the eighteenth century and earlier, being favored on theoretical grounds by a number of the orthoëpists, though John Walker in his *Critical Pronouncing Dictionary*, 2nd ed. (1797) says that "entirely sinking the *ch* in *sedule* seems to be the prevailing mode, and too firmly fixed by custom to be altered." He seems not to have heard the pronunciation now current in British English with [š-].

[81] The difference between the less usual British English pronunciation (cited second) and the American is due to American retention of secondary stress on the penultimate syllable of polysyllables in *-ary*, *-ery*, and *-ory*, to be discussed below. But the British pronunciation of the word in question with stress on the first syllable seems to be dying out; it is seldom if ever heard from younger-generation speakers.

[82] This has been alluded to, pp. 25, 177, and 220–21.

regard to such words is by no means consistent: a Bostonian may, for instance, have [ɑ] in *half* (and then perhaps only some of the time), but not in *can't,* or vice versa. An intermediate [a] is sometimes heard in America as a variant of this [ɑ]. According to the late John S. Kenyon, "The pronunciation of '*ask*' words [his term for the words under discussion] with **a** or **ɑ** has been a favorite field for schoolmastering and elocutionary quackery,"[83] and one cannot but agree when one hears American actresses (mainly actresses, but quite a few actors also) pronounce [a] in words like *hat, and, happy,* and others spelled with *a* which were not affected by the aforementioned shift.[84]

The use of [ɑ] in what Kenyon calls the "*ask*" words, supposed by some naïve American speakers to have higher social standing than [æ], is fraught with danger. With speakers of Standard British English, who use it naturally, in the sense that they acquired it when as children they were learning to talk, it never occurs in a great many words in which it might be expected if one were going only by analogy; thus, *bass, crass, mass,*[85] and *lass* have [æ], in contrast to the [ɑ] of *grass, class, glass,* and *pass;*[86] *plastic* has [æ], but *plaster* has [ɑ]; *ample* has [æ], but *sample* and *example* have [ɑ]; *romance* and *fancy* have [æ], but *dance, glance* and *chance* have [ɑ]; *can't* 'cannot' has [ɑ], but *cant* 'hypocritical talk' has [æ]; *mascot, massacre, mastiff,* and *bastard* have [æ], but *master* has [ɑ], and *masquerade* may have either [æ] or [ɑ]. It is obvious that few status-seekers could master such complexities, even if there were any real point in so doing. There is none, actually, for no one really worth fooling would be really fooled by such a shallow display of linguistic virtuosity.

Somewhat less noticeable, perhaps because it is more widespread in American English than the use of [ɑ] or [a] in the *ask* words, is the Standard British English loss of [r] before a consonant or in final position in an utterance (that is, before a pause) heretofore alluded

---

[83] *American Pronunciation,* 10th ed. (Ann Arbor, Mich., 1961), p. 183.

[84] Jayne Crane Harder has dealt effectively with "elocutionary quackery" in "The Influence of the Teaching of Elocution on Modern English Pronunciation" (unpublished dissertation, University of Florida, 1956). See also the same writer (as Jayne Crane), "Quest for a Standard: A Study of Stage Diction," *Southern Speech Journal,* XV (1950), 280–85.

[85] Similarly with *Mass,* the sacrament, though this may sometimes occur with [ɑ̄].

[86] But *classical, classicism, classify, passage, passenger, passable,* and *passive* all have [æ]. *Ass* may have either [æ] or [ɑ].

to (pp. 55–56), though the American treatment of this sound is as a rule somewhat less consistent and hence more complicated to describe than the British. In American English it may, for instance—to some extent depending upon the speech area—be retained preconsonantally in stressed syllables but lost in final position, particularly in final unstressed syllables (in *further* ['fɜrðə], for instance); or it may be lost under the same conditions as in Standard British English; or it may even, as in parts of the deep South, be lost before a vowel, as in *Carolina* and *far away*. Postvocalic [r] is lost, in one way or another, in eastern New England, in New York City, and in most of the coastal South.87 Away from the Atlantic Coast, it is retained in all positions. There are other less striking phonological differences, like the British slightly rounded "short *o*" in contrast to the unrounded [ɑ] in *got, stop, collar,* and the like heard in American English except for western Pennsylvania and eastern New England (pp. 58 and 173).

Though there are signs of its return, British English long ago lost its secondary stress on the penultimate syllables of polysyllables in *-ary, -ery,* and *-ory* (for example *military, millinery, obligatory*). This subordinate stress is regularly retained in American English. Many Americans, it is true, are fond of ['dɪkšən(ə)rɪ] as a pronunciation of *dictionary*—presumably it gives a certain social "tone" to the word— but few if any who use this pronunciation pronounce other such words in any save the usual American and older British fashion, that is, as *sécretàry, mónastèry, térritòry,* and the like. In my native usage (that of the area dominated by Baltimore), *stationery* 'writing paper' was by many speakers distinguished from *stationary* 'fixed' by omission of the secondary stress. Such stress was also frequently lacking in *primary, confectionery, cemetery,* and *library* (sometimes reduced to disyllabic ['laɪbrɪ]), but it regularly occurred as in all types of American English in all other such words. A restoration of the secondary stress in British English, at least in some words, is more likely due to spelling-consciousness than to any transatlantic influence. I have noted it from well-educated younger-generation British speakers in *secretary* and, for the first time about twenty years ago, in *extraordinary* (as [ɪk'strɔdɪ‚nɛrɪ]). Brian Foster, in "Recent American Influence on Standard English," says that "it is increasingly common" for *secretary*, in which secondary stress "is now to be heard from some excellent British speakers" (p. 356).

87 Kurath and McDavid, pp. 170–72.

The fact seems to be that, if we leave the very important matter of intonation, a handful of word choices, and the as yet unascertained question of voice quality out of consideration, the remaining distinctive features of British and American English are comprised in the pronunciation of a smallish number of words, some of them rather infrequently used words. It is nonetheless true that British speech is likely to be unclear to some Americans according to their own testimony, though it is doubtful that there are many such nowadays. It must be remembered, however, that unsophisticated people are very provincial in their reaction to any type of speech which differs from their own, and may even take a certain pride in their provincialism. Nationalistic prejudice, evincing itself frequently in a kind of obstinate refusal to tolerate differences, however slight they may be, has something to do with this reaction. It is not, however, wholly a matter of nationalism, for the Georgia "cracker" is likely to be almost as vexed—and because of this vexation perhaps indisposed to listen carefully—by the speech of an older-generation Boston Brahmin as by that of an Oxford professor of classical literature. And, be it said in all justice, the Oxonian, from whom we should expect a more enlightened linguistic attitude, is not at all unlikely to be equally intolerant of American speech—or, for that matter, of the folk speech of his own countrymen.

The type of American speech that one nowadays hears most frequently in nationally televised "commercials" is highly standardized and essentially synthetic. Spoken by trained speakers who, with the possible exception of the evangelical ministry in those parts of the country which Mencken called the Bible Belt, are probably as influential a group of persuaders as any in the United States, this speech evinces few if any regional or individual characteristics discernible to the untrained ears of those who listen glazed-eyed to it. In it the usage of the majority of Americans is reflected in the following respects: (1) *r* is carefully articulated in all positions; (2) medial *t* is voiced,[88] so that *matter* and *madder* are homophones, or practically so, and the naked ear has difficulty distinguishing "Atoms for Peace" from "Adams for Peace"; and (3) [hw-] occurs in the *wh*-words (see p. 39).[89] Unstressed syllables are frequently given somewhat more

[88] The sound is called a "voiced flap consonant" by Edward Artin, pronunciation editor of *Webster's Third New International Dictionary* (Springfield, Mass., 1961), who uses a special symbol in transcribing it (p. 41a).

[89] Occasionally [hw-] occurs by overcorrection in *w*-words as well, for instance *water*.

attention than natural, traditional speech gives them; for instance [ɛ] is often preferred to [ə] in the unstressed final syllable of *president*, [o] to [ə] in the unstressed initial syllables of *obey, o'clock,* and the like, and [i] to [ɪ] or [ə] in the unstressed initial syllables of *effect(ive), efficient,* and the like. The plural of *process* is quite likely to end in [-iz]. The names of the days of the week end in [-de] rather than in traditional [-dɪ].

Those who are professionally concerned with public speaking, either as teachers or as performers, sometimes attempt to justify such distortions of what is still the natural usage of cultivated speakers on the grounds that they make for greater clarity. Actually, they seldom if ever do so. In "Cultural Levels and Functional Varieties of English,"[90] John S. Kenyon quotes the statement of the great English phonetician Henry Sweet that "we cannot make words more distinct by disguising them," in reference to the use of full vowels in unstressed syllables where Standard English, whether British or American, has [ə] or [ɪ]. Kenyon reports the following momentarily confusing utterance from a radio announcer: "This program will be heard again tomorrow from one two three." No one could possibly be confused by "one [tə] three." Other instances of such "overpronunciation" cited in Kenyon's article are *ay man* ("a man"), *cahnsider, tooday, too go* ("to go"), and *Coalumbia*; "Sun day [for *sundy*] will be Mother's Day" was misheard as "Some day will be Mother's Day."

The glamour girls and the efficient, wholesome-looking women who on television extol the glories of cosmetics, shampoos, "washday products" (for *soap* has become practically a dirty word in such rarefied circles), refrigerators, and cleansers for the "food preparation area" (kitchen) and what is discreetly referred to as the "bathroom bowl" follow much the same patterns as their male counterparts. In addition, they are quite likely, when they think of it, to substitute [a] for Standard [æ] in, say, *dishpan hands.*

The extent of the influence and prestige of those who speak the commercials may be gauged by the astronomical sums spent on such advertising. Who can say that their standardized form of speech, based to a large extent upon writing, may not in time become the basis for, or for that matter may itself become, a nationwide caste dialect?

[90] *College English,* X (1948), 2–6, and conveniently reprinted in *Readings in Applied English Linguistics,* ed. Harold B. Allen (New York, 1958), pp. 215–21.

BRITISH AND AMERICAN SPELLING

Finally, there is the matter of spelling, which looms larger in the consciousness of those who are concerned with national differences than it deserves to do. Somewhat exotic to American eyes, though by no means unfamiliar to those of the educated, are *gaol, kerb* (of a street), *pyjamas, tyre* (around a wheel), *cyder, cypher, syren, cheque* (for drawing money from bank), and *shew.* But *jail, curb, pajamas, tire, cider, cipher, siren, check,* and *show* are also current in England in varying degrees. *Shew,* prevalent in the eighteenth century, was in fact called "obs[olete] exc[ept] in legal documents" by the *OED* (then the *NED*) in 1914. H. C. Wyld's *Universal Dictionary of the English Language* (London, 1932) states that it is archaic. But it is nevertheless still current, if very rare.[91] The spelling, like that of *sew,* indicates a pronunciation no longer current.

Noah Webster, whom many regard as a sort of linguistic mahatma, is responsible for excising the *u* from a group of words spelled in his day prevailingly in *-our: armour, behaviour, colour, favour, flavour, harbour, labour, neighbour,* and the like. The resultant American *-or* spellings are today far more obnoxious to the English than the alternative forms with *-our* are to Americans, who, in addition to reading a great many books printed in England, are quite accustomed to seeing *Saviour* and *glamour* in books printed in their own country. All these words have been current in earlier British English without the *u,* though most Englishmen today are probably unaware of the fact; Webster was making no radical change in English spelling habits. Furthermore, the English had themselves struck the *u* from a great many words earlier spelled *-our,* alternating with *-or: author, doctor, emperor, error, governor, horror, mirror,* and *senator,* among others. Perhaps they might also have shortened the remaining *-our* words if the self-righteous and nationalistic-minded Webster had not put their backs up by doing so first. As it is, they are so offended by what they regard as American misspellings of those words in which they retain the *u* that American books are sometimes reset before their publication in England, even though money might be saved by using the American plates.

Webster is also responsible for the American practice of using *-er* instead of the customary British *-re* in a number of words, for instance

---

[91] It is, for instance, consistently used in the Randolph Quirk and C. L. Wrenn *Old English Grammar* (London, 1955), occurring on pp. 6, 9, and elsewhere.

calibre, centre, litre, manoeuvre, metre (of poetry or of the unit of length in the metric system),[92] *sepulchre,* and *theatre.* The last of these spellings has nowadays probably a wider currency in American English than has *theater;* it is consistently used, for instance, in the announcement of course offerings of the Department of Speech in the University of Florida ("Theatre Appreciation," "History of the Theatre," and "Aesthetics of the Theatre"), and the yellow classified section of my telephone directory lists only "Theatres." Except for *litre,* which did not come into English until the nineteenth century, all these words occur in earlier British English with *-er.*

The fact that *c* before *e* indicates [s] must have irritated Webster. At one time he wanted to have *acre* spelled *aker,* but he was still left with *lucre* and *mediocre,* in the case of which he seems to have given up fighting the good fight. There was also *ogre,* about which little could be done; **oger* would have suggested [ˈo̯jər].

The American use of *-se* in *defense, offense,* and *pretense,* in which the English usually have *-ce,* is also attributable to the precept and practice of Webster, though he did not recommend *fense* for *fence,* which is simply an aphetic form of *defense* (or *defence*). Spellings with *-se* have occurred in earlier British English for all these words, including *fence. Suspense* is now usually so spelled in British English.

Webster proposed dropping final *k* in such words as *almanack, musick, physick, publick,* and *traffick,* bringing about a change which has occurred in British English as well, though not because old Noah recommended it. The single word with older *ck* after *o* in which he neglected to drop the *k* is *havock,* everywhere spelled without it nowadays. His *burdoc, cassoc,* and *hassoc* seem to have got nowhere.[93]

Though he was not the first to recommend doing so, Webster is doubtless to be credited with the American spelling practice of not doubling final *l* when adding a suffix except in words stressed on their final syllables, for example *grôvel, groveled, groveler, groveling,* but

---

[92] The homophone meaning an instrument for measuring is of different origin and is written *meter* in British as well as American English: thus *gas meter, barometer, thermometer.* Here the *-er* is the familiar English suffix of nouns of agency.

[93] Webster, who loved tinkering with all aspects of language, had contemplated far flashier spelling reforms, for instance, lopping off the final *e* of *-ive, -ine,* and *-ite* in final syllables (thus *fugitiv, medicin, definit*), using *oo* for *ou* in *group* and *soup,* writing *tung* for *tongue,* and deleting the *a* in *bread, feather,* and the like, but in time gave them up.

propél, propelled, propeller, propelling, propellant. Modern British spelling usually doubles *l* before a suffix regardless of the position of the stress, thus *grovelled, groveller,* and so forth.

The English use of *ae* and *oe* (or *æ* and *œ*) looks strange to Americans in *anaemic, paediatrician, gynaecology, haemorrhage, oesophagus, homoeopathy, manoeuvre,* and *diarrhoeia,* but not in *encyclopaedia* and *aesthetic,* which are fairly common in American usage. Some words earlier written with one or the other of these digraphs long ago underwent simplification, for example *phaenomenon, poenology,* and *oeconomy.* Others are in process of simplification: *hemorrhage, hemorrhoids,* and *medieval* are frequent British variants of the forms with *ae,* but *haemophilia, haematic, haemostatic,* and *haemoglobin* seem not to have lost the *a* as yet.

THE STUDY OF AMERICAN ENGLISH

Interest in American English has been very lively and scholarship very productive in recent years. In 1889, however, long before the publication of the revered H. L. Mencken's *The American Language,* the American Dialect Society was formed at Harvard for "the investigation of the English dialects in America with regard to pronunciation, grammar, vocabulary, phraseology, and geographical distribution,"[94] as the result of a suggestion made by Charles Hall Grandgent, then a young instructor, later to become a distinguished professor of Romance languages at Harvard.[95] One of the aims of the Society has been the preparation of a great American dialect dictionary. Although much preliminary work has been done toward this end, the completion and publication of such a work still lies in the future.

According to the authoritative historical sketch of the American Dialect Society by Louise Pound,[96] who was its president from 1938 to 1941, the "leading spirits" behind its foundation were Sheldon, Grandgent, and Francis James Child, the great editor of *English and Scottish Popular Ballads* (1883–98), who was the first president. George Lyman Kittredge, then on his way to an assistant professorship at

---

[94] As set forth by Edward S. Sheldon, then an assistant professor, later professor of Romance philology at Harvard. Sheldon became the first secretary of the Society.

[95] Grandgent was the Society's first treasurer.

[96] *Publication of the American Dialect Society,* No. 17 (April 1952), pp.

Harvard,[97] the poet James Russell Lowell, and John Matthews Manly, later of the University of Chicago, were among the earliest members.

The publication of the Society was *Dialect Notes*, which ran from 1890 to 1939. There was no publication during the war period 1939–44. The successor to *Dialect Notes* is called simply the *Publication of the American Dialect Society* or, more usually, *PADS*. It is issued twice yearly, some of its issues being full-length monographs, including Frederic G. Cassidy's *A Method for Collecting Dialect* (1953), Sumner Ives's *The Phonology of the Uncle Remus Stories* (1954), David W. Maurer's *Whiz Mob: A Correlation of the Technical Argot of Pickpockets with Their Behavior Pattern* (1955), Einar Haugen's *Bilingualism in the Americas* (1956), and Dwight L. Bolinger's *Interrogative Structures of American English* (1957). The titles give some notion of the scope of interests of the Society.

H. L. Mencken testifies that it was "a chance encounter" with *Dialect Notes* around 1905 which urged him to a systematic study of American English, and says "I was a steady customer of *Dialect Notes* after my discovery of its riches."[98] The first edition of his own zestful and stimulating book appeared in 1919; revised editions appeared in 1921 and 1923; then, in 1936, the great fourth edition, "corrected, enlarged, and rewritten." This was followed, in 1945 and 1948, by two fat supplements—in all a total of more than 2500 pages. An abridgment, with revisions, has been prepared by Raven I. McDavid, Jr., (New York, 1963), with the chapter on slang, cant, and argot under the charge of David W. Maurer.

The year 1925 saw the publication of George Philip Krapp's *The English Language in America* and the first issue of *American Speech*. Krapp's two-volume work is still indispensable; in addition to its learning, it is written with style and grace. *American Speech*, now published by the Columbia University Press, is, like the various publications of the American Dialect Society, both lively and learned. It was founded by H. L. Mencken, Kemp Malone, Louise Pound,[99] and Arthur Garfield Kennedy, who, though not many years Miss Pound's junior, had been her student at the University of Nebraska. Accord-

[97] He was president of the Society in 1897, succeeding Sheldon and Grandgent in that office.

[98] *The American Language: Supplement I,* Preface, p. ix.

[99] According to Mencken, her "early work put the study of American English on its legs" (*Supplement I,* Preface, vi). Miss Pound died, full of years and honors, in 1958.

ing to Malone, "the idea was Mencken's."[100] As it was planned, it was not to be "so academic as to attract only the austerest scholars as contributors and subscribers" (L. Pound, *loc. cit.*); and to this day, though it has always maintained the highest scholarly standards, it continues to demonstrate that sound scholarship need not be dull.

One of the most monumental scholarly undertakings of the present century is the *Linguistic Atlas of the United States and Canada* (Providence, R.I., 1939–43), under the direction of Hans Kurath, with the aid of a large staff of highly trained helpers. Work on this huge project began in 1931. An outgrowth of the interest in dialect geography which had begun in Europe, it has successfully carried through a study of the language—its phonology, morphology, syntax, and vocabulary—in a great number of communities in each region of the country, communities which have been carefully selected on the basis of their economic, social, and cultural history. Settlement history is obviously very important.

In each of these communities at least two informants have been interviewed by means of a questionnaire which is carefully and expertly devised to elicit characteristic locutions in response. According to Raven McDavid, who has been the chief field worker, an interview takes from four to seven hours under favorable circumstances. One informant is ideally an elderly native of the community whose speech has been relatively uncontaminated by schooling and can thus be presumed to represent old-fashioned usage; the other one middle-aged, with, say, a high school education. In addition, in many communities, particularly in those cities which are centers of culture and fashion, cultured informants have been interviewed.

Thus far, only the New England materials have been published, in the huge *Linguistic Atlas of New England*, with an accompanying *Handbook of the Linguistic Geography of New England* by Kurath and others (Washington, D.C., 1939; 2nd printing, New York, 1954). Pending the publication of the complete materials for regions other than New England, three important works based upon the materials for the Atlantic States have appeared as "Studies in American English" published by the University of Michigan Press: Kurath's *A Word Geography of the Eastern United States,* which demonstrates that there is a well-defined American Midland type of speech, the Midland

---

[100] The story of the beginnings of the journal is told by the four founders in "*American Speech,* 1925–1945: The Founders Look Back," *American Speech,* XX (1945), 241–46.

area on the Atlantic coast lying between the traditionally recognized North and South;[101] E. Bagby Atwood's *A Survey of Verb Forms in the Eastern United States* (1953); and the work which has been previously cited a number of times, Kurath and McDavid's *The Pronunciation of English in the Atlantic States* (1961). The best brief treatment of American linguistic geography is McDavid's "The Dialects of American English," which comprises Chapter 9 of W. Nelson Francis's *The Structure of American English*, cited in the previous footnote.

Two other monumental works, the four-volume *Dictionary of American English*, edited by Sir William Craigie and James R. Hulbert, and the originally two-volume *Dictionary of Americanisms* of M. M. Mathews, both published by the University of Chicago Press, have already been alluded to a number of times. Both works were prepared according to the historical principles laid down by the *OED*, of which Craigie was also an editor.

Although interest in the study of the living spoken language in Great Britain antedates that in America, British scholarship has lagged somewhat behind in the years under discussion. Linguistic atlases of England and Scotland are, however, now well under way; the first two volumes of the *Survey of English Dialects* by Harold Orton and Wilfred J. Halliday were published in Leeds in 1962. The *Introduction to a Survey of Scottish Dialects* (Edinburgh, 1952) by Angus McIntosh is a noteworthy sign of things to come. Since American English is a development of British English, it is inevitable that such investigations will enhance our knowledge of American

[101] The Midland extends on the coast only from southern New Jersey to midway through Delaware, but its boundaries widen considerably as one goes westward; the southern boundary, for instance, goes through northern Maryland, then turns sharply southwestwards and runs along the crest of the Blue Ridge in Virginia through North Carolina and upper South Carolina; the northern boundary swings northwestward and goes along the northern part of Pennsylvania. These boundaries were first shown in the map which is Figure 3 in Kurath's book. It has been frequently reproduced, for instance in Margaret M. Bryant's *Modern English and Its Heritage*, 2nd ed. (New York, 1962), p. 100; in Albert H. Marckwardt's *American English* (New York, 1958), p. 136; in *Introductory Readings on Language,* ed. Wallace L. Anderson and Norman C. Stageberg (New York, 1962), p. 331; and in W. Nelson Francis's *The Structure of American English* (New York, 1958), p. 580, where the boundaries are tentatively extended westward.

English, for, as Kurath has pointed out, in the Preface to *The Pro-nunciation of English in the Atlantic States,* while some of the divergencies between present-day American English and British English reflect "unsettled usage in Standard English during our Colonial period," others unquestionably stem from English dialect speech. We shall never, alas, have any tape recordings of either the British Standard or the folk speech of the seventeenth and eighteenth centuries, but the scientific study of modern folk speech, conservative as such speech always is in comparison with Standard, cannot fail to throw light on certain features of American English.

THE ESSENTIAL ONENESS OF ALL ENGLISH

We have now come to an end of our comparative survey of the present state of British and American English. He who looks for differences is sure to find them. We can only hope that he does not choose to magnify them. All too often treatments of the subject have been of what Robert A. Hall, Jr., has somewhere called the "Old Curiosity Shop" variety—even Mencken is in some measure guilty of this—playing up isolated differences in a wholly misleading way. What should have emerged from the present treatment is a conception of the essential unity of the English language in all its national, regional, and local manifestations. What, then, it may be asked, *is* the English language? Is it the speech of London, of Boston, of New York, of south Georgia, of Melbourne, of Montreal, of Calcutta? A possible answer might be, none of these, but rather the sum of them all, along with all other blendings and developments which have taken place wherever what is thought of as the English language is spoken by those who learned it as their mother tongue.[102] The most important of these

---

[102] The fears of Sir David Eccles, former British Minister of Education, as reported in *Time* (June 22, 1962, p. 33), that English may split up into a number of mutually unintelligible dialects, as Latin did in a quite different sort of world from that in which we live, have often been voiced before, and are quite unjustified by the facts. As Philip B. Gove, editor-in-chief of the Merriam-Webster dictionaries, pointed out in an Associated Press interview inspired by Sir David's contention that "we must get down to the job of preserving meanings [those in his own type of English?] and standards of purity [to be decided by whom?] for the English language," an American says "gasoline" and a Briton says "petrol," but "that doesn't mean they don't know each other's tank is empty." Air travel, intermarriage, exchange of radio and television programs, and the printed word, Gove

happen to be Standard British English and the English spoken by
Americans—and it should be clear by now that their importance is
due, not to any inherent virtues which they may possess, but wholly
to the present importance in the affairs of the English-speaking world
—some might go so far as to say of western European civilization—of
those who speak them.

---

went on to say, have brought American English and British English closer
together than ever before. And, as we have seen, they were never really very
far apart.

CHAPTER X

New Words from Old
Coinages and Adaptations

IN THE present state of our knowledge, there is, as we have seen, little point in speculating about the ultimate origins of words. But we can know with varying degrees of certainty a good deal about the making of words in historical times, and our principal concern in this chapter will be an examination of the various processes involved in the making.

ROOT CREATIONS

It is unlikely that very many words have come into being during the historical period which have not been suggested in one way or another by previously existing words.[1] An oft cited example of a word completely without associations with any existing word or words is *Kodak*, which made its first appearance in print in the *U.S. Patent Office Gazette* in 1888[2] and was, according to George Eastman, who invented the word as well as the device which it names, "a purely arbitrary combination of letters, not derived in whole or in part from any existing word,"[3] though according to his biographer a very slight asso-

---

[1] A good many given names, encountered primarily in the American Deep South and the Southwest, but of a type current all over the United States, are doubtless pure root creations, for example, *Lugen, Zedro* (suggested by *Pedro?*), *Velpo, Phalla, Morta* (*Marta?*), and *Venrean.* I have cited these and scores of others in "Onomastic Individualism in Oklahoma," *American Speech*, XXII (1947), 257–64, and in "Bible Belt Onomastics, or Some Curiosities of Anti-Pedobaptist Nomenclature," *Names*, VII (1959), 84–100.

[2] M. M. Mathews, *A Dictionary of Americanisms on Historical Principles* (Chicago, 1951).

[3] From a letter written by Eastman to the late John Matthews Manly in 1906, quoted from Carl W. Ackerman's *George Eastman* (New York, 1930)

ciation was in fact involved in his use of the letter *k*, for his mother's family name began with that letter. *Nylon, Dacron,* and *Orlon* are similarly etymologyless words.

TRADE NAMES

Most trade names, however, are clearly suggested by already existing words: *Vaseline,* for instance, was made from German *Wasser* 'water' plus Greek *elaion* 'oil';[4] *Kleenex* by *clean* and *Cutex* by *cuticle* plus a rather widely used but quite meaningless pseudoscientific suffix *-ex; Socony* by the initial letters of *Standard Oil Company of New York;* and *Uneeda* by "you need a," a process now rather old-fashioned in the naming of products.[5]

ECHOIC WORDS

Sound alone is the basis of a limited number of words, called echoic or onomatopoeic, like *bang, burp, splash, tinkle, ping, bobwhite,* and *cuckoo.* Leonard Bloomfield distinguishes between words which are actually imitative of sound, like *meow, moo,* and *bow-wow*—though as we have seen these differ from language to language—and those which he appropriately calls symbolic ("somehow illustrating the meaning more immediately than do ordinary speech-forms. . . . To the speaker it seems as if the sounds were especially suited to the meaning"), like *bump* and *flick,* but the distinction between these need not really concern us here.[6] Such words frequently show doubling, sometimes with slight variation, as in *bow-wow, choo-choo,* and *peewee,* the last of which by its sound is merely suggestive of tininess—a factor which could hardly be imitated in sound save by a

---

by H. L. Mencken, *The American Language: Supplement I* (New York, 1945), p. 342, n. 1.

[4] H. L. Mencken, *The American Language,* 4th ed. (New York, 1936), p. 172, n. 3.

[5] Louise Pound, "Word-Coinage and Modern Trade-Names," *Dialect Notes,* IV (1913), 29–41, discusses various processes. Though many of the proprietary names cited designate products no longer existing, Miss Pound's conclusion still holds good: ". . . the present day reveals a fluctuating and bewildering variety of commercial terms without apparent limits of kind or quantity."

[6] *Language* (New York, 1933), p. 156.

reduction in volume—and is hence symbolic, though as the name of a bird it is, like its variant *peewit* (or *pewit*), actually a fair imitation of the bird's cry.

EJACULATIONS

Sounds supposedly imitative of more or less instinctive vocal responses to emotional situations have frequently become words in their own right. One of these, *ouch*, is something of a mystery: it does not appear in British writing except as an Americanism. The *OED* derives it from German *autsch*, an exclamation presumably imitative of what a German exclaims at fairly mild pain, such as stubbing a toe or hitting a thumb with a tack hammer—hardly anything more severe, for when one is suffering really rigorous pain one is not likely to have the presence of mind to remember to say "Ouch!" The vocal reaction, if any, is likely to be a shriek, a scream, or a long-drawn-out [o] or [ɔ], followed sometimes by something like [č], in any event difficult to represent in writing. But regardless of the origin of *ouch*, it may be regarded, in American English, as a conventional representation of the sounds supposedly, if not indeed actually, made when one is in pain. The interesting thing is that the written form has become so familiar, so completely conventionalized, that Americans (and Germans) do actually say "Ouch!" when they have hurt themselves so slightly as to be able to remember what they *ought* to say under the circumstances.

Other such written representations, all of them highly conventionalized, of what are thought to be "natural utterances" have also become actual words, for instance, *ha ha,* with the variant *ho ho* for Santa Claus and other jolly fat men, and the girlish *tehee* which the naughty but nonetheless delectable Alison gives utterance to in Chaucer's *Miller's Tale,* in what is perhaps the most indecorously funny line in English poetry. Now, it is likely that, if Alison were a real-life girl (rather than better-than-life, as she is by virtue of being the creation of the male wishful thinking of a superb artist), upon receipt of the misdirected kiss she might have tittered, twittered, giggled, or gurgled under the decidedly improper circumstances in which she had placed herself. But how to write a titter, a twitter, a giggle, or a gurgle? Chaucer was confronted with the problem of representing by alphabetical symbols whatever the appropriate vocal response might have been, and *tehee,* which was doubtless more or less conventional in his day, was certainly as good a choice as he could have made. The form with which he chose to represent girlish glee has remained conventional. When we encounter it in reading, we think—and, if reading aloud, we actually say—[ti'hi],[7] and the effect seems perfectly realistic to us. But it is highly doubtful that anyone ever uttered *tehee*, or *ha ha*, or *ho ho*, except as a reflection of the written form. Laughter, like pain, is too paroxysmal in nature, too varying from individual to individual, and too unspeech-like to be represented accurately by symbols which are not even altogether adequate for the representation of speech sounds.

It is somewhat different with a vocal manifestation of disgust, contempt, or annoyance which might be represented phonetically (but only approximately) as [č]. This was as early as the mid-fifteenth century represented as *tush*, and somewhat later less realistically as *twish*. *Twish* became archaic as a written form, but [tʌš] survives as a spoken interpretation of *tush*. As in the instances cited, and in others to be cited, sounds came first; then the graphic representation, always somewhat inadequate; then finally a new word in the language based on an interpretation of the graphic representation of what was in the beginning not a word at all, but—to use a modern term in describing it—merely something in the nature of a sound-effect.

Pish and *pshaw* likewise represent "natural" emotional utterances of disdain, contempt, impatience, irritation, and the like, and have become so conventionalized as to have been used as verbs.[8] Both began as something like [pš]. W. S. Gilbert combined two such utterances to form the name of a "noble lord," Pish-Tush, in *The Mikado*, with two similarly expressive ones, Pooh-Bah, for the overweeningly aristocratic "Lord High Everything Else."[9]

Pugh is imitative of the disdainful sniff with which many persons react to a bad smell, resembling a vigorously articulated [p]. But, as with the examples previously cited, this has been conventionalized because of the written form into an actual word pronounced [pju] or

[7] It was presumably [te'he] in Alison's pre-vowel-shift pronunciation.

[8] See the citation in *Webster's Third New International Dictionary* (Springfield, Mass., 1961), which combines both, s.v. *pish* (". . . pished and pshawed a little at what had happened").

[9] Yum-Yum, the name of the delightful heroine of the same opera, is similarly a conventionalized representation of sounds supposedly made as a sign of pleasure in eating. These have given us a new adjective, *yummy*, as yet more or less confined to juvenile use—but give it time.

prolongedly as ['pi'ju]. *Pooh* (sometimes with reduplication as *pooh-pooh*) is a variant, with somewhat milder implications. The reduplicated form may be used as a verb, as in "He pooh-poohed my suggestion." *Fie,* used for much the same purposes as *pugh,* is now archaic; it likewise represents an attempt at imitation. *Faugh* is probably a variant of *fie;* so doubtless, is *phew.* *Ugh,* in its purest form a tensing of the stomach muscles followed by a glottal stop (p. 51, n. 2), has not been conventionalized to quite the same extent when used as an exclamation of disgust or horror. As a grunt supposedly made by a comedy Indian it is, one hopes only facetiously, pronounced [ʌg].

The palatal click, articulated by placing the tongue against the palate and then withdrawing it by sucking in the breath, is an expression of impatience or contempt. It is also sometimes used, or at least used to be, in reduplicated form (there may in fact be three or more such clicks) in scolding children, as if to express shock and regret at some antisocial act. Its best-known written form nowadays is *tut(-tut),* which has become a word in its own right, pronounced not as a click but according to the spelling. However, *tsk-tsk,* which apparently is intended to represent the same click, is gaining ground, though as yet unlisted in dictionaries. Teen-agers read it in the comic strips as ['tɪsk'tɪsk]. Older written forms are *tchick* and *tck* (with or without reduplication). *Tut(-tut)* has long been used as a verb, as in Bulwer-Lytton's "pishing and tutting" (1849) and Hall Caine's "He laughed and tut-tutted" (1894), both cited by the *OED.*

A sound which we frequently make to signify agreement may be represented approximately as [ˌm'hm]. This is written as *uh-huh,* and the written form is altogether responsible for the pronunciation [ˌʌ'hʌ]. The *p* of *yep* and *nope* was probably intended to represent the glottal stop frequently heard in the pronunciation of *yes* (without *-s*) and *no,* but one also frequently hears [yɛp] and [nop], pronunciations based on the written forms.

There is, so far as I know, no written representation of the so-called Bronx cheer. Eric Partridge has suggested, however, that Hamlet's "Buz, buz!" (II.ii.396), spoken impatiently to Polonius, is intended to represent the vulgar noise also known as a "raspberry."[10]

THE USE OF PREFIXES AND SUFFIXES

New words are, however, much more commonly acquired by other processes, the most common of these being the use of prefixes and

[10] *Shakespeare's Bawdy* (New York, 1948), pp. 12, 83.

suffixes. Many of these affixes were at one time independent words, like the insignificant-seeming -ly of many adjectives, such as *manly*, *godly*, and *homely*, which has developed from Old English *līc*[11] 'body,' and the *a-* of *aside, alive, aboard*, and *a-hunting*, which was earlier *on*, with the usual old loss of -*n* in this word when unstressed and followed by a consonant (see p. 211). When unstressed, as it inevitably came to be when used so frequently as a suffix,[12] the vowel of *līc* was shortened. Old English, as we have seen (p. 121) regularly added -*e* to adjectives to make adverbs of them, thus *riht* 'right,' *rihte* 'rightly'; and adjectives formed with -*līc* acquired adverbial forms in exactly the same way, thus *cræftlic* 'skillful,' *cræftlice* 'skillfully.' With the late Middle English loss of both final -*e* and final unstressed -*ch*, earlier Middle English -*lich* and *liche* fell together as -*li* (-*ly*). Because of these losses, we do not ordinarily associate Modern English -*ly* with *like*, the Northern dialect form which ultimately was to prevail in all dialects of English, and which stands in the same relationship to non-Northern *līch* as *dike* to *ditch*. The full form has more recently been used again as a suffix—history thus repeating itself—as in *gentleman-like* and *godlike*, which are quite distinct creations from *gentlemanly* and *godly*.[13]

Other affixes surviving from Old English times include *be-*, the unstressed form of *by* (OE *bī*), as in *believe, beneath, beyond, behalf, between*; *for-*, either intensifying, as in *forlorn*, or negating, as in *forbid, forswear*; -*y* (OE -*ig*), as in *thirsty, greedy, bloody*;[14] -*ness*, which

---

[11] Surviving in *lich-gate*, the roofed gateway of a churchyard where the body of the deceased is set down to await the clergyman. Though the Old English word might be applied to either a living or a dead body, in later times the meaning 'dead body' came to prevail, as in the aforementioned *lich-gate* and in *lich-owl*, another name for the screech-owl, whose cry was supposed to be an omen of death.

[12] When so used, it originally meant something like 'having the body or appearance of': thus the literal meaning of, say, *manly* is 'having the body or form of a man.'

[13] The earliest instances of this new use of *like* cited in the *OED* are from the latter part of the fifteenth century.

[14] The diminutive -*y* (or -*ie*) of *Kitty, Jackie*, and *baby* is from another source and occurs first in Middle English times. The -*y* occurring in loanwords of Greek (*phlebotomy*), Latin (*century*), and French (*contrary*) origin may represent Greek -*ia* (*hysteria*), Latin -*ius, -ium, -ia* (*radius, medium, militia*), or French -*ie* (*perjury*), -*ee* (*army*). It is not a living suffix in the sense that the diminutive -*y* is still available to us for forming new diminutives (for example *Esky*, the name of the bulbous-eyed, girl-watching old

may be affixed to practically any adjective (or participle) to form an abstract noun, as in *manliness, dedicatedness, obligingness*; *un-*, for an opposite or negative meaning, as in *undress, unafraid, un-English*; *-dom* (OE *-dōm*, earlier an independent word which has developed into *doom*, in Old English meaning 'judgment, statute,' that is, 'what is set,' and related to *do*), as in *freedom, filmdom, gangsterdom*;[15] *-ing*, to form verbal nouns;[16] *-ful*, to form adjectives, as in *baleful, sinful, wonderful*, and, with secondary stress, to form nouns as well, as in *handful, mouthful, spoonful*; *-less* (OE *-lēas* 'free from,' also used independently and cognate with *loose*), as in *wordless, reckless, hopeless*; *-ship* (OE *-scipe*), to form abstract nouns, as in *lordship, fellowship, worship* (that is, 'worth-ship'); *-ed*, to form adjectives from nouns, as in *storied, crabbed, top-hatted*; *-en*, also for adjectives, as in *golden, oaken, leaden*; and *-er* (OE *-ere*), to form nouns of agency, as in *singer, baby-sitter, do-gooder*, a suffix which, when it occurs in loan-words, for instance *butler* (from Anglo-French *butuiller* 'bottler, manservant having to do with wines and liquors') and *butcher* (from Old French, literally 'dealer in flesh of billy-goats'), goes back to Latin *-ārius*, but which is nevertheless cognate with the English ending.

Still other affixes which go back at least to Old English times are *-ster* (OE *-estre*), originally feminine, as in *spinster* 'female spinner' and *webster* 'female weaver,' but later losing all sexual connotation, as in *gangster* and *speedster*; *-hood* (OE *-hād*), as in *manhood* and *priesthood*, earlier an independent word meaning 'condition, quality'; *-ish* (OE *-isc*), to form adjectives, as in *English* and *womanish*; *-some* (OE *-sum*), likewise adjective-forming, as in *lonesome, wholesome, winsome* (OE *wynn* 'joy' plus *sum*); *under-*, as in *understand, undertake, underworld*; *up-*, as in *upright, upheaval, upkeep*; *out-* (OE *ūt-*) as in *outside, outfield, outgo*; *after-*, as in *aftermath, aftereffect, afternoon*; *-ward*, as in *homeward, toward, outward*; *mis-*, as in *misdeed, misalign,*

---

gentleman who is a sort of mascot for the magazine *Esquire*), and similarly the *-y* from Old English *-ig*, with which we continue to form adjectives (for example *jazzy, loony, tubby*).

[15] This has been called a "dead" suffix; but, as the last two examples indicate, it is by no means so. See Harold Wentworth, "The Allegedly Dead Suffix *-dom* in Modern English," *PMLA*, LVI (1941), 280–306.

[16] Quite distinct from the archaic *-ing* used to indicate derivation from, as in *king* (OE *cyning*, literally 'son, or ideal representative, of the race, or kin'), *atheling*, and *lording*, and frequent in Old English patronymics, as in *Æðelwulfing* 'son of Æðelwulf.'

mispronounce; *with-* 'against,' as in *withhold, withstand, withdraw*; and *-th*, for abstract nouns, as in *health, depth, sloth.*

Many of these affixes are still living, in that they may be used for the creation of new words. Most have been, and many can still be, affixed to non-native words, as in some of the examples cited, for instance *obligingness, mispronounce*; also *Czardom, Romish, orderly* (*-liness*), *sugary* (*-ish*), *pocketful, coffeeless.* Others very common in Old English times, notably *ge-*, have not survived at all; *and-* 'against, toward,' the English cognate of Latin *anti-*, survives only in *answer* (OE *andswaru*, literally 'a swearing against') and, in unstressed form with loss of both *n* and *d*, in *along* (OE *andlang*).

Those languages with which English has had the closest cultural contacts—Latin, Greek, and French—have furnished a number of freely used affixes for English words. The assimilation of native and foreign began quite early and has never ceased, though in earlier times it was the English suffix which was joined to the borrowed word rather than the other way round, as in Old English *grammatisc* 'grammatish,' later supplanted by *grammatical.*[17] Since English has a lexicon culled from many sources, it is not surprising that one finds a good many hybrid creations, like Greek-French *autocade* (the *auto-* of *automobile* plus the *-cade* of *cavalcade*).[18] It should likewise be noted that the *auto* of *automobile*, taken from French, in which it was also a hybrid creation, has itself become a new combining element, as in *autocar, autotruck, autobus, autocamp*,[19] quite distinct in significacation from the *auto-* 'self' of *autointoxication, autoerotic,* and *automat,* which have no suggestion of automotiveness. The second element of *automobile* also, it should be noted, has acquired a suffixal function, as in *bookmobile* 'library on wheels' and *bloodmobile* 'blood bank on wheels.'

[17] For other examples, see A. Campbell, *Old English Grammar* (Oxford, 1959), pp. 206–07. Albert C. Baugh, *A History of the English Language*, 2nd ed. (New York, 1957), pp. 215–16, has an excellent brief discussion of this type of derivation—loan-word plus native suffix—in Middle English times.

[18] It is likely that the *-cade* combinations were at first thought of as blends —the fusing, or telescoping, as it were—of two different words (see pp. 286–87). But *-cade* seems now to have lost its earlier association with *cavalcade* and to have become a free compounding element, at least in the world of entertainment, with the meaning 'spectacular display,' as in *aquacade, musicade, motorcade.*

[19] As also in German *Autobahn.*

One of the most commonly used prefixes of non-native origin is Greek *anti-* 'against,' which, in addition to its occurrence in long-established learned words like *antipathy, antidote,* and *anticlimax,* has been rather freely used since the seventeenth century for new, mostly American, creations, for instance *anti-Federalist, anti-Catholic, anti-tobacco, anti-slavery, anti-saloon, anti-allergent,* and *anti-acid-forming. Pro-* 'for' has been somewhat less productive.

Other foreign forms which have been affixed to English words (whatever their ultimate origin) include the -*(i)an* of *Nebraskan, Miltonian* (Lat. -[i]*ānus*), used to form adjectives from nouns and the neuter plural -*(i)āna* of the same Latin ending, as in *Americana, Menckeniana* —limited though the use of the latter ending might be nowadays; Latin -*orium,* as in the late Robert Ripley's *Odditorium* 'place where oddities are on display' (with a pun on *auditorium*), *pastorium* 'Baptist parsonage,' and *washatorium* 'self-service laundry'; and -*or,* as in *chiropractor* and *realtor,* words which were never known to the ancients, who were probably just as happy without them. The -*ician* of *beautician* and *mortician* is Latin, from -*ic* plus -*ian.* While these must be regarded as mere linguistic bijouteries, they at least indicate the viability of the suffixes. Still others are the -*ese* of *Federalese, Johnsonese,* and *journalese,* coming to us directly from Old French but ultimately going back to Latin -*ēnsis;* the verb-making -*ize* of *pasteurize, criticize,* and *harmonize,* along with a host of other more recent flowerings, of which we shall have more to say later; and *ante-, de-, dis-, ex-, inter-, multi-, non-, neo-, post-, pre-, pseudo-, re-, semi-, sub-, ultra-, -able, -al, -ette, -mania, -oid, -phile (-philia),* and -*phobe* (-*phobia*), all more or less freely adaptable. *Super-,* as in *Superman, supermarket,* and *superhighway* has even become an independent adjective in childish and familiar usage, as in "Our new car's super"; there is also a reduplicated form *superduper* 'very super.' The independent use of *super* as a noun dates from the mid-nineteenth century; it is a clipping of *supernumerary (actor),* though in New York City it may be used for the superintendent of an apartment house.

NEW AFFIXES AND NEW USES
OF OLD ONES

As has doubtless always been true, linguistically naïve misunderstanding has created new suffixes in our day. In German *Hamburger* 'pertaining to, or associated with, Hamburg,' for instance, the -*er* is affixed to the name of the city. This adjectival suffix may be joined to any place name in German, for example, *Kassler Rippenspeer* 'Kassel spareribs,' *Münchner Bier* 'Munich beer,' *Braunschweiger Wurst* 'Brunswick sausage,' *Wiener Schnitzel* 'Vienna cutlet,' and the like. In English, however, the *-burg-*, and, to a lesser extent the *-furt-* of *Frankfurter* 'pertaining to Frankfurt,' have been taken as suffixal elements: witness the scores of *-burger* combinations which have appeared within the past twenty years or so—most of them probably ephemeral, though *cheeseburger* has certainly acquired a permanent place in the American culinary vocabulary (*O tempora, O mores!*).[20] The same misunderstanding of *Frankfurter* is indicated by *shrimpfurter* and a few other such gaucheries. *Burger* is entered independently as a noun in *Webster's Third New International Dictionary*, denoting a sandwich containing a patty of meat or some other food (*any* other food, in fact) capable of being made into a patty. **Furter* has not as yet made the grade; it is doubtless dying even as a suffix. Purists will not lament its demise.

Whereas the proliferating of *-burger* is limited only by the number of edibles and near-edibles which can be patted into cakes, that of *-copter*, which is also due to a misunderstanding, is more or less limited to aviation enthusiasts. In *helicopter*, the source of the various new combinations, the *-o-* is the combining element between Greek *helix* 'spiral' and *pter(on)* 'wing,' but the word has been blunderingly analyzed as *heli-copter* rather than as *helico-pter*[21] and, in addition to the independent *copter*, such combinations as *gyrocopter* and *hoppicopter* have come into being.[22]

Though no man can say why—fashion would seem to be the principal determinant—certain affixes have been particularly popular during certain periods. For instance, *-wise* affixed to nouns and adjectives to form adverbs was practically archaic until, approximately, the 1940's, occurring only in a comparatively few well-established words, such as *likewise, lengthwise, otherwise,* and *crosswise.* The *OED* cites a few examples of its free use in modern times, for instance, *Cardinalwise* (1677), *festoon-wise* (1743), and *Timothy* or *Titus-wise* (1876).

[20] Many of these were recorded in the pages of *American Speech* between 1939 and 1944.

[21] An etymologically correct **pter* would of course present certain difficulties in pronunciation.

[22] These facts are pointed out by Svante Stubelius in his *Balloon, Flying-Machine, Helicopter*, Gothenburg Studies in English, No. 9 (Göteborg, 1961), pp. 268–70.

But around 1940 began a mighty proliferation of words in -*wise*, for instance *budgetwise, saleswise, weatherwise, healthwise,* and literally scores of others which can hardly be written off as ephemeral. Because of its economy in circumventing such phrases as *in respect of* and *in the manner of,* many such new coinages are likely to become permanent additions to the language, despite all the objurgations of older-generation speakers, who of course get along well enough without them, just as they always have done. The sudden resuscitation of this suffix—an independent word so used even in Old English times, as in *rihtwīs* 'rightwise,' developing into Modern English *righteous*—is incapable of explanation. There are no inhibitions whatever on its free employment in either American or British English,[23] as in the winning coinage of Mrs. Lyndon B. (Lady Bird) Johnson: "Fabric-wise, I like this room best."[24]

Type has enjoyed a similar vogue, and is well on its way to being a freely used suffix, though previously it was restricted to such words as *electrotype* and *prototype.* With it, adjectives may be formed from nouns, as in "Both Methodists and Episcopalians have Catholic-type bishops with considerable authority"[25] and ". . . undraped girls, in a 'Las Vegas-type revue.' "[26] Like -*wise,* -*type* is also economical, enabling us to short-cut such locutions as *bishops of the Catholic type* and *a revue of the Las Vegas type.*

The suffix -*ize* has been heretofore alluded to. Ultimately from Greek -*izein,* it has had a centuries-old life as a means of making verbs from nouns and adjectives—not only in English, but in other languages as well, for instance French -*iser,* Italian -*izare,* Spanish -*izar,* and German -*isieren.* Many English words with this suffix are borrowings from French, for instance (with z for French s) *authorize, moralize, naturalize*; others are English formations (though some of them may have parallel formations in French), for instance *concertize, patronize, fertilize*; still others are formed from proper names, for instance *Bowdlerize, mesmerize, Americanize.*

---

[23] For example, "The balletgoers see lively, leaping girls and boys whirling over the stage American-wise . . ." in the London *Tatler,* November 11, 1960, p. 39; "Alex Comfort's *Come Out to Play* may not be the most accomplished of books, constructionwise, but . . ." in the London *Spectator,* November 10, 1961, p. 675.

[24] Quoted in *Time,* November 17, 1961, p. 34.

[25] Jacksonville *Florida Times-Union,* December 5, 1960, p. 1.

[26] *Time,* December 29, 1961, p. 13.

This suffix became very productive around 1950, and dozens of new creations have come into being: *moisturize, sanitize, glamourize, personalize* 'to mark with name, initials, or monogram,'[27] *tenderize,* and a good many others. The most widely discussed of all these creations, however, must surely be *finalize,* which descended to general usage from the celestial mists of bureaucracy, where nothing is merely ended, finished, or concluded. It is a great favorite of administrators of all kinds and sizes—including the academic, for one comes upon it in the "directives" of university presidents, deans, and department heads. The verb would seem to be of American origin,[28] though certainly not regarded as alien corn by the English, who by and large prefer spelling it and other such words with the French-derived *-ise.*[29] Dwight D. Eisenhower gave it his imprimatur in a State of the Union Message, so that it automatically became "President's English" and has retained this exalted status, having occurred in the usage of his successor. When *Webster's Third* quite properly listed the word, bellows of anger and groans of outraged propriety issued from editorial writers (notably in the New York *Times* and in *Life*), who seem with a few honorable exceptions to regard themselves as custodians of the English language.[30]

[27] In other senses, for example 'personify,' this word is considerably older, but is almost certainly a new creation in the sense specified.

[28] Kelsie B. Harder, in *American Speech,* XXXVI (1961), 239, cites an early use (1943) in a letter written by an officer of the Royal Australian Naval Volunteer Reserve to Lieutenant (later President) John F. Kennedy. H. L. Mencken in *The American Language: Supplement I* (New York, 1945), p. 402, n. 12, states that a New South Wales correspondent of *John o' London's Weekly* reported in 1936 that the word was used in Australia at the end of World War I. Harder admits the possibility, which seems to be also an extreme probability, that the term is nevertheless in its present manifestation an independent American coinage.

[29] It is listed by Sir Ernest Gowers, along with *casualise, civilianise, editorialise,* and *publicise* (the last two of which will not seem in the least strange to Americans except in their spelling), as one of the darlings of British bureaucratese, in his *Plain Words: Their ABC* (New York, 1954), p. 54.

[30] Apparently they were unaware that the word is also entered in *Webster's New International Dictionary,* 2nd ed. (Springfield, Mass., 1934), in the *American College Dictionary* (New York, 1947), in *Webster's New World Dictionary of the American Language* (Cleveland, Ohio, 1953), and the *Funk and Wagnalls Standard Dictionary,* International Edition (New York, 1958).

Greek formed nouns of action from verbs in -izein by modifying the ending to -ismos or -isma, as reflected in many pairs of loan-words in English, such as ostracize–ostracism and criticize–criticism. The suffix -ism may be used as an independent word, as in creeds and isms. Such use of suffixes must be rather rare, though -ology has also been so used to mean 'science,' as in "Chemistry, Geology, Philology, and a hundred other ologies."[31] Prefixes have fared somewhat better; anti, pro, con, and ex are all used as nouns.

De-, a prefix of Latin origin with privative force, is still much alive. Though many words beginning with it are from Latin or French, it has for centuries been used for the formation of new words. Demoralize was claimed by Noah Webster as his only coinage, and it is a fact that he was the first to use it in English; but it could just as well be from French démoraliser. The prefix is used before words of whatever origin, as in defrost, dewax, and debunk. Gowers cites, from a collection of "septic verbs" made by Sir Alan Herbert, such poisonous specimens as debureaucratise, dewater, deinsectize, and deratizate 'get rid of rats,'[32] reporting defeathered geese from a directive issued by the British Ministry of Food. Two other de- words from Herbert's Index seem considerably less septic nowadays than they must have done when the list was made—decontaminate and dehumidify, which we have learned to take in our stride, though what point there was in coining them in the first place is difficult to see; they seem to be merely pompous ways of saying 'clean out' and 'dry out.' The Chamber of Horrors (London, 1952) of "Vigilans," a glossary "of official jargon both English and American," with an introduction by Eric Partridge, lists dehydrofreezing (called an "American term," like most of those which the English disapprove of), derequisition, and derestricted, among others. Dis-, likewise from Latin, is freely used in the same privative function, particularly in officialese, as in disincentive 'deterrent,' disassemble 'take apart,' and dissaver 'one who does not save his money.' Other voguish affixes are non-, from Latin, used according to Gowers "to turn any word upside-down," as in non-sick 'healthy,' presumably,[33] and non-availability 'lack'; -ee, from French, as in draftee, trainee, donee, and escapee 'escaper'; and re-, from Latin, as

---

[31] Cited from 1811 in OED, whose latest citation is from 1884. As we have seen, burger, which is commonly regarded as a suffix, has a vigorous independent existence. Bus, it should be noted, is part of the suffix of omnibus.

[32] Plain Words: Their ABC, p. 55.

[33] Gowers cites "Institutions for the care of the non-sick" (p. 57).

in *redecontaminate* 'clean out again,' *recivilianize* 'return to civilian life,' and *recondition* 'repair, restore.'

The very popular *cafeteria*, characterized by a Swiss observer of American life as a place for "grasping food from a counter, swallowing it in record time, and rushing back to work," which has "not merely ruined the health of millions of Americans, but has also affected their mentality, humour and outlook on life," for, "with his power and ingenuity for shortening life's pleasures in order to gain time for remunerative occupation and toil, the American has invented mass-feeding,"[34] is of Mexican Spanish origin, originally designating an establishment for coffee-drinking rather than for food-eating. The word has provided us with a suffix *-teria*, which used to carry implications of self-service and hence speed, as in *washateria, bookateria, shaveteria,* and *sodateria*, though it need no longer do so, for the suffix is used in the names of mere retail business establishments, like *hateria* 'hat shop' and *snacketeria* 'snack shop or counter.'

The *-teria* suffix began in the 1950's to be supplanted by *-rama*, from Greek *horama* 'view.' John Lotz suggests that the widespread use of this suffix stems from *Cinerama*, the wide-screen motion picture which was first shown in New York in 1952, and there is every reason to believe that he is right.[35] Lotz points out that *Cinerama* "was obviously coined on the analogy of *panorama* and the less frequent *cyclorama*." The first of its offshoots was doubtless *liquorama*, the name given to his window display by the dealer in spirits whose shop was next door to the theater where Cinerama made its debut.

Panorama, diorama, and *cyclorama*, which first appeared, according to the *OED*, in 1796, 1823, and 1840 respectively, are of course made up of Greek *pan-* 'all,' *di-* 'through,' and *kyklos* 'circle' plus *horama*; hence the *-o-* is correctly retained in these words, as it is not in *Cinerama* and other recent creations such as *beautyrama* 'beauty shop,' *bowlerama* 'bowling alley,' *icecreamerama*,[36] *Bridge-A-Rama* 'a large

[34] J. Henry Wild, *Glimpses of the American Language and Civilization* (Bern, 1945), pp. 44–45.

[35] "The Suffix '-Rama,'" *American Speech*, XXIX (1954), 156–58. *Futurama*, the name of the General Motors exhibit during the New York World's Fair of 1939–40, as Lotz points out, seems not to have created the vogue.

[36] The most nauseating specimen cited by William M. Ryan in his aptly titled "A Plethorama," *American Speech*, XXXVI (1961), 230–33. It presumably designates a party of some sort with ice cream as the *pièce de résistance*.

bridge party, the project of a University Women's Club to raise money for a fund to aid co-eds,' and, to cite a British example, *sexerama*.[37]

In the early examples cited by Lotz, the implication of *-rama* is 'spectacular display,' but more recent creations do not necessarily sustain the idea of a view; they may imply either largeness or nothing at all.[38] Ryan cites uses of the suffix to designate a process (*Slenderama*, a reducing method) or merely a product (*Coolerama*, pajamas; *Taperama*, Scotch tape).

As we have seen, many affixes can be shown to have been at one time independent words. Such words become affixes when they can no longer stand alone, that is, when they are no longer regarded as independent words. An Old English adjective in *-līc* thus may be regarded as a compound until the ending has gone through the various phonetic changes which reduced it to *-ly*. It is likely that the first of these changes, the shortening of the vowel because of lack of stress, was insufficient to disguise the origin of the suffix, and that analysis of such compounds was still possible and even usual, just as we still analyze *postman* as *post* plus *man* although for the second element of this compound we no longer say [mæn]; instead, the vowel is reduced to schwa, thus, ['pos(t)mən].

COMPOUNDS

Putting two or more words together to make a new word with a meaning in some way different, if only in being more specific, from that of its separate elements in juxtaposition—for instance, a *blackboard* is not the same thing as a *black board*[39]—has been very common in English, as in the other Germanic languages as well, from earliest times. Old English has *blīðheort* 'blithe-heart(ed),' *eaxlgestella* 'shoulder-companion, that is, comrade,' *brēostnet* 'breast-net, that is,

[37] *"Accatone* [an Italian motion picture] has the breath of life in it and deserves a better fate than to be billed as just another sexerama . . ." (*Spectator*, November 3, 1961, p. 627).

[38] The only "Beautyrama" with which I am personally acquainted is situated in a notably rundown neighborhood and is considerably smaller and, viewed from without, less pretentious than most establishments dedicated to the beautification of the American homemaker.

[39] The fact is that nowadays many blackboards are green, or some other color. A blackboard may thus be defined as a slab of slate or similar material fixed to a wall or mounted in a standing frame for writing upon with chalk. They are sometimes referred to in Educationese as *chalkboards*.

corslet,' *leornungcniht* 'learning retainer (knight), that is, disciple,' *wǣrloga* 'oath-breaker, devil (warlock),' *woroldcyning* 'world-, that is, earthly-king,' *fullfyllan* 'to fulfill,' and many other such compound words.

The compounding process has gone on continuously. In the early 1960's, for instance, the American people heard over their radio and television sets of a *manshoot*, that is, the propelling of an astronaut into outer space. The creation, parallel with *turkey shoot*, did not seem particularly strange—shocking as it may have been to some from a purely humane point of view—but merely new.

As far as writing is concerned—and we are not overmuch concerned with it at the moment—compound adjectives are usually hyphenated, like *one-horse, loose-jointed,* and *front-page,* though some which are particularly well established, like *outgoing, overgrown, underbred,* and *forthcoming,* are written solid. It is similar with compound verbs, like *overdo, broadcast, sidestep,* beside *double-date, baby-sit,* and *goose-step,* though these sometimes occur as two words. With the writing of compound nouns the situation is likewise somewhat inconsistent: we write *ice cream, Boy Scout, real estate, post office, high school* as two words; we hyphenate *kick-off, go-between, fire-eater, higher-up;* we write solid *firearm, icebox, postmaster, highball.* But hyphenation varies to some extent with the dictionary one consults,[40] the style books of editors and publishers, and individual whim, among other things—including chronology, for the preference in recent years has been to write compounds solid: the *high-brow* of *Webster's New Collegiate Dictionary* (Springfield, Mass., 1949) has become *highbrow* in *Webster's Seventh New Collegiate* (Springfield, Mass., 1963); *egghead,* a new creation, was so written from the beginning. Compound prepositions like *upon, throughout, into,* and *within* are always written solid, as are compound adverbs like *nevertheless, moreover,* and *henceforth,* and compound pronouns like *whoever* and *myself.*

A more significant and interesting characteristic of compounds—one which tells us whether we are dealing with two or more words used independently or as a unit—is their tendency to be more strongly stressed on one or the other element, in contrast to the more or less level stress of the same words when they constitute a phrase. (For

[40] For instance, the *American College Dictionary* has *whole-hearted;* *Webster's Third New International Dictionary* has *wholehearted.*

present purposes it is necessary to distinguish only two degrees of stress, primary and secondary.) In compound nouns it is usually the first element which receives primary stress (*bláckbèrry*, *hándbrèadth*, *cówbòy*)[41] and in adverbs and prepositions the last (*nèverthelèss*, *withóut*); for verbs and pronouns it is impossible to generalize (*bróadcàst*, *fulfíll*; *sómebody* [or *sómebòdy*], *whoéver*). Without this type of stress in compounds, the close connection between the constituents which gives them their special meanings would not be readily apparent. It alone makes the difference between a *man eating crow*, with more or less even stress on *man* and *eat*, and a *man-eating crow* (an unprecedented zoological phenomenon), with primary stress on *man* and considerably reduced stress on *eat*; in effect it welds together the elements and thus makes the difference between *hótbèd* 'heated bed of earth for growing plants' and *hót béd* 'midsummer sleeping place'; between *híghbròw* 'intellectual' and *hígh bŕów* 'result of receding hair'; between *good-bý* 'farewell' and *good búy* 'bargain'; between *gréenhòuse* 'heated glass structure for plants' and *gréen hóuse*

---

[41] In *Boy Scout* and *ice cream* the primary stress may be on either element. Frequently, it may be usually, these particular compounds may have level stress. Under such circumstances, according to Leonard Bloomfield, we are dealing with a phrase rather than a compound, "although there is no denotative difference of meaning" (*Language*, p. 228). From a historical point of view, however, we may follow Otto Jespersen, who in turn is following Henry Sweet (*A New English Grammar, Logical & Historical* [Oxford, 1900] I, 286–90). Jespersen considers such combinations as representative of "a new type of compounds" which "has sprung up in ModE, in which each part is more independent," and in which level stress is approximated or even completely achieved, citing as examples, among others, *lead pencil, plum pudding, toothbrush, ground floor, downhearted,* and *old-fashioned*. But, as Jespersen says, "individual pronunciations vary not a little," and "very often instead of the fully equal stress of the theory we have either fore-stress or end-stress" (*A Modern English Grammar on Historical Principles* [Copenhagen, 1909] I, 154–55). Daniel Jones, *English Pronouncing Dictionary*, 11th ed. (London, 1951) records only one primary stress in *toothbrush*, and H. C. Wyld, *Universal Dictionary of the English Language* (London, 1932) records secondary stress for the first syllable of *old-fashioned*. The plain fact is that in every one of these compounds there usually occurs what Jespersen calls unity-stress, and it seems likely that the unity-stress principle will prevail. It is similar with *public house* 'drinking place' and *headmaster*, for which only level stress is recorded in the dictionaries, but which according to my own observation frequently have only secondary stress on their first elements.

'house painted green'; between *wildflówer hunter* 'one who hunts flowers growing in a natural state' and *wild flówer-hunter* 'mad botanist'; between *mákeùp* 'cosmetics' and *màke úp* 'to reconcile'; between *hándòut* 'gift to beggar' and *hànd óut* 'driver's turning signal'; between *héadhùnter* 'savage' and *héad húnter* 'top man on safari'; between *lóudspèaker* 'sound amplifier' and *lòud spéaker* 'noisy talker'; between *báby-sìts* 'takes care of infant(s) while parents go to movies or party' and *bàby síts* 'infant rests weight on buttocks'—but one could go on and on with this sort of thing. A classical example is *líghthòuse keeper* and *lìght hóusekeeper*.

It is a general principal that when complete loss of secondary stress occurs, phonetic change occurs as well. For instance, *Énglish mán,* having in the course of compounding become *Énglish-màn,* proceeded to become *Énglishman* [-mən]. The same vowel-reduction has occurred in *highwayman* 'robber,'[42] but not in *businessman*; in *gentleman* and *horseman* (as also in the previously mentioned *postman*), but not in *milkman* and *iceman*.[43] It is similar with the [-lənd] of *Maryland, Iceland, woodland,* and *highland* as contrasted with the secondarily stressed final syllables of such newer compounds as *wonderland, movieland,* and *Disneyland*; with the *-folk* of *Norfolk* and *Suffolk* (there is a common American pronunciation of the former with [-ˌfok] and, by assimilation, with [-ˌfɔrk]); and with the *-mouth* of *Portsmouth,* the *-combe* of *Wyecombe,* the *-burgh* of *Edinburgh* (usually [-brə]), and the *-stone* of *Folkestone.* Even more drastic changes occur in the final syllables of *coxswain* ['kɔksn], *Keswick* ['kɛzɪk], and *Durham* ['dʌrəm] (though in *Birmingham,* as the name of a city in Alabama, the *-ham* is pronounced as the spelling suggests it "should" be) and in both syllables of *boatswain* ['bosn], *forecastle* ['foksl], *breakfast, Christmas* (that is, Christ's mass), *cupboard,* and *Greenwich,*[44] to cite only a few of many examples. Perhaps it is lack

---

[42] Though, as John S. Kenyon and Thomas A. Knott point out in their *Pronouncing Dictionary of American English* (Springfield, Mass., 1951), the secondary stress is retained when the word is used to mean 'one who oversees the building and upkeep of roads.'

[43] Pronunciation with [-mən] is recorded for this word by Kenyon and Knott, which saves it from the ignominy of having become practically archaic before it ever had a chance of attaining to what might be regarded as the final stage of *man* as part of a compound.

[44] Except for Greenwich Village in New York and Greenwich, Connecticut, this is as an American place name usually pronounced as spelled, rather than as ['grɛnič] or ['grɛniǰ]. The usual English pronunciation has ['grɪn-].

of familiarity with the word—just as the landlubber might pronounce *boatswain* as ['bot,swen]—which has given rise to an analytical pronunciation of *clapboard*, traditionally ['klæbə(r)d], on the part of younger-generation speakers. *Grindstone* and *wristband* used to be respectively ['grɪnstən] and ['rɪzbənd] Not many people have much occasion to use either word nowadays; consequently, the older tradition has been lost, and the words now have secondary stress and full vowels instead of [ə] in their last elements. The same thing has happened to *waistcoat*, now usually ['west,kot]; even among those who use the word at all, that is, the English, the traditional ['wɛskət] has become old-fashioned. Lack of familiarity can hardly explain the phenomenon in this instance, nor will it do for the new analysis of *forehead* (see p. 47). Perhaps a consciousness of the spelling of the word on the part of those who distrust cultural tradition is responsible. It is ironical that literacy has engendered this distrust.

Such phonetic changes as we have been considering have the effect of welding the elements of certain compounds so closely together that, judging from sound (and frequently also from their appearances when written), one would sometimes not suspect that they were indeed compounds. In *daisy*, for instance, phonetic reduction of the final element has caused that element to be identical with a suffix. Geoffrey Chaucer, without benefit of either the *OED* or scientific training in historical linguistics, guessed better than he could have known for certain when he referred to "The dayesyë, or elles the yë (eye) of day" in the Prologue to *The Legend of Good Women*, for the word is really and truly from the Old English compound *dægesēage* 'day's eye.' The *-y* of *daisy* is thus not an affix like the diminutive *-y* of *Katy* or the *-y* from Old English *-ig* of *hazy*; instead, the word is from a historical point of view a compound.

Such closely welded compounds have been called "amalgamated" by Arthur G. Kennedy,[45] who lists, among a good many others, *as* (OE *al* 'all' plus *swā* 'so'), *garlic* (OE *gār* 'spear' plus *lēac* 'leek'), *hussy* (OE *hūs* 'house' plus *wif* 'wife'),[46] *lord* (OE *hlāf* 'loaf' plus *weard* 'ward'), *marshal* (OE *mearh* 'horse' plus *scealc* 'servant'), *nostril* (OE *nosu* 'nose' plus *þyrel* 'hole'), and *sheriff* (OE *scīr* 'shire' plus *(ge)rēfa* 'reeve'). Many proper names are such amalgamated compounds, for

---

[45] *Current English* (Boston, 1935), p. 350.

[46] A beautiful example of pejoration. The two words following illustrate the opposite semantic development, melioration.

instance, among place names, *Boston* ('Botulf's stone'), *Sussex* (OE
sūð 'south' plus *Seaxe* 'Saxons'; compare *Essex* and *Middlesex*),
Norwich[47] (OE *norð* 'north' plus *wīc* 'village'), and *Bewley* (Fr. *beau*
'beautiful' plus *lieu* 'place'). The reader will find plenty of other interesting examples in Eilert Ekwall's *Concise Oxford Dictionary of
English Place-Names,* 4th ed. (Oxford, 1960). It is similar with surnames (which are of course sometimes place names as well), for
instance *Durward* (OE *duru* 'door' plus *weard* 'keeper'), *Purdue* (Fr.
pour 'for' plus *Dieu* 'God'), and *Thurston* ('Thor's stone,' ultimately
Scandinavian); and with a good many given names as well, for instance *Ethelbert* (OE *æðel* 'noble' plus *beorht* 'bright'), *Alfred* (OE *ælf*
'elf' plus *rǣd* 'counsel'), and *Mildred* (OE *milde* 'mild' plus *þryð*
'strength').

The making of a compound is uninhibited by any considerations
other than those dictated by meaning. A compound may be used in
any grammatical function: as noun (*wishbone*), adjective (*foolproof*),
adverb (*overhead*), verb (*gainsay*), or preposition (*without*). It may be
made up of two nouns (*baseball, mudguard, manhole*);[48] of an adjective followed by a noun (*bluegrass, madman, first-rate*); of a noun
followed by an adjective or a participle (*bloodthirsty, trigger-happy,
homemade, heart-breaking, time-honored*); of a verb followed by an
adverb (*pinup, breakdown, setback*); of an adverb followed by a verb
form (*upset, downcast, forerun*); of a verb followed by a noun which
is its object (*daredevil, blowgun, touch-me-not*); of a noun followed by
a verb (*hemstitch, pan-fry, typeset*); of an adverb followed by an adjective or a participle (*overanxious, oncoming, well-known*); of a preposition followed by its object (*overland, indoors*); and of a participle
followed by an adverb (*washed-up, carryings-on, worn-out*). There are
in addition a number of phrases which have become welded into compounds, for example *will-o'-the-wisp, happy-go-lucky, hop-o'-my-
thumb, mother-in-law, tongue-in-cheek, hand-to-mouth, lighter-than-
air, love-in-a-mist.* Many compounds are made up of adjective plus
noun plus the ending *-ed*, for example *bald-headed, bowlegged, hairy-
chested.*

[47] Traditionally pronounced to rime with *porridge*, as in the old nursery
jingle about the man from Norwich who ate some porridge. The name
of the city in Connecticut is, however, pronounced as the spelling seems to
indicate.

[48] The first noun is in a few traditional compounds the genitive form, for
example *bird's-eye, marksman,* and *daisy.*

CLIPPED FORMS

An abbreviation, or clipped form, must be regarded as a new word, particularly when, as it frequently does, it supplants the longer form altogether. Thus, *mob* can be said to have supplanted *mobile vulgus* 'movable, or fickle, common people,' and *omnibus*, literally 'for all' is in the sense 'motor vehicle for paying passengers' almost as archaic as *mobile vulgus*, having been strangely clipped to *bus*—strangely only because *bus* is no root, but merely part of an ending *-ibus* occurring in the dative (and ablative) plural forms of all Latin nouns of the third declension, that to which *omnis* 'all' belongs. But there is really no reason why English usage should reflect, or even particularly respect, the grammatical features of other languages from which it has borrowed words. Certainly it has not done so here, nor with *burger* and *copter* (see p. 271). *Periwig*, like the form *peruke* (Fr. *perruque*) of which it is a modification, is completely gone; only the abbreviated *wig* survives, and those who use it are not likely to be even slightly aware of the full form. *Taxicab* has so completely superseded *taximeter cabriolet* that no one associates it with the longer forms, if indeed they are known at all, and has supplied us with two new words, *taxi* and *cab*.[49] *Pantaloons* seems quite archaic.[50] The clipped form *pants* may be said to have won the day completely. *Bra* seems similarly to be pushing out *brassière*, which in French means a shoulder-strap (it is a derivative of *bras* 'arm') or a bodice fitted with such straps.[51] British English *perm*, from *permanent wave*, has found little favor with the American homemaker and those who have dedicated their lives to her beautification. No drinker nowadays imbibes *geneva* as the principal ingredient of his martinis; the clipped *gin*, first noted by Bernard Mandeville in 1714 in his *Fable of the Bees*, has driven out the full form, which, incidentally, has nothing to do with the Swiss city in which John Calvin flourished, but which has come to us by way of Dutch (p. 345). *Whisk(e)y* and *brandy* are similarly clippings of *whiskybae* and *brandywine*.

[49] As a shortening of *cabriolet*, *cab* is almost a century older than *taxicab*.

[50] I can, however, remember hearing it used in all seriousness by my maternal grandfather (1857–1924), who considered *trousers* non-U ("Let the tailors call 'em that") and *pants* inexpressibly low. He was a very conservative man in almost every respect.

[51] The woman's garment worn for uplifting, exaggerating the proportions, or otherwise modifying the contour of the breasts is in French called a *soutien-gorge*.

Other abbreviated forms more commonly used than the longer ones include *phone, zoo, extra, flu, auto,* and *ad. Zoo* is of course from *zoological garden* with the sound-change from [zoǝ-] to [zu-] because of the spelling. *Extra,* which is probably a clipping from *extraordinary,* has become a separate word. *Auto,* like the full form *automobile,* is rapidly losing ground to *car,* an abbreviated form of *motor-car.* In time *auto* may become archaic. *Advertisement* has become *ad* in American English, but was clipped less drastically to *advert* in British English, though *ad* is rapidly gaining ground in England.

Clipped forms occur in practically all, if not indeed in all walks of life, for instance the collegian's *lab, exam, lit, math, Bus Ad* (for *Business Administration,* a fully developed course of study in American universities, the pronunciation varying, depending upon the school, as [bʌs æd] and [bíz æd]); the housewife's *perk (percolate), vac (vacuum cleaner,* also 'to clean with a vacuum cleaner'), *fridge (refrigerator,* pretty much confined to British use); the oil-field worker's *reefer*[52] *(refrigerator car), toolie (tool dresser), forams (foraminifera);*[53] and the criminal drug addict's *Chino*[54] *(Chinese), benny (benzedrine), Harry (heroin);*[55] and the cowboy's *tarp (tarpaulin), wrango (wrangler), bronc (bronco).*[56] Many of the clipped forms recognizable as such which have been hitherto mentioned are by no means characteristic of informal speech. They occur in all varieties; this is to say, there are practically no situations in life so exalted that one would not say *car* (for *motor-car), phone, zoo, cab,* and *flu.* As for *mob, bus, wig,* and the names of the alcoholic drinks which have been cited, these are the only terms extant; between them and their full forms no choice is possible.

A special type of abbreviation consists of what is left over after an initial unstressed syllable has been lost, as in childish " 'Scuse me" and

[52] To the drug addict this word means 'marijuana cigarette.'

[53] Lalia Phipps Boone, *The Petroleum Dictionary* (Norman, Okla., 1952).

[54] The *o*-suffix is of fairly frequent occurrence in unconventional English, for instance *righto, kiddo, cheerio, daddy-o, ammo, blinko, stinko, blotto, combo, billy-o, bingo,* and a good many others. Eric Partridge, *Dictionary of Slang and Unconventional English,* 3rd ed. (New York, 1950), records *like Jimmy-o* as a variant of *like Billy-o, dekko* 'look,' *blindo* 'drunk' (hence synonymous with *stinko* and *blotto),* among a number of others.

[55] From "A Glossary of Terms Commonly Used by Underworld Addicts," in Chapter 10 of David W. Maurer and Victor H. Vogel, *Narcotics and Narcotic Addiction* (Springfield, Ill., 1954).

[56] Ramon F. Adams, *Western Words* (Norman, Okla., 1944).

"I did it 'cause I wanted to." Frequently this phenomenon has resulted in two different words, for instance *fender, fence, cute, squire,* and *sport,* which are simply aphetic forms of *defender, defense, acute, esquire,* and *disport.* Sometimes, however, an aphetic form may occur simply as a variant of the longer form, for instance *possum* (from *opossum*) and *coon* (from *raccoon*). Early Modern English *pothecary* and *spittle* (or *spital*) are aphetic forms of *apothecary* and *hospital.* The meanings of *etiquette* and the aphetic form *ticket* have become rather sharply differentiated; the primary meaning of French *étiquette* is preserved in the English shortening.

BACK FORMATIONS

Back formation—the making of a word from a word which is mistakenly assumed to be a derivative of it, as in *to burgle* from *burglar,* the final *ar* of which suggests that the word is a noun of agency and hence *ought* to mean 'one who burgles'[57]—has been the source of a smallish number of new words. In origin the final consonant [-z] of *pease* is not, as it seems to the ear to be, the English plural suffix *-s;* it is in fact not a suffix at all. But by the seventeenth century *pease* was mistaken for a plural, and a new singular, *pea,* was derived from a word which was itself singular,[58] precisely as if we were to derive a form *chee* from *cheese* under the impression that *cheese* was plural; then we should have *one chee, two chees,* just as we now have *one pea, two peas.* *Cherry* has been derived by an identical process from Old English *ciris,* a Latin loan-word (compare Fr. *cerise*), the final *s* having been assumed to be the plural suffix. Similarly, *sherry wine* was once *sherris wine,* to cite one of the English spellings for Xeres[59] (now Jerez), the city in Spain where the wine was originally made. The wonderful one-hoss *shay* of Holmes's poem was so called because of the notion that *chaise* was what it sounds like, a plural form, and the heathen *Chinee* of Bret Harte's poem is similarly explained.[60]

[57] Similarly with facetious *to ush* from *usher* and *to buttle* from *butler.*
[58] It had an unchanged plural.
[59] In Spanish *x* formerly had the value [š], so that the English spelling was perfectly sound phonetically.
[60] Other nouns in the singular which look like plural forms are *alms* (OE *ælmysse,* from Lat. *eleēmosyna*), *riches* (ME *richesse* 'wealth'), and *molasses.* Nonstandard *those molasses* assumes the existence of a singular *that *molass,* though such a form is not indeed heard. A story is told of a Southern "colonel" who, in the course of reproving his small colored servitor

The adverb *darkling* 'in the darkness' (*dark* plus adverbial *-ling*, a suffix which in Old English denoted direction, extent, or something of the sort) has been misunderstood as a present participial form, giving rise to a new verb *darkle*, as in Lord Byron's "Her cheek began to flush, her eyes to sparkle,/And her proud brow's blue veins to swell and darkle" (*Don Juan*, VI,101), in which *darkle* is construed to mean 'to grow dark.' A few years previously, in his "Ode to a Nightingale," John Keats had used *darkling* in "Darkling I listen; and, for many a time,/I have been half in love with easeful Death . . . ," where it presumably has the historical adverbial sense. It is not here implied that Byron misunderstood Keats's line; the examples merely show how easily the verb might have developed as a back formation from the adverb.[61] *Grovel*, first used by Shakespeare (*OED*), comes to us by way of a similar misconception of *groveling* (*grufe* 'face down' plus *-ling*), and *sidle* is likewise from *sideling* 'sidelong.'[62]

There is another species of back formation, in which the secondary form could just as well have been the primary one, and in which no misunderstanding is involved. *Typewriter*, of American origin, came before the verb *typewrite*; nevertheless, the ending *-er* of *typewriter* is actually the noun-of-agency ending, so that the verb could just as well have come first, only it didn't. It is similar with *housekeep* from *house-*

---

for spilling a jug of molasses, said, "You git down theah, suh, and lick them every one up," but it is doubtless apocryphal. I am informed, however, on unimpeachable feminine authority, that those who sell women's hose sometimes refer to a single stocking, or perhaps to a pair collectively, as a "very nice hoe."

License, pulse, and *appendix* sound like plurals. I have heard the back formation *licent* a good many times from unsophisticated speakers, usually in the phrase "licent tag," and the fact that *pulse* and *appendix* in non-standard use frequently take plural verbs indicates the existence, somewhere in the tortuous maze of the *psyche linguistica* of the common man, of assumed singular forms *pult* and *appendick*, even though these may never be heard.

[61] The earliest citation of the newer verb in the *OED* is from the year 1800, when it occurs in Tom Moore's "Ode to Anacreon." Could Byron, who first used the word in 1819, have picked it up from his friend Moore?

[62] Compare the now forgotten back formation *to quisle* 'to act as a traitor,' from Vidkun Quisling, the Norwegian traitor, executed in 1945. An intentional humorous assumption of *-ing* as a participial ending occurs in J. K. Stephen's immortal "When the Rudyards cease from Kipling,/And the Haggards ride no more."

keeper (or *housekeeping*) and *baby-sit* from *baby sitter.* The adjective *housebroken* 'excretorily adapted to the indoors' is older than the verb *housebreak;* but, since *housebroken* is actually a compounding of *house* and the past participle *broken,* the process might just as well have been the other way around—the usual way—except that it wasn't.

BLENDS

The blending of two existing words to make a new word was doubtless an unconscious process in the oldest periods of our language. The *haþel* 'nobleman' in line 1138 of the late fourteenth-century masterpiece *Sir Gawain and the Green Knight* is apparently a blend of *aþel* (OE *æðele* 'noble') and *haleþ* (OE *hæleð* 'man'). Other early examples[63] are *flush* (*flash* plus *gush;* the *American College Dictionary* says "in some senses further blended with *blush*) [1548]; *luncheon* (*lump* plus *nuncheon* 'noon drink') [1580]; *twirl* (*twist* plus *whirl*) [1598]; *dumfound* (apparently *dumb* plus *confound*) [1653]; and *flurry* (*flutter* plus *hurry*) [1698]. *Lunch,* a clipping of *luncheon,* has itself been blended with *breakfast* to make *brunch.*

Lewis Carroll (Charles Lutwidge Dodgson[64]) made a great thing of such blends, which he called "portmanteau words," particularly in his "Jabberwocky" poem. Two of his creations, *chortle* (*chuckle* plus *snort*) and, to a lesser degree, *galumph* (*gallop* plus *triumph*) have become established in the language. His *snark,* a blend of *snake* and *shark,* though widely known, failed to find a place because there was no need for it.

Recent years have seen a mighty proliferation of conscious blendings. Perhaps the most successful of these—certainly the most well established—are *smog* (*smoke* plus *fog*) and *motel* (*motor* plus *hotel*).[65] *Urinalysis* (*urine* plus *analysis*), of American origin also, first appeared in 1889 and has since attained to scientific respectability.[66] *Cafetorium*

[63] The dates of earliest occurrence are those given in the *OED.*

[64] His endearing passion for "fooling around" with language is indicated by his pen name: *Carolus* is the Latin equivalent of *Charles,* and *Lutwidge* must have suggested to him German *Ludwig* (on phonological grounds, Latin *Ludovicus* seems less likely), the equivalent of English *Lewis. Charles Lutwidge* thus became (in reverse) *Lewis Carroll.*

[65] There are also, at least in Florida, *botels* for those who arrive in boats.

[66] That the English are perfectly well able to do this sort of thing is indicated by *breathalyser* and *bloodalyser* (*breath, blood* plus *analyser*) 'apparatus used by British police for testing whether one has been drinking' (*Spectator,* January 22, 1961, p. 920).

(*cafeteria* plus *auditorium*) has made a great deal of headway in the American public school systems, and would seem to be a useful term for a large room planned for the double purpose indicated by it. *Beatnik* is a blend of *beat* in its recent sense 'eccentric' and, according to the *Webster's Third New International Dictionary,* Yiddish *nudnik* 'boring person,' though it seems likely on chronological grounds that *sputnik,* with the same suffix, has had a great deal to do with the widespread dissemination of the term, if indeed it did not figure in its coining. Boy Scouts frequently have *camporees* (*camp* plus *jamboree*[67]). A number of eating establishments now feature *broasted* (*broiled* plus *roasted*) chicken.

The news magazine *Time* has originated a number of blends, of varying degrees of ingenuity. Some of these are widely known, but they cannot be said to be really current in speech. *Cinemactor* (*cinema* plus *actor*) is probably the one which comes first to mind, but it is not likely ever to be taken very seriously. Walter Winchell in his column made great use of the blend as a stylistic device. His most successful creation, and the one most worthy to survive, though it doubtless will not do so, is *to infanticipate* 'to be expecting a baby' (*infant* plus *anticipate*); but even this, though amusing and very widely known, cannot really be said to be in current use.

The number of examples which have been cited might be multiplied without any citations of trade names, in the making of which blending has in recent times played an important part; but there is no point in doing so. Blends are easy to create, which is doubtless why there are so very many of them, and they are at the moment very popular. It would have been very surprising if John Fitzgerald Kennedy's program of medical care for the elderly had not become *Medicare.*

ACRONYMS

The use of the initial letters of the . words in phrases (*O.K., Y.M.C.A.*), sometimes of syllables (*TB, TV, PJs* 'pajamas'), as if these were words has long been common. Usually the motive for this is either brevity or catchiness, though sometimes euphemism may be involved, as with *B.O., B.M.,* and *VD*—all listed in the *Webster's Third New International.* Perhaps *TB* also was euphemistic in the beginning, when the disease was a much direr threat to life than it now is

---

[67] According to the *American College Dictionary*, this word is itself "apparently" a blend of *jabber* and French *soirée,* with the -*m*- from *jam.*

and its very name was uttered in hushed tones. A few forms so abbreviated have undergone expansion for some special reason, such as aural clarity; for instance A.M. and P.M., which are to the British railway signalman *ack emma* and *pip emma*. These expansions were also used in the British military services as early as World War I.

The "New Deal" of Franklin Delano Roosevelt, the first of our chief executives to be known by his initials only, dealt out among its other blessings a good many alphabetically named government agencies: *NRA, HOLC, OPA, WPA,* and others, the whole business being summarized in a famous *bon mot* by Al Smith—"alphabet soup." Such lavish use of initials in circles so exalted was bound to confer dignity and status upon what had hitherto been regarded as a more or less informal sort of abbreviation like, to cite a few earlier examples, *P.D.Q., I.W.W., G.O.P.,* and *O.K.*

It is inevitable that it should have dawned upon some waggish genius that the initial letters of words in certain combinations frequently spelled other words, or at least made pronounceable sequences of letters: thus, though C.O.D. has never actually been so treated, it might have been pronounced like *cod.* This is in fact what children sometimes do with the initial letters of their names if they are lucky enough to have a vowel in the middle. There had to be a learned word to designate such a process, and *acronym* was coined from Greek *akros* 'tip' and *onyma* 'name,' by analogy with *homonym.* The British seem to have beaten us to the discovery of the joys of making acronyms, even though the impressively learned word to designate what is essentially a letters game was probably born in America. In any case, as early as World War I days the *D*efence [*sic,* in British spelling] of the *R*ealm *A*ct had come to be called *Dora* and a member of the *W*omen's *R*oyal *N*aval Service had come to be called (with the insertion of a vowel) a *Wren.* *Wren* furnished the pattern in World War II for *Wac* (*W*omen's *A*rmy *C*orps) and a number of others—our happiest being *Spar* 'girl Coast Guard,' from the motto of the U.S. Coast Guard, *Semper Para*tus. The euphemistic *-fu* words—the most widely known are *snafu* and *tarfu*—are also among the acronymic progeny of World War II. The process has in some instances been reversed, for example *Wave,* which resembles a genuine acronym, but which one would suspect preceded the phony-sounding supposed source, *W*omen *A*ccepted for *V*olunteer *E*mergency Service.

The business of shooting people through space, into orbit, and ultimately to the moon and other planets has been organized by

NASA, pronounced ['næsə] or ['nɑsə], from *N*ational *A*eronautics and *S*pace *A*dministration. It may well be that in time acronyms will be as common as coinage from Greek roots in the naming of scientific developments. The best known scientific acronym is *radar*, from *ra*dio *de*tecting *a*nd *r*anging, but there are a good many others less widely current, like the more recent *laser* (*l*ight *a*mplification by *s*timulated *e*mission of *r*adiation), a General Electric development described as a "pencil-thin beam of light" with "the potential to transmit the contents of a multi-volume encyclopedia in the wink of an eye."

The use of acronyms for trade names is well understood and has been established for a long time. Louise Pound said of them in 1913—she did not of course use the word *acronym* to designate them, for the very good reason that it had not yet been coined—that "there are probably many terms so built; but they are not always easy to recognize, especially by those unfamiliar with the inventor's or the manufacturer's name, or with the story of the naming," and cites *Reo* (automobile, made by the *R. E. O*lds Company), *Sebco* (extension drill, made by the *S*tar *E*xpansion and *B*olt *Co*mpany), and *Pebeco* (tooth powder, made by *P. Be*iersdorf and *Co*mpany, Hamburg, Germany).[68]

FOLK ETYMOLOGY

Folk etymology—the naïve misunderstanding of a more or less esoteric word which renders it into something more familiar and hence seems to furnish it with a new etymology, false as it may be—has been a minor source of new words. Spanish *cucaracha* 'wood louse' has thus been modified to *cockroach*, though the justly unpopular creature so named is neither a cock nor a roach in the earlier sense of the word (that is, a freshwater fish). Notions of verbal delicacy have largely done away with what looks like the first element of an English compound (but which, as we have just seen, really isn't anything of the sort), with the consequence that *roach* has come to mean what *cucaracha* originally meant.

A very neat example of how the folk-etymological process works is furnished by the experience of a German teacher of ballet who attended classes in modern dance at an American university in order to observe American teaching techniques. During one of these classes, she heard a student describe a certain ballet jump which he referred to as a "soda box." Genuinely mystified, she inquired about the term.

---

[68] "Word-Coinage and Modern Trade-Names," *Dialect Notes*, IV, 38.

The student who had used it and other members of the class averred that it was precisely what they always said and that it was spelled as they pronounced it—*soda box*. What they had of course misheard from their instructor was the practically universal ballet term *saut de basque* 'Basque leap.' One cannot but wonder how widespread the folk-etymologized term is in American schools of the dance.[69]

All of us sometimes hear a new word imperfectly, and frequently when among friends we ask, "How do you spell it?"—as if such knowledge were necessarily a sure clue to either its standard pronunciation or its meaning. But often we think that we have understood and go on thinking so, perhaps for years, like the woman who told me with considerable amusement at her own naïveté that it was only after her marriage that she realized that the name of a certain piece of furniture which she thought of as a *Chester drawers* was really a *chest of drawers*. Sometimes our misunderstanding is aided by sheer and amazing coincidence. As a child too young to read, I misheard *artificial snow* as *Archie Fisher snow,* a plausible enough boner for one who lived in a town in which a prominent merchant was named Archie Fisher. In any case, Mr. Fisher displayed the stuff in his window, and for all an innocent child knew he might even have invented it.

When this sort of misunderstanding of a word becomes widespread, we have acquired a new item in the English lexicon—one which usually completely displaces the old one and frequently seems far more appropriate than the displaced word. Thus *isinglass*, which, though not really glass, is at least glasslike in that one can see through it after a fashion, makes far more sense to English-speaking people than obsolete Dutch *hysenblas* 'sturgeon bladder.'[70] Similarly, *crayfish* seems more fitting than would the normal modern phonetic development of its source, Middle English *crevice,* taken from Old French,[71] which language in turn took it from Old High German *krebiz* 'crab' (Modern *Krebs*). And *taffrail*, since it actually came to designate a rail around the stern of a ship, made better sense to seafaring men than Dutch *tafereel* 'picture' (in reference to the carvings once decorating the stern).

---

[69] For this example, which is fresh as far as I know, I am indebted to my colleague, Ernest H. Cox, who got it from the American husband of the baffled *Ballettmeisterin*.

[70] The Dutch now say *vislijm*, that is, 'fish-lime (glue).'

[71] The Modern French form is *écrevisse*.

Other examples of folk etymology follow, many of them well known and often cited in other works:[72]

ACORN: Middle English *akern*, Old English *æcern* 'oak or beech mast'—nothing to do with *corn*;

BELFRY: Middle English *berfrey* 'tower'—nothing to do with *bell*;

BRIDEGROOM: Middle English *bridegome*, Old English *brȳd* 'bride' plus *guma* 'man'—nothing to do with *groom*;

CARRYALL: French *cariole*—nothing to do with *carry* or *all*;

COLD SLAW: Dutch *koolsla*, compound of *kool* 'cabbage' plus *sla* 'salad'—nothing to do with *cold*;

CONTREDANSE, CONTRADANCE: French mistranslation of English *country dance*, reborrowed by English—nothing to do with French *contre* 'counter';

CURTAIL: older *curtal*, from French *courtault* 'shortened'—nothing to do with *tail*;

CUTLASS: French *coutelas*, ultimately Latin *cultellus* 'little knife'—nothing to do with either *cut* or *lass*;

CUTLET: French *côtelette* 'little rib,' ultimately Latin *costa* 'rib'—nothing to do with *cut*;

FEMALE: Old French *femelle* 'little woman'—nothing to do with *male*;

GREYHOUND: Scandinavian *grey* 'dog, bitch' plus *hound*—nothing to do with *grey* 'color';

HANGNAIL: earlier *angnail*, from Old English *ange* 'painful' plus *nægl* 'nail'—nothing to do with *hanging*;

HELPMATE: *help* plus *meet* 'fitting,' misunderstood as a compound in two occurrences in Genesis ii as "an help meet for him," subsequently influenced by *mate*, with which it has nothing to do;

HICCOUGH: variant spelling of imitative *hiccup* showing influence of *cough*;

HUMBLE PIE: pie made of *umbles* 'inferior parts of deer,' formerly fed to menials;

JERUSALEM ARTICHOKE: from Italian *girasole* 'sunflower'—nothing to do with Jerusalem;

MANDRAKE: from the herb *mandragora*—nothing to do with *man* or *drake*;

---

[72] Particularly George H. McKnight, *English Words and Their Background* (New York, 1923), Chapter 13, and James Bradstreet Greenough and George Lyman Kittredge, *Words and Their Ways in English Speech* (New York, 1901), Chapter 23.

-MOST (as in *foremost, utmost,* and so forth): Old English *-mest,* for which see p. 121;

MUSKRAT: Algonquian *musquash*—nothing to do with either *musk* or *rat*;

PENTHOUSE: Middle English *pentis,* aphetic form of Old French *apentis,* connected with *pend* 'hang'—nothing to do with either *pent* 'confined' or *house*;

PICKAX: Middle English *picois,* from Old French—nothing to do with *ax*;

REINDEER: Scandinavian *hreinn,* the name of the animal, plus *deer* 'animal'—nothing to do with *rein*;

SALTCELLAR: Middle English *saltsaler,* the second element from Old French *saliere* 'pertaining to salt,' ultimately Latin *salārium,* whose specific meaning 'money paid to soldiers for purchase of salt' accounts for *salary*—nothing to do with *cellar* 'basement';

SHAMEFACED: earlier *shamefast,* Old English *sceamfæst,* that is, 'bound by shame';

SIRLOIN: French *sur* 'above' plus *loin*—nothing to do with *sir*;

TITMOUSE: Middle English *titmose*—nothing to do with *mouse*;

TUBEROSE: Latin *tūberōsa* 'tuberous,' misinterpreted as *tube* plus *rose*;

WELSH RAREBIT: what solemn people have done with humorous *Welsh rabbit*;

WOODCHUCK: Algonquian *otchek*—nothing to do with either *wood* or *chucking*; and

WORMWOOD: Old English *wermōd*[73] 'absinthe'—nothing to do with *worm* or *wood.*

Note that all of the forms which have just been cited, with the possible exception of *cold slaw,* are standard, even though they are the results of what were once blunders. A classical example of folk etymology, *sparrow grass* (from *asparagus*) is no longer widely current, but was once apparently standard usage, judging by its occurrence in the writings of older periods. The last citation of the *OED* (from 1865) is interesting: "I have heard the word sparrowgrass from the lips of a real Lady—but then she was in her seventies." The word was country usage in western Maryland, and doubtless elsewhere, as recently as the 1930's; it may still be. Hucksters frequently shortened it to *grass.*

---

[73] The name of what is, after the olive, the most expendable ingredient of the martini cocktail is a French borrowing, as *vermout(h),* of the German form of this word, *Wermut.*

Chaise lounge for *chaise longue* 'long chair' is not yet standard in that it is not used by the really cultivated. Judging by the fact that it is listed as a variant in *Webster's Third*, it seems to be on the way to social respectability. A dealer informs me that the prevailing pronunciation, both of those who buy and of those who sell, is either [šɛz laʊnǰ] or [čes laʊnǰ], the first of these in some circles being considered somewhat elite, not to say snobbish, in that it indicates that the user has "had" French. In any case, as far as speakers of English are concerned, the boner is remarkably apt, as indeed are many of the folk-etymologized forms which have been cited. And there can be little doubt that the aptness of the blunder has much to do with its ultimate acceptance.

COMMON WORDS FROM PROPER NAMES

A large number of words have come to us from proper names—enough to have made up a dictionary of 476 pages with an average of between four and five entries to the page, with 165 additional pages of "border-liners and potential candidates."[74] From names of persons, to begin with, the three best-known examples are probably *lynch* (by way of *Lynch's law*, from the Virginian Captain William Lynch [1742–1820], who led a campaign of "corporeal punishment" against those "unlawful and abandoned wretches" who were harassing the good people of Pittsylvania County, such as "to us shall seem adequate to the crime committed or the damage sustained"),[75] *boycott* (from another captain, Charles Cunningham Boycott [1832–97], who, because as a land agent he refused to accept rents at figures fixed by the tenants, was the best-known victim of the policy of ostracization of the Irish Land League agitators), and *sandwich* (from the fourth Earl of Sandwich [1718–92], said to have spent twenty-four hours at the gaming table with no other refreshment than slices of meat between slices of bread). The following words are also the unchanged names of actual people: *ampere, bloomer,*[76] *bowie* (knife), *brougham,*

---

[74] Eric Partridge, *Name into Word* (New York, 1950).

[75] From the compact drawn up by Captain Lynch and his neighbors, cited by Mathews, *Dictionary of Americanisms*, s.v. *lynch law*.

[76] Usually in the plural, from Mrs. Amelia Jenks Bloomer (1818–94), who publicized the most unbecoming female garb ever known to man. One could devise no more appropriate name for voluminous drawers for women than the surname of the lady's unfortunate husband, though since he had nothing to do with their design or with advocating their adoption it would be more just to call them *jenkses*. But the innocent must suffer with the guilty.

burke,[77] *cardigan, chesterfield* (overcoat or sofa), *davenport, derby, derrick,*[78] *derringer, gage* (plum),[79] *graham* (flour), *guy, hansom, jaeger* (underclothes), *lavaliere, macintosh,*[80] *maudlin,*[81] *maverick, ohm, pinchbeck* (alloy or sham jewelry), *pompadour, pullman, shrapnel, solon* (legislator), *timothy* (grass), *titian* (color), *valentine, vandyke* (beard or collar), *watt, zeppelin.* Comparatively slight spelling modifications occur in *dunce* (from John Duns[82] Scotus [d. *ca.* 1308], who was in reality anything but a dunce—to his admirers he was *Doctor Subtilis*) and *praline* (from Maréchal Duplessis-Praslin [d. 1675]). *Tawdry* is a clipped form of *Saint Audrey,* and first referred to the lace bought at St. Audrey's Fair in Ely. *Epicure* is an anglicized form of *Epicurus.*

Kaiser and *czar* are from *Caesar,* and *faro,* the name of a card game, is simply a spelling for *Pharaoh,* though what the connection is would be difficult to say. *Volt* is a clipped form of the surname of Count Alessandro Volta (d. 1827), and *farad* is derived likewise from the name of Michael Faraday (d. 1867). The name of an early American politician, Elbridge Gerry, is blended with *salamander* in the coinage *gerrymander. Slumber Jay,* the name of an electric logging device used in oil fields, is the result of folk etymologizing; it is from the name of the German inventor, Schlumberger, whose name acquired a French pronunciation when his invention was sold to a Frenchman.[83] The following are derivatives of personal names: *begonia, bougainvillaea, bowdlerize, camellia, chauvinism, comstockery, dahlia, jeremiad,*

[77] Meaning 'to hush up, stifle' and now rather rare in American English, though listed in all American dictionaries. The word is from William Burke, a notorious murderer (hanged, 1829) who, doubtless thinking to advance the study of anatomy and line his own pockets at the same time, smothered besotted derelicts lured from the streets and the public houses and sold their bodies to the medical school of the University of Edinburgh.

[78] The name of a famous hangman who operated at Tyburn in the early seventeenth century.

[79] Usually preceded by *green-,* from Sir William Gage, who introduced the fruit into England.

[80] Mostly British, frequently clipped to *mac.*

[81] Long an English spelling for Old French *Madelaine,* ultimately from Latin *Magdalen,* that is, Mary Magdalene, who was frequently represented as lachrymose by painters.

[82] Like many personal names, this is from a place name—Duns, Scotland, the birthplace of John, whose full style means 'John of Duns the Scotsman.'

[83] Boone, *Petroleum Dictionary.*

lewisite, lobelia, masochism, mercerize, mesmerism, nicotine, onanism, pasteurize, platonic, poinsettia, sadism, spoonerism, wistaria, zinnia. *Bobby* 'British policeman' is from the pet form of the name of Sir Robert Peel, who made certain reforms in the London police system. It has almost driven out the synonymous *peeler. Pantaloon,* in the plural the old-fashioned name (see p. 282) for what used to be the most distinctive masculine garment, is only a slight modification of French *pantalon,* which in turn is from Italian *Pantalone,* the name of a silly senile Venetian of early Italian comedy who wore such close-fitting nether coverings. *Pantalone,* in Italian meaning 'Venetian' and then 'buffoon,' is from *San Pantaleone,* the name of the patron saint of Venetians. Derivatives of the names of two writers—*Machiavellian* and *Rabelaisian*—are of such wide application that capitalizing them hardly seems necessary, any more than *platonic.*

The names of the following persons in literature and mythology (if gods, goddesses, and muses may be considered persons) are used unchanged: *atlas, babbitt, calliope, galatea, gamp* (mostly British), *hector, hermaphrodite, mentor, mercury, nemesis, pander, psyche,*[84] *trilby* (mostly British), *volcano.*[85] *Benedick,* the name of Shakespeare's bachelor *par excellence,* has undergone only very slight modification in *benedict* 'unmarried man.' *Don Juan, Lothario, Lady Bountiful, Mrs. Grundy, man Friday,* and *Pollyanna* (which even has a derivative, *Pollyannaism*), though written with initial capitals, probably belong here also.

The following are derivatives of personal names from literature and mythology: *aphrodisiac, bacchanal, herculean, jovial, malapropism, morphine, odyssey, panic, quixotic,*[86] *saturnine, simony, stentorian, tantalize, terpsichorean, venereal, vulcanize.* Despite their capitals, *Gargantuan* and *Pickwickian* should doubtless be included here also.

Names may be used generically or because of some supposed appropriateness, like *billy* (in *billycock, hillbilly, silly billy,* and alone as the name of a policeman's club), *tom(my)* (in *tomcat, tomtit, tomboy, tommyrot, tomfool*), *john* 'toilet' (compare older *jakes*), *johnny* (in

[84] With a good many derivatives and compoundings, for example *psychology, psychiatric, psychosomatic, psychometric, psychotherapy, psychopathy.*

[85] The Italian form of *Vulcan,* Latin *Volcānus.*

[86] In view of the prevailing fashion for a pseudo-Spanish pronunciation of the don's name, one wonders how long it will be before this adjectival derivative of it will be pronounced [ki'hotɪk].

stagedoor johnny, johnny-on-the-spot), *jack* (in *jackass, cheapjack, steeplejack, lumberjack, jack-in-the-box, jack-of-all-trades,* and alone as the name of a small metal piece used in a children's game known as *jacks*), *rube* (from *Reuben*), *hick* (from *Richard*), and *toby* 'jug' (from *Tobias*).

Place names have also furnished a good many common words. The following, the last of which exists only in the mind, are unchanged in form: *arras, babel, bourbon, billingsgate, blarney, buncombe* (see p. 297), *champagne, cheddar, cheviot, china, cologne, grubstreet, guinea, homburg, japan, java* 'coffee,' *limerick,*[87] *lisle, mackinaw, madeira, madras, magnesia, meander, morocco, oxford* (shoe or basket-weave cotton shirting), *panama, sauterne, shanghai, shantung, suède* (French name of Sweden), *tabasco, turkey, tuxedo, ulster, utopia.*

The following are either derivatives of place names or place names which have different forms from those which are known to us today: *bayonet, bedlam, bock, brummagem, calico, canter, cashmere, copper, damascene, damask, damson, frankfurter, gamboge, gauze, hamburger, hock, italic, jeans* (pants), *laconic, lawn* (fabric), *limousine, mayonnaise, milliner, roman* (type), *romance, sardonic, sherry* (see p. 284), *sodomy, spaniel, spartan, stogy, stygian, wiener, worsted. Damascene, damask,* and *damson* all three come from *Damascus. Canter* is a clipping of *Canterbury* (*gallop*), the easy-going pace of pilgrims to the tomb of St. Thomas Becket in Canterbury, the most famous and certainly the "realest" of whom are a group of people who never lived at all save in the poetic imagination of Geoffrey Chaucer and everlastingly in the hearts and minds of those who know his *Canterbury Tales. Bock* and *hock* are likewise abbreviated forms, the first from *Eimbocker* in Prussia and the second from *hockamore,* which shows what the English did to *Hochheimer (Wein).*

VERNACULAR, SLANG, AND ARGOT

The specialized languages of games, trades, criminal activities, and the like have contributed a number of new words and phrases, or at least new uses of old ones, like *roughneck, roustabout, wildcatter, logrolling, crestfallen, to tilt at, to fence, fair play, to cross swords, to ante up, knockout, below the belt, mark* 'dupe,' *to bowl over, in the chips, on the lam, to take the rap,* and many others. The line between these

---

[87] A newer stanzaic form for humorous verse is called the *clerihew,* from the middle name of its originator, Edward Clerihew Bentley.

and slang would be difficult to draw. In any case, slang has been for a long time one of the most productive forms of language. Among its more recent contributions to general language are *to goof*, *hip* (formerly *hep*), *square* 'conventional,' and the reduplicated *booboo*; new compounds, like *soap opera* and *hillbilly*; different meanings, like *skirt* 'woman,' *pad* 'lodgings,' *eye* 'detective,' and *to take a powder* 'to run away.' There are a limited number of what are doubtless pure root creations, for example *snide, bazooka,* and the reduplicated *heeby-jeebies*.[88] A good many slang terms are merely clipped forms, like the aforementioned once slangy *mob*, which was reprehended, along with a number of other such abbreviations, by Jonathan Swift in a famous paper printed in the *Tatler* of September 28, 1710.[89] *Bunk* is an abbreviation of *Buncombe*, the name of a county in North Carolina, whose representative in Congress in the early 1800's once remarked in the course of a particularly dull and windy speech that

[88] There are many books dealing with slang. The seven-volume *Dictionary of Slang and Its Analogues* (London, 1890–1904) by John S. Farmer and William Ernest Henley—the "Invictus" poet—is practically a classical work. Partridge's *Dictionary of Slang and Unconventional English* is a valuable collection; so, for American slang, are *The American Thesaurus of Slang*, 2nd ed. (New York, 1953), by Lester V. Berrey and Melvin Van den Bark, and the *Dictionary of American Slang* (New York, 1960), edited by Harold Wentworth and Stuart Berg Flexner. Partridge has also written *Slang Today and Yesterday* (London, 1933). H. L. Mencken's *The American Language*, 4th ed. (New York, 1936) has an excellent discussion in Chapter 9, which is amplified in *Supplement II* (New York, 1948). References to earlier works will be found in some of these more recent ones. A very prolific American writer on argot is David W. Maurer. His *Whiz Mob: A Correlation of the Technical Argot of Pickpockets with Their Behavioral Pattern* was published by the American Dialect Society in 1955, and his *The Argot of the Racetrack* by the same Society in 1951. There are a good many word lists and articles on argot and specialized vernaculars in other publications of the American Dialect Society and in *American Speech*. Eric Partridge has a *Dictionary of the Underworld* (London, 1949), and there is a *Dictionary of American Underworld Lingo* (New York, 1950), edited by Hyman E. Goldin, Frank O'Leary, and Morris Lipsius, described in the Introduction to the work as "two long-term convicts and a prison chaplain," who were assisted by more than a score of "expert advisers whose qualifications were born of years of criminal activity and years of imprisonment alike."

[89] He did not call such terms *slang*, however; the word appeared first in print in 1756, according to the *OED*.

he was "only talking for Buncombe." *Kook* 'eccentric person' is a shortening of *cuckoo*, which with the same meaning or used as an adjective meaning 'crazy' is also slang.

LITERARY COINAGES

At what would seem to be another extreme, but is not necessarily so, literary men have also coined new terms, like Gelett Burgess' *blurb*, Will Irwin's *highbrow*, and H. L. Mencken's *Bible Belt* and the less viable *booboisie* and *ecdysiast*. Henry Bradley in his still valuable *The Making of English* (New York, 1924; first published 1904) points out that "it is a truth often overlooked, but not unimportant, that every addition to the resources of a language must in the first instance have been due to an act (though not necessarily to a voluntary or conscious act) of some one person," and devotes an entire chapter (pp. 215–40) entitled "Some Makers of English" to illustrating this truth. He cites among others *lovingkindness* (Coverdale), *peacemaker* (Tindale), *braggadocio* and *derring-do*[90] 'chivalry' (Spenser), *lonely, dwindle,* and *orb* 'globe' (Shakespeare), *pandemonium, irresponsible,* and *impassive* (Milton), and *raid, gruesome, uncanny,* and *glamour* (Scott).[91] To these Stuart Robertson and Frederic G. Cassidy add a good many more recent examples.[92] I. Willis Russell, as chairman of the New Words Committee of the American Dialect Society, has made extensive collections of new words. These have been published in the *Encyclopædia Britannica Yearbook* and in *American Speech*.

ONE PART OF SPEECH TO ANOTHER

A very prolific source of new words from old is the happy facility of Modern English, because of its paucity of inflection, for converting words from one grammatical function to another with no change in form. Thus, the name of practically every part of the body has been converted to use as a verb—one may *head* a committee, *shoulder* or *elbow* one's way through a crowd, *hand* in one's papers, *finger* one's

---

[90] This stemmed from Spenser's misunderstanding of Middle English *durryng (dorryng) don* 'daring to do,' as in Chaucer's *Troilus and Criseyde,* V.837: "In durrvng don that longeth to a knyght" ('In daring to do what appertains to a knight').

[91] Bradley makes it clear that the first *known* occurrences are in the works of the authors named; there may have been earlier ones.

[92] *The Development of Modern English,* 2nd ed. (New York, 1954), pp. 215–31.

tie, *thumb* a ride, *back* one's car, *leg* it along, *foot* a bill, *toe* a mark, and *tiptoe* through the tulips—without any modification of form such as would be necessary in other languages, for instance German, in which the suffix *-(e)n* is a necessary part of all infinitives. It would not have been possible to do this in Old English times either, when infinitives ended in *-(a)n* or *-ian*. But Modern English does it with the greatest ease; to cite a few nonanatomical examples, *to contact, to chair* (a meeting), *to telephone, to date, to park, to proposition,* and *to M.C.* (or *emcee*). Verbs may also be used as nouns. One may, for instance, take a *walk,* a *run,* a *drive,* a *spin,* a *cut,* a *stand,* a *break,* a *turn,* or a *look.* Nouns are just as freely used as adjectives, or practically so as attributives (*head bookkeeper, face card, cover girl, stone wall*), and adjectives and participles are used as nouns, for instance *commercial* 'sales spiel on a television or radio show,' *formals* 'evening clothes,' *clericals* 'clergyman's street costume,' *devotional* 'short prayer service subsidiary to some other activity,' *private* 'noncommissioned soldier,' *elder, painting,* and *earnings.*

Adjectives may also be converted into verbs, as with *better, round, tame,* and *rough.* In advertising "literature" we have been urged to "pleasure up" our smoking with a particular brand of cigarette, though some would doubtless have preferred a rival brand which "gentles the smoke and makes it mild." One wonders why it would not *mild* it as well as gentle it; it could perfectly well do so in English. Even adverbs and conjunctions are capable of conversion, as in "the *whys* and the *wherefores*" and "*but* me no *buts*" (in which *but* is first used as a verb, then as a pluralized noun). Transitive verbs may be made from older intransitive ones, as has happened fairly recently to *to shop* ("Shop Our Fabulous Sale Now in Progress"; "It's smart for all/To shop Duvall") and *to sleep* ("Her [a cruising yacht's] designer has claimed that she can sleep six"[93]).

VERB-ADVERB COMBINATIONS

There are a good many combinations of verbs and adverbs which are used primarily as verbs, for instance *slow down, check up, fill in* 'furnish with a background sketch,' *break down* 'analyze,' and *set up,* but which are easily convertible into nouns, though usually with shifted stress, as in *to check úp* contrasted with *a chéckup.* Some such

[93] Let this not be supposed an instance of peculiarly American linguistic depravity; the citation is from the London *Daily Telegraph and Morning Post* of August 13, 1956 (p. 3).

combinations are also used as adjectives, for instance *sit-down strike, sit-in demonstration,* and *drive-in theater.*

As with the verb-adverb combinations, change of form is sometimes involved when verbs, adjectives, and nouns shift functions, the functional shift being often indicated by a shift of stress: compare *upsét* (verb) and *úpset* (noun), *prodúce* (verb) and *próduce* (noun), *pérfect* (adjective) and *perféct* (verb).[94] Not all speakers make the functional stress distinction in *ally* and *address,* but many do.

In this chapter we have surveyed in some detail how English has used its own resources for enriching its vocabulary. Some of the newer forms cited will probably not be approved by all, though it should be noted that they differ from forms universally accepted only in being of more recent coinage or adaptation, not in the process by which they have come into being. In a subsequent chapter we shall examine another important process, borrowing, by which the English language has enriched itself—a process which has already been referred to many times.

[94] Jespersen, *Modern English Grammar,* I, 173–84, cites the varying stress according to grammatical function in *affix, absent, compact, conduct, content, insult, minute, object, perfume, progress, rebel, record, subject,* along with a good many others.

CHAPTER XI

Words and Meanings

IN CONSIDERING meaning, we cannot here be concerned with those larger philosophical aspects of language which have increasingly in recent years engaged the attention of scholars like Rudolf Carnap, Charles W. Morris, I. A. Richards, Ernst Cassirer, and Susanne K. Langer, nor with the "general semantics" of Alfred Korzybski, whose disciples with evangelical zeal unwittingly made *semantic* a vogue word meaning little more than 'verbal.' These approaches are certainly of great interest and value, but are not directly connected with such changes in meaning in the course of the development of the English language as we shall examine in this chapter.

DEVICES FOR SIGNALING MEANING

The educated man or woman is by long tradition expected to possess what is frequently referred to as "a good command of language." Actually, as has been pointed out in our introductory chapter, a child of five or so already has a "good command," in the sense that he uses without effort practically all the devices by which meaning is signaled vocally, sometimes with the aid of gestures. No normal child of even tenderer years would fail to understand, and to make an appropriate response to, such an utterance as "Is your mother busy?" or to distinguish it from the utterances "Your mother is busy" and "Your mother is busy?" It will be noted that the words in these utterances are identical in form and in meaning. What, then, are the linguistic devices by which the child distinguishes any one of these utterances from the others? Word order and intonation do the trick; in "Your mother is busy?" intonation alone (the rising tone beginning on the first syllable of *busy*) does it.

After we have mastered the use of such devices—we did so more or less unconsciously, of course, long before we could make any analysis of what we do or how we do it—about all that we acquire, except for a few more or less sophisticated "literary" constructions, are vocabulary items. Though we should as educated persons be able to analyze the linguistic devices by which we communicate with one another, we actually acquire these devices without formal instruction. But in the process we acquire only the most useful, everyday words—usually words which have been a part of the English language from the earliest times (*mother, moon, busy, ready, good, run, have, to, and*), along with some words of foreign origin which have been a part of it for a very long time (*giant, chase, catch*) or which for some other reason have been thoroughly naturalized—more or less homely words which continue for all our lives to provide our basic word hoard. But such equipment, common to all speakers of a language, does not comprise what is meant by "a good command of language."

WHY STUDY WORDS?

The fact is that, if we are going to be able to talk about anything very far beyond our day-to-day, bread-and-butter living, if we are going to associate in an easy manner with cultivated people, if we are going to read books which such people have found to be important and significant, then we must have at our command a great many words that the man in the street and the man with the hoe neither know nor use. This is not to imply that there is anything wrong in being a common man; his name is Legion, he is the salt of the earth and "a man for a' that." But it is assumed that most people, even though they may have no real intellectual aspirations, want to be—or at least to pass for—something more than, or at least different from, common men and women.

To begin the study of language with an examination of its word stock is, however, to put the cart before the horse, for words come later to us in our linguistic development than sentences—even the child's first meaningful utterances are sentences, though many of them may consist of only a single word each. But the fact remains that most people find the study of words and their meanings interesting and colorful. Witness in newspapers and magazines the number of "letters to the editor," usually sadly misinformed, which are devoted to the uses and misuses of words. These are frequently etymological in nature, like the old and oft recurring wheeze that sirloin is so called because King Henry VIII (or James I or Charles II) liked a loin of beef so well that he knighted one, saying "Arise, Sir Loin" at the conferring of the accolade.

WHY MEANING VARIES

The attribution of some sort of meaning to combinations of distinctive speech sounds and in a few instances to single sounds is a matter of social custom, and like other customs may vary in time, place, and situation: thus *tonic* may mean 'soft drink made with charged water' in parts of eastern New England, though elsewhere it usually means 'liquid medicinal preparation to invigorate the system' or in the phrase *gin and tonic*, 'quinine water'; in the usage of musicians the same word may also mean the first tone of a musical scale. It is also true that many words in frequent use, like *nice, God,* and *democracy,* have among speakers and writers of the same intellectual and social level meanings which are more or less subjective, and hence loose. All meanings of what is thought of as the same word have, however, certain elements in common—elements which may be said to operate within a certain field of meaning. If this were not true, there would be no communication.[1] But this is quite different from assuming the existence of "fixed," or "real," meanings.

Even though words do not have such inflexible meanings as we might prefer them to have, but only a field of meaning in which they operate and which may be extended in any direction or narrowed likewise, it is possible to be irritated at what we may consider a too-loose use of words. For instance, after relating that he had seen a well-dressed man take the arm of a blind and ragged beggar and escort him across a crowded thoroughfare, a rather sentimental man remarked, "That was true democracy." It was, of course, only ordinary human decency, as likely to occur in a monarchy as in a democracy, and by no means impossible under a totalitarian form of government like, say, that of Oliver Cromwell or Adolf Hitler. The semantic element of the word *democracy* which was in the speaker's mind was kindness to those less fortunate than oneself. He approved of such kindness, as indeed we all do; it was "good," and "democracy" was also "good." Hence, as soft-minded people are quite prone to do, he equated "democracy" with goodness.

We are defeating the purpose of accurate communication when we use words thus loosely. It is true that some words are by general consent used with a very loose meaning, and it is very likely that we could not get along without a certain number of such words—*nice,* for in-

[1] It is neither appropriate nor necessary here to go into the vexed philosophical question of what constitutes meaning—the "meaning" of *meaning*—which belongs in the realm of general semantics.

stance, as in "She's a nice girl" (meaning that she has been well brought up, is kind, gracious, and generally well-mannered, or, with the word stressed, merely that she is chaste), in contrast to "That's a nice state of affairs" (meaning that it is a perfectly awful state of affairs). There is certainly nothing wrong with expressing pleasure and appreciation to a hostess by a heartfelt "I've had a very nice time," or even "I've had an awfully nice time." To seek for a more "accurate" word, one of more limited meaning, would be self-conscious and affected.

A large number of educated speakers and writers, for whatever reason, refuse to use *disinterested* in the sense 'uninterested,' a sense which it previously had and lost for a while, and reserve the word for the meaning 'impartial, unprejudiced.' The meaning 'uninterested' has gained ground at a terrific rate, and it is possible that before long it will completely drive out the other one. There will have been no great loss to language *qua* communication. We shall merely have lost a synonym for *impartial* and acquired on all levels another way of saying 'uninterested.' Educated readers of the future will be no more annoyed by the change than they are by similar changes that have given some of the words used in, say, the plays of Shakespeare and in the King James Bible different meanings for us from those which they had in early Modern English. Uneducated readers will be baffled and misled, to be sure; but simple people today frequently misinterpret the King James Bible (the only literature in early Modern English which they are likely ever to read) with complete satisfaction to themselves. It is hardly feasible to expect language to stand still for the sake of ignorant people, who as a matter of fact manage quite well enough, as do the rest of us so long as our less informed fellows are restrained from forcibly imposing their interpretations of what they read, whether sacred or profane, upon us. How long they can be so restrained in a democracy, where numbers are all-important, is a very important question, but it is outside the scope of the present discussion.

ETYMOLOGY AND MEANING

There is a widespread belief, held even by some quite learned people, that the way to find out what a word means is to find out what it previously meant—or, preferably, if it were possible to do so, what it originally meant—a notion similar to the Greek belief in the etymon. Such is the frequent method of dealing with borrowed words, the mistaken idea being that the meaning of the word in current English and the meaning of the non-English word from which the English word is derived must be, or at any rate ought to be, one and the same. As a matter of fact, such an appeal to etymology to determine present meaning is as unreliable as would be an appeal to spelling to determine modern pronunciation. Change of meaning—semantic change, as it is called—may, and frequently does, alter the so-called etymological sense (that is to say, the earliest sense we can *discover*, which is not necessarily the very earliest sense), which may have become altogether obsolete. The study of etymologies is of course richly rewarding. It may, for instance, throw a great deal of light on present meanings, and it frequently tells us something of the workings of the human mind in dealing with the phenomenon of meaning, but it is of very limited help in determining for us what a word "actually" means.

Certain popular writers, overeager to display their learning, have asserted that words are misused when they depart from their etymological meanings. Thus Ambrose Bierce once declared that *dilapidated*, because of its ultimate derivation from Latin *lapis* 'stone,' could appropriately be used only of a stone structure.[2] Such a notion if true would commit us to the parallel assertion that only what actually had roots could properly be eradicated, since *eradicate* is ultimately derived from Latin *rādix* 'root,' that *calculation* be restricted to counting pebbles (Lat. *calx* 'stone'), that *sinister* be applied only to leftists, and *dexterous* to rightists. By the same token we should have to insist that we could *admire* only what we could 'wonder at,' inasmuch as the English word comes from Latin *ad* 'at' plus *mīrāri* 'to wonder,'[3] or that *giddy* persons must be divinely inspired, inasmuch as *gid* is a derivative of *god*.[4] Or that only men may be virtuous, because *virtue* is derived from Latin *virtus* 'manliness,' itself a derivative of *vir* 'man.' Now, alas for the wicked times in which we live, *virtue* is applied exclusively to women. *Virile,* also a derivative of *vir*, has retained all of its earlier meaning, and has even added to it.

From these few examples, it must be obvious that we cannot ascribe anything like "fixed" meanings to words. What we actually encounter

[2] In his *Write It Right* (New York, 1928), cited in Stuart Robertson, *The Development of Modern English,* 2nd ed., rev. Frederic G. Cassidy (New York, 1954), p. 234.

[3] Compare Hamlet's use of *admiration* in the sense 'wonderment, amazement' in "Season your admiration for a while/With an attent eare" (I.ii. 192–93).

[4] Compare *dizzy*, which may in very early times have had the same meaning. See Henry Bradley, *The Making of English* (New York, 1904), pp. 198–200. *Enthusiastic,* from the Greek, also had this meaning.

much of the time are meanings that are variable, and that may have wandered from what their etymologies suggest. To suppose that invariable meanings exist, quite apart from context, is to be guilty of a type of naïveté which may vitiate all our thinking.

HOW MEANING CHANGES

Change of meaning—a phenomenon common to all languages— while frequently unpredictable, is not wholly chaotic. Rather, it follows certain paths which we might do well to familiarize ourselves with. Much, probably most, of the illustrative matter which is to follow, like that which precedes, has come from many books read over a long period of years. Some of the examples are by now more or less stock ones, but they make their point better than less familiar ones would do, and hence are used without apology, but with gratitude to whoever first dug them out. It is likely that many of them will be found in James Bradstreet Greenough and George Lyman Kittredge's old, but still good, *Words and Their Ways in English Speech* (New York, 1901).

GENERALIZATION AND SPECIALIZATION

An obvious classification of meaning is that based on scope. This is to say, meaning may be generalized (extended, widened) or it may be specialized (restricted, narrowed). When we increase the scope of a word, we reduce the elements of its contents. For instance, *tail* (from OE *tægl*) in earlier times seems to have meant 'hairy caudal appendage, as of a horse.' When we eliminated the hairiness (or the horsiness) from the meaning, we increased its scope, so that in modern English the word means simply 'caudal appendage.' The same thing has happened to Danish *hale*, earlier 'tail of a cow.' In course of time the cow was eliminated, and in present-day Danish the word means simply 'tail,' having undergone a semantic generalization precisely like that of the English word cited; the closely related Icelandic *hali* still keeps the cow in the picture. Similarly, a *mill* was earlier a place for making things by the process of grinding, that is, for making meal. The words *meal* and *mill* are themselves related, as one might guess from their similarity. A mill is now simply a place for making things: the grinding has been eliminated, so that we may speak of a woolen mill, a steel mill, or even a gin mill. The word *corn* earlier meant 'grain' and is in fact related to the word *grain*. It is still used in this general sense in England, as in the "Corn Laws," but specifically it may mean either oats (for animals) or wheat (for human beings). In

American usage *corn* denotes maize, which is of course not at all what Keats meant in his "Ode to a Nightingale" when he described Ruth as standing "in tears amid the alien corn." The building in which corn, regardless of its meaning, is stored is called a barn. *Barn* earlier denoted a storehouse for barley; the word is in fact a compound of two Old English words, *bere* 'barley' and *ærn* 'house.' By elimination of a part of its earlier content, the scope of this word has been extended to mean a storehouse for any kind of grain. American English has still further generalized by eliminating the grain, so that *barn* may mean also a place for housing livestock.

The opposite of generalization is specialization, a process in which, by adding to the elements of meaning, the semantic content of a word is reduced. *Deer,* for instance, used to mean simply 'animal' (OE *dēor*) as its German cognate *Tier* still does. Shakespeare writes of "Mice, and Rats, and such small Deare" (*King Lear* III.iv.144). By adding something particular (the family *Cervidae*) to the content, the scope of the word has been reduced, and it has come to mean a specific kind of animal. Similarly *hound* used to mean 'dog,' as does its German cognate *Hund.* To this earlier meaning we have in the course of time added the idea of hunting, and thereby restricted the scope of the word, which to us means a special sort of dog, a hunting dog. To the earlier content of *liquor* 'fluid' (compare *liquid*) we have added 'alcoholic.' But generalization, the opposite tendency, has occurred in the case of the word *rum*, the name of a specific alcoholic drink, which in the usage of those who disapprove of all alcoholic beverages long ago came to mean strong drink in general, even though other liquors are much more copiously imbibed today. The word has even been personified in *Demon Rum.*

Meat once meant simply 'food,' a meaning which it retains in *sweetmeat* and throughout the King James Bible ("meat for the belly," "meat and drink"), though it acquired the meaning 'flesh' much earlier and had for a while both the general and the specialized meaning. *Starve* (OE *steorfan*) used to mean simply 'to die,' as its German cognate *sterben* still does.[5] Chaucer writes, for instance, "But as hire man I wol ay lyve and sterve" (*Troilus and Criseyde* I.427). A specific way of dying had to be expressed by a following phrase, for example "of hunger, for cold." The *OED* cites "starving with the cold," presumably dialectal, as late as 1867. The word came somehow to be primarily associated with death by hunger, and for a while there

---

[5] An even earlier meaning may have been 'to grow stiff.'

existed a compound verb *hunger-starve*. Usually nowadays we put the stress altogether on the added idea of hunger and lose the older meaning altogether. Although the usual meaning of *to starve* now is 'to die of hunger,' we also use the phrase "starve to death," which in earlier times would have been tautological. An additional, toned-down meaning grows out of hyperbole, so that "I'm starving" may mean only 'I'm very hungry.' The word is of course used figuratively, as in "starving for love," which, as we have seen, once meant 'dying for love.' This word furnishes a striking example of specialization and proliferation of meaning.

PEJORATION AND AMELIORATION

Change in meaning is frequently due to ethical, or moral, considerations. A word may, as it were, go downhill, or it may rise in the world; there is no way of predicting what its career may be. *Politician* has had a downhill development in American English; in British English it is still not entirely without honor. *Knave* (OE *cnafa*), which used to mean simply 'boy'—it is cognate with German *Knabe*, which retains the earlier meaning—is another example of pejorative (from Lat. *pējor* 'worse') development; it came to mean successively 'serving boy'[6] (specialization), like that well-known knave of hearts[7] who was given to stealing tarts, and ultimately 'bad human being,' so that we may now speak of an old knave, or conceivably even of a knavish woman. On its journey downhill this word has thus undergone both specialization and generalization. *Boor,* once meaning 'peasant,'[8] has had a similar pejorative development, as has *lewd,* earlier 'lay, as opposed to clerical,' and thereafter 'ignorant,' 'base,' and finally 'obscene,' which is the only meaning to survive.[9] The same fate has befallen the Latin loanword *vulgar,* ultimately from *vulgus* 'the common people'; the earlier

---

[6] Cf. French *garçon* 'boy,' which in a similarly specialized use means 'waiter.'

[7] Actually a further specialization: the jacks in card games are called the knaves in upper-class British usage.

[8] Its cognate *Bauer* is the usual equivalent of *jack* or *knave* in German card-playing, whence English *bower* (as in *right bower* and *left bower*) in certain card games such as euchre and five hundred.

[9] The development of *nice*, going back to Latin *nescius* 'ignorant,' has been just the opposite. The Old French form used in English meant 'simple,' a meaning retained in Modern French *niais*. In the course of its career in English it has had the meanings 'foolishly particular' and then merely 'particular' (as in *a nice distinction*), among others.

meaning is retained in *Vulgar Latin*, the Latin which was spoken by the people up to the time of the early Middle Ages and was to develop into the various Romance languages. *Censure* earlier meant 'opinion.' In the course of time it has come to mean 'bad opinion'; *criticism* is well on its way to the same pejorative goal, ordinarily meaning nowadays 'adverse judgment.' The verbs *to censure* and *to criticize* have undergone a similar development. *Deserts* (as in *just deserts*) likewise started out indifferently to mean simply what one deserved, whether good or bad, but has come to mean 'punishment.' A few more examples of this tendency must suffice. *Silly* (OE *sǣlig*), earlier 'timely,' came to mean 'happy, blessed,' and subsequently 'innocent, simple'; then the simplicity, a desirable quality under most circumstances, was misunderstood (note the present ambiguity of *a simple man*), and the word took on its present meaning. Its German cognate *selig* progressed only to the second stage, though the word may be used facetiously to mean 'tipsy.'

Like *censure* and *criticize*, *praise* started out indifferently; it is simply *appraise* 'put a value on' with loss of its initial unstressed syllable (aphesis). But *praise* has come to mean 'value highly.' Here what has been added has ameliorated, or elevated, the semantic content of the word. Amelioration, the opposite of pejoration, is well illustrated by *knight*, which used to mean 'servant,' as its German relative *Knecht* still does.[10] This particular word has obviously moved far from its earlier meaning, denoting as it usually now does a very special and exalted man who has been signally honored by his sovereign and who is entitled to prefix *Sir* to his name. *Earl* (OE *eorl*) once meant simply 'man,' though in ancient Germanic times it was specially applied to a warrior, who was almost invariably a man of good birth, in contrast to a *ceorl* (*churl*), or ordinary freeman. When under the Norman kings French titles were adopted in England, *earl* failed to be displaced, but remained as the equivalent of the Continental *count*.

CHANGES DUE TO SOCIAL CLASS

The meaning of a word may vary even with the group in which it is used. For all speakers *smart* has the meaning 'intelligent,' but there

---

[10] It must not be supposed that, because German cognates have frequently been cited as still having meanings which have become archaic in English, German words are necessarily less susceptible to semantic change than English ones. With different choices of examples it is possible that a contrary impression might be given.

is a specialized class usage in which it means 'fashionable.' The meaning of *a smart woman* may thus vary with the social level of the speaker; it may, indeed, have to be inferred from the context. The earliest meaning of this word seems to have been 'sharp,' as in *a smart blow.* It is interesting to note that *sharp* is also used nowadays in the sense 'up-to-date, fashionable,' as in *a sharp dresser*, by certain groups of speakers who admire this particular type of "sharpness."

Similarly, a word's meaning may vary according to the circumstances under which it is used. *Hall* (OE *heall*), for instance, once meant a very large roofed place, like the splendid royal dwelling-place Heorot in which Beowulf fought Grendel. Such buildings were usually without smaller attached rooms, though Heorot had a "bower"[11] (*būr*), earlier a separate cottage, but in *Beowulf* a bedroom to which the king and queen retired. For retainers the hall served as meeting-room, feasting-room, and sleeping-room. Later *hall* came to mean the largest room in a great house, used for large gatherings such as receptions and feasts, though the use of the word for the entire structure survives in the names of a number of manor houses such as Little Wenham Hall and Speke Hall in England. There are a number of other meanings, all connoting size and some degree of splendor, and all a far cry from the modern American use of *hall* as a narrow passageway leading to rooms.[12] The meaning of *hall* must be determined by the context in which it occurs.

Akin to what we have been considering is modification of meaning as the result of a shift in point of view. *Crescent,* from the present participial form of Latin *cresco,* used to mean simply 'growing, increasing,' as in Pompey's "My powers are Cressent, and my Auguring hope/Sayes it will come to'th'full" (*Antony and Cleopatra* II.i.10–11). The new, or growing, moon was thus called the crescent moon. There has been, however, a shift in the dominant element of meaning, the emphasis coming to be put entirely on shape, specifically on a particular shape of the moon, rather than upon growth. *Crescent* has thus come to mean 'new-moon-shaped.' Similarly, in *veteran* (Lat. *veterānus*, a derivative of *vetus* 'old'), the emphasis has shifted from age to military service, though not necessarily long service: a veteran need not have grown old in service, and we may in fact speak of a

[11] Note that this word survives only in the sense 'arbor, enclosure formed by vegetation.'

[12] In British English the reduced meaning of *hall* refers to the vestibule or entrance passage immediately inside the front door of a small house.

young veteran. The fact that etymologically the phrase is self-contra-
dictory is of no significance as far as present usage is concerned. The
word is of course extended to other areas, for instance *veteran politician*; in its extended meanings it continues to connote long experience
and usually mature years as well.

THE VOGUE FOR WORDS
OF LEARNED ORIGIN

When learned words acquire popular currency, they almost inevitably acquire at the same time new, less exact, meanings, or at least
new shades of meaning. *Philosophy,* for instance, earlier 'love of
wisdom,' has now a popular sense 'practical opinion or body of opinions,' as in "the philosophy of salesmanship," "the philosophy of Will
Rogers," and "homespun philosophy." An error in translation from
a foreign language may result in a useful new meaning, for example
psychological moment, now 'most opportune time,' rather than 'psychological momentum,' which is the proper translation of German
psychologisches Moment, the ultimate source of the phrase. The popular misunderstanding of *inferiority complex,* first used to designate
an unconscious sense of inferiority manifesting itself in assertive behavior, has given us a synonym for *diffidence, shyness.* It is similar
with *guilt complex,* now used to denote nothing more psychopathic
than a feeling of guilt. The term *complex* as first used by psycho-
analysts more than half a century ago designated a type of aberration
resulting from the unconscious suppression of more or less related
attitudes. The word soon passed into voguish and subsequently into
general use to designate an obsession of any kind—a bee in the bonnet,
as it were. Among its progeny are *Oedipus complex, herd complex,*
and *sex complex.* The odds on its increasing fecundity would seem to
be rather high.

Other fashionable terms from psychoanalysis and psychology, with
which our times are so intensely preoccupied, are *subliminal,* which
has been widely used in reference to a very sneaky kind of advertising
technique; *behavior pattern,* meaning simply 'behavior'; *neurotic,*
with a wide range of meaning, including 'nervous, highstrung, artistic
by temperament, eccentric, or given to worrying'; *compulsive* 'habit-
ual,' as in *compulsive drinker* and *compulsive criminal*; and *schizo-
phrenia* 'practically any mental or emotional disorder.'

It is not surprising that the newer, popular meanings of what were
once more or less technical terms should generally show a considerable

extension of the earlier, technical meanings. Thus, *sadism* has come to mean simply 'cruelty' and *exhibitionism* merely 'showing off,' without any of the earlier connotations of sexual perversion, as in fact the word *psychology* itself may mean nothing more than 'mental processes' in a vague sort of way. An intense preoccupation in the mid-twentieth century with what is fashionably and doubtless humanely referred to as *mental illness*—a less enlightened age than ours called it *insanity*, and people afflicted with it were said to be *crazy*—must to a large extent be responsible for the use of such terms as have been cited. Also notable is the specialization of *sick* to refer to mental imbalance.

The greatest darling among the loosely used pseudoscientific vogue words of recent years is unquestionably *image* in the sense 'impression that others subconsciously have of someone.' A jaundiced observer of modern life might well suppose that what one actually is is not nearly so important as the image of oneself that one is able—to use another vogue word—to project. If the "image" is phony, what difference does it make? Everyone must get along; all must be allowed to have what the political orators refer to as human dignity, whatever the phrase means.

From an interview with two eminent psychiatrists syndicated by the Women's News Service,[13] one may learn that Governor Nelson Rockefeller's campaign headquarters before the political conventions of 1960 "had an 'image division,' set up to help project a favorable impression." One of the sages being interviewed declared, after consulting his badly clouded crystal ball: "There is no doubt that Mr. Kennedy appeals to women. He is the image of their little boy. . . . But they will not vote for him because they do not want a boy in the White House. Women want a father image as president—especially if they have weak husbands." "Many psychologists have said," according to the same gentleman, "that President Eisenhower's great personal hold on the public is due to the fact that he creates a strong father image" and moreover "has nurtured this image by never taking a single act not compatible with the subconscious concept of the ideal father." Images do not necessarily have to be those of persons, for a quarterly report of the Standard Oil Company of New Jersey states that "a current advertising campaign featuring the skillful, courteous service available at Esso stations is proving remarkably effective not only at building a

[13] Published in the Jacksonville *Florida Times-Union*, February 9, 1960, p. 10.

favorable dealer service image in the public mind but also at encour-
aging and stimulating dealers and service station attendants to measure up to this image."[14]

The awesome prestige of science and technology in our day is indicated by the diversion of terms previously associated with them to
humbler activities. A Reading *Clinic*, for instance, is a department of
a college or university for the "diagnosis" and correction of the reading
difficulties of students (why not "patients"?) who have not hitherto
learned to read—at least, not without moving their lips. A Retail
Hardware Salesmanship *Clinic* is, as far as the layman is able to determine, nothing more than a conference of hardware salesmen. An Auto
Clinic is a hospital for ailing cars. The exact nature of the "second
annual Evangelism Clinic at the Pine Grove [Florida] Baptist
Church,"[15] with the pleasantly alcoholically named Rev. Tom Collins
as "principal inspirational speaker," is difficult to determine. A
Writing *Laboratory* (or *Lab*) is a classroom with chairs, tables, and
dictionaries where students of what used to be unassumingly called
Freshman English write themes under the supervision of graduate
assistants, who in due time will probably wish to be regarded as "lab
assistants." Similarly, an *intern* may nowadays just as well be a beginning teacher in a public school as an M.D. serving in a hospital. By a
sort of inverted snobbery, *workshop*, sharing much the same range of
meaning as *laboratory*, has become quite voguish, for instance *Writers'
Workshop*.

There are a good many special types of transfer of meaning. *Long*
and *short*, for instance, are on occasion transferred from the spatial
concepts to which they ordinarily refer and made to refer to temporal
concepts, as in *a long time, a short while*; similarly with such nouns
as *length* and *space*. Metaphor is involved when we extend the word
foot 'lowest extremity of an animal' to all sorts of things, as in *foot of
a mountain, tree,* and so forth. The meaning of the same word is specialized or restricted when we add to its original content something
like 'approximate length of the lowest extremity of the male human
animal,' thereby making the word mean a unit of measure; we do
much the same thing to *hand* when we use it as a unit of measure for
the height of horses.

[14] Quoted in the *New Yorker*, December 3, 1960, p. 100.
[15] Gainesville, Florida, *Sun*, February 10, 1960, p. 14.

TRANSFER FROM ONE SENSE TO ANOTHER

Meaning may be transferred from one sense to another (synesthesia), as when we apply *clear*, with principal reference to sight, to hearing, as in *clear-sounding*. *Loud* is transferred from hearing to sight when we speak of *loud colors*. *Sweet*, with primary reference to taste, may be extended to hearing (*sweet music*), smell ("The rose smells sweet"), and to all senses at once (*a sweet girl*). *Sharp* may be transferred from feeling to taste, and so may *smooth*. *Warm* may shift its usual reference from feeling to sight, as in *warm colors*, and along with *cold* may refer in a general way to all senses, as in *a warm (cold) welcome*.

Abstract meanings may evolve from more concrete ones. Latin *cantus* 'the act of singing' came to acquire the more abstract meaning 'song.' The compound *understand*, as Leonard Bloomfield points out, must in prehistoric Old English times have meant 'to stand among, that is, close to'—*under* presumably having had the meaning 'among,' like its German and Latin cognates *unter* and *inter*.[16] But this literal, concrete meaning gave way to the more abstract meaning which the word has today. Bloomfield cites parallel shifts from concrete to abstract in German *verstehen* ('to stand before'), Greek *epistamai* ('I stand upon'), Latin *comprehendere* ('to take hold of'), and Italian *capire*, based on Latin *capere* 'to grasp,' among others.

The first person to use *grasp* in an abstract sense, as in "He has a good grasp of his subject," was coining an interesting metaphor. But the shift from concrete to abstract, or from physical to mental, has been so complete that we no longer think of this usage as metaphorical: *grasp* has come to be synonymous with *comprehension* in such a context as that cited, though the word has of course retained its physical reference. It was similar with *glad*, earlier 'smooth,' though this word has completely lost the earlier meaning (except in the proper name *Gladstone*, if surnames may be thought of nowadays as having meaning) and may refer only to a mental state. Likewise, meaning may shift from subjective to objective, as when *pitiful*, earlier 'full of pity, compassionate,' came to mean 'deserving of pity'; or the shift may be the other way round, as when *fear*, earlier 'danger,' something objective, came to mean 'terror,' a state of mind.

ASSOCIATION OF IDEAS

Interchange of meaning may be due simply to association of ideas. Latin *penna*, for instance, originally meant 'feather,' but came to be

16 *Language* (New York, 1933), pp. 425, 429–30.

used to indicate an instrument for writing, whether made of a feather or not, because of the association of the quill with writing. Our word *pen* is ultimately derived from the Latin word, though it comes to us by way of Old French. Similarly, *paper* is from *papyrus*, a kind of plant, and the two were once invariably associated in people's minds, though paper is nowadays made from rags, wood, straw, and other fibrous materials, and this association has been completely lost. Sensational magazines used to be printed on paper of inferior quality made from wood pulp; these were referred to by writers, somewhat derisively, as wood-pulp magazines, or simply as the *pulps*, in contrast to the *slicks*, those printed on paper of better quality. Such "literature" has come up in the world, at least as far as its physical production is concerned, and many magazines whose reading matter is considered by serious-minded people to be of low quality are actually printed on paper with no pulp content. These are nevertheless still referred to as "the pulps," and a writer who keeps the wolf from his door by supplying them with stories and articles is known as a "pulp writer." Thus, because of an earlier association the name of a physical product, wood pulp, has been applied to a type of periodical with reference to the literary quality of its contents. *Silver* has come to be used for eating utensils made of silver—an instance of specialization—and sometimes, by association, for the same articles even when not made of silver, so that we may even speak of ten-cent-store silver. The product derived from latex and earlier known as *caoutchouc* soon acquired a less difficult name, *rubber,* from association with one of its earliest uses, making erasures on paper by rubbing. *China* 'earthenware' originally designated porcelain of a type first manufactured in the country for which it is called, and the name of a native American bird, the *turkey*, derives from the fact that our ancestors somehow got the notion that it was of Turkish origin.[17] These names, like others which might be cited, arose out of associations which have long since been lost.

THE EFFECT OF LATIN MEANINGS

In olden times, when every educated person knew Latin, Latin semantics might affect English word meanings. *Thing*, for example, meant in Old English 'assembly, sometimes for legal purposes,' a meaning which it had in the other Germanic languages and has re-

[17] In French the same creature is called *dinde*, that is, "d'Inde." The French of course thought that America was India at the time when the name was conferred.

tained in Icelandic, as in *Alþing* 'all-assembly,' the name of the Icelandic parliament. English *thing* thus acquired from Latin *rēs*, which was used in much the same sense and was translated by *thing*, 'case at law' as one of its meanings. This meaning was subsequently lost, but because of the association, originally at one small point, the English word came to acquire every meaning that Latin *rēs* could have, which is to say, practically every other meaning of *thing* in present English. German *Ding* has had, quite independently, the same sense-history.

SOUND ASSOCIATIONS

Similarity or identity of sound may likewise influence meaning. *Fay,* from Old French *fee, fae* 'fairy' has influenced *fey,* from Old English *fǣge* 'fated, doomed to die' to such an extent that *fey* is practically always used nowadays in the sense 'spritely, fairy-like,' as in "It may sound an odd criticism to make of a creature who is first cousin to a fairy, but Miss [Leslie] Caron's Ondine was at the start of the evening rather too fey."[18] Here there is an association of meaning at one small point: fairies are mysterious; so is being fated to die, even though we all are so fated.

TABOO AND EUPHEMISM

It will by now be apparent that many factors must be taken into account in any discussion of change in meaning. It is not surprising that superstition should play a part, as when *sinister,* the Latin word for 'left' (the unlucky side) acquired its present baleful significance. The verb *die,* of Germanic origin, is not once recorded in Old English. This does not necessarily mean that it was not a part of the Old English word stock; however, in the writings that have come down to us, roundabout, toning-down expressions such as "go on a journey" are used instead, perhaps because of superstitions connected with the word itself—superstitions which survive into our own day, when people (at least those whom we know personally) "pass away," "go to sleep," or "go to their Great Reward." Louise Pound collected an imposing and—to the irreverent—amusing list of words and phrases used in referring to death in her article "American Euphemisms for Dying, Death, and Burial."[19] Miss Pound concludes that "one of mankind's

[18] London *Spectator,* January 20, 1961, p. 76.

[19] *American Speech,* XI (1936), 195–202. Reprinted in *Selected Writings of Louise Pound* (Lincoln, Nebr., 1949), pp. 139–47.

gravest problems is to avoid a straightforward mention of dying or burial."

Name-shifting is especially frequent, and probably always has been, when we must come face to face with the less happy facts of our existence, for life holds even for the most fortunate of men experiences which are inartistic, violent, and hence shocking to contemplate in the full light of day—for instance, the first and last facts of human existence, birth and death, despite the sentimentality with which we have surrounded them. And it is certainly true that the sting of the latter is somewhat alleviated—for the survivors, anyway—by calling it by some other name, such as "the Great Adventure," "the flight to glory," and "the final sleep," which are among the many terms cited by Miss Pound in the article just alluded to. *Mortician* is a much flossier word than *undertaker* (which is itself a euphemism with the earlier meanings 'helper,' 'contractor,' 'publisher,' and 'baptismal sponsor,' among others), but the *loved one* whom he prepares for public view and subsequent interment in a *casket* (earlier a jewel-box, as in *The Merchant of Venice*) is just as dead as a *corpse* in a *coffin*. But such verbal subterfuges are apparently thought to rob the grave of some of its victory; the notion of death is made more tolerable to the human consciousness than it would otherwise be. Birth is much more plainly alluded to nowadays than it used to be, particularly by young married people, who seem to be strangely fascinated by the unpleasant clinical details attendant upon it. The free use of *pregnant* is not much older than World War II. A woman *with child, going to have a baby,* or *enceinte* used to terminate her condition by her *confinement*, or, if one wanted to be really fancy about it, her *accouchement*.

Ideas of decency likewise profoundly affect language. All during the Victorian era, ladies and gentlemen were very sensitive about using the word *leg, limb* being almost invariably substituted, sometimes even if only the legs of a piano were being referred to. In the very year which marks the beginning of Queen Victoria's long reign, Captain Frederick Marryat noted in his *Diary in America* (1837) the American taboo on this word, when, having asked a young American lady who had taken a spill whether she had hurt her leg, she turned from him, "evidently much shocked, or much offended," later explaining to him that in America the word *leg* was never used in the presence of ladies. Later, the captain visited a school for young ladies where he saw, according to his own testimony, "a square pianoforte with four limbs," all dressed in little frilled pantalettes. For reasons which it would be difficult to analyze, a similar taboo was placed upon *belly, stomach* being usually substituted for it, along with such nursery terms as *tummy* and *breadbasket* and the advertising copy writer's *midriff*. *Toilet*, a diminutive of French *toile* 'cloth,' in its earliest English uses meant a piece of cloth in which to wrap clothes, subsequently coming to be used for a cloth cover for a dressing table, and then the table itself, as when Lydia Languish in Sheridan's *The Rivals* says, "Here, my dear Lucy, hide these books. Quick, quick! Fling *Peregrine Pickle* under the toilet—throw *Roderick Random* into the closet. . . ."[20] There are other related meanings. The word came to be used in America as a euphemism for *privy*—itself in turn a euphemism, as are *latrine* (ultimately derived from Lat. *lavāre* 'to wash') and *lavatory* (note the euphemistic phrase "to wash one's hands"). But *toilet* is now frequently replaced by *rest room, comfort station, powder room,* or the intolerably coy *little boys'* (or *girls'*) *room*. It is safe to predict that these evasions will in their turn come to be regarded as indecorous, and other expressions substituted for them.

Euphemism is likewise resorted to in reference to certain diseases. Like that which attempts to prettify, or at least to mollify birth, death, and excretion, this type of verbal subterfuge is doubtless deeply rooted in fear and superstition. An ailment of almost any sort, for instance, is nowadays often referred to as a *condition* (*heart condition, kidney condition, malignant condition,* and so forth), so that *condition,* hitherto a more or less neutral word, has thus had a pejorative development, coming to mean 'bad condition.'[21] *Leprosy* is no longer used by the American Medical Association because of its repulsive connotations; it is nowadays replaced by the colorless *Hansen's Disease*. *Cancer* may be openly referred to, though it is notable that in the syndicated horoscopes of Carroll Righter, a well-known Hollywood astrologer, the term is no longer used as a sign of the zodiac; those born under Cancer are now designated "Moon Children." The taboo has been removed from reference to the various specific venereal diseases, formerly *blood diseases* or *social diseases*.

[20] It should be pointed out that about fifty years ago the direction for the disposal of *Roderick Random* would have been as risible as that for *Peregrine Pickle,* when *closet* was frequently used for *water closet,* now practically obsolete in American English.

[21] Note that, although *to have a condition* means 'to be in bad health,' *to be in condition* continues, confusingly enough, to mean 'to be in good health.'

Old age and its attendant decay have probably been made more bearable for many elderly and decrepit people by calling them *senior citizens.* A similar verbal humanitarianism is responsible for *under-privileged* 'poor,' the previously mentioned *sick* 'insane,' *social justice* 'charity,' *exceptional child* 'a pupil of subnormal mentality,'[22] and a good many other voguish euphemisms, some of which have been cited in another connection. In the last cited example, pejoration has also operated—unless it can be conceived generally that being below par intellectually is a desirable thing, as the schools would seem to have supposed. One wonders whether to the next generation an "exceptional man" will be thought of as a dull and stupid man, that is, an exceptional child grown to maturity, and whether the "exceptional bargains" offered by the stores had not better be passed up in favor of merely average ones. Sentimental equalitarianism has led us to attempt to dignify humble occupations by giving them high-sounding titles: thus a *janitor* (originally a doorkeeper, from *Janus,* the door-keeper of heaven in Roman mythology) has in many parts of America become a *custodian* and there are many engineers who would not know the difference between a slide rule and a cantilever. H. L. Mencken cites, among a good many others, *demolition engineer* 'house-wrecker,' *sanitary engineer* 'garbage man,' and *extermination engineer* 'rat-catcher.'[23] The meaning of *profession* has been generalized to such an extent that it may include practically any trade or vocation. The writer of a letter to the editor of *Life* comments as follows on the publication of a picture of a plumber in a previous issue: "I think you have done an injustice to the plumbing profession" (August 6, 1951); and a regional chairman of the Wage Stabilization Board informed a waitress who complained of the smallness of her tips, according to an Associated Press item of June 19, 1952, that "if tipping were viewed by your profession as a true incentive for better, faster and more agreeable service, this might go a long way toward relieving the situation." Long ago James Fenimore Cooper in *The American Democrat* (1838) denounced such democratic subterfuges as *boss* for *master* and *help* for *servant,* but these seem very mild nowadays. One of the great concerns of the democratic and progressive age in which we live would seem to be to ensure that nobody's feelings shall ever be hurt—at least, not by words.

[22] Note that the child who exceeds expectations has been stigmatized by the schools as an *over-achiever.*

[23] *The American Language,* 4th ed. (New York, 1936), pp. 289–91.

It is characteristic of the human mind, in varying degrees of course, to identify words with objects, persons, and ideas—to think much of the time not in terms of the actual situations of flesh-and-blood life, but in relation to words, like that oft quoted little girl who, upon first seeing a pig, remarked that it was certainly rightly named, for it was a very dirty animal. But a pig by any other name—even if it were called a rose—would smell as bad. What one happens to call it—*Schwein, lechón, porco,* or *pig*—makes no difference in the nature of the creature, nor is one name any more appropriate than another. To suppose that our term is superior—that a pig really *is* a pig and hence that we who speak English are more perceptive than foreigners in calling it by its "right" name—is so naïve that no one would own to such a belief. Yet it is certainly true that in their everyday lives people frequently act as though they thought words were identical with what they designate.

During World War II the name of a widely known and highly satisfactory pencil was changed from Mikado to Mirado—a hardly noticeable change, involving a single letter. Yet it is doubtful that the manufacturer would have gone to such trouble and expense as must have been involved in making that little change had he not been convinced that, with Japan as our enemy, many patriots would refuse to buy a pencil named for its emperor, although no one in his right mind could imagine that the pencil was a whit superior because of the change of name.

THE FATE OF INTENSIFYING WORDS

Intensifiers constantly stand in need of replacement, being so frequently used that their intensifying force is worn down. As an adverb of degree, *very* has only an intensifying function; it has altogether lost its independent meaning 'truly,' though as an adjective it survives with older meanings in such phrases as "the very man for the job" and "this very afternoon." Chaucer does not use *very* as an intensive adverb; the usage was doubtless beginning to be current in his day, though the *OED* has no contemporary citations. As everyone must be aware, the *verray* in the well-known line "He was a verray, parfit gentil knyght" is an adjective modifying *knyght*: the meaning is approximately 'He was a fully accomplished gentle knight in the widest sense of the term.'

For Chaucer and his contemporaries *full* seems to have been the usual intensive adverb, though Old English *swīðe* (the adverbial form of *swið* 'strong') retained its intensifying function until the middle of the fifteenth century, with independent meanings 'rapidly' and 'instantly' surviving much longer. *Right* was also widely used as an intensive in Middle English times, as in Chaucer's description of the Clerk of Oxenford: "he nas [that is, *ne was*] nat right fat," which is to say 'He wasn't very fat.' This usage survives formally in *Right Reverend,* the title of a bishop,[24] in *Right Honourable,* that of members of the Privy Council and a few other dignitaries; and in *Right Worshipful,* that of most lord mayors, as also in the more or less informal usages *right smart, right well, right away, right there,* and the like.

Sore, as in *sore afraid,* was similarly long used as an intensive modifier of adjectives and adverbs; its use to modify verbs is even older. Its cognate *sehr* is still the usual intensive in German, in which language it has completely lost its independent use.

In view of the very understandable tendency of such intensifying words to become dulled, it is not surprising that we should cast about for other words to replace them when we really want to be emphatic. "It's been a very pleasant evening" seems quite inadequate under certain circumstances, and we may instead say, "It's been an *awfully* pleasant evening"; *very nice* may likewise become "*terribly* nice." In negative utterances, *too* is coming to be widely used as an intensive: "Newberry's not too far from here"; "Juvenile-court law practice is not too lucrative."

Prodigiously was for a while a voguish substitute for *very,* so that a Regency "blood" like Thackeray's Jos Sedley might speak admiringly of a shapely woman as "a prodigiously fine gel" or even a "monstrous fine" one. The first of these now-forgotten intensifiers dates approximately from the second half of the seventeenth century; the second is about a century earlier. An anonymous contributor to the periodical *The World* in 1756 deplored the "pomp of utterance of our present women of fashion; which, though it may tend to spoil many a pretty mouth, can never recommend an indifferent one," citing in support of his statement the feminine overuse of *vastly, horridly, abominably, immensely,* and *excessively* as intensifiers.[25]

[24] The dean's title *Very Reverend* has exactly the same meaning, but is, naturally, less exalted in its connotations.

[25] Reprinted in Susie I. Tucker's useful little collection, *English Examined: Two Centuries of Comment on the Mother Tongue* (Cambridge, Eng., 1961), p. 96.

SEMANTIC CHANGE IS INEVITABLE

It is a great pity that language cannot be the exact, finely attuned instrument that deep thinkers wish it to be. But the facts are, as we have seen, that the meaning of practically any word is susceptible to change of one sort or another, and some words have so many individual meanings that we cannot really hope to be absolutely certain of the sum of these meanings. But it is probably quite safe to predict that the members of the human race, *homines sapientes* more or less, will go on making absurd noises with their mouths at one another in what idealists among them will go on considering a deplorably sloppy and inadequate manner, and yet manage to understand one another well enough for their own purposes.

The idealists may, if they wish, settle upon Esperanto, Ido, Ro, Volapük, or any other of the excellent scientific languages which have been laboriously constructed. The game of constructing such languages is still going on; it is assumed that these will not be susceptible to the kind of change which we have been considering here, any more than to changes in structure such as have been undergone by those languages which have evolved over the eons. But most of the manifold phenomena of life—disease, famine, birth, death, sex, war, atoms, isms, and people, to name only a few—will doubtless remain as messy and hence as unsatisfactory to those unwilling to accept them as they have always been, no matter what form of speech we employ when we have to deal with them verbally.

CHAPTER XII

Foreign Elements in the English Word Stock

THUS far we have dealt only incidentally with the non-English elements in the English lexicon. In the present chapter we shall make a rapid survey of these, along with some examination of the various circumstances—cultural, religious, military, and political—surrounding their adoption.

LATIN LOAN-WORDS IN GERMANIC

Long before Anglo-Frisian began its separate existence, while it was merely a regional type of Germanic, those who spoke it had acquired, along with the other Germanic tribes, a number of Latin words—loan-words which are common to several or to all of the Germanic languages to this day. Unlike a good many later borrowings, they are for the most part concerned with military affairs, commerce, agriculture, or with refinements of living which the Germanic peoples had acquired through a fairly close contact with the Romans since at least the beginning of the Christian era. *Wine* (OE *wīn*, Lat. *vīnum*), for instance, denotes an appurtenance of the good life which the Germanic peoples learned about from the Romans. It is to be found in one form or another in all the Germanic languages—the same form as the Old English in Old Frisian and Old Saxon, *Wein* in Modern German, *wijn* in Modern Dutch, *vin* in Danish and Swedish.[1] It was brought to Britain by the Germanic warrior-adventurers who in the mid-fifth century, as we have seen, became the first English people. Their not-so-remote ancestors had known malt drinks very well—*beer*

[1] The Balto-Slavic and Celtic peoples also acquired the same word from Latin.

and *ale* are both Germanic words, and mead was known to the Indo-Europeans. Apparently the principle of fermentation of fruit juices was a specialty of the Mediterranean peoples, for the word for the juice of the vine after it had passed through this benevolent, civilizing, and eupeptic process comes from the Romans. Roman merchants had penetrated into the Germania of these early centuries, Roman farmers had settled in the Rhineland and the valley of the Moselle, and Germanic soldiers had marched with the Roman legions.[2]

There are about 175 such words, most of them indicating special spheres in which the Romans excelled, or were thought to do so by the Germanic peoples.[3] Many of these words have survived into Modern English. They include *ancor* 'anchor' (Lat. *ancora*), *butere* 'butter' (Lat. *būtyrum*), *cealc* 'chalk' (Lat. *calc-*), *cēap*[4] 'marketplace, wares, price' (Lat. *caupō* 'tradesman,' more specifically 'wineseller'), *cēse* 'cheese' (Lat. *cāseus*), *disc* 'dish' (Lat. *discus*), *cempa* 'kemp, warrior' (Lat. *campio[nem]*), *cetel* 'kettle' (Lat. *catillus* 'little pot'), *cycene* 'kitchen' (Lat. *coquīna*), *mīl* 'mile' (Lat. *mīlia [passuum]* 'a thousand [paces]'), *mynet* 'coin, coinage, Modern English *mint*' (Lat. *monēta*), *mangere* '-monger, trader' (Lat. *mangō*), *piper, -or* 'pepper' (Lat. *piper*), *pund* 'pound' (Lat. *pondo* 'measure of weight'), *sacc* 'sack' (Lat. *saccus*), *sicol* 'sickle' (Lat. *secula*), *strǣt* 'paved road, street' (Lat. *[via] strāta* '[road] paved'),[5] and *weall* 'wall' (Lat. *vallum*).

[2] See Robert Priebsch and W. E. Collinson, *The German Language*, 4th ed., rev. (London, 1958), pp. 264–65.

[3] For a detailed classification, see Mary S. Serjeantson, *A History of Foreign Words in English* (London, 1935), Appendix A, pp. 271–77.

[4] Obsolete as a noun except in proper names such as *Chapman, Cheapside* (once simply *Cheap,* then *Westcheap*), *Eastcheap, Chepstow, Wincheap* (the name of a street in Canterbury, the first element of which Eilert Ekwall in his *Street-Names of the City of London* [Oxford, 1954], p. 182 n., tentatively derives from Old English *wægn* 'wain,' hence 'a market where goods were sold in wagons'). The adjectival and adverbial use of *cheap* is of early Modern English origin and is, according to the *OED,* a shortening of *good cheap* 'what can be purchased on advantageous terms.' *To cheapen* is likewise of early Modern English origin and used to mean 'to bargain for, ask the price of,' as when Defoe's Moll Flanders went out to "cheapen some laces."

[5] The earlier meaning survives in *Watling Street,* the name of what was a Roman road from London past St. Alban's to Wroxeter, near Shrewsbury. Edgware Road in London is part of the old Watling Street. Old English *strǣt* survives in a good many place names, for example *Stratford* 'ford by

Since all these are popular loan-words, resting upon a purely oral tradition, they have gone through all phonological developments which occurred subsequently to their adoption in the various Germanic languages. *Chalk, dish,* and *kitchen,* for instance, show respectively in their initial, final, and medial consonants the Old English palatization of *k*; in addition, the last-cited word in its Old English form *cycene* shows mutation of Vulgar Latin *u* in the vowel of its stressed syllable. German *Küche* and *Münze* (corresponding to OE *mynet*) show the same mutation. An earlier *a* has been mutated by *i* in a following syllable in *cetel* and *kemp* (compare Ger. *Kessel, Kämpfe*). It is similar with the German development of the same words. All have undergone the High German sound shift (see pp. 98–99), the *d* of Latin *discus* occurring as *t* in *Tisch,* the medial *t* of *monēta* and *strāta* as *z* [ts] and *ss* in German *Münze* and *Strasse,* the *p* of Latin *pondo* and *piper* as *pf* and *ff* in German *Pfund* and *Pfeffer,* and the postvocalic *k* of Latin *secula* as *ch* in German *Sichel.* The fact that none of these early loan-words has been affected by the First Sound Shift (see pp. 91–94) indicates that they were borrowed long after this shift had completed itself.

POPULAR AND LEARNED LOAN-WORDS

It is important at this point to make a distinction between popular and learned loan-words, one which was first made a good many years ago by Alois Pogatscher.[6] Popular loan-words, as has been pointed out, are of oral transmission and are part of the vocabulary of everyday communication, like those words which have been cited. For the most part they are not felt to be in any way different from English words; in fact, those who use them are seldom aware that they are of foreign origin. Learned words, on the other hand, owe their adoption to more or less cultural influences. The principal such influence in Old English times was, as we should expect, the church.[7] Learned

---

which a paved Roman road crossed a river,' *Stratton* 'a *tūn* (enclosure) on a Roman road,' *Streatley, Streatham, Stradbroke, Stradishall* (OE *Strǣt-gesell* 'place on a Roman road'), and a good many others listed in Eilert Ekwall's *Concise Oxford Dictionary of English Place-Names,* 4th ed. (Oxford, 1960), s.v. *strǣt, strēt.* Other old highways were Ermine Street and Icknield Street.

[6] *Zur Lautlehre der griechischen, lateinischen und romanischen Lehnworte im Altenglischen* (Strassburg, 1888).

[7] The word *church* (OE *cir(i)ce*) itself is, however, the English development of a West Germanic word ultimately from Greek *kyriakon* 'of the

words may in time become part of the living vocabulary, even though their use may be confined to a certain class or group; or they may, as with *clerk* (OE *cleric, clerc* from Lat. *clēricus*), pass into the usage of the common people. *Cleric* was once more taken from Latin as a learned word to denote a clergyman, since *clerk* had acquired other meanings, including 'scholar,' 'scribe,' 'one in charge of records and accounts in an organization,' and 'bookkeeper.' It was later to acquire yet another meaning, 'one who waits upon customers in a retail establishment,' in American English, the equivalent of the British 'shop assistant.' The earliest English meaning has survived in legal usage, in which a priest of the Church of England is described as a "clerk in holy orders."

LATIN WORDS BORROWED
IN OLD ENGLISH TIMES

The approximate time at which a word was borrowed is often indicated by its form: thus, as Miss Serjeantson points out,[8] Old English *scōl* 'school' (Lat. *schola*, ultimately Greek) is obviously a later borrowing than *scrīn* 'shrine' (Lat. *scrīnium*), which must have been adopted before the Old English change of [sk-] to [š-] in order for it to have acquired the later sound. At the time when *scōl* was borrowed, this sound change was no longer operative. Had the word been borrowed earlier, it would have developed into Modern English *shool*. The medial consonant of Old English *fefer* 'fever'[9] (Lat. *febris*), on the other hand, reflects a late Latin change. *Febrile*, a learned loan, came into English centuries later—specifically in the seventeenth century.

Among the early English loan-words from Latin, some of which were acquired from the British Celts, are *tæfl* 'gaming board' (Lat. *tabula*), *candel* 'candle' (Lat. *candēla*), *sealtian* 'to dance' (Lat. *saltāre*), *sealm*[10] (Lat. *psalmus*, taken from Greek), *leahtric* 'lettuce' (Lat.

Lord.' The pagan Germanic peoples were perfectly familiar, if only through their pillagings of churches in Roman provinces, with a number of words pertaining to Christianity. *Devil* (OE *dēofol*) is such a word, and may even be directly from Greek *diabolos*, according to A. Campbell (*Old English Grammar*, [Oxford, 1959] p. 199). *God* is, on the other hand, a native Germanic word.

[8] *History of Foreign Words in English*, p. 13.

[9] It should be remembered that Old English *f* between vowels stood for [v].

[10] The learned form *psalm* is of course a later borrowing.

lactūca), *eced* 'vinegar' (Lat. *acētum*), *Læden* 'Latin' (Lat. *Latīna*), *mægester* 'master' (Lat. *magister*), *cyst* 'box' (Lat. *cesta*), *peru* 'pear' (Lat. *pirum*), *senop* 'mustard' (Lat. *sināpi*), *regol* 'rule' (Lat. *regula*), *port* 'harbor' (Lat. *portus*), *mynster* 'monastery' (Lat. *monasterium*), *cese* 'cheese' (Lat. *cāseus*), *tīgle* 'tile' (Lat. *tēgula*), *sicor* 'secure' (Lat. *sēcūrus*), *stær* 'history' (Lat. *historia*, with aphesis and an unusual vowel development),[11] *crisp* 'curly' (Lat. *crispus*), *segn* 'mark, banner' (Lat. *signum*), and *ceaster* 'city' (Lat. *castra* 'camp').[12]

Somewhat later, after approximately A.D. 650, and hence not showing English sound changes, such learned loan-words as the following occur: *plaster*[13] (medical) (Lat. *emplastrum*), *alter* 'altar' (Lat. *altar*), *magister* 'master,' *martir* 'martyr' (Lat. *martyr*), *templ* 'temple' (Lat. *templum*), *(a)postol* 'apostle' (Lat. *apostolus*), *dēmon* (Lat. *daemōn*), *mæsse, messe* (Lat. *missa*, later *messa*), *circul* 'circle' (Lat. *circulus*), *paper* (Lat. *papȳrus*), *cālend* 'month's beginning' (Lat. *calendae* 'calends') *cometa* 'comet,' *balsam* (Lat. *balsamum*), *sōn* 'musical sound' (Lat. *sonus*), *fers* 'verse' (Lat. *versus*), and *cristalla* 'crystal' (Lat. *crystallum*). Since Latin borrowed freely from Greek, it is not surprising that some of the loans cited are of Greek origin, for example (to cite their Modern English forms), *apostle, demon, paper, comet, balsam,* and *crystal.* This is of course the merest sampling of Latin loan-words in Old English. Somewhat more than five hundred in all occur in the entire Old English period up to the Conquest. This is not actually a large number as compared with the Latin borrowings in later times. Miss Serjeantson lists, aside from the words from the Continental period, 111 from the period from approximately A.D. 450 to 650, and 242 from approximately A.D. 650 to the time of the Norman Conquest.[14]

[11] Sound changes in the early Latin loan-words are treated in detail by Campbell, *Old English Grammar,* Chapter 10.

[12] This survives in *Chester, Castor, Caister,* and as an element in the names of a good many English places, many of which were once in fact Roman stations, for instance *Manchester, Gloucester, Worcester, Casterton, Chesterfield, -ton, Lancaster,* and *Exeter* (earlier *Execestre*). The differences in form are mostly dialectal.

[13] Where only a single form is cited, as here, it is unchanged in Modern English, and where no Latin form is given, it is to be assumed that it is the same as the Old English form.

[14] Appendix A, pp. 277–88.

Many of these words, particularly those from the later period, were certainly never widely used, or even known. Some occur only a single time, or in only a single manuscript. Many were subsequently lost, some to be reborrowed, often with changes of meaning, at a later period from French or from Classical Latin. For instance, our words *sign* and *giant* are obviously not from Old English *segn* and *gīgant*, but are later borrowings from Old French *signe* and *geant*. In addition, it should be mentioned that a learned and a popular form of the same word might coexist in Old English, for instance *Latin* and *Laeden*, the second of which might also mean 'any foreign language.'

These loan-words, the later learned ones as well as the earlier popular ones, were usually made to conform to Old English declensional patterns, though occasionally, in translations from Latin into Old English, Latin case forms, particularly of proper names, may be retained, for example "fram Agustō þām cāsere" from the translation of Bede's account of the departure of the Romans from Britain: 'from Augustus the emperor,' with the Latin ending *-ō* in close apposition with the Old English dative endings in *-m* and *-e*. As with earlier borrowings, there came into being a good many hybrid formations: that is, native endings were affixed to foreign words, for example *-isc* in *mechanisc* 'mechanical,' *-dōm* in *pāpdōm* 'papacy,' and *-ere* in *grammaticere* 'grammarian,' and hybrid compounds such as *sealmscop* (Lat. *psalma* and OE *scop* 'singer, bard'). Infinitives took the Old English ending *-ian*, for example the grammatical term *declinian* 'to decline.'

LATIN WORDS BORROWED
IN MIDDLE ENGLISH TIMES

Many borrowings from Latin occurred during the Middle English period. Frequently it is impossible to tell whether a word is from French or from Latin, for instance *complex, miserable, nature, relation, register, rubric,* and *social,* which might be from either language, judging by form alone. Depending upon its meaning, the single form *port* may come from Latin *portus* 'harbor,' French *porter* 'to carry,' Latin *porta* 'gate,' or Portuguese *Oporto* (that is, *o porto* 'the port,' the city where "port" wine came from originally)—not to mention the nautical use of the word for one side of a ship, the origin of which is uncertain.

In the period between the Norman Conquest and 1500, many Latin words having to do with religion appeared in English, among them *collect*[15] 'short prayer,' *dirge, mediator,* and *Redeemer* (first used with reference to Christ: the synonymous *redemptor* occurs earlier). To these, legal terms might be added, for instance *client, subpoena,* and *conviction,* as well as words having to do with scholastic activities, for instance *simile, index, library,* and *scribe,* and with science,[16] for instance *dissolve, equal, essence, medicine, mercury, opaque, orbit, quadrant,* and *recipe.* These are only a few out of hundreds of Latin words which were adopted before 1500: a longer list would include verbs (for example *admit, commit, discuss, interest, mediate, seclude*) and adjectives (for example *legitimate, obdurate, populous, imaginary, instant, complete*).

LATIN WORDS BORROWED IN MODERN ENGLISH TIMES

The great period of borrowings from Latin and from Greek by way of Latin is the Modern English period. The century or so after 1500 saw the introduction of, among many others, the words *area, abdomen, compensate, composite, data, decorum, delirium, denominate, digress, edition, education, fictitious, folio, fortitude, gradual, horrid, imitate, janitor, jocose, lapse, medium, modern, notorious, orb, pacific, penetrate, querulous, resuscitate, sinecure, series, splendid, strict, superintendent, transition, ultimate, urban, urge,* and *vindicate.*[17]

---

[15] Stressed on the first syllable. The word was in Middle English also used as a noun in other senses, now obsolete. The verb, with stress on the second syllable, occurs considerably later, in the sixteenth century. The prayer was presumably so called in the Gallican liturgies because it was a sort of summarization (Lat. *collectus,* past participle of *colligere* 'to gather together'). The *Catholic Dictionary,* 3rd ed., ed. Donald Attwater (New York, 1958), derives the word from *oratio ad collectam* 'prayer at the gathering,' that is, a prayer said at one of the appointed stations where the people gathered in order to proceed together to the Mass. The *OED* states that there was apparently no connection originally between the Roman and the earlier Gallican uses.

[16] The word *science* itself is from Old French, and originally had a much broader meaning than it has at present. In the Middle Ages "the seven sciences" was often synonymous with "the seven liberal arts," that is, grammar, logic, rhetoric, arithmetic, music, geometry, and astronomy (*OED*).

[17] Some of these words are derived from French by the *OED*.

GREEK LOAN-WORDS

Even before the Conquest a number of Greek words had entered English by way of Latin, in addition to those very early loans discussed above (pp. 325–26, n. 7) which may have come into Germanic directly from Greek, such as *church*. Latin and French are the immediate sources of most loan-words ultimately Greek from the Middle English period on, for instance (from Latin) *allegory, anemia, anesthesia,*[18] *aristocracy, barbarous, chaos, comedy, cycle, dilemma, drama, electric, epoch, enthusiasm, epithet, history, homonym, metaphor, mystery, oligarchy, paradox, pharynx, phenomenon,*[19] *rhapsody, rhythm, theory, zone;* (from French) *center, chronicle, character, democracy, diet, dragon, ecstasy, fantasy, harmony, lyre, machine, nymph, pause, rheum, tyrant.* Straight from Greek (though some are combinations unknown in classical times) come *acronym, agnostic, anthropoid, autocracy, chlorine, idiosyncrasy, kudos, oligarchy, pathos, phone, telegram,* and *xylophone,* among many others.

The richest foreign sources of our present English word stock are Latin, French, and Greek (including those words of Greek origin which have come to us by way of Latin and French). Many of the Latin and Greek words which have been cited were in the beginning confined to the language of erudition, and some of them still are; others have passed into the stock of more or less everyday speech. It must be remembered in this connection that in earlier periods Latin was to the English the language of literature, science, and religion. Although Greek had tremendous prestige as a classical language, there was comparatively little first-hand knowledge of it in western Europe until the advent of refugee Greek scholars from Constantinople. Hence, most of the Greek words which appear first in early Modern English occurred, as far as the English were concerned, in Latin works, though their Greek provenience would usually have been recognized. Latin was, in fact, in every respect a living language among the learned

---

[18] In its usual modern sense 'drug-induced insensibility,' this word was first used in 1846 by Oliver Wendell Holmes, who was a physician as well as a poet.

[19] A few words in *-on* from Greek, though in other respects completely naturalized, retain Greek plurals in *-a,* for example *phenomena, criteria, automata.* There is a tendency among the half-educated to use these plurals as if they were singulars. Singular *phenomena* occurs as early as the sixteenth century, and a new plural *phenomenas* in the seventeenth. The blundering *phenominae* is recorded from the eighteenth century.

all over Europe throughout the medieval and early modern periods. Petrarch, it will be remembered in this connection, translated Boccaccio's story of the patient Griselda into Latin to insure that such a highly moral tale should have a wider circulation than it would have had in Boccaccio's Italian, and it was this Latin translation that Chaucer used as the source of his *Clerk's Tale*. More, Bacon, and Milton all wrote in Latin, just as Bede and other learned men had done centuries earlier.

AFFIXES FROM LATIN AND GREEK

Not only entire words such as have been cited were taken from Latin and Greek (including Greek by way of Latin and Latin by way of French), but many affixes commonly used in English as well. These were originally for the most part adverbs and prepositions. They have become completely naturalized, as has been shown (pp. 269–70).

EARLY CELTIC LOAN-WORDS

It is likely that even before the beginning of Latin borrowing in England, the English must have acquired some words from the Celts. As has been pointed out, some of the Latin loans of the period up to approximately A.D. 650 were acquired by the English indirectly through the Celts. It is likely that *ceaster* and *-coln*, as in *Lincoln*[20] (Lat. *colonia*), were so acquired. Phonology is not much help to us as far as such words are concerned, since they underwent the same prehistoric Old English sound-changes as the words which the English brought with them from the Continent.

There are, however, a number of genuinely Celtic words acquired during the early years of the English settlement. We should not expect to find many, for the British Celts were a subject people, and a conquering people are unlikely to adopt many words from those obviously inferior people whom they have conquered. The very insignificant number of words from American Indian languages which have found a permanent place in American English strikingly illustrates this fact. The Normans are exceptional in that they ultimately gave up their own language altogether and became Englishmen, in a way in which the English never became Celts. Probably no more than a dozen or so Celtic words other than place names were adopted by the English up

[20] *Lindon colonia*. The first word is connected with British *llyn* 'lake.'

to the time of the Conquest.[21] These include *bratt* 'cloak,' *cumb* 'combe, valley,' *brocc* 'badger,' *torr* 'peak,' and *bannuc* 'a bit.' Just as many American place names are of Indian origin, so many English place names are of Celtic provenience: *Cornwall, Devon, Avon, Usk, Dover, London, Carlisle,* and scores more.

More recent times have seen the introduction of a few more Celtic words into English: from Irish Gaelic in the seventeenth century *shamrock, brogue, leprechaun, tory, galore,* and subsequently *banshee, shillelagh, blarney, colleen*; from Scots Gaelic, in addition to *loch, clan,* and a few rarely used words which entered English in late Middle English times, *bog, plaid, slogan, cairn, whiskey,* and some others less familiar; from Welsh, *crag,* occurring first in Middle English, is the best known; others of more recent introduction include *cromlech* and *eisteddfod.*

SCANDINAVIAN LOAN-WORDS
IN OLD AND MIDDLE ENGLISH

Most of the Scandinavian words in Old English do not actually occur in written records until the Middle English period, though there can of course be no doubt of their currency long before the beginning of this period. In the latter part of the eleventh century the Scandinavians became gradually assimilated to English ways, though Scandinavian words had been in the meanwhile introduced into English. As we have seen, many Scandinavian words closely resembled their English cognates; sometimes, indeed, they were so nearly identical that it would be impossible to tell whether a given word was Scandinavian or English. Sometimes, however, if the meanings of obviously related words differed, semantic contamination might result, as when Old English *drēam* 'joy' acquired the meaning of the related Scandinavian *draumr* 'vision in sleep.' Jespersen cites also *brēad* 'fragment,'[22] *blōma* 'lump of metal,' and poetic *eorl*

---

[21] There were, however, doubtless some Celtic loan-words in Germanic and also in Latin: Old English *rice* as a noun meaning 'kingdom' and as an adjective 'rich, powerful' (cf. Ger. *Reich*) is almost certainly of Celtic origin, borrowed before the settlement of the English in Britain. The Celtic origin of a few others (for example OE *ambeht* 'servant,' *dūn* 'hill, down') has been seriously questioned.

[22] The usual Old English word for the food made from flour or meal was *hlāf,* as in "Ūrne gedæghwāmlīcan hlāf syle ūs tō dæg" 'Our daily bread give us today.'

'warrior, noble' (ModE *bread, bloom* 'flower,' *earl*). The last of these words acquired the meaning of the related Scandinavian *jarl* 'underking, governor.' Similarly, the later meanings of *dwell* (OE *dwellan, dwelian*), *plow* (OE *plōh*), and *holm* 'islet' (same form in Old English) coincide precisely with the Scandinavian meanings, though in Old English these words meant respectively 'to lead astray, hinder,' 'measure of land,' and 'ocean.'[23]

Late Old English and early Middle English loans from Scandinavian were made to conform wholly or in part with the English sound and inflectional system. These include (in modern form) *by* 'town, homestead,'[24] *carl* 'man' (cognate with OE *ceorl*, the source of *churl*), *fellow, hit* (first 'meet with,' later 'strike'), *law, rag, riding* 'administrative division of Yorkshire,'[25] *sly, swain, take* (completely displacing *nim*, from OE *niman*), *thrall*, and *want*. The Scandinavian provenience of *sister* has already been alluded to (p. 105).

A good many words with [sk] are of Scandinavian origin, for, as we have seen, early Old English [sk], written *sc*, came to be pronounced [š]. Such words as *scathe, scatter, score, scowl, scot* 'tax' (as in *scotfree* and *scot and lot*), *scrape, scrub, skill, skin, skirt* (compare native *shirt*), and *sky* thus show by their initial consonant sequence that they entered the language after this change had ceased to be operative. All have been taken from Scandinavian.

Similarly the [g] and [k] before front vowels in *gear, geld, gill* (of a fish), *kick, kilt,* and *kindle* point to Scandinavian origins for these words, since the velar stops became in Old English under such circumstances [j] and [č] respectively. The very common verbs *get* and *give* come to us not from Old English *gitan* and *gifan*, which began with [j], but instead from cognate Scandinavian forms in which the palatal-

[23] Otto Jespersen, *Growth and Structure of the English Language,* 9th ed. (Oxford, 1954), pp. 64–65.

[24] As in *bylaw* 'town ordinance.' The word also occurs in place names, for instance *Derby, Grimsby,* and *Rigsby*.

[25] Yorkshire was divided by the Scandinavians into three districts, each appropriately called a *þriðjungr* 'third part,' adapted in late Old English as *þriðing* or *þriding*. In East Riding and West Riding the initial *þ* has been assimilated to the final *t* of *east* and *west*, the resultant *East Triding* and *West Triding* being subsequently simplified. In *North Riding* the earlier initial consonant has been absorbed by the identical final consonant of *north*.

ization of [g] in the neighborhood of front vowels did not occur.[26]

As a rule the Scandinavian loans involve little more than the substitution of one word for another (such as *window*, from *vindauga*, literally 'wind-eye,' replacing *eyethurl*, literally 'eye-hole,' from OE *ēagþyrl*), the acquisition of new words for new concepts (such as certain Scandinavian legal terms) or new things (such as words for various kinds of warships with which the Scandinavians made the English acquainted), or the more or less sporadic and invariably slight modification in the form of an English word due to Scandinavian influence (like *sister*). More important and more fundamental is what happened to the Old English pronominal forms of the third person plural: all the *th-* forms, as we have seen (pp. 144 and 158) are of Scandinavian origin. Of the native forms in *h-* (p. 123), only *'em* (ME *hem*; OE *him*) survives, and it is commonly but mistakenly thought of as a reduced form of *them*.

SCANDINAVIAN LOAN-WORDS
IN MODERN ENGLISH

A number of Scandinavian words have entered English during the modern period. The best known of these are *scud, rug, muggy,* and *ski*, the last of these dating from the latter years of the nineteenth century. *Skoal* (Danish *skaal*) has had a recent alcoholic vogue. It comes as a surprise to learn that it first appears in English as early as 1600, though its early use seems to have been confined to Scotland. The *OED* reasonably suggests that it may have been introduced through the visit of James VI of Scotland (afterwards James I of England) to Denmark, whither he journeyed in 1589 to meet his bride. *Geyser* (1763; for a heater for bath water, 1871), *rune* (1685),[27] *saga* (1709), and *skald* (ca. 1763) are all from Icelandic. The recently introduced *smörgåsbord* (1926), usually written in English without the diacritics, is from Swedish.

FRENCH LOAN-WORDS IN MIDDLE ENGLISH

No loan-words unquestionably of French origin occur in English earlier than 1066. Leaving out of the question doubtful cases, some

---

[26] Native forms of these verbs with [j-] occur throughout the Middle English period side by side with the Scandinavian forms with [g-] which were ultimately to supplant them. Chaucer consistently used *yive, yeve,* and preterit *yaf*.

[27] Old English had the cognate *rūn* 'secret, whisper,' which became Modern English *roun*. The last citation in the *OED* is from 1567.

of the earliest loans which are unquestionably French are (to cite their Modern English forms) *service, juggler, prison,* and *castle.*[28] *Capon* could be French but was most likely taken directly from Latin.

The Norman Conquest made French the language of the official class in England. Hence it is not surprising that many words having to do with government and administration, lay and spiritual, are of French origin: the word *government* itself, along with Middle English *amynistre,* later replaced by the Latin-derived *administer* with its derivative *administration.* Others include *attorney, chancellor, country, court, crime* (replacing English *sin,* which thereafter came to designate the proper business of the Church, though the State has from time to time tried to take it over), *(e)state,*[29] *judge, jury, noble, royal;* in the religious sphere, *abbot, clergy, preach, sacrament, vestment,* among a good many others. Words designating English titles of nobility except for *king, queen, earl, lord,* and *lady*—namely, *prince, duke, marquess, viscount, baron* and their feminine equivalents—date from the period when England was in the hands of a Norman French ruling class. Even so, the earl's wife is a *countess,* and the peer immediately below him in rank is a *viscount* (that is, 'vice-count'), indicating that the earl corresponds in rank with the Continental count. In military usage, *army, captain, corporal, lieutenant* (literally 'place-holding'), *sergeant* (originally a serving-man or attendant), and *soldier* are all of French origin.[30]

French names were given not only to various animals when served up as food at Norman tables—*beef, pork, veal,* and *mutton,* for instance—but also to the culinary processes by which the English cow, pig, calf, and sheep were prepared for human consumption, for instance *boil, broil, fry, stew,* and *roast.* English *seethe* is now used

---

[28] Campbell, *Old English Grammar,* p. 221: "Even after 1066 French words flow into the literary language more slowly than Norse ones, and they do not occur frequently until the last hand of the *OE Chron[icle]* begins," that is, in 1132.

[29] *State* is an aphetic form. Both it and the full form *estate* were obviously borrowed before French loss of *s* before *t* (Mod. Fr. *état*).

[30] *Colonel* does not occur in English until the sixteenth century (as *coronnel,* whence the pronunciation). French *brigade* and its derivative *brigadier* were introduced in the seventeenth century. *Major* is Latin, occurring first (as an adjective) in *sergeant major* in the latter years of the sixteenth century; the nonmilitary adjectival use in English is somewhat earlier. The French equivalent has occurred in English since the end of the thirteenth century, its Modern English form being *mayor.*

mostly metaphorically,[31] as in *to seethe with rage* and *sodden in drink;* another Old English culinary verb, *brǣdan,* with a rather general meaning, survived into early Modern English as *brede;* the last citation in the *OED* is from 1509. Other French loans from the Middle English period, chosen more or less at random, are *dignity, enamor, feign, fool, fruit, horrible, letter, literature, magic, male, marvel, mirror, oppose, question, regard, remember, sacrifice, safe, salary, search, second* (replacing OE *ōðer*), *secret, seize, sentence, single, sober,* and *solace.*

Borrowing from French has gone on ever since, though never on so large a scale. It is interesting to note that the same French word may be borrowed at various periods in the history of English, like *gentle, genteel,* and *jaunty,*[32] all from French *gentil*—the last two of seventeenth-century introduction, as one might suppose from their pronunciations. It is similar with *chief,* first occurring in English in the fourteenth century, and *chef,* in the nineteenth—the doublets show by their pronunciation the approximate time of their adoption: the Old French affricate [č] survives in *chief,* in which the vowel has undergone the expected shift from [e:] to [i:]; *chef* shows the Modern French shift of the affricate to the fricative [š].[33]

Carriage, courage, language, savage, village, and *viage* (later modernized as *voyage*) came into English in Middle English times and have come to have initial stress in accordance with English patterns. Chaucer and his contemporaries could have it both ways in their poetry—for instance either *couráge* or *cóurage,* as also with other French loans, for instance *colour, figure, honour, pitee, vertu, valour.*

[31] It was occasionally so used in Old English, as in *Beowulf,* lines 190 and 1993 (in the preterit singular form *sēað*).

[32] *Gentile* was taken straight from Latin *gentīlis,* meaning 'foreign' in post-Classical Latin.

[33] In words of French origin spelled with *ch,* the pronunciation is usually indicative of the time of adoption: thus *chase, chamber, chance, chant, change, champion, charge, chattel, chaste, check, choice* were borrowed in Middle English times, whereas *chauffeur, chamois, chevron, chic, chiffon, chignon, douche,* and *machine* have been taken over in Modern English times. Since *chivalry* was widely current in Middle English, one would expect it to begin in Modern English with [č]; the word has, as it were, been re-Frenchified, perhaps because with the decay of the institution it became more of an eye-word than an ear-word. Daniel Jones's *English Pronouncing Dictionary,* 12th ed. (London, 1963) records [č-] as current, but labels such pronunciation old-fashioned.

This practice is still evidenced by such doublets as *dívers* and *divérse* (showing influence of Lat. *dīversus*). The position of the stress is frequently evidence of the period of borrowing: compare, for instance, older *válour* with newer *velóur*, *cárriage* with *garáge*,[34] or *véstige* with *prestíge*.

French words might come into English from two dialects of French, the Norman spoken in England (Anglo-Norman) and the Central French (that of Paris, later Standard French). Just as the pronunciation of *ch* and in most instances the position of the stress in words of French origin indicate their relative age as English words, so we may frequently tell by the form of a word whether it is of Norman or of Central French provenience. For instance, Latin *c* [k] before *a* developed into *ch* [č] in Central French, but remained in the Norman dialect; hence *chapter*, from Middle English *chapitre* (from Old French), ultimately going back to Latin *capitulum* 'little head,' a diminutive of *caput*. Compare also the doublets *chattel* and *cattle*, from Central French and Norman respectively, both going back to Latin *capitāle* 'possession, stock,' *capital* in this sense being a Latin loan. Old French *w* was retained in Norman French, but elsewhere became [gw] and then [g]: this development is shown in such doublets as the frequently cited *wage–gage* and *warranty–guarantee*. There are a good many other phonological criteria.

The century and a half between 1250 and the death of Chaucer was a period during which the rate of adoption of French loan-words was greater than it had ever been before or has ever been since. According to Jespersen, nearly half (42.7 per cent) of the French borrowings in Middle English belong to this period.[35] His estimate is based on the dates of earliest occurrence in writing as supplied by the *OED*, and he is quite aware that these may be somewhat later, by as much as fifty years, than the actual first use of the more popular words; nevertheless it is likely that he is not far out of the way, as subsequent studies based on the completed *OED* have shown.

Let us pause to examine the opening lines of the *Canterbury Tales*,

[34] This word has principal stress on its first syllable in British English, as ['gæˌraž] or [-ˌrɑɟ], with pseudo-French vowel in its second syllable. A completely Anglicized pronunciation, with reduction of the [ɑ] of the second syllable—hence riming with *carriage*—is also current in British use, though it would be regarded as eccentric, not to say substandard, in America.

[35] *Growth and Structure*, pp. 86–87.

written toward the end of this period. The italicized words are of French origin:

Whan that Aprille with hise shoures soote
The droghte of *March* hath *perced* to the roote
And bathed every *veyne* in swich *licour*
Of which *vertu engendred* is the *flour;*
Whan Zephirus eek with his swete breeth   5
Inspired hath in every holt and heeth
The *tendre* croppes, and the yonge sonne
Hath in the Ram his half[e] *cours* yronne,
And smale foweles maken *melodye,*
That slepen al the nyght with open eye—   10
So priketh hem *nature* in hir *corages—*
Thanne longen folk to goon on *pilgrimage[s]*,
And *Palmeres* for to seken *straunge* strondes,
To ferne halwes kowthe in sondry londes
And *specially* from every shires ende   15
Of Engelond to Caunturbury they wende
The hooly blisful martir for to seke
That hem hath holpen whan þat they were seeke.
Bifil that in that *seson* on a day,
In Southwerk at the *Tabard* as I lay   20
Redy to wenden on my *pilgrymage*
To Caunterbury with ful *devout corage,*
At nyght were come in to that *hostelrye*
Wel nyne and twenty in a *compaignye*
Of sondry folk by *aventure* y-falle   25
In felaweshipe, and *pilgrimes* were they alle
That toward Caunterbury wolden ryde.[36]

In these twenty-seven lines there are 189 words. Counting *pilgrimage*

---

[36] From the Ellesmere MS (now in the Huntington Library, California), as given in *A Six-Text Print of Chaucer's Canterbury Tales,* Part I, ed. Frederick J. Furnivall for the Chaucer Society (London, 1868), p. 1. As in other citations from old texts, except for the chapter from Banckes's *Herball* (pp. 169–70), *v* has been used for older *u* with consonantal value. A necessary *-e* has been added in the eighth line and an obvious omission of *-s* rectified in the twelfth. Note the scribe's inconsistent use of *th* and þ in the eighteenth line; other manuscripts of the *Canterbury Tales* use þ much more than does the Ellesmere.

and *corage* only once, twenty-four[37] of these words come from French. Such a percentage is doubtless also fairly typical of cultivated London usage in Chaucer's time.[38] It will be noted, as has been pointed out before, that the indispensable, often used, everyday words—auxiliary verbs, pronouns, and particles—are of native origin. To the fourteenth century, as Miss Serjeantson points out (p. 136), we owe most of the large number of still current abstract terms from French ending in *-ance, -ence, -ant, -ent, -tion, -ity, -ment* and those beginning in *con-, de-, dis-, ex-, pre-,* and the like, though some of these do not actually show up in writing for another century or so.

LATER FRENCH LOAN-WORDS

Loans from French since the late seventeenth century are, as we should expect, less completely naturalized by and large than most of the older loans which have been cited, though some, like *cigarette, picnic, police,* and *soup,* seem commonplace enough. These later loans[39] also include *aide-de-camp, amateur, ballet, baton, beau, bouillon, boulevard, brochure, brunette,*[40] *bureau, café, camouflage, chaise longue* (see p. 293), *champagne, chaperon* (in French, a hood or cap formerly worn by women),[41] *chemisette,*[42] *chi-chi* 'chic gone haywire,' *chiffonier* (in France, a rag-picker), *chute, cliché, commandant, communiqué, connoisseur, coupé* ('cut off,' past participle of *couper,*

[37] *Aprille* is from Latin, but the French form with *v* for Latin *p* was also widely current in Chaucer's day, occurring (as *Averylle*) in one of the better MSS of the *Canterbury Tales*. Regardless of the written form, the word is to be stressed on the first syllable and the final *e* is not to be pronounced.

[38] According to Serjeantson, "the proportion of French words used by Chaucer varies, sometimes being ten or eleven per cent, and sometimes rising as high as fifteen per cent" (p. 151).

[39] In the forms cited, the French accents and other diacritics have been used, though many of the words cited with such markings are now printed without them in English.

[40] Its antonym *blond(e)* occurs as early as the late fifteenth century.

[41] The English meaning is explained, doubtless correctly, as deriving from the notion that a married woman shields the younger girl as a hood shields the face. (See *OED*, s.v. *chaperon* 3, quotation for 1864.)

[42] *Chemise* is of Middle English introduction, though pronounced as if modern. *Shimmy,* both for the undergarment and the wiggling dance of the 1920's, is a back formation from it, like *shay* from *chaise,* which because of the final sibilant was mistakenly regarded as a plural.

used of a closed car with short body and practically always pronounced [kup] in American English), *coupon, crêpe, crochet, débris, début(ante), de luxe, dénouement, détour, élite, embonpoint,*[43] *encore, ensemble, entrée, envoy, etiquette, fiancé(e), flair, foyer* (British ['fwɑje] or ['fɔɪje]; American ['fɔɪər]), *fuselage, genre, glacier, grippe, hangar, hors d'oeuvre, impasse, invalid, laissez-faire, liaison, limousine, lingerie, massage, matinée,*[44] *mêlée, ménage, menu, morale, morgue, naïve, négligé* (as *negligee*), *nuance, passé, penchant, plateau, première, protégé, rapport, ration,*[45] *ravine, repartee, repertoire, reservoir, restaurant, reveille* (British [rɪ'vɛlɪ]; American ['rɛvəli]), *revue, risqué, roué, rouge, saloon* (and its less thoroughly Anglicized variant *salon*), *savant, savoir faire, souvenir, suède, surveillance, svelte, tête-à-tête, vignette,* and *vis-à-vis.* There are also a fairish number of loan translations from French, for example *trial balloon* (*ballon d'essai*), *marriage of convenience* (*mariage de convenance*), and *that goes without saying* (*ça va sans dire*).[46] The suffix *-ville* in the names of so many American towns is of course of French origin; of the American love for it, Matthew Arnold declared, with some justice: "The mere nomenclature of the country acts upon a cultivated person like the incessant pricking of pins. What people in whom the sense of beauty and fitness was quick could have invented, or could tolerate, the hideous names ending in *ville,* the Briggsvilles, Higginsvilles, Jacksonvilles, rife from Maine to Florida; the jumble of unnatural and inappropriate names everywhere?"[47] *Chowder, depot* 'railway station,' *gopher, levee* 'em-

---

[43] Compare the loan translation *in good point,* which occurs much earlier, for example, in Chaucer's description of the Monk in line 200 of the General Prologue of the *Canterbury Tales:* "He was a lord ful faᵗ and in good poynt."

[44] Earlier, as its derivation from *matin* implies, a morning performance.

[45] The traditional pronunciation, riming with *fashion,* indicates the French origin of this word meaning originally 'portion of food given to a soldier.' It has acquired within the past twenty years a pronunciation based on a mistaken analogy with Latin-derived *nation* and *station,* which came into English during the medieval period.

[46] The last two examples are cited by Winfred P. Lehmann, *Historical Linguistics* (New York, 1962), pp. 215–16.

[47] *Civilization in the United States* (Boston, 1888), reprinted in *American Social History as Recorded by British Travellers,* ed. Allan Nevins (New York, 1923), p. 509. Pylesville, in Harford County, Maryland, would really have set the pins to pricking in Arnold's soul. Fortunately, he seems not to have encountered this seat of American culture and fashion.

bankment,' *picayune, prairie, praline, shivaree (charivari),* and *voyageur* are Americanisms of French origin.

LOAN-WORDS FROM SPANISH

English has taken words from various other European languages as well, as we should expect in the light of the external history of the language, involving as this does the contact of English-speaking people with Continental Europeans as a result of cultural exchanges of one sort or another, of trade, of exploration, and of colonization. Moreover, a good many non-European words entered English by way of Spanish, and to a smaller extent by way of Portuguese, mostly from the sixteenth century on. Spanish words and words of Spanish transmission, many coming from the New World, include *alligator (el lagarto* 'the lizard'), *anchovy, armada, armadillo* (literally 'little armed one'), *avocado* (ultimately Nahuatl *ahuacatl,* confused with Sp. *abogado* 'advocate, lawyer'), *barbecue, barracuda, bolero, cannibal (Caribal* 'Caribbean'), *cargo, cask (casque), castanet, chocolate* (ultimately Nahuatl), *cigar, cocoa, cockroach* (see p. 289), *cordovan* (leather; an older form, *cordwain,* comes through French), *cork,*[48] *corral, desperado, domino* 'cloak or mask,' *embargo, flotilla, galleon, guitar, junta, key* 'reef' *(cayo), maize* (ultimately Arawak), *mescal* (ultimately Nahuatl), *mantilla, mosquito* 'little fly,' *mulatto, negro, palmetto, peccadillo, plaza,*[49] *potato* (ultimately Haitian), *punctilio, sherry* (see p. 284), *silo, sombrero, tango, tomato* (ultimately Nahuatl), *tornado,*[50] *tortilla,* and *vanilla*—many of these, for instance *barbecue, barracuda,* and *tortilla,* being more familiar to Americans than to the English, though they may have occurred first in British sources. A good many words were adopted from Spanish in the nineteenth century by Americans: *adobe, bonanza, bronco, buckaroo (vaquero), calaboose (calabozo), canyon, chaparral* 'scrub oak' (whence *chaps,* or *shaps,* 'leather pants worn by cowboys as protection against such vegetation'), *cinch, frijoles, hacienda, hoosegow (juzgado,* in Mexican Spanish 'jail'),

[48] Occurring somewhat earlier than the other words cited, this is an aphetic form of *alcorque* 'cork shoe,' taken into Spanish from Arabic but ultimately going back to Latin *quercus* 'oak.' The *American College Dictionary* suggests a blending with Spanish *corcho,* from Lat. *cortex* 'bark.'

[49] From Latin *platēa,* also the ultimate source of the English loan-word *place,* which occurs in Old English times, and of the Italian loan-word *piazza.*

[50] A blend of *tronada* 'thunderstorm' and *tornar* 'to turn.'

lariat (la reata 'the rope'), *lasso, mesa, mustang, patio, pinto* 'bean,' *pueblo, ranch, rodeo, sierra, siesta, stampede (estampida), stevedore (estivador* 'packer'), *vamoose (vamos* 'let's go'). *Tamale, mescal,* and *mesquite* are ultimately Nahuatl, entering American English before the nineteenth century, like similar loans in British English, by way of Spanish. *Chili,* also of Nahuatl origin, entered British English in the seventeenth century, but it is likely, as M. M. Mathews points out, that its occurrence in American English in the nineteenth century— "at the time we began to make first hand acquaintance with the Spanish speakers on our Southwestern border"—is not a continuation of the British tradition, but represents an independent borrowing of a word for which Americans had had till that time very little if any use.[51] No words came into English direct from Portuguese until the modern period; those which have been adopted include *albino, flamingo, madeira* (from the place), *molasses, pagoda, palaver,* and *pickaninny (pequenino* 'very small'). There are a few others considerably less familiar.

LOAN-WORDS FROM ITALIAN

From yet another Romance language, Italian, English has acquired a good many words, including much of our musical terminology. As early as the sixteenth century *duo, fugue, madrigal, violin,* and *viola da gamba* 'viol for the leg' appear in English; in the seventeenth century, *allegro, largo, opera, piano*[52] 'soft,' *presto, recitative, solo,* and *sonata;*[53] in the eighteenth, when interest in Italian music reached its apogee in England, *adagio, andante, aria, cantata, concerto, contralto, crescendo, diminuendo, duet, falsetto, finale, forte*[54] 'loud,' *libretto, maestro, obbligato, oratorio, rondo,*[55] *soprano, staccato, tempo, trio,*

[51] *Some Sources of Southernisms* (University, Ala., 1948), p. 18.

[52] As the name of the instrument, a clipped form of eighteenth-century *pianoforte,* the earliest occurrence cited by the *OED* is in 1803.

[53] In regard to this word the *OED* manages to antedate itself by eleven years. Its first citation is from 1694, though elsewhere (s.v. *piano* 'soft') there is a citation of Purcell's *Sonnatas* [*sic*] *in Three Parts,* the date of which is 1683.

[54] The identically written word pronounced with final *e* silent and meaning 'strong point' is from French.

[55] The literary terms *rondeau* and *rondel* are from French. Though their English meanings differ, they are simply variant forms, *rondeau* being the later development. *Rondeau* was taken into Italian from French and written *rondo,* entering English in this form as a musical term.

trombone, viola, and *violoncello;*[56] and in the nineteenth, *alto, cadenza, diva, legato, piccolo, pizzicato, prima donna,* and *vibrato.* Other loan-words from Italian include *artichoke, balcony, balloon, bandit, bravo, broccoli, cameo, canto, carnival, casino, cupola, dilettante,*[57] *firm* 'business association,' *fresco, gondola, grotto, incognito, inferno, influenza, lagoon, lava, malaria (mala aria* 'bad air'), *maraschino, miniature, motto, pergola, piazza, portico, regatta, replica, scope, stanza, stiletto, studio, torso, umbrella, vendetta,* and *volcano,* not to mention those words of ultimate Italian origin, like *cartoon, citron, corridor, gazette,* and *porcelain,* which have entered English by way of French. *Macaroni* (Mod. It. *maccheroni*) came into English in the sixteenth century,[58] *vermicelli* in the seventeenth, and *spaghetti* and *gorgonzola* (from the town) in the nineteenth. *Ravioli* (as *rafiol*) occurs in English in the fifteenth century, and later as *raviol* in the seventeenth century. Both forms are labeled obsolete and rare; it is indeed likely that the single occurrence of each form cited by the *OED* is the only one. The modern form thus can hardly be considered as continuing an older tradition, but is instead a reborrowing, perhaps by way of American English in the twentieth century. *Lasagna* and *pizza* are also doubtless of twentieth-century introduction into English—probably in America, where Italian cooking is more popular than in England, despite the excellent Italian restaurants in Soho.

LOAN-WORDS FROM HIGH GERMAN

High German has made comparatively little impact upon English. Much of the vernacular of geology and mineralogy is of German origin, for instance *cobalt, feldspar* (a half-translation of *Feldspath*), *gneiss, kleinite* (from Karl Klein, mineralogist), *lawine* 'avalanche,' *loess, meerschaum, nickel* (originally *Kupfernickel,* perhaps 'copper demon,' partially translated as *kopparnickel* by the Swedish mineralogist Von Cronstedt, from whose writings the abbreviated form entered English in 1755), *quartz, seltzer* (ultimately a derivative of Selters, near Wiesbaden), and *zinc. Carouse* occurs in English as early as the sixteenth century, from the German *gar aus* 'all out,' meaning the same

[56] The clipped form *cello* does not occur until the late nineteenth century.

[57] Frequently pronounced as if French, by analogy with *debutante.*

[58] Its doublet *macaroon,* though designating quite a different food, entered English by way of French in the seventeenth century. *Maccaroni* was the plural of *maccarone;* the singular form was taken into French and adapted as *macaron,* whence the English form *macaroon.*

as *bottoms up*. Originally adverbial, it almost immediately came to be used as a verb, and shortly afterwards as a noun. Other words taken from German include such culinary terms as *sauerkraut* (occurring first in British English, but the English never cared particularly for the dish, and the word may to all intents and purposes be considered an Americanism, independently reborrowed), *noodle* (*Nudel*), *delicatessen, wienerwurst, braunschweiger, schnitzel, pretzel, zwieback,* and *pumpernickel*. *Liederkranz, knackwurst,* and *sauerbraten* are fairly well known, but can hardly be considered completely naturalized. *Liverwurst* is a half-translation of *Leberwurst*. *Hamburger* and *frankfurter* have been discussed in another connection (pp. 270–71). The vernacular of drinking includes *lager, bock* (from *Eimbocker Bier* 'beer of Eimbock,' shortened in German to *Bockbier*), *schnapps, kirsch(wasser),* and *katzenjammer* 'hangover' (though more widely known from *The Katzenjammer Kids*). Other words from German include *drill* 'fabric,' *plunder* (*plündern*), *hamster, waltz, landau* (from the place of that name), and the dog names *dachshund, Doberman(n) pinscher, poodle* (*Pudel*), and *spitz*. *Alpenstock, edelweiss, hinterland, leitmotiv, poltergeist, rucksack, schottische, yodel (jodeln),* and the not yet thoroughly naturalized *Gestalt, Weltanschauung* and *Weltansicht*. *Ablaut, umlaut,* and *schwa* (ultimately Hebrew) have been frequently used as technical terms in this book. *Blitz(krieg)* and *Luftwaffe* had an infamous success in 1940 and 1941, but they have since receded.

Seminar and *semester* are of course ultimately Latin, but they entered American English by way of German—*seminar,* as M. M. Mathews says, probably "independent of the British borrowing of about the same date,"[59] that is, the late nineteenth century, when many American and English scholars went to Germany in pursuit of their doctorates. *Semester* is known in England, but the English have little use for it save in reference to foreign universities. *Academic freedom* is a loan translation of *akademische Freiheit*. *Bummeln* is used by German students to mean 'to loiter, waste time,' and may be the source of American English *to bum* and the noun in the sense 'loafer,' though this need not be an academic importation.

On a less elevated level, American English uses such expressions as *gesundheit* (when someone has sneezed), and *nix* (*nichts*), and German-Americans have doubtless been responsible for adapting the German

[59] *A Dictionary of Americanisms on Historical Principles* (Chicago, 1951).

suffix -*fest*, as in *Sängerfest*, to English uses, as in *songfest* and *gabfest*. *Biergarten* has undergone translation in *beer garden; kindergarten* is frequently pronounced as though the last element were English *garden*. Yiddish (that is, *Jüdisch* 'Jewish') has been responsible for the introduction of a number of German words and minced forms of German words, some of them having special meanings in Yiddish: *kibitzer, phooey, schlemiel, schmaltz, schnozzle, shmo, shnook,* and others less widely known to non-Jews. By way of the Germans from the Palatinate who settled in southern Pennsylvania in the early part of the eighteenth century come a number of terms of German origin little known in other parts of the United States, such as *sots* 'yeast,' *snits* 'fruit cut for drying,' and *smearcase* 'cottage cheese' (*Schmierkäs*). *Kriss Kingle* or *Kriss Kringle* (*Christkindl* 'Christ child') and *to dunk* have become nationally known.

LOAN-WORDS FROM LOW GERMAN

Dutch and other forms of Low German have contributed a number of words to English, to a large extent by way of the commercial relationships existing between the English and the Dutch and Flemish-speaking peoples from the Middle Ages on. Even before the beginning of the Modern English period the words *boor* (*boer*), *booze, brake, hop* 'twining plant,' *kit, luck, pickle, spool,* and *snap* occur, among others less well known; later, *brandywine, cambric, duffel* (from the name of a place), *easel, frolic* (*vrolijk* 'joyful,' cognate with Ger. *fröhlich*), *gimp, gin* (short for *genever*, borrowed by the Dutch from Old French, ultimately Lat. *juniperus* 'juniper'; *genever* was confused in English with *Geneva*), *isinglass* (a folk-etymologized form of *hysenblas*, see p. 290), *landscape, mahlstick, rant, skate, split, wagon* (the related OE *wægn* gives modern *wain*), and *wiseacre* (Middle Dutch *wijsseggher* 'soothsayer'). It is not surprising in view of their eminence in seafaring activities that the Dutch should have contributed a number of nautical terms, as the Scandinavians had done earlier, though these latter have not survived. From Dutch nautical usage come *buoy, cruise, deck* (Dutch *dec* 'roof,' then in English 'roof of a ship,' a meaning which later got into Dutch), *luff, marline* (the name of the fish, *marlin*, is short for *marlinespike*), *pea jacket, scow, skipper* (*schipper* 'shipper, that is, master of a ship'), *sloop, taffrail* (see p. 290), *yacht,* and *yawl*. *Trek, commandeer, commando, outspan,* and *apartheid* have come to English from South African Dutch (Afrikaans). Americanisms of Dutch origin include *boss* (in the beginning a democratic euphemism to avoid having to refer to one's master as one's master), *bowery, coleslaw* (*koolsla* 'cabbage salad'), *cooky, dope, pit* 'fruit stone,' *Santa Claus* (*Sante Klaas,* from *Sant Nikolaas* 'Saint Nicholas'), *sleigh, snoop, spook,* and *waffle.*

LOAN-WORDS FROM THE EAST

As early as Old English times words from the East doubtless trickled into the language, then always by way of other languages. *Mancus* 'coin' and *ealfara* 'pack horse' have been cited as commercial loans from Arabic. Neither word has survived, and the second occurs only once in the Old English writings which have come down to us.[60] A number of words ultimately Arabic, most of them having to do in one way or another with science or with commerce, came in during the Middle English period, usually by way of French or Latin. These include *amber, camphor, cipher,*[61] *cotton, lute, mattress, orange, saffron, sugar, syrup,* and *zenith.* The Arabic definite article *al* is retained in one form or another in *almanac, alchemy, alembic, algorism, alkali, azimuth* (as [for *al*] plus *sumūt* 'the ways'), *elixir* (*el* [for *al*] plus *iksīr* 'the philosopher's stone'), and *hazard* (*az* [for *al*] plus *zahr* 'the die'). In *admiral,* occurring first in Middle English, the Arabic article occurs in the final syllable: the word is an abbreviation of some such phrase as *amīr-al-baḥr* 'commander (of) the sea.' Through confusion with Latin *admīrābilis* 'admirable,' the word has acquired a *d*; *d*-less forms occur, however, as late as the sixteenth century, though ultimately the blunder with *d*, which occurs in the first known recording of the word—in Layamon's *Brut,* written around the end of the twelfth century—was to prevail. *Alcohol* (*al-kuḥl* 'the kohl, that is, powder of antimony for staining the eyelids'),[62] *alcove,* and *algebra,* all beginning with the article, were introduced in early Modern times, along with a good many words without the article, for instance *apricot, assassin* (originally 'hashish-eater'), *caliber, candy, carat, caraway,*

---

[60] Serjeantson, p. 214.

[61] From Arabic *ṣifr* by way of Medieval Latin. The Italians modified the same Arabic word as *zero,* by way of **zefiro* (*OED*). This Italian form entered English in the early Modern period.

[62] The modern meaning, which occurred in the European languages borrowing the word, has come about in a rather complicated way. Its development from a specific powder to any powder to essence (or "spirit," as in obsolete *alcohol of wine*) to the spirituous element in beverages is traced in the *OED* for anyone who wishes to follow it.

fakir, giraffe, garble, harem, hashish, henna, jinn (plural of *jinnī*), *lemon, magazine* (ultimately an Arabic plural form meaning 'storehouses'), *minaret, mohair, sherbet,* and *tariff.* Some of these were transmitted through Italian, others through French; some were taken directly from Arabic. *Coffee,* ultimately Arabic, was taken into English by way of Turkish. Other Semitic languages have contributed little directly, though a number of words ultimately Hebrew have come to us by way of French. Regardless of the method of their transmission, most of us must be aware of the ultimate or immediate Hebrew origin of *amen, behemoth, cabbala, cherub, hallelujah, jubilee, rabbi, Sabbath, seraph, shekel,* and *shibboleth.* Both *Jehovah* (*Jahveh*) and *Satan* are Hebrew. Yiddish uses a very large number of Hebrew words and seems to have been the medium of transmission for *kosher, tokus* 'backside,' *mazuma, matzo* (plural *matzoth*), and *goy.*

Persian and Sanskrit are not exotic in the same sense as Arabic, for both are Indo-European; yet the regions in which they were spoken were far removed from England, and they were to all intents and purposes highly exotic. Consequently, such words as Persian *caravan* (in the nineteenth century clipped to *van*) and *bazaar* must have seemed as exotic to the English in the sixteenth century, when they first became current, as Chinese *kumquat* and Japanese *sukiyaki* seem to most people past middle age today. *Tiger, paradise, satrap, scarlet, azure, taffeta,* and *musk* occur, among others, in the Middle English period. None of these are direct loans, coming directly from Latin or Old French; later, from the same two direct sources, come *naphtha, tiara,* and a few Persian words borrowed through Turkish, such as *giaour.* In addition, some Persian words were borrowed in India: *cummerbund* 'loin-band,' which first appears (as *combarband*) in the early seventeenth century, to reappear within the last thirty years or so as a name for an article of men's semiformal evening dress frequently replacing the low-cut waistcoat. The word in this sense obviously returned to English by way of Englishmen posted for one reason or another in India, for the last citation in the *OED* is from 1869 and defines it in effect as a belt worn to protect one from the onslaught of cholera; it is similar with *seersucker,* an Indian modification of Persian *shīr o shakkar* 'milk and sugar,' the name of a fabric which came into vogue in America less than half a century ago, and with *khaki* 'dusty,' recorded in English first in 1857 but not widely known in America until much later, when it was at first pronounced in the traditional fashion ['kɑkɪ], though ['kækɪ] seems to prevail nowadays. Direct from

Persian, in addition to *caravan* and *bazaar*, come *dervish, divan, shah,* and *shawl. Chess* is directly from Old French, an aphetic form of *esches,* but the word is ultimately Persian, as is *check* (in all its senses), from the variant Old French form *eschecs.* The words go back to Persian *shāh* 'king,' which was taken into Arabic in the specific sense 'the king in the game of chess,' whence *shāh māt* 'the king is dead,' the source of *checkmate.* The derivative *exchequer* (OF *eschequier* 'chess board') came about through the fact that accounts used to be reckoned on a table marked with squares like a chess (or *checker,* in British English usually *chequer*) board. *Rook* 'chess piece' is also ultimately derived from Persian *rukhkh* 'castle.'

From Sanskrit come, along with a few others, *avatar, mahatma, swastika,* and *yoga* ('union,' akin to English *yoke*). *Swastika* denotes in English a symbol of the Nazi party in Germany, but is actually little known in that country, where the name of the figure is usually *Hakenkreuz* 'hook-cross'; the word occurs in English first in the latter half of the nineteenth century. It usually has [æ] in the first syllable in British English, in contrast to American [ɑ]. Sanskrit *dvandva, sandhi,* and *svarabhakti* are pretty much confined to the vernacular of linguistics; nonlinguists get along without them very well indeed. *Ginger,* which occurs in Old English (*gingifere*) is ultimately Prakrit. From Hindustani come *bandanna, chintz, cot, dinghy, dungaree, gunny* 'sacking,' *juggernaut, jungle, loot, maharaja* (and *maharani*), *nabob, pajamas, pundit, sahib, sari,* and *shampoo,* along with a number of other words which are much better known in England than in America (for instance *pukka, durbar, babu,* and *bangle* 'claspless ringlike bracelet'[63]). *Pal* is from Romany, or Gypsy, which as we have seen (p. 83) is an Indic dialect. The non-Indo-European languages called Dravidian spoken in southern India have contributed a few fairly well-known words, for instance *copra, curry, mango, pariah,* and *teak.* Of these, *curry* and *pariah,* from Tamil, are direct loans; the others have come to us by way of Portuguese, *mango* from Portuguese by way of Malay.

Other English words from languages spoken in the Orient are comparatively few in number, but some are quite well known. *Silk* may be ultimately from Chinese, although there is no known etymon in that language; as *seoloc* or *sioloc* the word came into English in Old English times from Baltic or Slavic. Miss Serjeantson cites *tea, catchup*

---

[63] This last word, while not unknown, is comparatively rare in American English, in which any ornament for the wrist is called a bracelet.

(*ketchup*),[64] and *japan* 'varnish' (from the Chinese name of the country, called *Nippon* by the Japanese), along with the names of some varieties of tea (*pekoe, oolong, bohea, souchong*) (p. 237). *Ginseng, kowtow, litchi,* and *pongee* have come direct from Chinese, along with the Americanisms of Chinese origin *chow, chow mein, chop suey,* and *tong* 'secret society.' From Japanese have come *banzai, geisha, hara-kiri, (jin)ricksha, kimono, sake* 'liquor,' *samurai,* and *soy(a),* along with the ultimately Chinese *tycoon, judo,* and *ju-jitsu. Kamikaze* had a certain vogue during World War II. The word, designating so-called suicide pilots, literally means 'divine wind.'

From the languages spoken in the islands of the Pacific come *bamboo, gingham, launch,* and *mangrove,* and others mostly adopted before the beginning of the nineteenth century by way of French, Portuguese, Spanish, or Dutch. *Rattan* (as *rattoon*), direct from Malay, appears first in Pepys's *Diary,* where it designates, not the wood, but a cane made of it: "Mr. Hawley did give me a little black rattoon, painted and gilt" (September 13, 1660). Polynesian *taboo* and *tattoo*[65] 'decorative permanent skin marking,' along with a few other words from the same source, appear in English around the time of Captain James Cook's voyages (1768–79); they occur first in his journals. *Ukulele* is Polynesian, entering American English by way of Hawaii around 1900. Captain Cook also first recorded Australian *kangaroo; boomerang* (as *wo-mur-rāng*), from the same source, occurs first somewhat later. *Budgerigar,* also Australian and designating a kind of parrot, is well known in England, where it is frequently clipped to *budgie* by those who fancy the birds, usually known as *parakeets* in America.

LOAN-WORDS FROM THE AFRICAN NEGROES

A few words from those languages spoken by Negroes on the west coast of Africa have entered English by way of Portuguese and Spanish, notably *banana* and *yam,* both appearing towards the end of the sixteenth century. It is likely, as M. M. Mathews points out, that *yam* entered the vocabulary of American English independently. In the South, where it is used more frequently than elsewhere, it designates

---

[64] The variant *catsup* has given rise to a pronunciation based on its spelling.

[65] Not the same as *tattoo* 'drum or bugle signal, (later) military entertainment' which is from Dutch *tap toe* 'the tap (is) to,' that is, 'the taproom is closed.'

not just any kind of sweet potato, as in other parts, but a red sweet potato, which is precisely the meaning it has in the Gullah form *yambi*. Hence Mathews thinks, very plausibly, that this word was introduced into Southern American English direct from Africa, even though there is no question of its Portuguese transmission in earlier English: "Our word came to us directly from headquarters, that is from Africa" he declares, pointing out that "we had in our midst the very people who gave the word to the Portuguese" (pp. 111–12). *Voodoo,* with its variant *hoodoo,* is likewise of African origin and introduced by way of American English. *Gorilla* is apparently African: it first occurs in English in the *Boston Journal of Natural History* in 1847, according to Mathews' *Dictionary of Americanisms,* though a plural form *gorillae* occurs in 1799 in British English. *Juke* (more correctly *jook*) and *jazz* are Americanisms of African origin. Both were more or less disreputable when first introduced, but have in course of time lost most of their earlier sexual connotations. Other African words transmitted into American English are *banjo, buckra, cooter* 'turtle,' the synonymous *goober* and *pinder* 'peanut,' *gumbo, jigger* 'sand flea,' recorded in the dictionaries as *chigoe,* and *zombi. Samba* and *rumba* are ultimately African, coming to English by way of Brazilian Portuguese and Cuban Spanish respectively. There can no longer be much doubt that *tote* is of African origin; the evidence presented by Lorenzo Dow Turner[66] seems fairly conclusive.

OTHER SOURCES:
SLAVIC, HUNGARIAN, TURKISH,
AND AMERICAN INDIAN

Very minor sources of the English vocabulary are Slavic, Hungarian, Turkish, and American Indian, with few words from these sources used in English contexts without reference to the countries from which they have been borrowed. Most of these have been borrowed during the Modern period, since 1500, and practically all by way of other languages. Thus Slavic *sable* comes to us in Middle English times not direct but by way of French. Later we acquired, also indirectly, *polka. Astrakhan* and *mammoth* are direct from Russian. Other Russian words which are known but hardly thoroughly naturalized are *bolshevik, borzoi, czar* (ultimately Lat. *Caesar*), *intelligentsia* (ultimately Latin), *kopeck, muzhik, pogrom, ruble, samovar, soviet,*

[66] *Africanisms in the Gullah Dialect* (Chicago, 1949), p. 203.

steppe, tovarisch, troika, tundra, ukase, vodka, and the fairly recent *sputnik.* Miss Serjeantson cites *hussar* and *coach* as Hungarian loans (p. 211); the first of these is ultimately from Italian *corsaro* 'corsair,'[67] but the second is apparently a direct loan from *kocsi. Goulash* and *paprika* are also direct loans; both are too recent to be entered in the *OED* proper, though they are in the 1933 Supplement from 1900 and 1898 respectively. *Jackal,* ultimately Persian, comes to English by way of Turkish; *khan* occurs as a direct loan quite early. Other Turkish words used in English include *fez, horde,* and *tulip,* from *tulipa(nt),* a variant of *tülbend* (taken by Turkish from Persian *dulband*), coming into English in modified form as *turban(d).* The flower was so called because it was thought to look like the Turkish headgear. *Coffee,* as has been pointed out, is ultimately Arabic, but comes to us direct from Turkish; the same is true of *kismet.* American Indian words do not loom large, even in American English, though many have occurred in American English writings. The noble savage has no longer much place in the American consciousness, and most of the 132 words borrowed from Algonquian dialects compiled by Alexander F. Chamberlain in 1902[68] have now gone out of use or are but dimly known, for instance *sagamore, squantum,* and *peag.* Many place names are of course taken from Indian languages.

ENGLISH REMAINS ENGLISH

Enough has been written to indicate the cosmopolitanism of the present English vocabulary. Yet English remains English in every essential respect: the words that all of us use over and over again, the grammatical structures in which we couch our observations upon practically everything under the sun remain as distinctively English as

---

[67] *Corsair* comes into English by way of French.

[68] Many of these are cited by H. L. Mencken in *The American Language, Supplement I* (New York, 1945), pp. 167–71. Those which have survived are, thanks to the European vogue of James Fenimore Cooper, about as well known transatlantically as in America: they include *moccasin, papoose, squaw, tomahawk,* and *toboggan.* Others with perhaps fewer literary associations are *opossum, skunk, moose, terrapin, pecan,* and *woodchuck.* Muskhogean words are more or less confined to the southern American states, for instance *bayou, catalpa,* and a good many proper names like *Tallahassee, Tuscaloosa,* and *Tombigbee.* Loans from Nahuatl, almost invariably of Spanish transmission, have been included as if Spanish (pp. 341–42).

they were in the days of Alfred the Great. What has been acquired from other languages has not always been particularly worth gaining: no one could prove by any set of objective standards that *army* is a "better" word than *dright* or *here*, which it displaced, or that *advice* is any better than the similarly displaced *rede*, or that *mercy* is any better than *mildheartness* (OE *mildheortnes*) and *loving-kindness*, or that *to contend* is any better than *to flite*. The fact that we have taken words from many sources is indicative of a cosmopolitan attitude which is the very opposite of the lexical provincialism of, say, Icelandic and to a lesser extent German. Those who think that *manual* is a better, or more beautiful, or more intellectual word than English *handbook* are of course entitled to their opinion. But such esthetic preferences are purely matters of style and have nothing to do with the subtle patternings which make one language different from another. For, as has been demonstrated time and again in this book, language is nothing so simple as words. The words we choose are nonetheless of tremendous interest in themselves, and they throw a good deal of light upon our cultural history.

But with all its manifold new words from other tongues, English could never have become anything but English. And as such it has given to the world, among many other things, some of the best books the world has ever known. It is not unlikely, in the light of writings by Englishmen in earlier times, that this would have been so even if we had never taken any words from outside the word hoard which has come down to us from those times. That what we have borrowed has given greater wealth to our word stock no man can gainsay, but the true Englishness of our mother tongue has in no way been lessened by such loans, as those who speak and write it lovingly can never forget.

Selected Bibliography

ABBOTT, E. A. *A Shakespearian Grammar.* London, 1897.

ADAMS, RAMON R. *Western Words: A Dictionary of the Range, Cow Camp and Trail.* Norman, Okla., 1944.

ALEXANDER, HENRY. *The Story of Our Language.* Toronto, 1940.

ALSTON, R. C. *An Introduction to Old English.* Evanston, Ill., n.d.

The American College Dictionary. New York, 1947.

American Speech: A Quarterly of Linguistic Usage. 1925–date.

ARMOUR, J. S. *The Genesis and Growth of English: An Outline of Philology for Students.* New York, 1935.

ARMSTRONG, LILIAS E., and IDA C. WARD. *A Handbook of English Intonation.* 2nd ed. Cambridge, Eng., 1931.

ATWOOD, E. BAGBY. *The Regional Vocabulary of Texas.* Austin, Tex., 1962.

———. *A Survey of Verb Forms in the Eastern United States.* Ann Arbor, Mich., 1953.

BARTLETT, JOHN RUSSELL. *Dictionary of Americanisms: A Glossary of Words and Phrases Usually Regarded as Peculiar to the United States.* 2nd ed. Boston, 1859.

BAUGH, ALBERT C. *A History of the English Language.* 2nd ed. New York, 1957.

BEHAGHEL, OTTO. *A Short Historical Grammar of the German Language,* trans. Emil Trechmann. London, 1899. (Original title *Deutsche Sprache.*)

BENDER, HAROLD H. *The Home of the Indo-Europeans.* Princeton, N.J., 1932.

BENSE, J. F. *A Dictionary of the Low-Dutch Element in the English Vocabulary,* pts. I–V. London, 1926–39.

BERREY, LESTER V., and MELVIN VAN DEN BARK. *The American Thesaurus of Slang.* 2nd ed. New York, 1953.

BLAIR, PETER HUNTER. *An Introduction to Anglo-Saxon England.* Cambridge, Eng., 1956.

BLOCH, BERNARD, and GEORGE L. TRAGER. *Outline of Linguistic Analysis.* Special Publications of the Linguistic Society of America. Baltimore, 1942.

BLOOMFIELD, LEONARD. *An Introduction to the Study of Language.* New York, 1914.

———. *Language.* New York, 1933.

BOONE, LALIA PHIPPS. *The Petroleum Dictionary.* Norman, Okla., 1952.

BRADLEY, HENRY. *The Making of English.* New York, 1904.

BROOK, G. L. *A History of the English Language.* London, 1958.

———. *An Introduction to Old English.* Manchester, Eng., 1955.

BRYANT, MARGARET M. *Current American Usage.* New York, 1962.

———. *A Functional English Grammar.* Boston, 1945.

———. *Modern English and Its Heritage.* 2nd ed. New York, 1962.

BÜLBRING, KARL D. *Altenglisches Elementarbuch. I. Teil: Lautlehre.* Heidelberg, 1902.

CAMPBELL, A. *Old English Grammar.* Oxford, 1959.

CARROLL, JOHN B. *The Study of Language: A Survey of Linguistics and Related Disciplines in America.* Cambridge, Mass., 1953.

CHOMSKY, NOAM. *Syntactic Structures.* The Hague, 1962.

CRAIGIE, W. A. *English Spelling: Its Rules and Reasons.* New York, 1927.

———, and JAMES ROOT HULBERT, eds. *A Dictionary of American English on Historical Principles.* 4 vols. Chicago, 1938–44.

CURME, GEORGE O. *A Grammar of the English Language,* Vols. II and III. Boston, 1931, 1935.

———. *Principles and Practice of English Grammar.* New York, 1947.

DARMESTETER, ARSÈNE. *La Vie des Mots.* Paris, 1887.

DAVIES, CONSTANCE. *English Pronunciation from the Fifteenth to the Eighteenth Century.* London, 1934.

Dialect Notes: Publication of the American Dialect Society, Vols. I–VI (1890–1939).

DIRINGER, DAVID. *Writing.* London, 1962.

DOBSON, E. J. *English Pronunciation, 1500–1700.* 2 vols. Oxford, 1957.

EKWALL, EILERT. *American and British Pronunciation.* Essays and Studies on American Language and Literature, II. Upsala, 1946.

———. *The Concise Oxford Dictionary of English Place-Names.* 4th ed. Oxford, 1960.

———. *Historische neuenglische Laut- Und Formenlehre.* 3rd ed., rev. Berlin, 1956.

EMERSON, OLIVER FARRAR. *A Middle English Reader.* New and rev. ed. New York, 1948.

ENTWISTLE, WILLIAM J. *Aspects of Language.* London, 1953.

EVANS, BERGEN, and CORNELIA EVANS. *A Dictionary of Contemporary American Usage.* New York, 1957.

FARMER, JOHN S., and WILLIAM ERNEST HENLEY. *Dictionary of Slang and Its Analogues.* 7 vols. New York, 1890–1904.

FOWLER, H. W. *A Dictionary of Modern English Usage.* Oxford, 1926.

———, and F. G. FOWLER. *The King's English.* 2nd ed. Oxford, 1906.

Francis, W. Nelson. *The Structure of American English.* With a chapter on American English dialects by Raven I. McDavid, Jr. New York, 1958.

Franz, W. *Shakespeare-Grammatik.* 2nd ed. Heidelberg, 1909.

Fries, Charles Carpenter. *American English Grammar.* New York, 1940.

——. *The Structure of English.* New York, 1952.

Funk and Wagnalls New Standard Dictionary of the English Language. New York, 1925.

Galinsky, Hans. *Die Sprache des Amerikaners: Eine Einführung in die Hauptunterschiede zwischen amerikanischem und britischem English der Gegenwart.* 2 vols. Heidelberg, 1951, 1952.

Gelb, I. J. *A Study of Writing: The Foundations of Grammatology.* Chicago, 1952.

Gleason, H. A., Jr., *An Introduction to Descriptive Linguistics.* Rev. ed. New York, 1961.

Goldin, Hyman E., Frank O'Leary, and Morris Lipsius, eds. *Dictionary of American Underworld Lingo.* New York, 1950.

Gowers, Sir Ernest. *Plain Words: Their ABC.* New York, 1954.

Graff, Willem L. *Language and Languages.* New York, 1932.

Gray, Louis H. *Foundations of Language.* New York, 1939.

Greenough, James Bradstreet, and George Lyman Kittredge. *Words and Their Ways in English Speech.* New York, 1901.

Greet, W. Cabell. *World Words: Recommended Pronunciations.* New York, 1944.

[Grose, Francis]. *A Classical Dictionary of the Vulgar Tongue.* London, 1785.

Grose, Francis. *A Provincial Glossary.* 2nd ed. London, 1790.

Hall, John R. Clark. *A Concise Anglo-Saxon Dictionary.* 4th ed., with a supplement by Herbert D. Meritt. Cambridge, Eng., 1960.

Hall, Robert A., Jr. *Hands Off Pidgin English!* Sydney, Australia, 1955.

——. *Linguistics and Your Language.* New York, 1960. (Originally pub. as *Leave Your Language Alone!* [Ithaca, N.Y., 1950].)

——. *Sound and Spelling in English.* Philadelphia, 1961.

Harris, Zellig S. *Structural Linguistics.* Chicago, 1960. (Originally pub. as *Methods in Structural Linguistics* [Chicago, 1951]).

Hill, Archibald A. *Introduction to Linguistic Structures.* New York, 1958.

Hockett, Charles F. *A Course in Modern Linguistics.* New York, 1958.

Horn, Wilhelm. *Laut und Leben. Englische Lautgeschichte der neueren Zeit (1400–1950),* rev. and ed. Martin Lehnert. 2 vols. Berlin, 1954.

Horwill, H. W. *A Dictionary of Modern American Usage.* Oxford, 1935.

[Hotten, John Camden, comp.]. *The Slang Dictionary: or, The Vulgar Words, Street Phrases, and "Fast" Expressions of High and Low Society.* London, 1869.

Hughes, John P. *The Science of Language.* New York, 1962.

Hulbert, James Root. *Dictionaries: British and American.* London, 1955.

JESPERSEN, OTTO. *Efficiency in Linguistic Change.* Copenhagen, 1941.

——. *Essentials of English Grammar.* New York, 1933.

——. *Growth and Structure of the English Language.* 9th ed. Oxford, 1954. (Originally pub. 1905.)

——. *Language: Its Nature, Development and Origin.* New York, 1922.

——. *A Modern English Grammar on Historical Principles.* 7 vols. Copenhagen, 1909–49.

——. *Negation in English and Other Languages.* Copenhagen, 1917.

——. *Progress in Language, with Special Reference to English.* 2nd ed. London, 1909.

——. *Selected Writings.* London, 1962.

JONES, DANIEL. *An English Pronouncing Dictionary.* 12th ed. London, 1963.

——. *The Pronunciation of English.* 4th ed. Cambridge, Eng., 1958.

JORDAN, RICHARD. *Handbuch der mittelenglischen Grammatik,* pt. I. 2nd ed. Heidelberg, 1934.

KENNEDY, ARTHUR G. *A Bibliography of Writings on the English Language from the Beginning of Printing to the End of 1922.* Cambridge, Mass., and New Haven, Conn., 1927.

——. *Current English.* Boston, 1935.

——. *English Usage: A Study in Policy and Procedure.* New York, 1942.

KENT, ROLAND G. *Language and Philology.* New York, 1932.

——. *The Sounds of Latin: A Descriptive and Historical Phonology.* Special Publications of the Linguistic Society of America. 3rd ed. Baltimore, 1945.

KENYON, JOHN S. *American Pronunciation.* 10th ed. Ann Arbor, Mich., 1961.

——, and THOMAS ALBERT KNOTT. *A Pronouncing Dictionary of American English.* Springfield, Mass., 1951.

KLUGE, FRIEDRICH. *Etymologisches Wörterbuch der deutschen Sprache.* 4th ed. Strassburg, 1889.

——, and F. LUTZ. *English Etymology.* Strassburg, 1898.

KÖKERITZ, HELGE. *Shakespeare's Pronunciation.* New Haven, Conn., 1953.

KOZIOL, HERBERT, and FELIX HÜTTENBRENNER. *Grammatik der englischen Sprache.* Heidelberg, 1956.

KRAPP, GEORGE PHILIP. *The English Language in America.* 2 vols. New York, 1925.

——. *Modern English: Its Growth and Present Use.* New York, 1909.

——. *The Pronunciation of Standard English in America.* New York, 1919.

KRUISINGA, E. *A Handbook of Present-Day English.* Pt. I, 4th ed., Utrecht, 1925; pt. II, 5th ed., Groningen, 1931, 1932.

KURATH, HANS. *A Word Geography of the Eastern United States.* Ann Arbor, Mich., 1949.

KURATH, HANS, et al. *Handbook of the Linguistic Geography of New England*. Providence, R.I., 1939.

——, et al. *Linguistic Atlas of New England*. 3 vols. in 6. Providence, R.I., 1939–43.

——, and RAVEN I. McDAVID, JR. *The Pronunciation of English in the Atlantic States*. University of Michigan Studies in American English, No. 3. Ann Arbor, Mich., 1961.

——, and SHERMAN M. KUHN, eds. *Middle English Dictionary*. Ann Arbor, Mich., 1952 (in progress).

LAIRD, CHARLTON. *The Miracle of Language*. New York, 1957.

Language: Journal of the Linguistic Society of America. 1925–date.

LARSEN, THORLEIF, and FRANCIS C. WALKER. *Pronunciation: A Practical Guide to American Standards*. London, 1930.

LEE, DONALD W. *Functional Change in Early English*. Menasha, Wis., 1948.

LEHMANN, WINFRED P. *Historical Linguistics: An Introduction*. New York, 1962.

LEHNERT, MARTIN. *Altenglisches Elementarbuch*. 4th ed., rev. Berlin, 1959.

LEONARD, STERLING A. *Current English Usage*. NCTE Monograph, No. 1. Chicago, 1932.

——. *The Doctrine of Correctness in English Usage, 1700–1800*. University of Wisconsin Studies in Language and Literature, No. 25. Madison, Wis., 1929.

LLOYD, RICHARD J. *Northern English*. 2nd ed. Leipzig and Berlin, 1908.

LONG, RALPH B. *The Sentence and Its Parts*. Chicago, 1961.

LUICK, KARL. *Historische Grammatik der englischen Sprache*. Leipzig, 1914–40.

MALONE, KEMP. "The Phonemes of Current English." In his *Studies in Heroic Legend and in Current Speech*, pp. 226–67. Copenhagen, 1959.

MARCKWARDT, ALBERT H. *American English*. New York, 1958.

——. *Introduction to the English Language*. New York, 1942.

——, and FRED G. WALCOTT. *Facts About Current English Usage*. New York, 1938.

MATHEWS, M. M. *The Beginnings of American English*. Chicago, 1931.

——. *Some Sources of Southernisms*. University, Ala., 1948.

——, ed. *A Dictionary of Americanisms on Historical Principles*. 2 vols. Chicago, 1951.

MAYHEW, A. L., and WALTER W. SKEAT. *A Concise Dictionary of Middle English from A.D. 1150 to 1580*. Oxford, 1888.

McINTOSH, ANGUS. *An Introduction to a Survey of Scottish Dialects*. Edinburgh, 1952.

McKNIGHT, GEORGE H. *English Words and Their Background*. New York, 1923.

——. *Modern English in the Making*. New York, 1928.

MENCKEN, H. L. *The American Language.* 4th ed. New York, 1936. (Originally pub. 1919.)

——. *The American Language: The Fourth Edition and the Two Supplements,* abridged and ed. Raven I. McDavid, Jr. New York, 1963.

——. *The American Language, Supplement I.* New York, 1945.

——. *The American Language, Supplement II.* New York, 1948.

MITFORD, NANCY, ed. *Noblesse Oblige: An Enquiry into the Identifiable Characteristics of the English Aristocracy.* London, 1956.

MOHRMANN, CHRISTINE, ALF SOMMERFELT, and JOSHUA WHATMOUGH. *Trends in European and American Linguistics, 1930–1960.* Utrecht, 1961.

MOORE, SAMUEL. *Historical Outlines of English Sounds and Inflections,* rev. Albert H. Marckwardt. Ann Arbor, Mich., 1951.

——, and THOMAS ALBERT KNOTT. *The Elements of Old English,* rev. James Root Hulbert. 10th ed. Ann Arbor, Mich., 1955.

MOORHOUSE, A. C. *Writing and the Alphabet.* London, 1946.

MOSSÉ, FERNAND. *Esquisse d'une Histoire de la Langue Anglaise.* Lyon, 1947.

——. *A Handbook of Middle English,* trans. James A. Walker. Baltimore, 1952.

——. *Manuel de L'Anglais du Moyen Age des Origines au XIVe Siècle.* Pt. I, *Vieil-Anglais.* 2 vols. Paris, 1950.

Names: Journal of the American Name Society. 1953–date.

NICHOLSON, MARGARET. *A Dictionary of American-English Usage.* New York, 1957.

ONIONS, C. T. *A Shakespeare Glossary.* 2nd ed. Oxford, 1919.

ORTON, HAROLD, and WILFRED J. HALLIDAY. *Survey of English Dialects,* Vols. I and II. Leeds, 1962.

The Oxford English Dictionary. 13 vols. Oxford, 1933. (Originally pub. 1884–1928 as *A New English Dictionary on Historical Principles,* re-issued with Supplement in 1933.)

PALMER, HAROLD E. *English Intonation.* Cambridge, Eng., 1922.

PARTRIDGE, ERIC. *Adventuring Among Words.* London, 1961.

——. *A Dictionary of Slang and Unconventional English.* 3rd ed. New York, 1950.

——. *Dictionary of the Underworld.* London, 1949.

——. *Name into Word.* New York, 1950.

——. *Shakespeare's Bawdy: A Literary and Psychological Essay and a Comprehensive Glossary.* New York, 1948.

——. *Slang Today and Yesterday.* London, 1933.

——, and JOHN W. CLARK. *British and American English Since 1900.* New York, 1951.

PAUL, HERMAN. *Grundriss der germanischen Philologie.* 2 vols. Strassburg, 1891, 1893.

PEDERSEN, HOLGER. *Linguistic Science in the Nineteenth Century: Methods and Results*, trans. John Webster Spargo. Cambridge, Mass., 1931.

PERRIN, PORTER G. *Writer's Guide and Index to English*. 3rd ed. Chicago, 1959.

PIKE, KENNETH L. *The Intonation of American English*. Ann Arbor, Mich., 1945.

POOLEY, ROBERT C. *Teaching English Grammar*. New York, 1957.

———. *Teaching English Usage*. New York, 1946.

POTTER, SIMEON. *Language in the Modern World*. Baltimore, 1960.

———. *Modern Linguistics*. London, 1957.

———. *Our Language*. London, 1950.

POUND, LOUISE. *Selected Writings*. Lincoln, Nebr., 1949.

POUTSMA, H. *A Grammar of Late Modern English*. 4 vols. Groningen, 1904–26. (Pt. I, 2nd ed. in 2 sections, 1928, 1929.)

PRICE, H. T. *Foreign Influences on Middle English*. Ann Arbor, Mich., 1947.

PRIEBSCH, R., and W. E. COLLINSON. *The German Language*. 4th ed., rev. London, 1958.

PROKOSCH, E. *A Comparative Germanic Grammar*. Special Publications of the Linguistic Society of America. Philadelphia, 1939.

———. *The Sounds and History of the German Language*. New York, 1916.

Publication of the American Dialect Society. 1944–date.

PYLES, THOMAS. *Words and Ways of American English*. New York, 1952; London, 1954.

QUIRK, RANDOLPH, and C. L. WRENN. *An Old English Grammar*. London, 1955.

RAO, G. SUBBA. *Indian Words in English*. Oxford, 1954.

REANEY, P. H. *A Dictionary of British Surnames*. London, 1958.

———. *The Origin of English Place-Names*. London, 1960.

ROBERTS, PAUL. *Understanding English*. New York, 1958.

———. *Understanding Grammar*. New York, 1954.

ROBERTSON, STUART. *The Development of Modern English*. 2nd ed., rev. Frederic G. Cassidy. New York, 1954.

ROSS, ALAN S. C. *Etymology*. London, 1958.

SAPIR, EDWARD. *Language: An Introduction to the Study of Speech*. New York, 1921.

SAUSSURE, FERDINAND DE. *Course in General Linguistics*, ed. Charles Bally and Albert Sechehaye in collaboration with Albert Reidlinger, trans. Wade Baskin. New York, 1959.

SCHLAUCH, MARGARET. *The English Language in Modern Times (Since 1400)*. Warsaw, 1959.

———. *The Gift of Language*. New York, 1955. (Originally pub. as *The Gift of Tongues* [New York, 1942].)

SCHMIDT, A. *Shakespeare-Lexicon.* 4th ed. 2 vols. Berlin and Leipzig, 1923.

SERJEANTSON, MARY S. *A History of Foreign Words in English.* London, 1935.

SHEARD, J. A. *The Words We Use.* New York, 1954.

SIEVERS, EDUARD. *An Old English Grammar,* trans. and ed. Albert S. Cook. 3rd ed. Boston, 1903.

SKEAT, WALTER W. *English Dialects from the Eighth Century to the Present Day.* Cambridge, Eng., 1911.

———. *An Etymological Dictionary of the English Language.* Oxford, 1882.

———. *Notes on English Etymology.* Oxford, 1901.

SLEDD, JAMES. *A Short Introduction to English Grammar.* Chicago, 1959.

———, and GWIN J. KOLB. *Dr. Johnson's Dictionary: Essays in the Biography of a Book.* Chicago, 1955.

———, and WILMA R. EBBITT, eds. *Dictionaries and* That *Dictionary: A Casebook on the Aims of Lexicographers and the Targets of Reviewers.* Chicago, 1962.

SMITH, HENRY LEE, JR. *Linguistic Science and the Teaching of English.* Cambridge, Mass., 1956.

STARNES, DEWITT T., and GERTRUDE E. NOYES. *The English Dictionary from Cawdrey to Johnson, 1604–1755.* Chapel Hill, N.C., 1946.

STRATMANN, FRANCIS HENRY. *A Middle-English Dictionary,* rev. Henry Bradley. Oxford, 1891.

STURTEVANT, E. H. *An Introduction to Linguistic Science.* New Haven, Conn., 1947.

———. *Linguistic Change: An Introduction to the Historical Study of Language.* New York, 1942. (Originally pub. 1917.)

———. *The Pronunciation of Greek and Latin.* 2nd ed. Special Publications of the Linguistic Society of America. Philadelphia, 1940.

SWEET, HENRY. *A New English Grammar, Logical and Historical.* 2 vols. Oxford, 1900, 1903.

TEN BRINK, BERNHARD. *The Language and Metre of Chaucer.* 2nd ed., rev. Friedrich Kluge, trans. M. Bentinck Smith. London, 1901.

THIEME, PAUL. *Die Heimat der indogermanischen Gemeinsprache.* Wiesbaden, 1954.

THOMAS, CHARLES KENNETH. *An Introduction to the Phonetics of American English.* 2nd ed. New York, 1958.

THORNTON, RICHARD H. *An American Glossary.* 2 vols. London, 1912. (A third volume is published in *Dialect Notes,* Vol. VI.)

TRAGER, GEORGE L., and HENRY LEE SMITH, JR. *An Outline of English Structure.* Studies in Linguistics: Occasional Papers, 3. Norman, Okla., 1951.

TUCKER, SUSIE I., ed. *English Examined: Two Centuries of Comment on the Mother-Tongue.* Cambridge, Eng., 1961.

TURNER, LORENZO DOW. *Africanisms in the Gullah Dialect.* Chicago, 1949.

ULLMAN, B. L. *Ancient Writing and Its Influence.* New York, 1932.

"VIGILANS." *Chamber of Horrors.* Introduction by Eric Partridge. London, 1952.

WALKER, JOHN. *A Critical Pronouncing Dictionary, and Expositor of the English Language.* . . . London, 1791.

WARDALE, E. E. *An Introduction to Middle English.* London, 1937.

WATERMAN, JOHN T. *Perspectives in Linguistics.* Chicago, 1963.

Webster's New World Dictionary of the American Language. Cleveland, Ohio, 1953.

Webster's Third New International Dictionary. Springfield, Mass., 1961.

WEEKLEY, ERNEST. *The English Language.* New York, 1929.

WENTWORTH, HAROLD, ed. *American Dialect Dictionary.* New York, 1944.

————, and STUART BERG FLEXNER, eds. *Dictionary of American Slang.* New York, 1960.

WHATMOUGH, JOSHUA. *Language: A Modern Synthesis.* New York, 1956.

WHITEHALL, HAROLD. *Structural Essentials of English.* New York, 1956.

WITHYCOMBE, E. G. *The Oxford Dictionary of English Christian Names.* New York, 1947.

WRENN, C. L. *The English Language.* London, 1952.

WRIGHT, JOSEPH. *The English Dialect Grammar.* Oxford, 1905.

————, and ELIZABETH MARY WRIGHT. *An Elementary Historical New English Grammar.* London, 1924.

—————. *An Elementary Middle English Grammar.* 2nd ed. London, 1928.

—————. *Old English Grammar.* 3rd ed. London, 1925.

WYLD, HENRY CECIL. *A History of Modern Colloquial English.* 3rd ed. New York, 1937.

————. *A Short History of English.* 3rd ed. New York, 1927.

————, ed. *The Universal Dictionary of the English Language.* London, 1932.

ZANDVOORT, R. W. *A Handbook of English Grammar.* 5th ed. London, 1957.

ZACHRISSON, R. E. *The English Pronunciation at Shakespeare's Time as Taught by William Bullokar.* Upsala, 1927.

————. *Pronunciation of English Vowels, 1400–1700.* Göteborg, Sweden, 1913.

Index of Words and Phrases

Subject Index

A

A, use of, 43
Abbreviations, 282–84
Accents in English, 245–47
Ackerman, Carl W., 263
Acronyms, 287–89
Adams, John, 189
Adams, Ramon F., 283
Adjectives: in early Modern English, 184–85; in Middle English, 152–53; in Old English, 119–21
Adverbs: in early Modern English, 184–85; in Old English, 121–22; and verbs combined, 299–300
Ælfric, 133–36, 156
Affixes, 266–76, 331
African languages, 3, 349–50
Agglutinative language, 66
Albanian language, 84
Alcuin, 137
Aleut language, 70
Alford, Dean Henry, 206, 207
Alfred the Great, 102, 103–04, 136–38, 183
Algeo, John Thomas, 136
Allen, H. C., 231
Allen, Harold B., 206, 253
Allophones, 51, 55
Alphabet: Arabic, 10; Cyrillic, 9–10, 26–27, 28; global, 9; Greek, 22–24, 26–27; Roman, 9–10, 24–27, 30–41, 50; Semitic, 22–24
Alphabet of the International Phonetic Association, 53–54
Altaic languages. *See* Ural-Altaic languages
Alveolar stops, 54
Amelioration, 308–09
American Dialect Society, 18, 256–57, 298
American English: accents in, 245–47; British attitude toward, 224–25; conservatism of, 220–21; idiom of, 240–43; influence of, on Standard British English, 225–32; morphology of, 238–40; national word choice in, 232–38; periodicals concerning, 257–58; pronunciation of, 247–53; purism in, 243–47; spelling of, 254–56; study of, 256–60; syntax of, 238–40; vocabulary changes in, 221–23. *See also* Pronunciation of American vs. Standard British English
American Indian languages, 16–17, 69–70, 331, 350–51
Ancrene Riwle, 142
Anderson, Wallace L., 259
Angles, 100–01
Animal languages, 6
Apocope: in early Modern English, 174–75; in Middle English, 156–57
Arabic alphabet, 10
Arabic language, 346–47
Argot. *See* Slang
Armenian language, 84
Armstrong, Lilias E., 246
Arnold, Matthew, 224, 340
Articulation, 54–57
Aryan languages. *See* Indo-European languages; Indo-Iranian languages
Attwater, Donald, 329
Atwood, E. Bagby, 195, 197, 198, 199, 201, 203, 259
Augustine, St., 102
Austen, Jane, 182
Australian languages, 69
Avesta, 84
Avestan language, 83–84. *See also* Indo-Iranian languages
Ayenbite of Inwit, 142

B

Back formations, 284–86
Back vowels, 61–62
Bacon, Francis, 331
Bailey, Nathan, 212
Baker, George, 45
Baltic languages, 84–85

A	4
B	5
C	6
D	7
E	8
F	9
G	0
H	1
I	2
J	3